To John,

With Best Wishes

THE LONG SHADOW OF THE LITTLE GIANT

Popular Music History
Series Editor: Alyn Shipton, Royal Academy of Music, London, and City University, London.

This series publishes books that challenge established orthodoxies in popular music studies, examine the formation and dissolution of canons, interrogate histories of genres, focus on previously neglected forms, or engage in archaeologies of popular music.

Published

Handful of Keys: Conversations with Thirty Jazz Pianists
Alyn Shipton

The Last Miles: The Music of Miles Davis, 1980–1991
George Cole

Jazz Visions: Lennie Tristano and His Legacy
Peter Ind

Chasin' the Bird: The Life and Legacy of Charlie Parker
Brian Priestley

Out of the Long Dark: The Life of Ian Carr
Alyn Shipton

Lee Morgan: His Life, Music and Culture
Tom Perchard

Being Prez: The Life and Music of Lester Young
Dave Gelly

Lionel Richie: Hello
Sharon Davis

Mr P.C.: The Life and Music of Paul Chambers
Rob Palmer

Trad Dads, Dirty Boppers and Free Fusioneers: A History of British Jazz, 1960–1975
Duncan Heining

Soul Unsung: Reflections on the Band in Black Popular Music
Kevin Le Gendre

Jazz Me Blues: The Autobiography of Chris Barber
Chris Barber with Alyn Shipton

An Unholy Row: Jazz in Britain and its Audience, 1945–1960
Dave Gelly

The Ultimate Guide to Great Reggae: The Complete Story of Reggae Told through its Greatest Songs, Famous and Forgotten
Michael Garnice

Bill Russell and the New Orleans Jazz Revival
Ray Smith and Mike Pointon

The Long Shadow of the Little Giant

The Life, Work and Legacy of Tubby Hayes

Simon Spillett

SHEFFIELD UK   BRISTOL CT

Published by Equinox Publishing Ltd.

UK: Office 415, The Workstation, 15 Paternoster Row, Sheffield, South Yorkshire S1 2BX
USA: ISD, 70 Enterprise Drive, Bristol, CT 06010

www.equinoxpub.com

First published 2015

© Simon Spillett 2015

British Library Cataloguing-in-Publication Data

A catalogue record for this book is available from the British Library.

ISBN-13   978 1 78179 173 8 (hardback)

Library of Congress Cataloging-in-Publication Data

Spillett, Simon.
    The long shadow of the little giant : the life, work and legacy of Tubby
Hayes / Simon Spillett.
        pages cm. -- (Popular music history)
    Includes bibliographical references and index.
    ISBN 978-1-78179-173-8 (hb)
  1. Hayes, Tubby. 2. Jazz musicians--England--Biography. 3.
Saxophonists--England--Biography. I. Title.
    ML419.H3525S65 2015
    788.7'16509292--dc23
    [B]

2014044380

Typeset by Atheus

Printed and bound by Lightning Source Inc (US), La Vergne, TN; Lightning Source
UK Ltd, Milton Keynes; and Lightning Source AU Pty Ltd, Scoresby, Vic

Contents

In a way, Tubby never grew up. Underneath it all was the basic thing that he sounded like when he was fifteen. He never had to try too hard – it was there, a natural thing.

Ronnie Scott

To Tubby
Thanks for the music —
Ronnie Scott

Acknowledgements

Writing a biography of someone who you already think you know well is a humbling experience and any writer worth their plaudits quickly realizes that the finished work is actually only as exhaustive – or as valuable – as its list of contributors. Thankfully, throughout the research and writing of this book, I've received invaluable information, assistance and encouragement from a wide range of people, all of whom cheered me on to complete what has, at times, been a far more laborious task than I'd ever anticipated. They form a remarkably diverse list, from Hayes's wife and lover to his offspring, his colleagues and his discographer. There have been almost as many methods of introduction as there are individuals – from the fan who came up to me on a gig one night to spill the contents of a carrier bag stuffed full of rare photographs, to the many musicians who've risked life and limb recovering rare tape reels in overcrowded attics, and those who've contacted me via email with fascinating anecdotes or discographical minutiae.

I'm indebted to Robert Savage and Vivien Van Namen who gave me an introduction to Liz Grönlund, Tubby's girlfriend. I will forever treasure the moment when Liz loaned me her scrapbooks and finally granted access to Tubby's tape archive. In establishing Savage-Solweig Records, Bob Savage has done Hayes fans everywhere a huge service by releasing several of Tubby's live gig appearances on CD. The help and kindness of all three has made this project much more than I'd ever envisioned it could be.

I wish to thank Tubby's ex-wife Maggie who gave me the most insightful three-hour interview during a visit to the UK in 2009. Her recollections transformed the earlier part of this study.

Tubby's son Richard has provided rare letters and photographs which highlighted his parents' relationship during the early 1960s, and has offered general encouragement and appreciation of my efforts to keep his father's music out there.

There are four other individuals to whom I owe a huge thank-you. First, long-term Hayes fan and collector Tony Prior, whom I met by accident in 2005 but who soon became a close friend. Tony's archive on Hayes was a revelation to me, filling many gaps in the recorded chronology of Tubby's work. He also deserves my thanks for being a great supporter of my own music.

My good friend, Canadian jazz fan Tom Davis, has been a tower of strength throughout our collaboration on the revised Tubby Hayes discography, which has run concurrently with the writing of this book. Indeed, Tom has proved unflappable even when scrambling out from under the avalanche of information I've sent him, for which he deserves a medal. Or some sort of therapy.

Barbara Schwarz, author of the first discography of Tubby Hayes (Blackpress, 1990), kindly sent me the entire contents of her research files on Hayes when she discovered I was writing this biography. Barbara's contribution was pivotal in providing documents that I may have struggled to attain myself and typifies a project characterized by people's willingness to share information and offer assistance. Rarely have a few parcels yielded so many gems!

I'd also like to thank the late Tony Ketley, a lifelong friend of Tubby's – or as he called him "The Fat Man" – who gave me an invaluable glimpse into Hayes *the man*, filling out details of his various romantic relationships and his sometimes disastrous personal life.

The list of musicians who have contributed to my research, either via interviews or by providing recordings, press clippings or technical information, forms a veritable who's who of British jazz: the late Vic Ash, Roy Babbington, Alan Barnes, the late Phil Bates, Ted Beament, Roger Beaujolais, the late Harry Beckett, Alan Berry, Keith Bill, Dave Bishop, Pete Blannin, Chris Bolton, Stan Bourke, Lennie Breslaw, Clive Burton, Leon Calvert, Mike Cappoci, Mike Carr, Les Cirkel, Andrew Cleyndert, Malcolm Cliff, the late Jeff Clyne, the late Les Condon, John Critchinson, Alec Dankworth, the late Sir John Dankworth, Brian Dee, the late Martin Drew, Keith Edwards, the late Bill Eyden, Digby Fairweather, Tony Fisher, the late Allan Ganley, Willie Garnett, Ernie Garside, Dave Gelly, Coleridge Goode, Dave Green, the late Ian Hamer, Jim Hart, the late Eddie Harvey, Chris Hodgkins, Jack Honeyborne, John Horler, Tommy Jones, Peter King, Tony and Pat Kinsey, the late Harry Klein, Dame Cleo Laine, Duncan Lamont, Chris Laurence, the late Bill Le Sage, the late Tony Levin, Miles Levin, Chris Levin, Jonathan Lewis, Mornington Lockett, Pete Long, Henry Lowther, Ron Mathewson, Steve Melling, Andre Messeder, Laurie Morgan, the late Dick Morrissey, Clive Morton, the late Danny Moss, the late Joe Mudele, Evan Parker, Vinnie Parker, the late Jack Parnell, John Patrick, Jim Philip, Jim Richardson, Stan Robinson, Daryl Runswick, the late Ronnie Simmonds, Len Skeat, Alan and

Kay Skidmore, Brian Smith, Louis Stewart, Bob Sydor, Trevor Taylor, Art Themen, Frank Toms, Trevor Tomkins, Clark and Sylvia Tracey, the late Stan and Jackie Tracey, Trevor Watts, Don Weller, Spike Wells, Bobby and Isabelle Wellins, the late Kenny Wheeler, the late Tommy Whittle, Dave Willis, John Withers and Bobby Worth.

Those who've generously contributed in varying ways from providing anecdotes, photographs, recordings, discographical details and press cuttings, to transferring and restoring tape reels and even driving me to and from gigs include: Paul Adams, Amity Alton-Lee, Derek Ansell, Peter Asher, Graham Attwood, Louis Barfe, Anthony Barnett, Colin Barnes, Roger Barnes, Tony Batchelor, Alan Bates, Mark Baxter, Roger Baycock, Dave Bennett, Cyril Bevan, Peter Bevan, Bill Birch, Don Bishop, Brian Blain, Colin Bleads, Susan Bould, Alan Brett, the late Brian Buckingham, Geoff Buller, Stu Cameron, Arnie Chadwick, Charles Clifton, Lee Cogswell, Derek Coleman, Fred Cohen, Bernie Collett, Eddie and the late Janet Cook, John Cooper, John Cox, Russell Crombie, Geoff Cronin, Tom Cunniffe, Michael Cuscuna, Brian J. Davies, the late Brian Davis, Peter Dawn, Peter Dennett, Stephen Didymus, Denis Dundon, Roger Eatough, Richard Evans, Maureen Eyden, Roger Farbey, Tony Fernley, Michael Fishberg, Dan Fleming, John Fordham, Mark Gardner, John Gaylor, Mark Gilbert, Brian Goddard, Alastair Graham, Bill Greig, Tony Hall, the late Vic Hall, Rod and Val Hamer, the late Rick Hardy, the late Colin Hare, Carl Hazeldine, Richard Henderson, Dudley Herbert, Pete Heyward, Tony Higgins, Wally Houser, the late Bill Hugkulstone, Roger Hunter, Colin Izod, Pete Keeley, Richard Kennard, Michael and Miki King, Ben Knowles, Paul Koehler, the late Jeffrey Kruger, Pete Lay, the late Don Leach, Fran Leslie, Matt Leviers, Oliver Lomax, the late Bob Lord, Amity Alton Lee, Alan K. Mais, Derek Martin, the late Jack Massarik, Cole Mathieson, Geoff Matthews, Peter Matthews, Ian McCann, Sam McMurray, the late Mike Melvoin, Al and Carole Merritt, Tony Middleton, John Miles, Robin Millard, Michele Monro, Alun Morgan, Brian Moulton, David Nathan, Colm "Red" O'Sullivan, Mike O'Sullivan, Dr Edward Orgill, Harry Owen, Paul Pelletier, Paolo Piangia-relli, Rodney Pledge, Alan Price, Carol Pyne, Keith Raison, Alan Reeves, Sir Tim Rice, Peter Rowan, Peter Rynston, Gordon Sapsed, Peter and Katrina Seal, Graham Sharpe, Darrel Sheinman, Bernard Shirley, Benny Simons, Jim Simpson, Mike Slade, Brian Smith, Robert Spanswick, Ralph Stevenson, Adrian Tattersfield, Roger Thomas, Les Tomkins, Peter Tongue, Alex Towers, Dave Trett, Jonny Trunk, Peter Vacher, Joop Visser, Steve Voce, the late Freddy Warren, Paul Watts, Simon Whittle, Paul Wilson, Dean Winsall, David Wirdnam, the late Peggy Wray and Peter Wright.

Finally, I'd like to thank my parents, Marianne and Richard, who once upon a time courted to Tubby Hayes's music and who have offered unflinching support throughout the decade it's taken to finally complete this book. They've seen more than a few screw-ups along the way, and have occasionally cast a cautious eye over my actions, but have always encouraged me to follow my own path, for which I will always remain thankful. Tubby Hayes may well have inspired me to write this biography, but it has been their example that has been inspirational in so many other ways. Thank you.

Simon Spillett
May 2014

Introduction

It was on a Sunday afternoon, some time in the autumn of 1987, which means that I must have been around thirteen years of age, when I first heard Tubby Hayes. I'd known jazz all my life. My Dad is a former trombonist who then possessed a formidable record collection, the contents of which I had only begun to take serious notice of earlier that year, just before I started secondary school. Suffice to say I wasn't a typical late-1980s teenager. As my classmates debated the merits of whoever was topping the charts, I was busy scribbling cartoons of a bereted Dizzy Gillespie in the margins of my exercise books. I'd recently taken up the trombone, for two reasons, the most obvious being that I was following my Dad's example – even at this early age I could spot the difference between, say, Frank Rosolino and J. J. Johnson – but also because the head of the school's music department (a haughty title for what in effect comprised a dilapidated classroom full of broken-down instruments) had promised that if I started to learn an instrument I could use the room for practice during break times. Having previously spent my mid-morning breaks and lunchtimes in a futile attempt to find a safe corner of the school playground not dominated by fearsome and intimidating older boys, the chance to hone my wobbly, rudimentary trombone skills in peace and (relative) quiet was grabbed with eager hands.

Most of my spare time on school nights and virtually all of my weekends were taken up by jazz, either in delving into my Dad's record collection, housed in our loft room, or in going through our bookshelf and reading every jazz book I could lay my hands on. Years later, during one of my periodic episodes of self-doubt, I was talking to a friend about how I wished I'd had a more formal jazz education. He stopped me and said, "but you had all your Dad's records. That was like going to college and learning the history without leaving the house." I'd never looked at it that way before, but it was true, and in so many ways those hour-upon-hour listening sessions in the loft at home helped shape me forever. It was then that I first heard Parker, Gillespie,

Coltrane, Getz, Mulligan, Miles and Rollins, some of the shaping forces of modern jazz, but also where I fell in love with the Benny Goodman Quartet, Bud Freeman's 'The Eel', Lester Young's solo on 'Shoe Shine Boy', Coleman Hawkins's 'Body And Soul', and encountered the music of Eric Dolphy, Roland Kirk, Chick Corea and even Tony Oxley for the first time. I'm quite sure that my Dad had never ever intended his record collection to become a jazz reference library, just that it simply comprised the things he liked to hear, but the fact that it gave me such a thorough and comprehensive exposure to the history of jazz at such a young age is a tribute to his innate good taste. I don't think I've ever really taken the opportunity to say thank you to him for helping me find my way, so I'll do it now – thanks, Dad.

The Sunday afternoons of my teenaged jazz weekends were spent in one of two ways – either in collective three-way listening sessions with my Dad and brother Carl, which inevitably ended up going towards the funkier, fusion-fuelled end of big band jazz in the 1970s – probably my brother's influence – or with Dad breaking out his collection of jazz video cassettes. Among the gems I can remember watching during this time were Clark Terry and Bob Brookmeyer's joint appearance on the BBC's *Jazz 625*, Bert Stern's magical *Jazz On A Summer's Day*, Miles Davis with John Coltrane and Gil Evans, and the wonderful *Sound of Jazz* with Coleman Hawkins, Gerry Mulligan, Thelonious Monk, Count Basie and Billie Holiday among its glittering cast. Then, on one particular afternoon, my Dad announced we were going to see "a British band." Admittedly, up to this point I hadn't paid much attention to British jazz musicians. I knew who Humphrey Lyttelton was simply because I'd tune into his Monday night radio show, but after that my knowledge was sketchy. The few bits I had listened to sounded, even to my naïve young ears, rather toothless after the American recordings I'd heard.

However, the band that shouted out of our TV speakers on this afternoon – and which equally importantly looked sharp as a tack in neatly cut Italian suits and college-boy haircuts – was an entirely different proposition. It was, of course, the Tubby Hayes Big Band, making a one-off appearance on BBC2's *Jazz 625* series in the spring of 1965. Contractual obligations for re-screening had meant that in 1984 the programme had been shown as part of a weekend of jazz on BBC2, itself an incredibly bold piece of scheduling, which is when – like innumerable jazz buffs up and down the UK – my Dad did the right thing and set the VHS recorder running. I've often wondered how and when – or indeed *if* – I'd have encountered Tubby Hayes's music were it not for that pivotal moment.

As we sat and absorbed the music, Dad gave me a sort of précis running commentary; Hayes was a virtuoso, who died very young, but who was the best modern jazz musician we'd got back in the 1950s and '60s, right up there with the American saxophonists. "We used to see him at Ronnie Scott's," he went on. "He'd be by the bar and always nodded a hello."

I already knew that my parents had seen a great many of the jazz icons – Duke Ellington, Basie, Ella Fitzgerald, Sonny Stitt, Buddy Rich, Woody Herman *et al.* – but suddenly, and, in retrospect, quite precociously for a hormone hamstrung teenager, I wondered how on earth they had courted to such distracting music. In a vivid mental scenario, I pictured them in their youth, Dad brylcreemed, suited and svelte and Mum looking like Stanmore's answer to Brigitte Bardot, sitting in Ronnie's old dimly lit basement drinking in all this wonderful jazz whilst their thoughts were more than likely on other things.

Watching Tubby and his band on *Jazz 625* that Sunday, I could have little dreamed how he and his music would affect the course of my life, or indeed that I would eventually get to know and work with four of the players I was listening to. But, as usual, my Dad had got there first. As we watched, he pointed out one of the band's two trombonists, Ken Wray, a wiry bespectacled man who looked more like a tax inspector than a hard bopper. "He gave me a couple of trombone lessons back in the Fifties," he said with all the vicarious pride one can muster when having briefly rubbed shoulders with the mighty.

And with that he hit the nail on the head. The music I was hearing wasn't made by men from Detroit, St Louis or New Jersey; it was made by men who hailed from Merseyside, Manchester and London's East End, who'd served their musical apprenticeships not in the heady glamour of the American Swing Era but in the rather blander world of the palais, and who, like Ken Wray, might well have even got their start in something as quintessentially English as a brass band. In sum, it was Made in England, but it didn't sound like it to me, at least not initially. In my relative inexperience, I could hear no difference between Tubby Hayes, Jimmy Deuchar and Allan Ganley skating through the murderously fast 'Suddenly Last Tuesday' and the kind of music on, say, my Dad's *Art Farmer Quintet* album with Hank Mobley and Elvin Jones – both sounded assured, confident and thoroughly authentic. I simply hadn't expected a *British* jazz group to sound that way. Although it was to be some time before I truly grasped how different was the lot of the average British jazz musician during the 1950s and '60s when compared to that of his counterparts in America (a realization that fuels this book), it was immediately clear that Hayes was a man of quite extraordinary gifts. On the *Jazz 625* show he played not only tenor saxophone, but also flute and vibraphone, and, as well as composing and arranging much of the music, he was also leading the band. The only other jazz musician I then knew of with such a diverse range of talents was Roland Kirk and recourse to my Dad's jazz reference books had shown me how rare was *his* example. Even then, my mind was struck not only by how difficult it must have been to do all these things so well, but to do them in a country an ocean away from the main jazz arena. When I found out Hayes had just turned thirty the day before the programme was filmed, I wondered where he'd found the time to become a master of so many skills. I suppose, in some subconscious way, the seeds of this study were sown then.

As luck would have it, my Dad owned a Tubby Hayes LP, *Tubbs' Tours*, a 1964 recording by the same band that had appeared on *Jazz 625* and featuring some of the same music. He'd picked up the record for just a few quid in a "junk" shop in Leighton Buzzard sometime in the 1970s, which itself says much about how Hayes's music had fallen into limbo in the years immediately after his death: discarded, second hand and no longer worth much. However, repeated playing of *Tubbs' Tours* over the next few months convinced me that my first impressions of Hayes were not wrong. Here was a tenor saxophonist equal to Sonny Rollins and Stan Getz, leading a big band as exciting as those of Herman and Rich. Yet, in many of the jazz encyclopaedias and reference books I thumbed through, he'd become little more than a footnote. In some, he wasn't mentioned at all. However, when I looked at the yellowing pages of *Melody Maker* and *Jazz News* which my Dad had saved from the 1960s, he was everywhere, the ubiquitous man-about-jazz, clearly dominating the local jazz scene. One *Melody Maker* headline shouted "Tubby a Triumph in New York," before going on to explain that Miles Davis, Paul Desmond and Zoot Sims had all turned up to hear Hayes on his first gig in America. *What?!* Given this sort of esteem how then had a figure of such titanic talent become so overlooked?

Fast-forward a few years to the early 1990s: I had abandoned the trombone for – surprise, surprise – the tenor saxophone and, threading in between the expected fixations with Getz, Coltrane and Rollins was an ongoing love of Tubby Hayes. In the interim I'd learned the sad truth that precious little of his recorded work had remained available but I had seized whatever I could get hold of, thus far a couple of cassette tapes of albums borrowed from one of my parents' friends and a recently issued LP called *For Members Only*, purchased from a well-known high-street record retailer in Watford and clutched with emblematic pride on the train journey home. Shortly afterwards, *Jazz FM magazine*, launched in conjunction with the ill-fated radio station, published an article on Hayes by Alun Morgan, accompanied by a series of atmospheric period photographs of the full-faced, wide-smiling saxophonist looking more like an innocent cherub than the hedonistic experienced professional he really was. I was hooked.

Whenever Hayes's name came up among the greying bunch of enthusiasts at my local jazz club, Merlin's Cave in Chalfont St Giles – at sixteen I was by far the youngest member of the audience – it was in reverential tones, accompanied by what, even at my unsubtle and green stage of the game, I could read as genuine affection. Hayes was clearly much more to this generation than a long-dead saxophonist – he was a lost leader, a fallen hero, a musician who, nearly twenty years after his death, continued to inspire awe, respect and wonder.

The most vociferous Hayes advocate in this circle was a man named Rick, a bluff, sometimes overbearingly difficult Londoner, whose conversation tended to be *at* rather than *with* you. However, what he lacked in social grace was atoned for in his enthusiasm for all things Tubby Hayes, and it was he who introduced me to the fascinating subterranean counter-culture of bootleg tapes. I still have my first ever acquisition in what was to become a series of cherished home-recorded rarities, a cassette of a BBC session from 1965 featuring Hayes and Victor Feldman, exchanged for, as I remember it, a copy of one of Joe Harriott's LPs.

If the jazz fans I'd met were still notably moved by Hayes and his music, what about the musicians? At the same club, I was making my first tentative attempts to sit in, the time-honoured tradition in which young musicians find out on the bandstand how little they know. As appalling as I was, and as unsettling as the experience sometimes was musically, I found that off the stand many of the older players were happy to talk to me about their youth. I remember having vivid Hayes-anecdote-filled conversations with players including Bill Le Sage, Duncan Lamont and Dick Morrissey. "I used to have to go on before him at the Marquee," said Morrissey. "Can you imagine how terrifying that was!?" It was the same awed reaction that I'd seen in fans like Rick, only this time it was accompanied by a professional musician's knowledge of the technical side of the game. If a player as accomplished as Morrissey found following Hayes "terrifying" it clearly said something.

However, it was to be another of the musicians I met at my local gig, and a man who would become my saxophone teacher, who would provide the best insights into Tubby Hayes: Vic Ash.

When I began my studies as a nervous, enthusiastic and painfully raw eighteen-year-old, one of the things that quickly cemented our friendship was my love of what Vic was fond of calling "the bebop era." He wasn't referring to goatees and berets and oop-bop-sh'bams but to the British jazz scene in the 1950s and 1960s. Often, at the end of our lessons, I'd amuse him by pulling out a yellowing copy of *Melody Maker* or some other jazz magazine from the 1960s featuring his picture or an article about him. If Tubby just happened to be on the same page, Vic was off and running, tripping over himself in a stream of superlatives.

Vic's enthusiasm matched that of all the other musicians I'd met who'd once worked with Tubby, and, after I turned to music as a profession at the age of twenty-one, it seemed that everyone I encountered in the business had a Tubby Hayes story of one kind or another. Indisputably larger than life during his twenty-three-year career, over two decades later Hayes had succeeded in becoming larger than death. Indeed, as more than one musician has observed during the course of the research of this book, even years after his passing Hayes has continued to have a near-tangible presence on the UK jazz scene, even for those too young to have heard him in person.

When *Jazzwise* magazine in 2004 asked saxophonist Theo Travis to name the album which had been his musical turning point, he chose Hayes's *Mexican Green*, not only for the music. "You only have to mention Tubby Hayes to people in a UK jazz club and a big smile comes to their face, and a story follows," he remarked. "He's one of those people about whom everybody has a story." Having grown up not far from where Hayes's drummer Tony Levin was living, Travis saw him as "a real person – he wasn't someone like Miles Davis, a legend that you only knew from far away. Again that was something that made it more real and close for someone just getting into the music."

Interestingly, although we had never met, Travis's views on Hayes's local importance were identical to mine: "Because it's English, it's just that one step closer to one's own experience. One can love all the classic stuff, but culturally, it's very far away – whereas [Tubby's music], though I was obviously not part of it in terms of time, is a stone's throw away geographically. That feeling that it's near you, almost within your grasp, I think it fires you up a bit."

My decision to write a biography of Tubby Hayes was prompted initially by one thing: my enthusiasm for his music, which, it cannot be avoided, should be the reason behind any study of a musician. However, beneath this was my mystification that no one had yet written at length about him. As one of the most colourful characters in British jazz, with a career rich in both professional achievement and personal strife, his life, it seemed to me, made ideal material for a thorough biography. Indeed, just playing the numbers game alone revealed Hayes to have been a truly extraordinary individual: he turned professional at the age of fifteen and, over a career of just twenty-three years, released twenty albums, wrote over seventy compositions and recorded on no fewer than thirteen instruments. But clearly there was much more to him than numeric achievement. There was the cultural tangibility, the charisma, the sense that someone who packed so much into such a short life must have left much more than music in his wake.

Having spent a great deal of time reading through the contemporary music press from his youth, and more specifically, from the time of his death aged thirty-eight in 1973, I was also alarmed that so many of the published accounts of his life either fudged the facts or ignored them altogether. The usual pat summary went something like "boy wonder multi-instrumentalist goes to America, comes home triumphant, gets hooked on drugs, undergoes heart surgery and dies on the operating table, a tragic victim of the jazz life." This treatment was usually accompanied by a morbid and over-sensationalized reference to Hayes's various addictions. But although the general arc of his life does have more than a trace of the Hollywood biopic to it – the public schoolboy who dared to play jazz by night! – Hayes, I believe, deserves far better than this. Indeed, in choosing to write this book at the beginning of the twenty-first century, this is certainly the last time in which Hayes's colleagues and contemporaries can help retell his story with first-hand accuracy. Since several of them have died in the years between their being interviewed and this book being completed, their recollections are now even more valuable.

My third motivation for writing about the music, life and times of Tubby Hayes is probably altogether far more personal. I make no secret of the fact that I am nostalgic for a world I never knew, the world in which my parents grew up and which, as I was born in 1974 and Hayes died in 1973, does not really overlap with mine. I have long held a fascination with post-war Britain, the nation that moved from war-winning pride through the innovative 1960s and on to the oddly bleak and ignominious 1970s, and its cinema, television, fashions, literature, music, politics and everyday society continues to intrigue me as much – if not more – in middle-age as it did when I was in my early teens.

Indeed, Tubby Hayes's story slots neatly into the cultural history of post-war Britain. He's one of the self-made generation who emerged after World War II, pushing their hopeful dreams uphill against the realities of austerity. In this he joins a whole raft of key contributors to the post-war English zeitgeist – a list that could also include such disparate figures as Ray Davies, John Osborne, Matt Monro and Ronnie Barker – but, although chronologically he aligns with the British jazzmen who came up fighting their way out of the dance bands of the 1950s, simply because he began so young Hayes truly came into his own a decade later. Certainly he recorded his finest work during that time. Representing the razor edge of London cool, he also enjoyed a sympathetic following among the early Mod movement and watching him on the BBC's *Jazz 625*, or in among the kitsch of the film *Dr Terror's House of Horror*, he becomes part of the much wider culture of the day. Indeed, Hayes is as British as James Bond and The Beatles, as much a product of the drab suburbia of London as The Kinks or Michael Caine, as quintessentially "1960s" as *The Avengers* and Hammer films. (For those seeking to explore the times through which Hayes lived in greater detail, I recommend Dominic Sandbrook's excellent and exhaustive three-part study of post-war UK, *Never Had It So Good*, *White Heat*, and *State of Emergency*.)

It's therefore unsurprising that my enthusiasm for the great British jazz survivors of this era is also tinged with nostalgia. Somehow they represent a link to what was undoubtedly a golden age for the UK and the fact that you may still be able to see them on a pub gig for the price of a pint and a raffle ticket has an odd compounded effect. On the one hand, it's tragic – if there's any justice, musicians of that sort of skill shouldn't be working in that sort of environment – but it is also simultaneously and paradoxically heartening to know that there remains an up-close tangibility to their world that you just can't find anywhere else. I'm sure Theo Travis would agree.

Although I believe that enthusiasm for a chosen subject is a requisite building block for any effective biography, it needs to be supplemented with technical accuracy. To this end, I would add that working as a professional musician on a jazz circuit which thankfully still boasts some of Hayes's playing colleagues among its number (and which, less thankfully, continues to persist with some aspects of presentation and promotion that the saxophonist himself would be familiar with) has aided me immeasurably in gaining a greater understanding of my subject. I have worked with – and happily now count among my personal friends – some of Hayes's closest musical associates, all of whom have provided me with candid, intimate accounts of their time with the various incarnations of his bands. I'd like to think that my being a musician may well have influenced their decision to open themselves so readily to my questions. It certainly says much that none of them have been stinting with their memories. Indeed, throughout the research and writing of this study there has been a wonderful sensation of being on the inside track, with access to both recordings and recollections that, had I not been a working player, may well have eluded me. I cannot say enough how music has been a double blessing in this regard.

When I began my tentative research back in 2003, I already had a sense that telling Hayes's story accurately would require the metaphorical unravelling of a huge and complex ball of wool. What I hadn't anticipated was just how long the process of unravelling would take or how much there was left to uncover. My first interview with one of Hayes's former colleagues, Allan Ganley – and I truly could not have started with a nicer bloke – revealed so much that instantly I realized I had begun a process that would be anything but cut and dried.

Files of press clippings, stacks of old *Melody Makers*, reams of notes and teetering boxes of tapes and CD-Rs have occupied my desk ever since, the sheer volume of material matching that of Hayes's enormous importance. Whilst I have fortunately never lacked research material (which began with the expedient annexing of my Dad's old *Melody Makers* – thanks again!), the completion of this project has been interrupted by the one thing that I didn't have when I began in 2003 – a successful career as a musician – but somehow the two have gone nicely hand-in-hand. In fact, one day there could well be another book in the fascinating experiences I've shared with some of Hayes's former colleagues.

Some of the information I've gleaned along the way has been usefully filtered into sleeve notes for various albums, but I've endeavoured to keep enough "fresh" material back to make this study read like a new work and not a simple regurgitation of already extant essays. I've also done my level best to avoid the worst kind of sycophancy; as partisan as I am about Hayes's music, I readily accept that, like all human beings, he had his personal flaws and occasional lapses in both taste and judgement. I've made no attempt to disguise these failings – nor to glorify them – but have tried to capture them as accurately and truthfully as possible. If this may periodically make for awkward reading, I make no apology whatsoever; I believe Hayes's gifts are sufficient enough to withstand the odd revelation about his personal behaviour.

Writing as a musician – and specifically as a tenor saxophonist – I've consciously tried to ensure that the narrative doesn't get too bogged down in technical speak and musical analysis. After all this is a book about Hayes's *life*, *work* and *legacy*, not a treatise on his improvisational style or a chronology of his mouthpiece changes. Suffice to say, as a player I remain wholly in awe of Hayes's skills, and writing this book – a project that has at times necessitated a thorough saturation in his playing to the virtual exclusion of all else – has only increased my respect for those talents, whether they be featured on a film soundtrack or in a blistering jazz club recording. Nothing I have heard from him – and this assessment includes material not intended for public consumption – has diminished my appreciation of his ability. Even those recordings made when he may have been taking this or that substance generally remain first-class technical examples of jazz saxophone playing. Occasionally readers will find that I've waxed a little more poetically about certain performances than others and that their own favourite album or solo may not have been examined at any great length. However, in my defence, I believe that there is enough appreciative description within this study to convince anyone that Hayes was every bit the saxophone giant that Getz and Coltrane were. Examining and documenting just how he came to this, an unprecedented position for a British jazzman, forms the main thrust of this study. Indeed, Hayes's story is as much about his uncompromising triumph over his environment and circumstances as it is about his musical development. I'd even venture so far to say that among local players of the generations too young to have encountered him live, his example should be even more widely revered. His roots were in the same suburbia that most of us know and have experienced all our lives, not in the steaming pressure cooker of New York, or the hallowed halls of academic jazz study. For me at least, this has been the biggest inspirational aspect of Hayes's career, the fact that the UK could produce an international contender – a player once described as "Britain's own Saxophone Colossus"[1] – through sheer hard graft alone. It's a work ethic that still governs those who played with Hayes, nearly half a century on, but it is something that one day might well disappear forever.

As I've written elsewhere in a different context, the root purpose of any essay about music is to ultimately motivate the reader to go and listen – I sincerely hope that is what I have achieved here. Together with that I hope to have emphasized effectively just how Hayes overcame obstacles and inhibiting circumstances to reach his stature as a musician. Ten years ago, the majority of his work had not been reissued, and locating some of his recordings required either vast sums of money or friends in the know. Now, all but a handful of his albums have reappeared on CD, and more recently as downloads. There have also been – sometimes as a by-product of the research for this study – a healthy showing of previously unissued club and concert recordings, each adding yet more substance to Hayes's recorded legacy. I'd urge the reader to hear them all, although a more selective discography is included for those who require an overview rather than the complete works.

Time and again in reading through appraisals of Tubby Hayes's music one encounters descriptions like "world class," or "equal to the best Americans," both of which ring true, but to my mind part of what constitutes Hayes's charm and appeal is that his music is, without doubt, born of Britain, something its initial American-style panache can occasionally mask. In this regard, both Hayes's music and life have a warranted place in the history of British post-war culture, yet another reason to question exactly why it has taken this long for him to receive a thorough celebration. As yet, no blue plaque adorns 34 Kenwyn Road in south-west London, Hayes's childhood home, although it has all the qualifications for such an award; surely if the National Trust can preserve the house of a Beatle, why not mount a plaque for a musician like Hayes? Are we wrong to seek such an acknowledgement? Possibly, but then the entire process of writing this book has been very much a search for Tubby Hayes, not only in the physical quest to locate some of his rarest music, and in the desire to tell his story, faithfully and in detail, but also in an attempt to ensure he receives the appreciation he so richly deserves. Some jazz writers and listeners continue to find Hayes overrated, glib and superficial – the very criticisms he faced during his heyday – and yet, whilst I cannot hope to convince everyone that he was a truly exceptional talent, I hope that at least some readers will come to appreciate him anew.

In a paradox, although my original intention was to take a somewhat revisionist stance, and to remove the fact from the folklore, much of what we have come to know as the Tubby Hayes legend emerges from this study intact. I sincerely hope that this book goes some way towards ensuring that Hayes's legacy endures and that, with a greater understanding of the background to his unique achievements, his example is not forgotten. Above all, I hope it brings new listeners to his music.

This then is the story of Tubby Hayes, The Little Giant, a figure who, in the words of one writer, "bestrides British Jazz like a colossus."[2]

It's small wonder that he continues to cast such an impressive shadow.

Simon Spillett
May 2014

1 A Face Not Built for Gloom (1935–51)

He was never as happy as when he had his mouth wide open and was shouting his head off.

Dorothy Hayes

Tubby was born Edward Brian Hayes on Wednesday January 30th, 1935. Virtually every previous biographical account of his life has begun by incorrectly stating the location of his birth as Raynes Park in south-west London, close to where his parents lived and in which he would spend a large part of his formative years.

Home births were by no means unusual in 1935, but Hayes's birth certificate gives the location as St Pancras Hospital in Camden. The birth was not registered until March of that year for reasons that can only be guessed at.

One might be the working itinerary of his father, also named Edward, but known to all as Teddy. A handsome, bespectacled man with a Ronald Colman moustache and a swathe of dark hair, Teddy Hayes was a professional musician, playing the violin and leading his own dance band. At the time of his son's birth this work was prolific as Britain had been swept by the dance band craze. Live music at ballrooms, theatres and dance halls was still the major force in popular entertainment and the social interaction of dancing formed its very infrastructure.

People the length and breadth of the British Isles were used to the sound of dance bands; such people might be the posh and well-to-do, able to afford a night at one of the plush night-clubs and hotels in London's West End, where darlings of the genre such as Bert Ambrose, Lew Stone and Jack Jackson held sway, or the average wage earner of the day, happy to foxtrot away in front of the semi-professional band at the local Palais.

Teddy Hayes's orchestra – or rather orchestras, as, by the mid-1930s he was proudly boasting he could provide anything from a salon quartet to a full gypsy orchestra – were typical of the era.

A publicity brochure advertising the services of "Hayes Orchestra" at this time asked whether the reader required music for a wide array of events: "Masonic? Ladies Festival? Annual Dinner and Dance? Reception? Wedding? Cabaret? Theatre?" adding that bands could be "supplied at the shortest notice." Alongside the agent-style puff was a list of the Teddy Hayes orchestra's "municipal engagements":[1]

Palace Pier, Brighton – 4 Seasons

Pavilion, Herne Bay – 3 Seasons

Pavilion, Burnham-on-Sea – 3 Seasons

Borough of Wembley – 2 Seasons

Herne Bay, Burnham-on-Sea and Wembley might not sound like the most exciting places in which to spend a musical career but Teddy was happy enough, and he was earning a good living, far better than many in 1935. Britain was still feeling the effects of the depression brought on by the Wall Street Crash in 1929. Economic downturn was the story everywhere, and in January 1935 the country's unemployment stood at a staggering 2,397,000. It was small wonder therefore that live entertainment flourished, almost as an antidote to the morbid fiscal atmosphere.

There were also renewed political tensions in Europe, surrounding the rise of a new German leader, Adolf Hitler, whose National Socialist Nazi party had swept to power in 1933. During the same month as the birth of the Hayes's son, a plebiscite in the Saarland region, taken from the German people at the end of World War I, resulted in a 90% vote in favour of rejoining the national borders, and, in March, in strict defiance of the Versailles Treaty, Hitler announced German rearmament.

International affairs, however, probably mattered little to Tubby's mother Dorothy in early 1935. A pretty dark-haired lady, with a good figure and a stylish dress sense, she was the ideal partner for Teddy, and together they made a striking couple. One of two sisters, she had been born Dorothy Roche and, like her husband, had a strong musical talent, receiving singing lessons as a child with an idea towards a career in classical music. Somewhere along the way though she'd changed direction and, by the time she and Teddy met, Dorothy was a revue artist, as likely to be in a dance troupe as an acting role. It appears that Dorothy had retired from the stage by the time of the birth of her son, leaving her husband to keep her in a style, if not exactly luxurious, then certainly less inhibited by the financial privations felt by many at the time.

Home for the Hayes family was 34 Kenwyn Road in the west Wimbledon area of south-west London, close to Raynes Park. Bordered by Wimbledon and New Malden, and effectively bisected by the Waterloo to Southampton railway line, Raynes Park was quintessential 1930s suburbia. The population of the area had begun to increase in the late-Victorian and Edwardian eras and the development of new housing and roads continued throughout the inter-war years, with the nearby A3 Kingston bypass and the A298 Bushey Road dual carriageway being built in the 1920s. Bus services to central London had run since 1914 and the London Underground network extended to adjacent South Wimbledon in 1926, making the suburb ideal commuter-belt territory.

Sharing the same 617-square-foot floor plan as the rest of the houses in the street, but with a slightly wider front garden, with both a hedge and a fence outlining its border with the pavement, the Hayes's home was by no means

Edward Brian Hayes 1936. Courtesy Liz Grönlund.

palatial, but Teddy's good earnings meant that the house had a telephone, still considered a domestic luxury, a radio and a gramophone player.

Brian, as the Hayes's always referred to their son, even into adulthood, grew up spoiled rotten. He was to be the couple's only offspring and this situation, together with a certain amount of monetary comfort, meant that he was indulged throughout his formative years, something that would have a great bearing on his adult character. Dorothy would hand-make a great many of his clothes and his surviving pre-school photographs show a well-dressed, happy-looking boy, with wavy blonde locks and the broad smile he would carry into adulthood. Years later the broadcaster Peter Clayton would comment that "Tubby's face wasn't built for gloom."[2] In his years as a toddler he certainly had plenty to smile about and, as if in practice for his later lifestyle, he grew up with a life of periodic disruption due to Teddy's workload. Indeed, most of the pictures of Tubby as a small child feature him with his mother at the various seaside locations where Teddy was working. One can easily understand the bond formed between mother and son as they often found themselves alone together as Teddy played matinee performances, week in week out, for several months at a stretch. Amusing a child at the seaside would have been easy enough for Dorothy, but one can also imagine her loneliness, as she was left to bring up her son almost single-handedly at times. It was by no means an easy task. Boisterous and confident, the young Brian was already showing clear signs of a distinctly artistic temperament.

Tubby with his parents, Edward and Dorothy, circa 1936.
Courtesy Liz Grönlund.

Osmosis would be the most pragmatic explanation behind his gifts. Teddy was a successful musician and Dorothy had her own talents, not just as a vocalist but as a skilled seamstress. Both were clearly creative and the young Brian was growing into a world where talent was all around him. Doubtless he sometimes watched his father's band in action during the long months spent away from home as a small child and he had also begun to show a fascination with drawing, a compulsion he shared with a later hero, Sonny Rollins. Surviving childhood sketches show a clear eye for detail and an indication that, had he chosen to pursue this career path, he could have made an excellent artist.

Tubby's behaviour was also alarmingly precocious: Dorothy would later describe him as "a little show-off." There was certainly a vanity to him, which would persist through his teenage years and into adulthood, and a definite will to have things his own way, another character trait that would not desert him in the years ahead. And, although he had a deep and affecting relationship with his mother, it was to be his father who became his first real hero. "Everything his father had he had to have too,"[3] Dorothy once remarked, and soon that "everything" would include the violin, Teddy's instrument of choice and the first of Tubby's many musical conquests.

At the outbreak of World War II in September 1939, Teddy was part way into his season at Brighton and, in the first of what would be many twists of fate linking the two men, unbeknown to Tubby, he would spent the opening days of the war in the same town as his future musical partner Ronnie Scott, who was staying in a hotel owned by an aunt and uncle.[4] Approaching five years of age, Tubby was old enough to appreciate the excitement of the conflict, but not yet old enough to comprehend the coming horror. Little is known about his life during the war years, or indeed about the extent of Teddy's participation in the conflict. He almost certainly would have been too old for call-up, although the presence of what appears to be an ARP helmet in a wartime snapshot of his son suggests he may have done his bit in local civil defence, hardly a position matching the glamour of his regular employment. Tubby may well have been evacuated for a brief time – the Hayes family had relatives in Maidenhead – but it is fairly certain that Teddy, Dorothy and Tubby remained in Raynes Park into 1940, when the Battle of Britain took the German offensive over the skies of the capital.

However, that same year an event occurred that had a far greater impact upon the young Tubby Hayes than either the new world of primary education he had just entered into or the unfolding spectacle of the war around him.

Teddy took his young son along to Archer Street in London's West End, the narrow, short road that runs, parallel with Shaftesbury Avenue, between Great Windmill Street and Rupert Street. Since the 1920s the street had acted as an open-air labour exchange for jobbing musicians, a tradition that would stretch forwards to the dawn of the '60s, and Monday afternoons would find throngs of players jamming the pavement eagerly looking for work. The jobs on offer, however, weren't jazz as Tubby Hayes's generation would know it, but commercial engagements, everything from Palais gigs to West End shows, Deb balls and hotel soirées. Sometimes the musicians came straight from other gigs, still in evening dress, and it was common practice for players to

"A face not built for gloom." Late 1930s. Courtesy Liz Grönlund.

carry their respective instrument cases in order to alert potential employers as to their skills. There were also other less chivalrous codes of conduct, designed to entrap the naïve, as clarinettist Vic Ash recalled: "Certain bandleaders [might] call out 'Trumpeter for Palais, Wednesday night, £5!' But as you got closer you would see [he] had two fingers spread on his lapel, indicating the job was in fact worth £2."[5]

But, by and large, there was a brotherly camaraderie amongst the job seekers, and Archer Street, or The Street as it was simply known to its regulars, was as much a social gathering as an exercise in career movement. There would be ribald humour, practical jokes and put-ons and, when the weather took a turn for the worse, as many bodies as possible would crowd into the Harmony Inn. Steaming cups of tea and endless games of table football passed the time if no work was forthcoming.

Archer Street was just one part of the booming band business and by the late 1930s music publishers, booking agencies and instrument shops dotted the map of the West End, each contributing in its own way to the ongoing appeal of dance music. Whilst the publishers and bookers oiled the wheels of the professional side of the business, the retailers were a magnet for the amateur, who might just fancy himself as another Nat Gonella or Harry Hayes. Shining rows of trumpets and saxophones were as ineluctable to the children of the 1930s as electric guitars were to be to the rock-and-roll generation years later and it was into the gleaming window of one such retailer, Joe Pausey's Saxophone Shop in Shaftesbury Avenue, that the five-year-old Brian Hayes gazed and realized instantly – and with a certainty that would extinguish any notions of it being just a passing childhood fad – that he had found something indisputably for him. "I'll never forget it," he remembered twenty years later: "I saw three saxes in the window, an alto, a tenor and a baritone. I knew right away and said I wanted the one in the middle." This sudden and compelling desire wasn't shared by Teddy. "[He] said I was too young to learn tenor," Hayes remembered, but like parents the world over Teddy diplomatically deferred his son's dream rather than brush it completely aside: "[He said] I could have one when I was twelve. I kept him to that promise."[6]

It's easy to understand Tubby's all-consuming fascination with the saxophone, and the tenor saxophone in particular. It is one of the most eye-catching of all the musical instruments, the result of a quite remarkable blend of practical mechanism and aesthetics. Uniting a wonderfully complex-looking series of levers and rods, gaping tone holes, spring work and circular keys operated by a series of pearl buttons, viewed close up there is a suggestion of something vaguely Jules Verne about its construction. It is clearly designed to do something quite complex, and the minutiae of the craftsmanship brings with it a sense that the instrument is not simply a practical tool but a work of art. By the time the young Tubby Hayes was peering through Joe Pausey's window, the tenor saxophone also had its first handful of jazz virtuosi.

Emerging from the band of Fletcher Henderson in the late 1920s, Coleman Hawkins had all but invented the instrument as a viable jazz voice, possessing a technical command unrivalled by any other player of the day, a tone cello-rich and lustrous throughout the entire register and a harmonic mind that had few equals. He had worked his way through a variety of bands besides Henderson's before striking out on his own, touring Europe as a soloist during the mid-thirties. However, his crowning glory came when he returned to the United States in 1939, just a few months before Tubby Hayes first set his heart on owning a saxophone, with a recording of the ballad 'Body And Soul', a performance which, in under three minutes, virtually defined his style and which, over seventy years later, can still overawe anyone encountering it for the first time.

But Hawkins had also returned to find a new rival, Lester Young, a Missouri-born performer who had done what was hitherto thought impossible in eschewing the heavy tone, thick vibrato and grandiose delivery favoured by his opposite number (adapted in varying degrees by nearly every other tenor player of the day, including Ben Webster, Don Byas and Chu Berry). Instead, Young offered a poetic and languid sound, lighter, airier and in many ways more flexible than that of Hawkins. His improvisations, whilst as harmonically sound as that of his predecessor, stressed melodic content first and foremost, almost if he were singing through his instrument. Young's early recordings, with Count Basie, Billie Holiday and others, soon caught the ear of a younger generation of American jazzmen, among them Dexter Gordon, Stan Getz and Zoot Sims, and would likewise transform the lives of English musicians of a similar age, such as Tommy Whittle and Don Rendell. From then on, throughout the Swing Era, tenor players of all abilities had two principal role models from which to choose, Hawkins or Young, with each camp thinking they knew best.

Tubby Hayes would have been unaware of these partisan allegiances in 1940, and like the thousands of people who have taken up the saxophone since its invention a century earlier, he found there was simply something about its look, its feel and its aura that captivated him. There was no way that he would forget his first encounter with the tool of his life's work and no way in which he would let his father forget the promise that, in the not too distant future, a tenor saxophone would be his for keeps.

In the meantime Teddy decided that his son's musical education was best served by learning the violin. Tubby began these studies under his father's tutelage in 1943, aged eight, and this start at such a young age, even on an instrument he would soon abandon, set in place several of the key musical foundation stones of his mature talent. Teddy was a stickler for accuracy and one can imagine that the young Tubby would have spent hours working on his instrument until his father was satisfied. Teddy also taught Tubby to read music at this time, another skill vital for the years ahead. In fact, it is impossible to overemphasize the importance of learning this, the most fundamental of musical requirements, so young. Children who learn to read music at an early age do so with a degree of receptivity not always found in more mature learners, or in those who have initially learned to play "by ear." The latter have to effectively "unlearn" their inherent skill, and the misbalance between what they can reproduce by sheer reflex and what they struggle to reproduce from a written score can inhibit further musical development. Aged eight, Tubby simply followed his father's example and learned what he was shown. The degree of natural talent involved – through osmosis – may or may not have been higher than that of an average learner, but without access to either some sort of formal musical certificates or recorded evidence it is impossible to judge.

Tubby moved to Rutlish School in nearby Merton in 1945.[7] The school, whose motto is "Modeste, Strenue, Sancte" (Be Modest, Be Thorough and Pursue Righteousness), was named in honour of William Rutlish, one-time embroiderer to Charles II, who upon his death in 1687 had left the princely sum of £400 for the education of "poor children of the parish." This charity existed until the 1890s when the chairman of the board of trustees, local landowner John Innes (after whom the famous garden compost is named) used the excess funds to build a school.[8]

Up until 1945 Rutlish had been a private school, subsisting solely on fee-paying pupils, but the 1944 Education Act had meant that by the end of World War II it had begun to accept a number of pupils through scholarship

Tubby in his Rutlish blazer, outside 34 Kenwyn Road, circa 1947. Courtesy Liz Grönlund.

entry. The effect of this system was to prove seismic and the Rutlish that Tubby Hayes encountered upon his arrival was an establishment struggling to cling onto its laurels. Many aspects of the school were straight out of *Tom Brown's Schooldays*. "Each entry year of about 90 boys was divided up evenly into eight houses: Argonauts, Crusaders, Kelts (sic), Parthians, Romans, Spartans, Trojans and Vikings," a school friend Alan Reeves recalls. "Tubby and I were Trojans." Discipline was rigid. "We were forbidden to run in the playground, and had to wear school caps at all times if wearing the school tie and blazer. To be caught in uniform out of school without a cap was a detentionable offence."[9]

Although young Brian Hayes appears not to have made too much of an academic splash during his initial year at the school, opinions differ as to his character. "He was quiet and kept his head down and got on with his work," Dudley Herbert comments,[10] whilst another school friend Don Bishop describes him as "full of fun, even then."[11] Alan Reeves recalls that Hayes "was not the most studious of pupils academically" but that he was "friendly and amiable." Everyone, however, remembers his nickname: "Even in those days, although he was named Edward Brian – I had heard him called Brian – he was always known as Tubby, which he was."[12]

For the moment Tubby's preoccupation was with sport, which would remain a lifelong passion. Indeed, among the photographs surviving from his childhood are several of him with a cricket bat or squaring up to the camera in a pair of boxing gloves. Boxing was a particular favourite and during his time at Rutlish he hero-worshipped Freddie Mills, the English fighter who had secured the World Light-Heavyweight Champion title in 1948. This fascination with the fight game was such that Tubby himself was often involved in informal boxing championships with fellow pupils such as Alan Reeves on nearby Cannonhill Common.[13] Hayes's talent for drawing also enabled him to produce an A3-sized "comic" book, telling the adventure of an imaginary American boxer, each scene lovingly sketched and scripted with a neat and fastidious eye for detail, a skill that would stand him in good stead in the musical career that lay ahead. Tubby's own beautifully annotated boxing scrapbooks were among the few early possessions he would retain until his death.[14]

Cricket was another enthusiasm. The 1948 Test Match, with the arrival of the sensational Don Bradman and his Australian squad, was also a magnet for his father, who considered it of such importance that he purchased the considerable luxury of a television set on which to watch the coverage.

Teddy was also keen to further encourage his son's musicality. Although Tubby had already been playing the violin for two years prior to his arrival at Rutlish, it was there that he first made a distinct musical impression on those outside his family. One morning before the school building was unlocked Alan Reeves discovered Tubby, in cap and blazer, "serenading us all solo on his violin."[15] Dudley Herbert remembers that he already had a tangible sense of style: "He displayed panache when playing with the school orchestra. He was a performer, even then. The other boys in the orchestra, which was led by our French master, would all be sitting with rather sullen faces and Tubby would be leaning forward and smiling. He had no nerves about him."[16]

Nerveless and precocious, Tubby clearly had much going for him musically, but, like countless parents before and since, Teddy and Dorothy decided that their son's musical future would benefit from piano lessons, and like innumerable children, their son baulked at the idea. Although he later expressed regret that he hadn't pursued these studies further (which also began to teach him the basis of musical theory) in order to aid his compositional skill, the deciding moment came when Teddy and Dorothy decided to groom Tubby for a public performance. "They tried to rush me I'm afraid. They said they'd like me to play a piece at a concert and I got the horrors and refused to go to lessons anymore!"[17]

In between sports, drawing and the piano, the young Tubby had also found a new interest in jazz, one which to his father's annoyance he seemed intent on indulging. Ironically, it had been Teddy who first introduced his son to a music that seemed a world away from the cosy dance band quaintness of his own orchestra. "I remember him switching on the radio when I was very young and listening to Benny Goodman's band or something on the short wave,"[18] he recalled twenty years later, but although early exposure to swing stylists such as Goodman might have initially caught his young ear, as the forties progressed a musical revolution was taking place that would transform jazz – and Tubby Hayes – forever.

World War II had been a catalyst in breaking down many barriers – sociological, moral, technological and artistic – and, as the conflict drew to its conclusion, there was a certainty that nothing could be quite the same again. Old ideologies had been toppled, empires were crumbling and convention was being thrown out the window. Unsurprisingly, this spirit of revolution had also surfaced in jazz.

The Swing Era of the late 1930s, which had rocketed men such as Benny Goodman to fame, and which had, for the only time in history, placed a music primarily based on instrumental jazz in the forefront of public taste, had now settled down into something tediously routine, especially to those young musicians employed in the big bands of leading black performers such as Count Basie, Earl Hines and Cab Calloway. It wasn't only the formulaic nature of the music that irked them. Swing may well have been a phenomenon created by men like Fletcher Henderson and Jimmy Lunceford but to the general public the princes of the music were virtually all white – Goodman, Artie Shaw, Tommy Dorsey and Glenn Miller. In a country where they faced social indignities on a daily basis, some black musicians thought the theft of music they had created the ultimate injustice.

There was also a deep dissatisfaction with the direction of the music itself and, as young players dreamt up new ways to escape the formula of swing, three figures emerged as central to the revolution: trumpeter Dizzy Gillespie, pianist Thelonious Monk and alto saxophonist Charlie Parker. All three had served time within the big swing bands (Gillespie with Cab Calloway, Monk with trumpeter Cootie Williams and Parker with Earl Hines and Jay McShann) and each was musically curious enough to want to experiment. The new music pioneered by these players, worked out in after-hours jam sessions, eventually acquired the nickname bebop, derived from its off-kilter rhythmic figures and stop-start melodies; by the close of World War II it had begun to be documented by small independent record labels in New York. The first handful of bebop 78s, including such seminal recordings as 'Ko-Ko' by Charlie Parker and Dizzy Gillespie's 'Groovin' High', set the tone for the whole movement and were virtual definitions of the language of modern jazz: new and complex melodies sat atop old chord progressions in a way that challenged both the player and the listener to a mind game that no previous style had offered – it was jazz seen through the prism of post-war cynicism, the height of hip.

Inevitably, but interminably, bebop filtered through to Europe. A few of the younger London musicians, who had befriended US servicemen stationed in the UK, had already come to know the name Charlie Parker: saxophonists Ronnie Scott and John Dankworth, two of the country's most promising musical figures then earning their keep in commercial dance bands, both remembered a young altoist by the name of Art Pepper (then serving as a military policeman) telling them about Parker after a wartime set at the Feldman club in Oxford Street. For the moment, however, he was just a name and a reputation, although enlightenment wasn't far away. The epiphany for Ronnie Scott and several other young players occurred soon after, at one of the informal listening sessions held at the record-lined flat of drummer Carlo Krahmer, an avid collector who through a variety of routes managed to secure many records not yet available in the UK. On this afternoon he played a 78 rpm by guitarist Tiny Grimes, titled 'Red Cross', made in late 1944, and featuring Charlie Parker in one of his last on-record appearances as a sideman. Grimes's riff was a typically trite throwaway, the sort of thing swing musicians were used to concocting on the spot, but Parker's improvisation was a clarion call from another place altogether. For Scott, hearing the altoist's playing was like opening a door onto another world; similar conversions were occurring all over London, often in the unlikeliest of places: clarinettist Vic Ash recalls saving up to buy the 78 of his first Parker–Gillespie recording – the blistering 'Shaw 'Nuff' – from a market stall in the East End's Petticoat Lane, and playing it until the grooves wore off. What was clear to all its converts was that bebop was music of its time, of *their* time.

Britain's record industry had been slow to grind back into action following World War II and it was some time before anything by Parker, Gillespie and the other revolutionaries became available domestically. Parlophone and HMV, the two major labels, eventually released several titles by Gillespie in 1947 but the time-lag between the UK and the US meant that many of these recordings were already several years old. Even so, in the austere circumstances of late forties London, which could give the feeling that a full-stop had been planted on progress, they still seemed like missives from the future. Ever enterprising, Carlo Krahmer saw a gap in this market and teamed with fellow enthusiast Peter Newbrook to form Esquire Records, a label operating along almost cottage industry lines which issued 78s by Parker, Sonny Stitt, Miles Davis and others, often dubbed from dreadful third-hand copies of the original American discs. Esquire also gave valuable early recording breaks to the small coterie of English musicians exploring the new music, amongst them Ronnie Scott, John Dankworth, pianist Tommy Pollard and drummers Laurie Morgan and Tony Crombie.

Like the founding fathers of the style in New York earlier in the decade, the English boppers were already earning good money in commercial dance bands. Some, like Ronnie Scott, who at nineteen had been recruited by the hottest new band on the London scene, that of trombonist Ted Heath, had already made an impression as fledgling swing players, but the frustrations of unsuitable outlets for their type of music soon surfaced. There was even open hostility from some established leaders who, having proffered a very polite type of dance music since before the war, didn't take kindly to their young upstart sidemen indulging willy-nilly in "reboppy" solos. The music press of the day also considered the new music to be bunk, a reaction typified by *Melody Maker*'s reviewer Edgar Jackson, a man of forthright opinions who more or less wrote his own epitaph with repeated attacks in print on Charlie Parker. Adding further to this dilemma was an ongoing feud between the American Federation of Musicians and the British Musicians' Union which, in an attempt to protect the interests of English performers, had placed an embargo on visiting American players. Its effect was nothing but negative: during the 1930s, Fats Waller, Coleman Hawkins and Benny Carter had all visited the UK and recorded with local players, and a young Dizzy Gillespie had even toured with the band of Teddy Hill, whilst the war itself had brought down certain barriers with the arrival of Major Glenn Miller's Army Air Forces

Orchestra and the US Navy band headed by former Artie Shaw saxophonist Sam Donahue; but if anyone expected the transatlantic strictures to loosen after the conflict ended they were to be bitterly disappointed.

For Ronnie Scott, John Dankworth, Tony Crombie and the other young British modernists there seemed only one solution, that of somehow getting to America. As pipe dreams went it was as tough as they came, but youthful determination kicked in. The first to go, Scott and Crombie, pooled their money and flew – via Iceland – to spend a few intoxicating weeks in New York. Once there, the guessing game was over. They caught Charlie Parker, Miles Davis, Tadd Dameron, Bud Powell and others at clubs such as the Three Deuces and the Royal Roost, before returning to London, broke but inspired.

Fortunately a more practical route to the jazz mecca opened up shortly afterwards with the relaunch of transatlantic cruise liners including the *Queen Mary*. These ships had always needed bands – quaintly referred to as "Geraldo's Navy," after the veteran bandleader who organized the secondment of these ocean-going musicians – and if it meant a few days' blowing sedate foxtrots and waltzes to placate the moneyed passengers, the incentive was a full day's turnaround in New York. Young jazz musicians flocked for the jobs and soon they were regularly hearing their heroes up close, often finding them not much older than themselves. A whole world denied them back home suddenly opened up. John Dankworth – one of the few of these transatlantic pioneers to have enjoyed a formal musical education – took an even more practical route to learning Charlie Parker's cipher, writing down whatever he could remember from a night spent listening at a club when he returned to the ship. For those left back home, the "Geraldo's Navy" men brought back the valuable teaching tools of more recordings, together with other hip ephemera gleaned from the jazz capital – everything from boxes of saxophone reeds purchased at Manny's, the music store frequented by Charlie Parker, to Ivy League ties, colourful shirts and socks.

Inspired by venues such as the Three Deuces, and desperate to create a playing environment of their own, the clique around Dankworth and Scott formed their own club late in 1948, Club XI, named after its still disputed list of eleven founder members. Unlike the venues they'd visited in New York, their effort had a distinctly austere British flavour. Held in Mac's rehearsal rooms in London's Windmill Street (a stone's throw from the famed Windmill Theatre), its amenities were crude and the lighting basic but it quickly became a magnet for true aficionados, who sat avidly soaking up the sounds of Dankworth's and Scott's respective bands, or who worked out bizarre half-speed dance steps to accompany the racing music. The atmosphere was often as raw and energized as the playing, but incredibly, for a venue that existed more on luck, love and spirit than on fiscal resources, the club soon acquired a European reputation.

The embargo on American performers didn't apply to continental Europe and so bebop bands such as Dizzy Gillespie's and that of former Parker trumpeter Howard McGhee were already visiting France and Sweden. Some of these visitors passed through London on their way to the continent and sought out Club XI; Gillespie's pianist John Lewis (later to form the successful Modern Jazz Quartet) dropped in one night on his way back from Paris, and among the other illustrious guests was Tadd Dameron, the lyrical bop composer who found himself briefly in the UK working as an arranger for Ted Heath. Even Benny Goodman called in, bringing with him an impressive – and then unknown – young pianist named Buddy Greco. These visits offered sure-fire endorsement of the local's efforts and, by 1949, bebop had a firm if somewhat limited foothold in London. Although its coterie of practitioners may have been confined and hermetic, they were already beginning to exert an influence on other young musicians, including Tubby Hayes.

Tubby's wartime wish finally came true on Christmas Day 1946, when Dorothy and Teddy at last presented him with his first tenor saxophone. It's unclear exactly what the instrument's provenance was, or its company of manufacture: later in life Hayes's only recollection about his first saxophone was that it was "a pretty beat-up one." Nevertheless, his progress appears to have been instantaneous and, according to one interview, he was proficient enough to be playing along with the Squadronaires dance band on the radio by Boxing Day. "I picked up the fingering right away," he remarked in 1960, adding modestly "I think my ear must have been pretty good."[19]

Frustratingly, Hayes gave very little away over the years about his early days as a learner. With the exception of one lesson "which taught me how to take the instrument out of its case, and cost me about twenty-five shillings,"[20] he maintained that he was largely self-taught. Indeed, his descriptions of his early efforts tended to be brief and rather uninformative, usually along the lines of "I practised pretty hard for a couple of years"[21] but, given the fact that he had a successful professional career with one of the top bands in the country barely four years after first taking up the saxophone, he can be forgiven for not offering much in the way of an explanation. The proof, he probably thought with some justification, was clear for all to hear. There is little doubt that he was a natural, and a prodigal one at that, but for all his inherent talent (and one cannot fail to recognize that his earlier efforts on the violin and piano contributed much to this rapid mastery of his new skill) there must have been a time when he simply settled down and got on with the basic groundwork of learning the mechanics of the instrument.

As anyone who has ever learned to play the saxophone to a degree of successful musical consistency is aware, there is much more to the task than simply learning the order of the keywork. A reasonable amount of digital dexterity can be achieved in a relatively short space of time, the very reason why so many amateur saxophonists with ambitions to play jazz can produce superficially impressive runs of notes without too much effort, but the difference between these callow efforts and a higher level of performance comes from a concentration on producing an effective and controlled tone, which is arguably harder to do and requires greater patience. This also

In the back garden at Kenwyn Road with his first tenor saxophone. Courtesy Liz Grönlund.

accounts for the number of would-be saxophonists who complain about, or even abandon, their playing because "it doesn't sound like the records I listen to."

Tubby would have without doubt worked on his control (through the near mesmeric process of playing sustained notes) along with the development of his technical velocity, achieved by the same old routine that has blighted many a child's piano lessons: scales and arpeggios and simple, sometimes mind-numbing, exercises designed to strengthen the fingers and heighten the hand/eye co-ordination. Later on in his career, he criticized his early playing for having a thin tone, but this might well have had nothing to do with a lack of application on his part, but rather on his following the fashionably "light" sound of the leading tenor saxophonists of the day.

Aside from a precociously quick grasp of the technicalities involved in playing his instrument, Hayes also boasted two other highly prized assets. He could read music fluently, the result of his earlier violin tuition, and, even more promisingly, he had an extremely receptive ear. It is not known whether he had perfect pitch – the uncanny ability possessed by some people to hear a note and identify exactly what pitch it is – but he certainly had relative pitch, whereby he could hear a melody and play it back instantly on his instrument without a delay in working out the relevant fingering – hence the early "sit-in" with the radio in the living room at Kenwyn Road.

The radio would have been an important part of Tubby's musical education, as indeed it was for virtually all of his generation. Exposure to his father's band meant he was familiar with the disciplined and sometimes over-fussy music that still ruled the airwaves after World War II, but, as the earlier encounter with Benny Goodman has illustrated, odd spots of jazz did make their way onto the BBC. Alongside American records, there were also appearances by British groups on the programme *Jazz Club* (begun in 1947 and later to be a regular source of employment for Tubby). Much of the music heard on these broadcasts in the late 1940s echoed the small-band swing from earlier in the decade, but the growing interest in "revivalism," a movement that sought to reinstate the values of early jazz from New Orleans, and which was making stars of players such as the young former guards officer Humphrey Lyttelton, meant there was also liberal helpings of even more backward-looking forms.

Bebop had taken a while to surface on the BBC and ironically it first did so in an unlikely place, on a show quaintly titled *Accordion Club*. Bandleader Tito Burns had assembled a group of young bop-influenced players including John Dankworth and Ronnie Scott, and for no other reason than his playing accordion, the band wangled a broadcast. The new music had therefore initially arrived via the back door, but as time went on more modern styles began to infiltrate *Jazz Club* and there were the infrequent occasions when the BBC might dare to play a recording by Charlie Parker, or by the brash new big bands led by Woody Herman and Stan Kenton.

Exactly *when* Tubby Hayes first heard Charlie Parker is undocumented, but he later revealed that the first Parker recording he owned was a 78 of 'Stupendous', a composition recorded for the Dial label in California in 1947 during an especially purple patch in the American's career.[22] Although he doubtless found delight in the playing of Parker's sidemen on the disc – including the tenor saxophonist Wardell Gray, among the first to transfer the language of bebop onto the larger horn – for Tubby Hayes, it was the leader who was the king. The altoist's example had also set him a formidable challenge: "I always wanted to sound like Parker. There weren't any tenor players playing like that then."[23]

Alongside Charlie Parker, other influences were beginning to affect Tubby's musical development, key amongst them being the altoist's hand-in-glove partner Dizzy Gillespie. Parker was a genius, quixotic, mercurial and gifted with a language that couldn't really be codified but in Gillespie Hayes had found an example that was more practically useful; his music was easier to comprehend and emulate: "He was sort of more accessible, he caught your attention more," he later remarked.[24] It was small wonder that throughout his life Hayes's work often contained the diminished scale runs that Dizzy had pioneered in the late 1940s, but what he lacked at this point – or rather hadn't yet sought out – was a definitive tenor saxophone playing role model.

When he did eventually find a tenorist who truly caught his ear, ironically, his first major influence was not an American, but a fellow Londoner, Ronnie Scott. Charismatic, assured and with a musical strength that made him stand out among his peers, Scott quickly became a new hero for the young Hayes, and, although he didn't yet know it, they already had much in common. Scott was an only child, doted on by his mother, and his father, a working musician, had left the family home when Scott was a toddler. Hayes's home life was to follow a similar pattern. Both men had a steely compulsion to have their own way that sometimes meant they rode rough-shod over others. They also shared a definite flair for putting their music and themselves across with absolute professionalism. However, the opportunity to meet and play with his idol was still some way off, and for the time being Hayes sought out rather more parochial playing partners. Principal among these was Mike Oliver, with whom he co-formed his first band, the Oliver–Hayes Boptet, a quartet that played at local youth clubs.

In the days before rock and roll made a vocation out of teenage delinquency, youth clubs were the closest thing young people got to making their own entertainment on their own terms and in this quaint and unthreatening environment – where demonstrating a skill like playing a musical instrument would instantly win friends – it was unsurprising that Tubby Hayes was already beginning to make a reputation for himself.

He had also become a beacon of musical modernity for his fellow Rutlish pupils, all of whom were startled at how quickly he had been able to assimilate the message of bebop. Dudley Herbert recalls that Hayes's quick musical ear even delighted the school's music teacher Roy Howard.

Alongside providing a useful guide to what was hip, Hayes also revelled in recounting tales of late-night jam sessions and the wild antics of his bebop-obsessed associates.[25] Later to become a professional jazz drummer who would go on to work with Dick Morrissey, Joe Harriott and Michael Garrick, a younger pupil, Colin Barnes, saw the saxophonist as an idol, retaining a vivid memory of the blazered Tubby playing during an assembly in front of the whole school: "Mr Blenkinsop, the headmaster, introduced him and it was all very sober and serious: 'And now Hayes will play the saxophone'. He played 'East Of The Sun' and we loved it."[26]

The school's attitude to Hayes's musical ambitions nevertheless remained inconsistent. Although there was pride in his precocious ability, and even special dispensation for him to keep his fashionable "Boston" hairstyle[27] – which he described to the head as "like a union card – without it I can't get work" – Hayes continued to shirk his academic studies. Indeed, fast approaching his final year of schooling, and showing no real sign of aligning himself to any subsequent career path, it had become clear that the distraction of music was now absolute. At home, when he wasn't playing, he'd be tuning into Armed Forces Network, the American radio station that had become a lifeline for many jazz-starved British fans. On occasion he'd also turn the dial to pick up French radio and when Charlie Parker played at the 1949 Paris Jazz Fair, the altoist's short-wave transmissions provided excuse enough for him to abandon his homework. There were also late-night bouts of saxophone practice, the Hayes's neighbours' reaction to which can only be imagined. The mornings after could be problematic for Tubby. He'd regularly doze off during maths lessons, incurring the wrath of a fearsome slipper-wielding master named Hathway. Alan Reeves also recalls him being hauled up as a bad example to his peers: "I recall our physics master, a Mr Butler, singling out Tubby in front of the class – as he had clearly not done his homework – to say 'you'll never do anything in your life!' How wrong could he be?"[28]

The decision terminating Hayes's schooling appears to have been taken sometime during 1950, when, according to legend, he overslept following a late-night gig and failed to turn up for an examination.[29] While, for Tubby, this early dismissal was a blessing, for his father the ramifications were harder-hitting: "My Dad paid out an unreturnable deposit to pay for my education till I was sixteen so he was pretty sick that I left at fifteen. He thought I was a nut not to stay at school."[30] Despite his reservations, Teddy recognized his son's determined talent and gave him a familiar qualified proviso: "[He] told me that I could try my hand at music for a year but after that I'd have to start earning a living."[31] There may well have been other factors at play in his father's mind at this time. Now ensconced in the BBC Revue Orchestra, Teddy had finally come off the road, but his wanderlust remained as strong as ever. Finally Dorothy tired of seeing his charm work its spell on other women and the marriage disintegrated. Soon after Tubby's departure from Rutlish, Teddy moved out, leaving Dorothy alone to deal with her now professional, and increasingly wayward, son.

Fame and success didn't occur overnight for Tubby Hayes. His prodigal talent may have already promised much more than mere novelty value, but upon leaving school the spade work of commercial gigs continued apace. As had been the pattern during his final year at Rutlish, this work, still often with Mike Oliver, comprised local weddings, tea-dances and suburban youth clubs but there were also odd sorties further afield. The night of his first gig in the West End was to prove equal parts triumph and disaster: borrowing his father's evening dress, Tubby had returned home the next morning minus his shirt and nursing a thundering hangover. For the time being Dorothy mitigated that her son had "not been used to drink and things like that,"[32] but within a short space of time he had begun sinking pints with the ease of a lifelong drinker. Having now entered a tough, adult profession wherein seasoned players would expect a newcomer to prove his mettle in all sorts of ways, Tubby Hayes was growing up as fast as a hothouse flower.

In some instances the growth came with an ignominious price, and his first regular engagement, at a pub in Woolwich, was no exception: "[We] used to travel all the way from Raynes Park for 10s a night plus what we got going round with a collecting box. We split it between the five of us. The leader was a coalman and we used to drive to our dates sitting on the empty coal sacks in his truck."[33] As the youngest member of the band, Hayes wasn't always guaranteed a place in the cab and often rode on the back of the lorry. It was hardly an auspicious start to his professional career and one can imagine some hard-fought battles to look cool after a trip across London on an open coal truck. There were perks, however, as the gig fee included "everything you could drink,"[34] something that, even at this early stage, he found a highly appealing prospect. But it was to be his youth that spelled the end of the gig: when the landlord discovered the saxophonist was only fifteen the band was instantly dismissed.

There were musical opportunities to be had closer to his home turf too and, in spring 1950, Hayes alighted on a new venue that had recently opened up in nearby Morden, the T and H Modern Rhythm Club.

The T stood for Les Tomkins, a young jazz fan and avid record collector who together with a bunch of like-minded friends was a regular attendee at dances held at nearby Wimbledon Palais. To supplement these trips, Tomkins thought that this nucleus needed a place to meet and play what he recalls as its collection of "swing, bebop and hot vocal discs." Early in 1950, he begun to lay the groundwork for the first of these club meetings and found suitable premises in Morden Assembly Rooms, handily adjacent to a pub called The Beverley, as the T and H, like most such gatherings of the time, was to be decidedly "dry."

The club was soon presenting live jazz alongside its record recitals, creating a rare oasis of modernism for a mixed ability group of local players. Exactly how Tubby Hayes first heard of the T and H isn't clear – although Les Tomkins recalled making extensive house-to-house leaflet drops advertising the club – but there is little doubt that he wanted a piece of the action.

Some time in May 1950, together with other assorted friends including Mike Oliver, he made his way to the club, intent on buttonholing Tomkins for a sit-in. Minus his tenor, Hayes – who Tomkins remembers as "a curly haired, rather corpulent lad"[35] – borrowed a baritone saxophone, got up in front of drummer Lennie Hastings and "proceeded to astound everybody." "All the musicians there were saying 'Who's *this*?'"[36] Answering the question at the end of the night Tubby gave Tomkins his card, which read "The Oliver–Hayes Boptet." His instant reaction was to enquire about the saxophonist's future availability.

Besides Tomkins, other jazz promoters were beginning to sit up and take notice. Bix Curtis – a former trumpet player who would shortly write himself into the history books by defying the authorities and bringing Coleman Hawkins to the UK for a concert – organized a guest spot for Hayes with the Toni Anton band at Acton Town Hall on July 9th. "[His] capacity for showmanship was as large as his jacket," wrote Mike Nevard in *Melody Maker* the following week, thus marking Hayes's first notice in the national press.[37]

The success of the T and H meetings at Morden soon prompted Les Tomkins to look for somewhat larger premises and during the summer of 1950 he moved the club to the Rosehill Community Centre in Sutton. Via agent Les Perrin (later to work for the Rolling Stones), he had also begun to organize a programme of visiting bands, as well as revamping the club's use of local performers, now engaging a pool of nine musicians, including Tubby, pianists Jack Honeyborne and Harry South and saxophonist Les Simons, all of whom alternated leadership of the club's resident group. Although he cannot recall the exact circumstances surrounding the break-up, Tomkins remembers that by the time of opening the new venue at Rosehill, "[Tubby's] former colleagues had been jettisoned and the real star was being featured."[38]

The relocated T and H's "Grand Opening Night" on Monday September 4th presented "Britain's Musician of The Year, leading his own Band of Radio and Recording Fame, The Great Johnny Dankworth Seven," with, at the foot of the bill, The Tubby Hayes Group. The booking of Dankworth was an especially shrewd piece of business. Since Club XI had disintegrated earlier that year, the altoist had been running his own seven-piece group, which, in keeping with its leader's character, presented a lighter and less intense brand of modern jazz which was proving enormously popular. Unsurprisingly, Dankworth's set at the T and H drew a large crowd and as the leader and his men made way for the intermission slot by the resident band, they experienced the familiar feeling of dread they'd felt dozens of times before when faced with the prospect of hearing a group of local amateurs. Listening to Tubby Hayes, however, provided a shock of an altogether different kind, as the leader remembered: "We sort of pooh-poohed [Tubby] when he did his first intermission thing, and then at the end we were rather frightened about going on because he couldn't be followed."[39] "This little kid got on stage and exploded! There's no other way to put it," Dankworth's trombonist Eddie Harvey recalled years later. "We couldn't believe it."[40]

Hayes's victory was sweet, but as if making musicians in the country's leading modern jazz group sit up and take note were not enough, two weeks later on September 18th he finally got the opportunity to play alongside his hero Ronnie Scott. Tomkins had booked the tenorist's Club Copacabana Sextet, another sure-fire draw, and as the evening progressed suggested Hayes might like to join Scott for a few numbers. Surprisingly, he found the younger saxophonist was far from enthusiastic. "I was scared stiff,"[41] Hayes confessed years later, but he wasn't the only one unnerved by this historic meeting. Ronnie Scott would tell the story of this initial encounter many times over the next forty-five years, but never better than in the sleeve notes to one of Hayes's albums in the early 1960s: "During the course of the evening, a chubby young man who appeared to be about twelve years old (he was, in fact, fifteen) came on to the stand with a tenor saxophone only a couple of sizes smaller than himself and asked if he could 'sit-in'. With rather patronising amusement, I agreed. He then proceeded to scare the daylights out of me. The conception, the spirit and fire, the confidence in one so young and inexperienced was absolutely astonishing."[42]

Word about the talents of the Raynes Park wunderkind was clearly spreading. Having rapidly become a local hero, he now took to looking elsewhere for opportunities to demonstrate his gifts. By the close of 1950, he was also venturing regularly to the White Hart in Acton, home of the faintly Goon Show-esque sounding Acton Bop Club, and to the Number 1 Jazz Club in Great Newport Street, where Les Tomkins remembers him taking part in sessions involving scat-singer Alan Dean and fellow tenorist Kenny Graham, whose Afro-Cubists, one of the most distinctive of British modern outfits, had also visited Rosehill.

THE T. & H. MODERN RHYTHM CLUB
ROSEHILL COMMUNITY CENTRE
SUTTON, SURREY

next Monday

SEPTEMBER 18th

RONNIE SCOTT

THE TERRY BROWN
QUINTET

THE JACK
HONEYBORNE
ALL STARS

with **Les Simons** and **Tubby Hayes**

WOOLLEY, 151 STAVORDALE ROAD, CARSHALTON, SURREY

"He scared me to death." The flyer for the T and H Modern Rhythm Club gig during which Ronnie Scott first encountered the teenaged Tubby Hayes. Author's collection.

Like Scott and Dankworth, Graham had been instantly won over by the teenaged Hayes but, unlike the stoic Scott, his affection for the youngster showed itself in an almost avuncular form. Indeed, it appears that it may well have been Graham who first furnished the young Hayes with the nickname The Little Giant around this time. At five foot, five inches tall, Hayes appreciated the sentiment but detested the name.

It may well be worth pausing at this point for a revised look at Hayes's oft-remarked-upon weight. Intriguingly, photos taken at various points during his time at Rutlish give the lie to legends of a "fat little boy" and show a full-faced yet handsome young man, with no suggestion of any obesity. The only sign of anything that might have given rise to his nickname is merely some teenage puppy-fat. His earliest publicity photos, taken some time in 1951, show a trimmer physique still: the only thing in excess is hair, as he had yet to lose the Boston.

Les Tomkins saw a further opportunity for Hayes early in 1951 when he read in *Melody Maker* that trumpeter Kenny Baker was forming a sextet.

Although he was no bebopper, Baker's fiery yet sweet playing had been a key part in the success of the first Ted Heath band, and now, frustrated at a lack of opportunity to play small-group jazz, he was looking to strike out on his own. When he discovered that the trumpeter was due to make a guest soloist appearance at Acton, Tomkins wasted no time in orchestrating a meeting between the star soloist and his young friend. Like Dankworth, Scott and Graham, Baker was immediately impressed and, as had been Tomkins's intention all along, by the end of the evening he had offered Hayes a job.[43]

Joining what amounted to the most exciting new jazz group in the country was vindication for Hayes, and when *Melody Maker* broke the news of Baker's new signing on February 10th, complete with a photograph of the band

Young man with a horn. Tubby sports the legendary "Boston" for his first publicity photograph, 1951. Author's collection.

caught during a break in rehearsals, among those who saw it and smiled with vicarious pride was his former school friend Alan Reeves. "It amazed us all, with a mother of one of my school friends saying 'What? Little Tubby?!'"[44] Hayes – the recalcitrant pupil who barely a few months before had been told he'd never amount to anything – had finally made it.

The biggest impression Hayes was making, however, was upon his fellow band mates. The personnel of Baker's sextet shifted subtly over the first few months of its existence, but the opening line-up featured two musicians with whom he would form fast friendships: veteran tenor saxophonist Jimmy Skidmore and, closer to his own age, clarinettist Vic Ash, also embarking on his first professional "name" job.

To his younger colleagues, Skidmore – arguably the first great jazz saxophonist the UK had produced – was a veritable fount of knowledge, a player who knew the business, and all its ups and downs, inside out. To be privy to such wisdom was bound to prove insightful, so much so that Hayes later declared the best thing about his stay with the Baker sextet had been getting the chance to work alongside Skidmore. The admiration was mutual: Skidmore's similarly talented tenor-playing son Alan remembers his father returning home from an early Baker gig raving about "this youngster – he's absolutely phenomenal."[45]

After a month of rehearsals, the Baker band made its debut at the No. 1. Jazz Club in Great Newport Street on Sunday March 4th and headed out on the road for the first time a week later for a concert at Manchester Hippodrome. Work for the group had yet to pick up and, as Baker organized a more widespread tour for later in the spring, Hayes continued to freelance with a bewildering array of players: he appeared with a big band led by the legendary British bop guru Denis Rose at the Downbeat Club in Archer Street on March 3rd and on March 9th drummer Billy Kaye's Contemporary Music Society presented him as a member of The Martin Feldman All Stars, a group led by the future comedian and actor. The contrast between the diligent Hayes and the leader – a self-confessed musical chancer – couldn't have been stronger. Years later Feldman delightfully confessed, "I have a write-up that describes me as the worst trumpet player in the world, which sums it up, I think."[46]

Even though Hayes had clearly moved on from the circle around the T and H Modern Rhythm Club he was still in regular contact with Les Tomkins, and on April 5th, 1951, he recorded a privately cut 12" 78 rpm acetate accompanying Tomkins's vocals at R. G. Jones Studio in Morden. Although the leader sings with spirit on both sides, the real value of the disc unsurprisingly lies in Tubby Hayes's full chorus solo on 'Good Bait' (he does not solo on the reverse). It would be nearly three years until he would set foot in a professional recording studio to make a commercially available recording featuring his solo skills, and consequently Tomkins's acetate is not only historically significant but musically revelatory – the first evidence of

The Kenny Baker Sextet, 1951. Baker (trumpet) leads David Milne (piano), Allan McDonald (bass), Pete Bray (drums), Vic Ash (alto saxophone), Jimmy Skidmore (tenor saxophone) and Tubby Hayes, aged sixteen. Courtesy Vic Ash.

Tubby Hayes, the youthful giant slayer, already capable of playing men with far more experience to a standstill.

So how does he sound to twenty-first-century ears? The answer is simple: impressive, extremely competent and confident, and, as would be the case throughout his career, like a consolidator rather than someone with a startlingly new voice. The tenor tone is light, edgy and cool, in line with the prevailing Stan Getz influence of the day, and the absence of any of the clichéd vocabulary of bebop is also telling. Indeed, throughout the solo, Hayes sounds very much like Getz did in the late 1940s, and, even if this can ultimately be dismissed as mere mimicry, it is still no mean achievement for one so young.

After Charlie Parker, Stan Getz had become the strongest force in shaping Hayes's musical language. "Back in 1951 *everyone* was trying to imitate Stan Getz," he remarked later,[47] but we also know that by this point he had heard some of the first recordings issued in the UK by Sonny Stitt and Sonny Rollins (including the classic August 1949 session made for Blue Note under Bud Powell's leadership) both of whom had transplanted the cadences of Charlie Parker to the tenor. There is nothing of this in the recording with Tomkins. In fact, listening to Hayes on 'Good Bait', one is instantly struck by how cool and reserved he sounds – a world away from the full-on drive of his mature music. Indeed, the disc only adds to the impression that his pre-1955 discography actually contains very little to support his early wunderkind reputation. However, this is a judgement informed by hindsight and one must not forget that, in the UK of the early 1950s, such an accomplished facsimile of the latest American style must have seemed hugely impressive, especially when delivered by a sixteen-year-old.

The folklore that has grown up around Hayes since his death has also loaded our expectations. His initial meeting with Ronnie Scott, a few months before the recording with Tomkins, has invariably been written up as some sort of tenor battle, the imagined soundtrack of which appears in the mind's ear as something akin to the two men's later Jazz Couriers collaboration. The truth is that, in the *very* early 1950s, Hayes was still a long way from being the machine-gunning technician he was to become later and that – not for the last time in his career – his talent was for following fashion rather than dictating it.

Further evidence of his youthful development was delivered a few weeks after his recording with Tomkins, on April 21st, 1951, when he made his first BBC appearance, playing two numbers alongside blind pianist Eddie Thompson in the "Jazz for Moderns" slot of *Jazz Club*. "Considering how [he] plays at the age of sixteen," *Melody Maker*'s Maurice Burman wrote presciently of Hayes, "he ought to top the poll by twenty – if Ronnie [Scott] will let him."[48]

2 Boy Wonder Tenorist (1951–55)

Every session is a clambake, a party, and being young and full of the zest of life he makes the most of it.

Patric Doonan, *Weekly Sporting Review*, 1955

The Kenny Baker Sextet begun to strike out to the provinces that same month, with the band's first ballroom gig, at South Parade Pier, Southsea, attended by a crowd of two thousand, giving a hopeful indication of future success. The group's first tour proper began on May 5th, 1951, following an unusual engagement at the Granada Theatre in Sutton, during which it performed for an exclusively school-aged audience, some of whom were barely a few years Tubby Hayes's junior. That same evening the band appeared in Ipswich, before heading off for gigs in Leicester, Chorlton-cum-Hardy, Leith, Leeds, Sheffield, Whitley Bay, Glasgow, Aberdeen and Cowdenbeath, a wide range of locations typical of a touring band's itinerary at the time.

Vic Ash remembered life on the road with Baker with a mix of horror and affection: "He had bought an old, barely roadworthy coach with no heater, as was usual in those days, in which to get around. It was not the most comfortable way to travel and was a hard introduction to youngsters like Tubby and me."[1] Travelling to and from gigs in the pre-motorway Britain of the early 1950s was an arduous task and every touring band faced the same hurdles. Then working the traditional jazz circuit, trumpeter Dickie Hawdon remembered well how time-consuming it could all be: "For a gig in Liverpool you left Alsop Place (behind Baker Street where all the bands used to meet) at around 8.30 am. You didn't get back until 7.30 the next morning."[2] Bassist Pete Blannin, another regular on the road, recalls how "everything took an age then, with no motorways. It used to take four or five hours to get to Manchester. The next morning you'd stumble off the coach absolutely knackered and there's all these people going to work, clean, fresh, smart with collars and ties, and we'd all be shattered."[3]

On the longer trips – and if they could afford it – bands stayed overnight, but, in the days before elaborate contractual "riders" stipulating high standards of accommodation, the musicians often had to find their own digs. A regular port of call was Mrs Mac's boarding house in Manchester. "It was home to all the touring bands," recalled Vic Ash. "It had one single bedroom for the bandleader and one large dormitory with eight beds in it, which the rest of us used for the privilege of five shillings night. You can imagine the grunts and groans and odours during the night!"[4] If places like Mrs Mac's were not available, a band would be forced to split up and scour the streets for a single room.[5]

Alongside the ways of the itinerant musician, the first Kenny Baker tour introduced Tubby Hayes to many things he'd grow used to in the coming years. He accompanied an American star – the vocalist Nellie Lutcher – for the first time, and developed a begrudging affection for the lethal food served by the nation's transport cafes (which, in the words of Benny Green, "dotted the country's highways like a run of acne"[6]). There were other vices too, such as the over-enthusiastic female fans that would make themselves readily available. "These girls would follow the bands around and offer their services, not for money," Vic Ash maintained, "but because they were such fans of jazz musicians."[7] Casual sex was available nationwide, with some of these "groupies" garnering quite a reputation for their accommodating manner. The most notorious of all was "Jean," a colourful lady from one of the big industrial towns in the north of England. "She was something else," one musician remembered. "She would only do oral, that's all, everything else was off the menu, but she would give a great blow-job." One day, one of Hayes's colleagues came down to breakfast at a boarding house to find the young man seated in closed-eyed reverie at the kitchen table. "Aaaah! First one of the day," Hayes beamed, as Jean surfaced, smiling. Jean was certainly exceptional: without stylistic prejudice, she would provide her services to musicians in both the modern and traditional fields of jazz. Benny Green even went so far as to joke that when Ronnie Scott enlarged his group to a big band the fan who had gained the most out of the decision had been Jean.[8]

Occasionally, faced with such an inconsistent lifestyle even a young man with the cast-iron constitution of Tubby Hayes could find it all too much. When the Baker band played the Winter Gardens in Ventnor that July, he passed out, according to the *Melody Maker*, suffering from the effects of heat. The headline "Tubby Keeps Going Despite Collapse"[9] and the accompanying description of his being advised to rest but refusing to let the band down is an eerie precursor to the kind of news Hayes would make during the 1960s. For the time being, however, he managed to keep his vices under control. "He'd drink a bit and maybe have a joint," Vic Ash remembered, "but in those days, Tubby wasn't doing anything heavy, maybe just the odd smoke."[10]

Ever since the "Jazz Age" the music had an associated narcotic culture, as the multitude of songs with the words 'Reefer' and 'Viper' in their title betrayed, and cannabis joints were by no means unknown to the young beboppers. Tubby had started smoking cigarettes at school and to indulge in something more illicit probably seemed little more than part of his rite of passage into the upper echelons of the music business. However, something far darker and more deadly came with the new music: heroin addiction.

News of Charlie Parker's habit had arrived in the UK through the distorted rumour-mill of jazz folklore. Parker was known to be a hedonist, and for some European fans ignorant of the ravages of his addiction, musical modernity and narcotic indulgence seemed to be logical bedfellows. Inevitably, several of the younger English modernists began to ape their American counterparts in ways other than simple musical flattery, progressing from cannabis to heroin. One, the drummer Phil Seamen, summed up this disturbing attitude when he stated "Bebop is heroin music."[11]

To his credit, Tubby Hayes's emulation of his American heroes at this time only went so far. "People always talk about Tubby's raving side, but by far the most impressive thing about him was his music," Vic Ash commented;[12] and in summer 1951 the impression Hayes was making upon listeners received its first international acknowledgement when Barry Ulanov, the editor of the American music magazine *Metronome* (second only to *DownBeat* as chronicler of the latest jazz news) wrote a glowing endorsement in *Melody Maker*: "One of the very few English jazzmen who create a fresh pattern and an original fabric of ideas in a bop setting is a youngster I heard with the Kenny Baker band, a 16 year old tenor saxophonist by the name of Tubby Hayes."[13]

Exactly how Tubby Hayes sounded whilst with Kenny Baker's sextet is, yet again, something of a guessing game. The only commercially issued recording by the band during Hayes's stay doesn't feature him in any capacity other than that of an ensemble player. Parlophone had cut a test session with the band at EMI's soon-to-be-legendary Abbey Road Studios in June 1951 and a month later, on July 24th, the group recorded two titles, issued on the dark blue label "Rhythm-Style" series: 'I Can't Get Started', a feature for Baker, and 'I Only Have Eyes For You', including solos from Vic Ash and Jimmy Skidmore.

In the absence of any other recorded evidence from the time, surviving concert programmes provide the best indication as to the Baker band's musical bias outside the studio. They make fascinating reading: bop standards such as 'Marmaduke', 'The Squirrel', 'Ow' and 'Wee Dot' rub shoulders with themes such as 'Ray Anthony's Boogie' and 'Music, Music, Music' and there is a heavy emphasis on the vocals of either Linda Ellington or Joan Brook. Given such unfocused prospects it was hardly surprising that, although he'd barely been professional for a few months, by the autumn of 1951 Hayes was already getting itchy feet. Even a revamped band, bringing in other musicians closer in age, including saxophonist Harry Klein and pianist Stan Tracey, couldn't stop his musical wanderlust.

The final gig with Baker was on November 3rd and instantly Hayes moved on to another six-piece line-up led by another trumpeter, Terry Brown, a player with an interesting pedigree who would eventually abandon performing to become a successful producer for the Philips and Pye labels, working in both the folk and jazz idioms. During the 1960s, Brown would go on to produce several of Tubby Hayes albums, but in 1951 he was one of a small handful of local modern jazz trumpeters. He was also hopelessly idealistic, believing that artistic integrity and show-business commerce needn't automatically cancel each other out. Initially he had made the outwardly sensible decision to pattern his new outfit on a well-known role model, the sextet of accordionist Tito Burns, which had scored as much of a commercial bullseye as was possible from modern jazz in the UK with its adaptation of the style of the famed Charlie Ventura Bop For The People group. The glaring fact that Ventura's original had eventually floundered didn't seem to enter the equation.

The limited circle of jazz venues across the capital meant that the band was soon working favourite haunts such as Studio 51 and the White Hart in Acton, as well as venues which at this distance in time sound like something from a far less sardonic age, such as the Maidstone Rhythm Club and the Boathouse Bop Club in Kew. It was by no means a glamorous existence, as Brown recalled: "We had no transport, and my extra-musical job was transporting the music stands and arrangements packaged together with string, and meeting up with jobsworth bus conductors."[14] Finally, after such an undignified start, a welcome three weeks of work outside of London presented itself at The West End Café in Edinburgh over Christmas 1951. "Sean Connery was one of the bouncers," Brown remembered,[15] but being let off the leash so far away from home proved to be the band's undoing. On New Year's Eve they were invited to a party held by an individual Brown recalled as a prominent "local bigwig," during which the leader's young sidemen got very drunk. "Tubby had discovered a local brew called Thompson's British Wine at five shillings a bottle. Thanks to Tubby over-imbibing somewhat we were all thrown out. Into the cold, cold snow."[16] The band split shortly afterwards.

If the ignominious death of Brown's sextet had been merely disappointing, Hayes's next job was nothing short of hilarious. Earlier the previous year, much to his sidemen's disgust, Kenny Baker had taken a holiday, leaving his band high and dry and without work. For Hayes, a lucky break came when bandleader Roy Fox offered a two-week engagement bridging the gap. He took the job, played the fortnight and, as a result, the bandleader made a note that should he ever need a tenorist, the young man would prove ideal.

Although American by birth, Fox had been a doyen in British society circles since the 1930s, but by the early 1950s he realized that a move with the times – albeit a considered one – had become necessary in order to survive. In February 1952, the prospect of working regularly with a band chockfull of bebop-obsessed contemporaries – Hank Shaw, Vic Feldman and bassist

Lennie Bush among them – coupled with regular money, seemed ideal to Tubby Hayes. The reality was less endearing. Despite the new blood, Fox's band remained unrequitedly square and proffered nothing more challenging than an innocuous dance repertoire. The leader was also notoriously bad at paying his men on time, leaving a string of unpaid debts. Within a couple of weeks, Hayes was already feeling the pinch. Les Tomkins remembers meeting the saxophonist in an especially despondent mood on one of Fox's gigs, and believes it to be the first time he had ever witnessed the effect of stimulants other than alcohol on his friend. It was brief trough, though, and within two weeks Hayes had left the band, appending a cynical commentary about the experience in his own scrapbook. Written in ink beneath a picture of the Fox and his musicians are the words "I joined this band in February 1952 and left in February 1952. Reason? NO MONEY."

Joining Tito Burns's group for a Scottish tour, Hayes's next career move looked more promising. Burns had upped his usual numbers to that of a fourteen-piece big band, containing friends Harry Klein and Benny Green in the saxophone section; however, the uncanny knack for joining bands just as they changed musical policy persisted when Hayes was recruited to Burns's regular sextet that May. "I had only two solos. The Champ and Intermission Riff,"[17] he later recalled with disgust.

The real issue was that Burns was first and foremost a shrewd businessman and throughout his sextet's existence he'd always somehow contrived to balance business with bebop. Indeed, he was among the first commercial bandleaders in Britain to adopt the style, employing young mavericks such as John Dankworth, Ronnie Scott and Tony Crombie when few other name bands would have touched them. However, by the summer of 1952, whatever saleable steam there had been in the music was fast running out, and Tubby Hayes found himself aboard a less than happy ship that was taking an age to sink. A photograph of Burns's group in Hayes's scrapbook, taken in Ramsgate during the summer of 1952, shows a glum-looking saxophonist apparently puffing his cheeks out in exasperation, and is titled "Tito's Happy Smiling Band." Like all of Hayes's employers, all Burns was attempting to do was keep alive a financially solvent working band. His only mistake was to employ a clutch of young bebop musicians, none of whom really sympathized with their leader's plight.

Away from his sideman duties, Hayes's reputation as a jazzman was still on the upsurge. Billed under straplines like "Boy wonder tenorist," there was certainly no shortage of opportunities to show off his skills. His diary for 1952 lists countless appearances at the Feldman Club in Oxford Street and at now-forgotten suburban venues such as the Beehive Club, London; the Lion's Den, Sutton; the Club 23, West Norwood; the Robin's Nest, Hornchurch; and the Royal Roost, Leytonstone. The list of musicians participating in these ad-hoc engagements makes fascinating reading: Hayes played alongside most of the prominent local modernists of the day including Joe Harriott, Danny

Moss, Les Condon, Victor Feldman, Hank Shaw, Leon Calvert, Vic Ash, Harry South, Bob Burns, Dickie Devere, Don Lusher, Eddie Thompson and Jimmy Skidmore. There were also occasional reunions with his old idol Ronnie Scott, like that at the Gearbox Club in Dartford in December 1952. But perhaps the most remarkable of all these ad-hoc gigs were the All-Nighter sessions held on Christmas and New Year's Eve at the Zan-Zeba Club, during which Hayes locked horns with Benny Green. The Zan-Zeba was located at 39 Gerrard Street, later to become the first home of Ronnie Scott's club.

The Robin's Nest, Hornchurch, October 1952. Courtesy Peter Tongue.

Tubby Hayes now had reason besides a full diary to feel satisfied. The previous autumn he had met Margaret Helen Yates, a pretty blonde who worked as a photo finisher at Wykeham Studios in Streatham. The couple's courtship was – typically for Tubby – brief and straight to the point. Already a jazz fan, Maggie had encountered the boyish saxophonist for the first time on a trip to Wimbledon Palais and despite his being five years her junior the

The soon-to-be Mrs Hayes: Margaret Yates, circa 1952. Author's collection.

attraction was instant and mutual: she found the young prodigy charming, funny, outrageous even, and, although by no means innocent, she was hardly prepared for his final gambit of the night. Returning to her cousin's flat, she discovered that her young beau was intent on much more than just a kiss goodnight. "I thought 'Oh, he's just a boy'. I thought I could handle him but he was very mature in *every* way."[18]

From then on the couple were, in Maggie's words, "inseparable," although the social strictures of the time presented a very real impasse for the young lovers. She remembers that an early visit to the Hayes family home wasn't to meet Dorothy – quite the opposite – but to assuage their mutual passion. Even trips away from their home turf could prove tricky. Terry Brown's disastrous Scottish tour of Christmas 1951 found "Mr and Mrs Hayes" ensconced in a boarding house, with "Mrs Hayes" the proud owner of a Woolworth's wedding ring hastily bought before the trip. But these youthful trysts also had their darker side. Between 1951 and their marriage in 1953, Maggie fell pregnant three times, with each pregnancy terminated in covert, back-street abortions.[19]

To the casual observer, Hayes's next career move might have looked even more musically disastrous than that he had made when joining Tito Burns. He was now recruited by veteran dance band leader "Bert" Ambrose, a legend whose West End residencies before World War II had made him the ultimate figure in musical high society. Like Roy Fox, Ambrose had realized that he had to make compromises for a post-war audience, but it had been done through gritted teeth. "The dance-music public has changed completely," he told *Melody Maker* in the spring of 1953. "It seems to be composed almost entirely of youngsters in their teens. There's been a revolution in the dance-music business. And they know what they they're paying for. Their musical knowledge is amazing. They ask for 'The Champ' or 'The Hawk Talks' and expect to get these numbers as they hear them on records."[20]

New Musical Express ran the story of Ambrose's resurgence as if it were the dramatic recovery of a dying patient. "Among the finest he has ever fronted," the paper declared of the new band, predicting that its formation would "bring him back into the public eye with a real bang."[21] Alongside Hayes, among the other young performers Ambrose had personally selected were saxophonist Jimmy Walker, Jamaican trumpeter Pete Pitterson and pianist Ken Moule, and although the veteran bandleader knew what he was looking for – in short, youth – he wasn't really familiar with the work of the newer names under his charge. Hayes later remembered the novel way in which he'd been recruited: "Bert phoned me up and said 'Are you Tubby Hayes?' I said yes. He said 'Can you play "The Champ?"' I said yes. And he said, 'You're in!'"[22]

Another new Ambrose signing was drummer Phil Seamen, the soon-to-be-legendary hell-raiser and a figure who was to play a dark and inconsistent part in Tubby Hayes's life in the decades ahead. The two men's relationship would always remain somewhat problematic. Maggie Hayes describes it as "destructive"[23] while bassist Jeff Clyne called it "a sort of a love–hate thing."[24] But in 1953, at the time they joined Ambrose, the two men were at their closest. Similarly wild and rebellious, both revelled in whatever merriment they could make. Inevitably, Ambrose found the behaviour of the young men under his direction almost as intolerable as the new music they played. Bassist Pete Blannin sometimes worked with the band and found the leader's attitude towards musical progress far less charitable during gigs than had been related in the press: "We would be playing the more commercial stuff and then he'd say 'Right. Now we're going to have the bebop band [within a band] play something for you' and then he'd walk off with his fingers in his ears. He was really a dance band guy."[25]

Together with the seismic changes to his musical policy, the veteran star also now faced the indignity of boarding the same coach as his sidemen, just one of many reminders that his day had passed: when he arrived at an engagement in Whitley Bay in Yorkshire to find his name advertised on a chalkboard he took exception to the lack of publicity and refused to perform. But there were occasional triumphs too, and when the band headed a Coronation Ball at Southampton Guildhall on May 29th, 1953 it must have seemed like a return to former glories.

On October 27th, 1953, close to the end of his stay with Ambrose, Tubby and Margaret were married. Hayes's proposal, Maggie recalls, had been as much practical as romantic. When she had moved into a downstairs flat in Brixton Hill earlier that year, her boyfriend had followed her, a situation

Mr and Mrs Hayes: Tubby marries Margaret Yates, Tuesday October 27th, 1953. Author's collection.

prompting an apoplectic reaction from her landlady. "I remember her saying that this was a respectable place and it wouldn't do. These days this sort of thing is just accepted but then an unmarried couple living together was a real taboo. When I told Tubby this, he just said 'Right then, we'll get married!'"[26]

Before the wedding could take place, Hayes had another dilemma to attend to: aged eighteen, he had received his call-up for National Service, an opportunity that many of his generation were to later describe as defining, but which to a successful, headstrong, professional musician with a good career already established for himself held little appeal. Dodging the call to arms was possible if you knew who to ask and there were several names in the business that had done just that, including Ronnie Scott, who had been summarily dismissed from his RAF medical after he turned up speeding on Benzedrine. Others preferred to use the services of a corrupt Harley Street doctor who'd take a substantial fee for declaring his "patient" medically unsound. Along these lines, a young saxophone student of Hayes, Bruce Miles, remembers his teacher's cryptic description of how he'd avoided National Service by "[paying] someone £100 to 'fix it' for him. I didn't bother to ask who or how!"[27]

According to Maggie Hayes, the wedding day was distinctly lacking in fuss. "We picked a Tuesday because we knew a lot of guys wouldn't be working and we went down to Lambeth Registry Office with just Tubby's mum and my mum. I made my own dress and I certainly don't remember Tubby buying a new suit."[28] The witnesses – trumpeter Les Condon and saxophonist Lennie Dawes – found the whole ceremony hilarious, the result of smoking several joints beforehand, while the reception – more or less an open house at Brixton Hill – had ended when MacBean, Kenny Baker's powerfully built roadie, jammed shut the bedroom door in an effort to get the last guests to go home and leave the newlyweds in peace.

There was no honeymoon for the couple and married life soon settled into some sort of routine. Tubby would get out of bed every morning and practise whilst still in his dressing gown ("Not scales and all that, but tunes"[29]) but any activity on the domestic front was alien to him. Maggie says,

> I did everything. He wasn't lazy but he just devoted himself to music. He wouldn't even knock in a nail as he was frightened of hurting his hands. We had a coal fire but if I didn't make it up Tubby would turn on the little electric heater as he didn't know how to make a fire. If I did light it and went out, he wouldn't put any coal on so when I got back it would be really low. He needed a woman to take care of him and that was my job. Music was all that mattered to him.[30]

The couple's flat soon became a familiar port of call to many London jazzmen and, although far from salubrious, it was the scene of many convivial evenings. "It was a really rough and ready place, very grotty," Eddie Harvey remembered. "In fact, one night at a party someone fell through the floorboards – it was that bad."[31] Occasionally there were early signs of the decay of Tubby and Maggie's relationship. Hayes could be possessive and was quick to anger when challenged. One night, he arrived home drunk with a group of friends and proceeded to pull Maggie into the kitchen by her hair, demanding she cook a meal, before he was pacified by drummer Lennie Breslaw.[32] Maggie, however, was no soft touch. Eddie Harvey remembered another evening during which the couple began a terrific argument.

> Tubby was swearing, you know. "You fucking bitch" and all that, and Maggie was giving as good as she got. Anyway, Tubby got really angry and proceeded to chase her out of the flat and down the hill. She was screaming and as she ran there were these two guys, bakers, who were obviously loading their van or something as it's about three in the morning, and all they see is this woman screaming and being chased by this guy. So they start to chase Tubby! I can see him now, running as fast as he could back into the flat![33]

During the same week as the wedding, Hayes had accepted an invitation to join the orchestra of Vic Lewis, then about to embark on a "Tribute to Stan Kenton" tour alongside the band of Ronnie Scott. After the disappointments of his stay with Ambrose, it seemed that the offer might at last afford him the chance to enter an enclave of genuine modernism. Lewis certainly had a controversial reputation for barrier-breaking music. Born in 1919, he was older than most of the other London modernists but, unlike Bert Ambrose or Roy Fox, his conversion to newer musical forms had been both sincere and successful. Having heard the Stan Kenton Orchestra on a wartime V-Disc, he had been determined to pattern something of his own in Kenton's image.

By and large he had succeeded, but the pressures of a circuit dominated by Palais edicts and strict tempos meant that commercial concessions were rarely far away. A surviving broadcast from January 1954, a few weeks after Tubby Hayes joined, gives a good indication as to the band's sometimes mixed aims: Hayes plays a Zoot Sims-like solo on the opener, Gerry Mulligan's 'Bark For Barksdale', and has a brief spot on Lewis's adaptation of 'Down By The Riverside', before the programme slides further down the ladder to novelties like 'O Mien Papa' and 'South Of The Border'. A far better testament to the band's ability came the following week, when Decca Records began a series of recording sessions for a new LP, centred on the music of Gerry Mulligan, whose piano-less quartet had recently turned the jazz world on its head. Released under the title *Mulligan's Music*, the recordings marked Tubby Hayes's first solo exposure on a commercially available disc.

Three years on from the acetate with Les Tomkins, he had clearly developed. He solos on seven of the eight titles (an eighth tenor solo on 'Walkin' Shoes' appears to be by his section mate, Les Wigfield) and plays with a sense of time and tone fittingly reminiscent of Stan Kenton's tenors of the day, such as Zoot Sims and Richie Kamuca. The sound is light, the swing breezy and the improvised lines by no means wholly locked into the bebop vernacular. Rather surprisingly, the one improvisation that is redolent of the steam-roller delivery for which Hayes would soon be renowned is that on 'Bark For Barksdale', wherein, at Lewis's request, he plays the baritone saxophone. The leader was undoubtedly thinking of Mulligan, but his young sideman sounds more akin to Cecil Payne or Serge Chaloff. Indeed, battling against a band whose enthusiasm borders on crudity, Hayes's playing is without doubt the best thing about the *Mulligan's Music* album. However, the music press of the day certainly saw nothing portentous in the recordings, with *Melody Maker* delivering a penny plain review which simply states "should go well with all who like honest-to-goodness swing."[34]

Piecing together the story of Hayes's musical development pre-1955 requires the ability to make lengthy leaps between very few recorded stepping stones. The rediscovery of early acetates with Les Tomkins, Eddie Thompson and others has rounded out the picture considerably but the next step on from his official studio debut was a short one indeed. Three days after the final session for *Mulligan's Music*, on Saturday January 23rd, 1954 the Vic Lewis Orchestra's "Tribute to Stan Kenton" tour reached Sheffield City Hall, where it was recorded in circumstances that remain unclear. It appears that Lewis himself may have arranged for the concert to be taped using stereo equipment – then a new form of sound reproduction – in order for it to be sent to Stan Kenton. In the late seventies, Lewis unearthed mono acetates of the entire concert which, in truncated form and running slightly fast, were released on an LP by the HEP label.

Alongside reruns of much of the recent *Mulligan's Music* material, Hayes is featured in a quartet spot with the band's rhythm section, playing a two-tempo

Publicity still, 1953. Author's collection.

reading of 'Too Marvellous For Words' which proves to be his most revealing recording thus far. The first ballad chorus is pure Roost-era Stan Getz – clean-toned, lyrical, reserved yet romantic – but, once at medium tempo, the shape and momentum of his improvisation takes on a more characteristic Hayesian slant, with suggestions of his future work for the Tempo label, albeit tempered slightly by the cooler, leaner tone. Even if the treatment seems a little contrived and the playing somewhat routine and formulaic, the results remain impressive, especially coming from one so young. Indeed, 'Too Marvellous For Words' is just the kind of precocious performance that was then making jaws drop in London's jazz club. A few days shy of his nineteenth birthday, Tubby Hayes was already a jazzman with much to say.

Early in 1954, *Melody Maker* published the results of its annual readers' poll and for the first time Hayes had entered the running. In later years jazz polls were seen as somewhat academic, but in the 1950s the results in papers like *Melody Maker* and *New Musical Express* were much anticipated – acting as a valid guide to who was hot and who was not. Hayes had come in at sixth place in the tenor saxophone category, taking him several steps closer to realizing Maurice Burman's earlier prediction:

1. Ronnie Scott 6151

2. Tommy Whittle 4826

3. Don Rendell 3211

4. Art Ellefson 1206

5. Kenny Graham 943

6. Tubby Hayes 851

The result was also a reminder that, despite all the necessary to-ing and fro-ing in commercial big bands, Hayes remained first and foremost a committed jazzman. Making a living, however, was still a concern. Vic Lewis's wage was barely enough and in March 1954 he left the band to join the Jack Parnell Orchestra, an appointment that would prove to be his last regular sideman job.

By the mid-1950s, Parnell was already something of a household name. A stint with Ted Heath's band in the late 1940s had effectively launched him as the UK's first real big band drum star, along the lines of American idols such as Gene Krupa and Buddy Rich. However, like those of Hayes's previous employers, his own bandleading efforts had been somewhat sabotaged by wilful and unsympathetic sidemen. The band into which Hayes now entered was no exception. With personalities as forthright as Phil Seamen, Ken Wray and Hank Shaw in his charge, Parnell faced an especially tough time keeping everyone happy, walking an awkward line between purism and novelty. The band recorded regularly for the Parlophone label; in among the pop songs, Hayes appears in a solo capacity on two titles: 'Sure Thing', taped on June 10th, 1954 and 'Trip To Mars', recorded late in September of the same year. The excellence of the band's performance makes one wish for more: Neil Hefti's 'Sure Thing' is pure Basie, with the tenorist in a lazy, Wardell Gray bag, whilst 'Trip To Mars' is a suitably ballistic Marty Paich arrangement complete with rocket sound effects. The short solo spots for Hayes, trumpeter Jo Hunter and trombonist Ken Wray are balanced by band passages which sound very close to the contemporary work of Stan Kenton and Woody Herman.

Despite these blasts of modernism, daily life in a commercial British big band continued to have more than its share of downtime and drudgery. Relieving this was simple – you drank more. Phil Seamen was Hayes's room-mate on Parnell's out-of-town trips and together the two men now embarked on a hedonistic lifestyle more commonly associated with later generations of rock stars. Pete Blannin depped on a Scottish tour made by the band during the summer of 1954 and was shocked to discover the disparity between his colleague's on- and off-stage behaviour:

> We were doing [a gig at] Greens Playhouse in Glasgow and I was
> sharing with Phil and Tubby. Phil was incredible. He had a whole

stack of band parts and they were pristine! He just played them at a rehearsal and that was it, he never needed to look at them again. Anyway, one morning, we're all in bed and there's this knock at the door and this guy comes in and says "C'mon Tubby – wake up! I've got a beer for you." That was how they'd start the day. It was crazy, but on the stand they were both perfectionists, total professionals.[35]

Alongside drink, Hayes also maintained his interest in another distraction – cannabis. Whereas Seamen was already locked in the throes of serious heroin addiction – still a rarity among British jazz artists at this time – the softer option of smoking a joint was open to everyone and Hayes had taken to pot with the same enthusiasm that he had for anything that took his fancy, musical or otherwise. He'd even done his bit for turning others on to it, including, allegedly, pianist Stan Tracey.[36]

However, the law was less naïve than it had been a few years earlier during the fiasco of a drug-bust at Club XI, and those who regularly used cannabis knew they now faced much more than a smacked wrist if caught. On September 11th, 1954, whilst the Parnell band was playing a two-week engagement at Blackpool's Winter Gardens, Tubby and Margaret were arrested for possession of what the press noted as "dangerous drugs."[37] Hayes, it was said, had been found in possession of 3.53 grams of Indian hemp, whilst his wife was caught with 1.63 grams. The couple knew the ramifications were serious, and the press announced that the saxophonist and his wife were both to appear at Blackpool Magistrates Court in November to face sentencing.

There was precious little Hayes could do ahead of the court hearing other than to keep working and hope for the best. He certainly couldn't make any further plans, and at any rate the combined experience of dancing to the tunes of leaders such as Bert Ambrose, Vic Lewis and Jack Parnell over the past eighteen months had convinced him that there was little satisfaction to be had in joining yet another touring band. His solos were undoubtedly the musical high spot of the Parnell show, enjoyed by fans and fellow musicians alike, and he had made repeated requests for a wage packet reflecting his contribution, but the bandleader simply refused to budge. Years later Parnell saw the funny side of their exchanges: "[Tubby] stopped the show night after night when we were playing. I told him to bugger off, and I think to myself now: Tubby Hayes! He only wanted a pound, and he didn't get it!"[38]

The Hayes's duly appeared before the court in Blackpool on November 12th charged with possession of a dangerous narcotic. Both had been advised to plead guilty. The arresting officer Chief Constable H. Barnes began by telling the court that a search of the house in which the couple had been staying whilst in Blackpool had revealed a tin of hemp found in Tubby's jacket and a small quantity of the drug wrapped in newspaper in his wife's coat. "It is obvious from other matters found there," Barnes concluded, "that these two people had been making their own cigarettes and smoking them."[39]

Tubby and Maggie,
Studio 51, London,
December 2nd, 1954.
Author's collection.

When it came to passing sentence, the judge took into account that neither Tubby nor Margaret had had any previous encounters with the police and discharged them from court with an order to pay £2. 6s. 6d. each in costs. Chairman of the bench G. W. Leavesley delivered a stern reminder that, although they had escaped imprisonment, the couple were not above the law: "If you are caught in the next twelve months taking drugs again, you will be brought back to this court and punished."[40]

The last weeks of 1954 were a merry-go-round of back-to-back club engagements for Hayes, taking in the Mapleton, Studio 51, the Café Anglais as well as other less celebrated suburban venues. Most of these appearances were nothing more than staged jam sessions, but alongside the good cheer to be had working with old friends, some of the musicians taking part, including Hayes, were beginning to realize that disorganized, ad-hoc situations weren't necessarily helping their musical progress. In trumpeter Jimmy Deuchar – one of the most theoretically minded of all London jazzmen – Hayes now found not only a sympathetic ear but also a simpatico musical partner, and across the closing months of the year the two men's efforts to present something far more cohesive began to get noticed. Delivering an overview of the London jazz scene during the previous twelve months in *Record Mirror*, promoter, compere and journalist Tony Hall – a figure familiar to all those who attended the Flamingo and Florida clubs – singled out the partnership for especial praise.

> These two together have done so much to improve the "theme" situation in British jazz. Not for them 'Lester Leaps' (except under extreme pressure from audiences at places like Chingford!) and played-to-death standards. For them, in the latter category, it's

things like 'Between The Devil And The Deep Blue Sea', 'This Time The Dream's On Me', 'I Can Dream Can't I?' In the theme department they turn to the newest unissued American discs. They come up with exciting Horace Silver compositions on various changes.[41]

Although no one in the UK was as yet calling it by the name by which it would subsequently become known, the music that Hayes and Deuchar were playing was already firmly rooted in the hard bop vein. As the name suggested, the style was a logical outgrowth – and in some aspects *reduction* – of the methods of bebop. The tempos could still be as maniacally demanding as those of the late 1940s, but the melodies were often simpler, and the accompaniment, although still engaging and stimulating, had taken on a new earthy directness. The first records that could truly be said to feature the new style were those made by Miles Davis for the Prestige label in late 1951, featuring saxophonists Sonny Rollins and Jackie McLean. Coming on the back of the measured, pastel voicing of Davis's nonet recordings – the famous *Birth of the Cool* – this new music seemed base, crude even, but its sizzling intensity communicated in a way that was far more invigorating. Indeed, one of the basic tenets of hard bop was to be an almost "take it or leave it" approach. The style also kicked sand at the notion that the jazz idiom had to develop along more decorous, formal lines, as was then beginning to occur in California, home of what critics were already calling West Coast Jazz.

By 1954, the British Esquire label was beginning to release some of the earliest efforts in the hard bop style recorded for Prestige in New York, including records by Davis and Sonny Rollins, while Vogue had licensed similar sessions from the Blue Note imprint, among them a further Davis sextet date with trombonist J. J. Johnson and saxophonist Jimmy Heath and Johnson's own 10" LP featuring the brilliant young trumpeter Clifford Brown. Tubby Hayes and his young colleagues digested as much of this music as they could, and within a relatively short space of time its influence began to permeate their respective styles: bassist Pete Blannin took on something of Percy Heath's drive, drummer Bill Eyden hero-worshipped Art Blakey and a pianist from South London new to Hayes's circle, Terry Shannon, displayed an uncanny understanding of the methods of Horace Silver and Sonny Clark.

The local guiding light for all these men remained Jimmy Deuchar, a player cut from the same cloth as Clifford Brown, and one of the few British modernists to have emerged with his musical aims seemingly fully formed. On a scene where some players' efforts at contemporary improvisation could still sound ragged and unformed, Deuchar's solo work had a formidable logic, something that had begun to exert a tremendous influence upon Tubby Hayes. As the two men further cemented their collaboration over the festive season of 1954 – and with gigs at places as unpromising as Streatham Baths Hall there was probably little else to do *but* strengthen relations – the saxophonist realized how much more he had yet to learn:

> Jimmy was the one who really made me start taking music seriously. I'd been on the road with big bands from 1952–54 and didn't worry much about anything, except having a ball. Then that Christmas came the group at the old Flamingo with Jimmy, Terry Shannon, Pete Blannin and Bill Eyden. Jimmy was so good that I had to try.[42]

The impact on those who heard this band in person was to prove unforgettable, with Tony Hall loudly predicting a great future for the unit in his regular magazine column. Sixty years later, he still stands by his earlier declaration that Deuchar and Hayes made a trumpet and tenor team every bit the equal of those in the bands of Horace Silver.[43] However, the pipe dream of a regular union between the two men burst on February 12th, 1955, when *Melody Maker* announced that Hayes was to form a new nine-piece touring band. At the age of just twenty, and after having spent barely four years as a professional musician, the saxophonist now faced the quite sudden prospect of becoming the youngest bandleader in the country. As such, the ensuing eighteen months would provide some of the best – and the worst – moments of his career.

Tubby Hayes and his Orchestra pose for an early publicity photo, spring 1955. Front row (left to right) Harry South, Pete Blannin, Tubby Hayes, Jackie Sharpe and Dickie Hawdon. Back row (left to right) Les Condon, Lennie Breslaw and Mike Senn. Author's collection.

It was small wonder that Tubby Hayes held ambitions to lead his own band. He was gifted, charismatic and precociously able and although barely out of his teens he felt he'd already taken more than his fill of working for other leaders. Much of the preceding four years had been spent bowing low to overly commercial musical policies or in being woefully under-appreciated by those that employed him. Even those leaders who had recognized Hayes's potential, such as Jack Parnell, had been hard put to find much space for him among programmes bursting with novelty numbers, popular songs and mambos. Nevertheless, there were those who *had* been listening and taking note.

Late during Hayes's stay with the Parnell band, his former employer Tito Burns had attended a concert at which the saxophonist had delivered a typically show-stopping solo feature. The audience's reaction to this dazzling display piqued Burns's interest. He already knew Hayes well: the two men's conflicting aims had brought their brief musical association to an abrupt end three years earlier, but by early 1955 even Burns himself had tired of the perpetual reinvention required to maintain a regular working group and had decided to use his already extensive musical connections in order to establish his own booking agency. The connections soon paid off and within a few weeks of starting his business Burns had signed a contract with Whetstone Entertainment Ltd, operators of a string of Northern ballrooms, and had also won a coveted deal as sole agent for the US Forces base at Burtonwood in Lancashire. Whoever Burns booked was assured of a healthy supply of work, and, keen to build a stable of young artists, he put the idea of leading a band to Hayes.

To Burns's surprise, the saxophonist was initially reluctant. Although no bad blood remained between the two men, the offer had struck Hayes as insufficient. The agent had volunteered his old band uniforms, music stands and a ready-made library, but Hayes was insistent that if a new band were to go out under his leadership it was by no means to be a second-hand echo of an already failed venture. This determination paid off and Burns eventually agreed to stump up the money for the new equipment and arrangements. The music press was soon ablaze with the news that Hayes was to become "Britain's youngest bandleader." *Melody Maker*'s breaking story on February 12th made much of the young man's intention to provide a new sound "with the unusual instrumentation of three tenors doubling baritones, two trumpets doubling mellophone, three rhythm and a girl vocalist"[44] but, if anything, the press were a little ahead of themselves, as Hayes had as yet only confirmed the availability of three potential recruits. Nevertheless, one can readily understand their enthusiasm. Burns too had wasted no time in ensuring the new band's pre-launch publicity was as captivating as possible, announcing that Hayes had already signed a two-year contract with Vogue-Decca Records.

As press and fans alike worked themselves into a minor frenzy over the potential of the new unit, there were those who cast a more considered eye, including another young bandleader who might well have been able to offer some cautionary advice – none other than Ronnie Scott. Indeed, there was a certain amount of timely irony to the formation of the new Tubby Hayes band. With its flexible three saxes, two brass line-up and jazz-heavy intentions, the group was almost a carbon copy of the line-up that Scott had led since his defection from Jack Parnell in 1952, but which, by early 1955, was dying a slow, unfortunate death. For Tubby Hayes, Scott remained something of a hero and, throughout the scrapbook that he kept from 1951 to 1956, there are various clippings documenting the older man's musical movements. This interest was by no means obsessive, nor was it yet competitive (at least on Hayes's part), but rather Hayes sensed a musical kindred spirit in the older man. In fact, despite its failure, Scott's nine-piece was actually a rather good role model on which Hayes could base his own band. The instrumentation was large enough to pack the punch of a big band, but not so big as to become unwieldy and, crucially, there remained plenty of space for individual solo statements.

Whilst Tito Burns inked in the diary for that spring, Hayes got around to the hands-on business of choosing his sidemen, using the opportunity not to cherry-pick from well-known names but to give breaks to those contemporaries he thought deserved a wider hearing.

The saxophone section centred upon altoist Mike Senn, a journeyman from the bands of Basil Kirchin, Kathy Stobart and Henry Hall who had recently quit the music scene and returned to the family confectionery business. Alongside Senn, Hayes recruited a new face, tenorist Jackie Sharpe. A jobbing London taxi driver at the time he received Hayes's offer, Sharpe was perhaps taking greater risks than any other member of the new band, selling his cab – and potentially his livelihood – in order to buy a baritone saxophone and make the move to music full-time. Settling the remainder of the personnel was to prove more difficult. Bassist Pete Blannin still had to work his notice on a society gig in Mayfair whilst Harry South, an old friend from the days of the T and H Club, had to extricate himself from commitments to the Tony Crombie band. Securing a trumpet section was even more time-consuming: after accepting a lucrative contract with the BBC Show Band, Jimmy Deuchar was unavailable and so Hayes turned initially to another Crombie alumnus, Les Condon. In principle, it was an inspired choice. Vociferously dedicated to the new music and well regarded in London jazz circles for his sharp dress sense and general air of hipster cool (his colleagues had nicknamed him The Dude), Condon hadn't yet displayed much in the way of matching musical coherence. Indeed, the Tony Crombie band from which he'd transferred – in which he'd played alongside fellow trumpeter Dizzy Reece – had boasted some of the most ragged ensemble work yet heard on the British jazz scene. The same triumph of spirit and camaraderie over musical appropriateness also informed Hayes's choice of drummer, Lennie Breslaw, another East-Ender who had made a name for himself on the suburban jazz club circuit.

The personnel finalized, there then followed several hectic weeks up until the band's first public performance, scheduled to take place at the South Parade Pier, Southsea on Friday April 1st, 1955. Throughout the build-up Tito Burns continued to court the press. Publications as varied as *Weekly Sporting Review* and *Record Mirror* devoted columns to coverage of the band's first rehearsal at Studio 51, with Tony Hall positively effusive in his verdict: "It was the most exciting and musically interesting – as well as swinging – sound I've heard since the Scott band started three years ago. Rough edges galore, of course. But that's only to be expected at this stage. I hope it's a great success."[45] However, by far the most perceptive documentation of the birth pangs of the Tubby Hayes orchestra was that contributed to the *New Musical Express* by Benny Green.

Green had been catapulted to musical fame as part of the Ronnie Scott band, but he had deep-seated reservations as to whether he was genuinely capable enough to sit among such fast company. Although undoubtedly a competent saxophonist, his real gift and, it would transpire, true vocation was as a writer. Indeed, such was his all-consuming fascination with literature that the rumours soon abounded that while the remainder of the Scott band were going to bed with whoever they could, Green was going to bed with a good book. Supporting this, television personality Michael Parkinson remembers an incongruous situation when, as a young jazz fan in Barnsley, he had the dubious pleasure of providing the Scott band with refreshments on the interval of a gig. Parkinson entered the dressing room to find most of the band members making merry in whatever way they saw fit, as Green sat soberly in the corner reading Dostoevsky.

Such were Green's talents as a wordsmith that in 1953 the *New Musical Express* hired him to contribute a regular column – a sort of insider view of the jazz scene. However, it quickly transpired that this was to be none of the trite prose found elsewhere in the music press. Green wrote with genuine wit and a sophisticated command of the language, a skill that sat somewhat at odds with his cab-driver speaking voice, and he had an uncanny knack for blowing apart the artifice that accompanied much of the dance band business.

NME liked to bill Green with various jocular straplines – "The Runyon of Rhythm" and so on – and reviewing the early rehearsals by the Tubby Hayes band in the paper's March 25th issue, he was dubbed "The Saxophone Player With A Twinkle In His Typewriter." Enormously impressed by Hayes, Green quickly took to task those who saw the leader's tender years as an impasse to the success of his new venture:

> Here and there, I have heard scepticism about this project. People wonder if one so young as Tubby can front a band. I remind them that age is a question less of years than experience and that Tubby has been with the best touring bands for a long while now.

He also offered up the first documented acknowledgement of what, if it didn't sound too pretentious, might be termed the Tubby Hayes Phenomenon.

> In some weird way that defies explanation, Edward Brian "Tubby" Hayes has, over the past two or three years become something of a legendary character to the teenagers of the provinces. He has somehow captured the imagination of the younger fans possibly because he is no older than they are and they can identify themselves with him and enjoy a sort of vicarious self-pride when he does something special, perhaps because the boisterous happy spirit is there for everyone to see. The boy is bursting at the seams with it. Whatever it is, it is a factor which cannot be ignored by those who are trying to assess his chances. The touring band leaders who have had Tubby in their bands and have lost him know what I mean.[46]

Green concluded his piece by mentioning some of those within the business who wished Hayes well, including Phil Seamen, Kenny Graham and himself, adding that should Mike Senn unexpectedly quit "well, Tubby has my number – I wouldn't mind."[47]

On March 10th, 1955, three weeks ahead of its public debut, the Tubby Hayes orchestra visited Decca Studios in West Hampstead to cut its first recording for the Tempo label. Just ahead of the session, *Melody Maker* had announced the recruitment of Dickie Hawdon to the band's trumpet section, to some observers a highly unlikely appointment. Hawdon had cut his teeth in traditional jazz circles with bands as dyed-in-the-wool as the Christie Brothers Stompers, but in recent years had surprised everyone with a titanic musical leap to the cool school sextet of Don Rendell. There were still problems in securing the personnel and so for the purposes of the recording Jimmy Deuchar temporarily joined Hawdon in the trumpet section. In the remarkably short time allotted them, the band cut four titles, Duke Jordan's 'Jordu', 'Orient Line' by Harry South, Horace Silver's 'May Ray' and Victor Feldman's 'Monsoon'.

Although Hayes had chosen an ambitious set of compositions – almost amounting to a modernist's manifesto – the band's performance revealed equal parts strength and weakness, as the music press were quick to highlight. Unsurprisingly, *Melody Maker*'s Edgar Jackson hacked the recordings to pieces. Reviewing the initial 78 rpm release of 'May Ray' and 'Orient Line' in the paper's May 14th edition, he described the notion of recording the new unit as "a mistake."[48] "A band needs time to develop a character and if one may judge from this record, Mr Hayes is no exception to this rule." *New Musical Express* was only slightly more charitable: "Rough but ready, willing and able. The band's tremendous wailing enthusiasm atones for the lack of polish. But that I'm sure will come before very long."[49]

"A lovely shouting little band." The octet on-stage at the Chiswick Empire, Sunday April 24th, 1955. Author's collection.

Sixty years on there remains a substantial body of truth in these contemporary assessments. The first recordings by the new Hayes band are indeed both bursting with youthful alacrity and lacking in mature refinement. However, it should be remembered that they are, above all, *debut* recordings and should be judged accordingly. Neither profound, nor especially well executed, they contain little in ensemble terms that presciently points towards the sort of high standard that the leader would demand in the coming decades, but where they do score is in Hayes's startling confidence. For one so young, he already sounds remarkably assured, and a well-assimilated understanding of the mechanics of modern jazz is evident throughout, especially on 'Jordu', a composition with a devilish series of descending modulations in its construction. What is perhaps even more remarkable, especially at this distance, is how unlike any other jazz saxophonist – American or British – he already sounds. Finding just the right setting for this gift was to prove difficult in the years immediately ahead.

Hayes arrived in Southsea on April 1st to find a stack of telegrams from friends and colleagues wishing him well for opening night, among them messages from Annie Ross, Tony Hall, Tito Burns and Harold Davison. The evening now had an added pressure: the band of drummer Basil Kirchin was also appearing in the town that same night and, although the two men were friends, Hayes knew the competition for an audience would be very real. The music press was also waiting with bated breath, poised to deliver its verdict on The Little Giant's big idea. In general, their reception was positive: Mike

Butcher's report in *NME* glowed with praise, especially for Hayes's quick-thinking attitude regarding the evening's programming. Finding themselves before a largely dance-hungry crowd, the band hastily reorganized from the heavily jazz-slanted set-list they intended to play to something far more commercial.

> Tubby proved he has an alert head on his young shoulders. He put in a lot of commercial material including some well-conceived medleys of current pops and familiar standards, relegated most of the jazz to a less conspicuous position, between more obviously popular offerings – and still managed to feature more good music in three hours than most of his competitors in thirty![50]

Butcher also praised the band's cohesion: "The ensemble gets a great fat sound and shows unmistakable evidence of painstaking rehearsal. Sure enough the band has its faults, including the occasional inaccuracies common to every new crew. But the success it deserves is unlimited."[51]

All of the press reviews singled out Tubby's own solo contributions, with *Music Mirror*'s Tony Hall making note of two tenor features, 'Imagination' and "the Sonny Rollins line on 'Way You Look Tonight'": "He is quite the most uncommercial tenorman in Britain. Certainly the most coloured [sic] sounding. Very Sonny Rollins-ish, in fact."[52] Mike Nevard of *Melody Maker* agreed: "[He is] a magnificent tenorist by any standards, with eloquent ideas, an admirable sound and swing and the authority which many musicians twice his age would envy."[53]

Having scored a somewhat qualified victory, it was clear from the outset that Hayes and his band were going to have a struggle on their hands as they tried to escape the expectations of the dance circuit. Indeed, their touring itinerary that spring wasn't exactly chock-full of outstanding jazz dates:

April 2nd – US Air Force base, Brize Norton

April 3rd – US Air Force base, Greenham Common

April 4th – Royal Festival Hall concert opposite John Dankworth and Don Rendell

April 8th – Chingford

April 9th – Chelmsford

April 10th – Chatham

April 14th – Amesbury

April 16th – Empire Rooms, Taunton

April 17th – Hackney Empire (compere Bob Monkhouse)

April 18th – Royal Festival Hall Recital Rooms

April 23rd – Peterborough

April 24th – Chiswick Empire (with David Nixon)

April 29th – Recording session for Decca

May 1st – debut appearance at The Flamingo Club

May 2nd – Manor House

May 5th – Acton

May 8th – Ramsgate

Bassist Pete Blannin remembers well the pressures they were under: "We tried to get a few commercial things in there to kind of keep the punters happy. You just did it – you had to play things they could dance to. You'd have this bloody big ballroom full of people who wanted to dance so you can't go playing 'Oop Bop Sh'Bam' and all that. It was a case of survival."[54] As his sidemen soon found out, the leader took it all in his stride. Off the stand, he rarely focused on their shaky fiscal future, preferring instead to indulge his passion for sport. Jack Sharpe in particular found him a fascinating character. "Though music was Tubby's life he had a lot of outside interests. He was a keen fight fan, and we

An impromptu cricket match on an unidentified Devon beach, summer 1955. Mike Senn fields while Bill Eyden keeps wicket. Courtesy Maureen Eyden.

used to go to all the small halls. He had all the books and a terrific knowledge of boxing. In the daytime, when he was away with the band, his spare time would be taken up watching cricket or football."[55]

Life on the road also fuelled the gradual realization that, although the man next to you was musically hand-in-glove, you needn't necessarily approve of everything he did. Even the leader wasn't above criticism. Pete Blannin found Hayes unashamedly self-centred: "He was a bit spoilt, I think. His upbringing, I guess. He liked to get his own way about everything. He could be very petulant at times."[56] Dickie Hawdon recalled his boss as "a bit of a hooligan," prone to living it up rather than taking care of business. Hawdon also remembered that the inconsistencies of being a co-operative band were enough to test even the most battle-hardened of campaigners. When they found themselves playing a percentage gig to a handful of people in Wisbech, the trumpeter's protestations to his leader ended in a fist-fight.[57] Under such duress, the only thing to really do was concentrate upon the music and, as the Tubby Hayes band toured across the UK during the spring of 1955, it grew in cohesiveness, artistic empathy and musicianship. Years after it had disbanded, its member still glowed with pride about its collective achievements: "It was a lovely shouting little band," Dickie Hawdon remembered,[58] whilst Jack Sharpe maintained "Tubby's band on the road was an education I would not have missed for anything: One of the happiest periods of my life."[59]

3 '56 not '45 (1955–58)

One we don't advise you stir the tea to . . .

Unidentified BBC announcer introducing
the Tubby Hayes band, January 4th, 1956

Away from his own unit, Hayes continued to make as many out-and-out jazz dates as he could, whenever possible in the company of Jimmy Deuchar. The trumpeter's dream of his own band including Hayes may well have fallen flat but the pair remained as musically tight as ever and on April 26th, 1955 Tony Hall produced a session for the Tempo label featuring both men under Deuchar's direction. The recording was actually something of a coup for Hall, who had raved almost weekly in the *Music Mirror* about his desire to record an album with a personally selected line-up. Hall's day job was in the promotions department of Vogue-Decca Records (he'd already held a similar position at the UK arm of Capitol Records) but his first love remained modern jazz. During the early 1950s he had served as the resident compere at the Feldman club and exposed to the myriad abilities of the local modernists had already begun making plans for his own brand of "dream" bands. For the time being, these ideas amounted to nothing more than indulgent fantasies but when Jeff Kruger opened the Flamingo club in the summer of 1952, Hall wasted no time in supplementing his role as emcee by assembling groups of players he liked, operating under the title of the Hall-Stars. However, when he began chivvying the powers that be at Vogue-Decca to take an interest in the kind of music he was presenting nightly in London's club land, he faced an uphill struggle. British jazz – of any stripe – wasn't a big seller, the Decca chiefs argued, and the names Hall was presenting were hardly household ones. Only after agreeing to take on all the organizational tasks necessary for a recording was he finally given the go-ahead. Not surprisingly, the work was all unpaid and strictly for kicks. "The people at Decca let me do these sessions, rather patronisingly thinking I would do my day job better if I was happy," he later remarked.[1]

Once a home for Revivalist jazz, the Tempo label had been launched in the late 1940s, during the first wave of post-war British traditionalism, but had quickly fallen by the wayside. By the time Hall came on board, it had been revamped, albeit modestly, and was tucked away in a tiny corner of the company's budget allowance – the ideal place to produce records that might be rather less saleable than Decca's other concerns. Initially Tempo had gone for a fairly safe bet, the sextet of Don Rendell, whose cool, West Coast-ish music wasn't likely to upset the corporate horses; Hall, however, had ideas above and beyond the local scene. Handsome, charismatic and well-spoken, he had a knack of getting to know those in important places and had already begun a transatlantic correspondence with various US record label bosses, with a view to exporting British jazz to the USA. John Dankworth had recently signed to the American Capitol label and there had already been some rather half-baked attempts to export the recordings of Ronnie Scott and others to the US; but Hall envisaged something far more authentic. His first success came through negotiations with Contemporary Records – the leading California-based label who boasted Shelly Manne, The Lighthouse All-Stars and Lennie Niehaus among its roster – securing a deal to produce his own album for issue in America. Although Contemporary was by no means an ideal place for the kind of music Hall loved – hard bop – it did have a UK licensing deal with Vogue-Decca, thus cutting down on everything from paperwork to promotion. Further persistence had also enabled him to pique the interest of other American companies including Imperial, Savoy and Blue Note.

On the afternoon of April 26th, 1955, Hall took his seat in the control booth of Decca's West Hampstead studio to direct his first export session. Owing to existing commitments, the logistics had taken some time to fix, but the producer could hardly believe his luck in assembling exactly the personnel he'd asked for: Jimmy Deuchar, Tubby Hayes, Ken Wray, Derek Humble, Victor Feldman, Lennie Bush and Phil Seamen. To aid the export drive, each of Deuchar's original themes was to be titled after a famous British beer. A little bit of local colour was a small price to pay for the opportunity to export the work of his favourite local players.

The four titles cut that day are a revealing barometer of the state of British modern jazz at the time, and the varying skills of their participants provide an accurate picture of the music's plusses and minuses. Throughout the session, the band play with the blend of stiff accuracy, overdone dynamics and enthused energy peculiar to British jazz of the day, and, almost ironically, the best of the four titles 'I. P. A. Special', was recorded at the very beginning of the session, when the participants might have been expected to sound at their most tentative. Tubby Hayes's performance in particular shows a remarkable assurance: the tone is full and clear, far more so than on the March octet date, and the shape of his improvisation, far from being a ceaseless stream of boppish semi-quavers, contains a thoughtful sense of balance, coursing through the changes at one moment only to pause, open the vibrato and stress a piquant choice of sustained note the next.

When the four titles recorded that day eventually appeared on the Contemporary label, issued in 1957 under the delightful title of *Pub Crawling With Jimmy Deuchar*, they didn't exactly set the US jazz scene alight. Nevertheless, Tony Hall was well satisfied – he had proved that, through little more than sheer determination, the hitherto impossible could be achieved. He was also delighted at the uniformly excellent critical reaction given the British issue of the music, a far more austere effort on a 10" LP with the rather more sober title of *Jimmy Deuchar Ensemble*. Unqualified victories for British jazz recordings were virtually unheard of but *NME*'s Mike Butcher led the cheers by describing the album as "just about the most successful set of its kind ever produced in Britain,"[2] even going so far as to align Deuchar with Clifford Brown. *Jazz Monthly*'s Alun Morgan heard similar authenticity when played a test-pressing of the LP in an informal "blindfold test" and was convinced that Tubby Hayes was none other than Sonny Rollins.[3] Even Edgar Jackson offered a rare endorsement, finding 'I. P. A. Special' "probably not only the best example of British jazz in the modern manner ever to find its way on to a record, but not far short of one of the best from anywhere."[4]

As the Hayes orchestra made its way between the dance halls of the British Isles that summer, it began to dawn on its members that their early hopes of success had been somewhat premature. Although the camaraderie was strong enough to overcome the hurdles of bringing modern jazz to the provinces, it couldn't always countervail musical differences and, in the first of many such instances over his career, Hayes now sensed that his rhythm section was not all that it might be. The doubts centred on Lennie Breslaw, a player whose appointment, some argued, had been more social than musical. Breslaw's own recollection of the end of his time with Hayes is brief and to the point: "We got into some argument about a number he didn't think I was making it on. He got aggressive and I got aggressive back."[5] "Lennie was a lovely guy but it just wasn't happening," Pete Blannin remembers. "Pretty soon Tubby realized that he wasn't what he wanted so we got Bill Eyden, who was fantastic."[6]

Phil Seamen may well have had a singular flamboyance, and ultimately the greater reputation, but Eyden's stock-in-trade was two-fold – incredible physical power behind the kit combined with genuine consistency – and, even though he was only twenty-five at the time he joined Hayes, he was already one of the finest jazz drummers ever to have emerged from the UK. "Bill was great," Blannin maintains. "Some guys are easy to play with, some aren't, but Bill was a dream for me. It became a whole different ball game. The band just lifted. That first night, we thought 'We've got something now!'"[7]

Criss-crossing the UK from Oldham to Minehead, the Tubby Hayes orchestra's itinerary for June, July and August 1955 was gruelling, but no less extensive than that of any other commercial band of the period. Squeezed in between one-nighters in Ashton-in-Makerfield and Huddersfield, their next recording session took place on July 14th, resulting in further 78 rpm singles of 'Tootsie Roll' and 'Fidelius', the latter a composition by Victor Feldman which had already been recorded by its composer in the company of Ronnie Scott. Both performances reveal how – in little under two weeks – Bill Eyden's presence had transformed the band.[8]

The Hayes band into which Eyden entered, however, remained in the grip of fiscal crisis. Another new face, trumpeter Ian Hamer, was recruited shortly afterwards – replacing Dave Usden – and his surviving contract makes fascinating reading. Hired at the block rate of £15 for three evening performances, Hamer was also guaranteed a further £3 for any other evening engagements with the additional heady promise of £20 per week should the band commence a residency. The latter looked extremely unlikely, but with work on the road beginning immediately, Hamer soon saw how much effort his leader would put into getting their music across to the public. Occasionally, all the showmanship could backfire:

> Tubby would bring the band off at the end of a number by swinging his sax down, like sax players do. Anyway, one night he'd had a bit to drink, and at the end of the tune, he brought his sax up and when it came down it slipped off the neck strap and went crashing onto the floor. There were bits and pieces everywhere. So he could carry on, Jack Sharpe lent him his tenor and the next thing you know, he did it again on the next number. I can remember the two of them out the back in the interval, trying to make one good sax between the two. It was hilarious.[9]

Privy to his leader's talents both on- and off-stage, Hamer also learnt about Tubby Hayes – ladies' man. Despite being married, it appears Hayes didn't think too rigidly of his commitment to Maggie. Away from home for long stretches, he lapped up the attention of the opposite sex and, as Hamer discovered, could prove unbelievably vain about how he projected his image. During the band's stop in Rhyl, the trumpeter found himself sharing a caravan with Hayes and Jack Sharpe and on their night off the two saxophonists had taken an inordinately lengthy time to get ready for an evening out, with Tubby immaculate in a clean, neatly pressed blue serge suit. Hamer had elected to stay in for the night and, as expected, was awoken several hours later by the arrival of his two friends. But, far from piling in with two acquiescent conquests as he'd imagined, the door flung open to reveal Tubby plastered from head to toe in mud. His evening hadn't gone quite as planned, and had been topped off by slipping over face forward outside the caravan. He didn't see the funny side.

For Hayes's next recorded venture on Tempo, Tony Hall decided to temporarily abandon the larger band in favour of documenting the tenorist with only his rhythm section. Ever since the Southsea debut that spring Hayes had made a point of featuring himself in a quartet format for all of his band's gigs, providing not only a breather for his fellow players but a genuine slice of jazz for those who'd come to listen rather than dance. Hall initially thought of capturing just four of these party-pieces and accordingly booked the Decca Studios for the afternoon of July 29th, but to his delight, he found Hayes, Harry South, Pete Blannin and Bill Eyden amenable to recording a further four titles. Released on two extended play 45s – appropriately titled *The Swinging Giant* – the results are unquestionably the highlight of Tubby Hayes's 1955 discography.

Whilst not expansive (none of the eight titles breaches four and a half minutes) the eight performances contain the best examples yet of the young saxophonist's fast maturing skills. The up-tempo themes – 'Peace Pipe', Harry South's blues 'Dance Of The Aerophragytes' and Horace Silver's 'Opus De Funk' – find Hayes at his bellicose, youthful best, hurtling through his choruses with both tangible excitement and apparent ease. Indeed, so characteristic are these three performances that they might well serve as a sort of statement of intent; the fire and energy we now think of as the musical hallmarks of Hayes's mature style are already displayed in abundance, albeit still in a somewhat prototypical manner. They are, perhaps, the first recordings in which Tubby Hayes can truly be said to sound like himself.

Two grooving medium-tempo themes – 'There Will Never Be Another You' and Johnny Mandel's 'Straight Life' – both contain genuinely relaxed improvisations, countering all the claims that Hayes's performances were all smoke and mirrors, while the session's two ballads, 'There's No You' and 'Imagination', are given elegiac and slightly rueful readings (a mood heightened by the period use of the echo chamber) which, like 'Sophisticated Lady' from the octet's book, also demonstrate a commendable maturity. *Music Mirror*'s Anne Kennedy-Wilson spoke for many when she described the sudden leap forward Hayes appeared to have made on the new issues: "You have to admit that he is blowing stronger and better these days," she wrote reviewing one of the EPs, drawing particular attention to the "richer and more fulsome tone he displays now."[10]

Others clearly agreed. A snapshot of Hayes's activities at the close of the year illustrates how popular he was now becoming: On December 21st there was a Flamingo gig co-led with Joe Harriott; the 23rd found him playing as part of an all-star line-up led by Vic Ash at Studio 51; on Christmas Eve there was an all-night session by the whole of Hayes's band at Club Americana in Coventry Street; Christmas Day featured another all-star bill with Ronnie Scott, Derek Humble, Jimmy Deuchar and Tony Crombie at the Florida Club; and finally the full Hayes band returned to the Downbeat Club on Boxing Day. One contemporary report of the gig at the Americana reveals that the

The Jazz Jamboree, Gaumont State, Kilburn, Sunday October 23rd, 1955. Mike Senn looks on admiringly as Hayes and Bill Eyden get to work. Author's collection.

band played for no less than *eleven* hours, an account capturing perfectly the kind of Herculean energy for which Hayes was famed. Indeed, now almost manically driven to create his niche, the saxophonist's hard work was at last beginning to pay off. Although Tommy Whittle had taken the tenor title in the *Melody Maker* readers' poll that autumn, Hayes's band were now placed fifth as the Most Promising New Band. Even more crucially, they had finally passed their BBC audition.

The Tubby Hayes orchestra's first BBC dance music broadcast was aired on the afternoon of Wednesday January 4th, 1956. While they were fully aware of the make-or-break power of Broadcasting House, none of the band were filled with joy at the prospect of playing a programme of what Ian Hamer recalled as "dance band shit."[11] Remarkably, a copy of the broadcast has survived, one of the earliest of Hayes's BBC appearances to do so, and the eleven titles it contains make for fascinating – and in some ways revelatory – listening. The period aura is heightened by an unidentified male compere, the very embodiment of the punctiliousness of Auntie. "Tubby and the boys are all set to bring you a bright bouncy tune to set the tea-cups rattling," he declares before the band launch into a programme including such fare as

'The Yellow Rose of Texas' and 'Oo-Bang-Jiggly-Jang'. Much of the weight of trying to pass themselves off as a commercial band falls to vocalist Bobby Breen, a performer whose versatility had made him a useful asset out on the road. But while Breen was a one-man commercial sales-pitch on live gigs – dancing, playing percussion, telling gags – even he couldn't help save the broadcast. The show's few "jazz" performances – 'Sophisticated Lady', a quartet feature for the leader in 'Almost Like Being In Love' and a version of Count Basie's 'Ain't It The Truth' ("one we don't advise you to stir the tea to") are so marooned in a sea of mush as to barely register. For the broadcast the band received the lavish collective fee of £43. 7s. 0d.; one can imagine they felt they'd earned every penny.

Tubby Hayes celebrated his twenty-first birthday three weeks later on January 30th, marking the occasion with a party held at the Downbeat Club, attended by friends including Flash Winston, Tony Hall, Pete Blannin, Harry Klein, Benny Green and Jeff Ellison. Green saw this coming-of-age as the perfect excuse to examine Hayes's career to date and, in an article in the *New Musical Express* on February 10th, he began by stating his incredulity at the saxophonist's recent milestone: "It is a very peculiar experience celebrating the twenty-first birthday of a veteran," he wrote, going on to explain with typical depth of perception how the youngster now cut a very different musical figure to those around him:

> Edward Brian "Tubby" Hayes, as from last Monday technically a man, is a significant figure on the British jazz scene today. The first tenor saxophone for several years to challenge the venerable triumvirate of Scott, Whittle and Rendell, he is in one very important way different musically from any of those three contemporaries. He has never had to shed a Dixieland conception of harmony, nor sit down and figure out exactly how to make himself sound like '56 and not '45. Flattening his ninths comes as naturally to him as screwing up the ligature on his mouthpiece, and for this reason his playing has a fluency very rare among modern jazz players in this country. He has the jump on most of his contemporaries, for there is no conflict of styles. He plays exactly as Tubby Hayes would wish him to play, and he never thinks about it. It comes easily. Tubby continues to blow his saxophone with the desperate intensity of a man wrestling the devil, very possibly unaware that he comprises almost single-handed the younger jazz generation in this country.[12]

Green's comments on Hayes's apparent superiority to many other local jazzmen weren't mere sycophancy. Nor was there any exaggeration in his declaration that Hayes was now a serious contender to topple the "venerable triumvirate" of Ronnie Scott, Don Rendell and Tommy Whittle. It was easy to see why. Nearly a decade older than Hayes, Scott, Rendell and Whittle had begun their careers during World War II, when a shortage of musicians had enabled promising youngsters to take positions in bands that otherwise might have not have been available to them. As such, by the time of the arrival of the first bebop records in the UK each man was already deeply versed in the vernacular of the day's popular swing bands. The same could also be said of their almost exact contemporaries across the Atlantic – men such as Dexter Gordon, Zoot Sims and Stan Getz, for example – but shaking off one idiomatic guise in order to don another was altogether far harder without regular first-hand exposure to its source. For this reason alone (it certainly was no reflection of the individual instrumental talents of these players) the work of the three English tenorists had not always seamlessly progressed from – or indeed even wholly abandoned – the earlier ground rules of swing – the very crux of Green's "'56 not '45" argument. Whittle sometimes echoed Don Byas, Rendell had something of the powder-puff elegance of Lester Young and, in his more bellicose moods, even Scott could revert back to a booting style in which it was possible to detect trace elements of early influences such as Charlie Ventura and Vido Musso. Against this backdrop, Tubby Hayes was, almost by default, bound to stand out. Whilst Scott and others may well have been curious about the work of distinctly forward-thinking players like Sonny Rollins, Hank Mobley and Frank Foster, these influences were slow in coming to the surface. Hayes, on the other hand, made no secret of his desire to keep abreast of the latest trends and was seemingly able to absorb and consolidate these newer styles with unusual ease and rapidity. Later in life, this appetite for fashion would occasionally get the better of him, but in the mid-1950s, there could be little doubt that Tubby Hayes was closer to the vanguard than virtually any other British modernist.

Comparison with the leading Americans, however, continued to be as insidious as it was unavoidable. The British jazz scene remained notoriously insular and insecure, a situation due not only to its relatively small number of exponents, but also to the ongoing embargo on visiting American bands. "US jazz men dislike the ban as well," John Dankworth had told *Melody Maker* the previous year following a promotional visit to America,[13] but it was hard to see exactly what they were losing out on. British musicians, on the other hand, were seemingly bereft of everything – the sustenance of a supportive network of fellow players, access to the latest innovations as they unfolded, the general energy of a scene far more robust and ambitious. Until a genuinely free exchange of musical ideas were permitted, they protested, their music would continue to exist under a bell jar.

The portcullis finally lifted in spring 1956. After years of interminable wrangling, the American Federation of Musicians and the British Musicians' Union had finally struck a deal centred around a man-for-man exchange, with the negotiating officials reasoning that such a literal interpretation ensured no player on either side of the Atlantic would lose out. Ironically, after years spent baulking against the ban, British musicians like Tubby Hayes greeted the news with mixed feelings. Yes, it was wonderful to finally have the chance to see their heroes in action, up close and over a tour's worth of performances, but *British* jazz musicians going to *the States*? How would *that* work? It was Ronnie Scott who best summed up the situation with the immortal statement that America needed English jazzmen like Damascus needed a synagogue.

The British half of the bargain began by exporting the Ted Heath orchestra – arguably the most saleable of local musical assets – for a short tour that included an appearance at Carnegie Hall, but for the fans left behind in the UK the musical windfall was far greater. The first American band to make an official public appearance on British soil since 1937 was that of Stan Kenton, and when the mighty behemoth drew into London that spring, everyone knew nothing would ever be quite the same again. The visit had ramifications other than musical ones. Although his music sounded at times like a jazz equivalent of an H-Bomb detonation, Kenton himself proved to be courteous, polite, deferential even, and was keen to ensure that his ambassadorial visit hit no awkward moments. When he fired two of his saxophonists for drug use, the bandleader plugged the gap with local players, including Don Rendell and Benny Green, an instant winner with the indigenous press. It was also an education the Englishmen would never forget, and, sceptical though he was about Kenton's musical preoccupations, Green admitted in *NME* that the American's tour was an example of how to get things right: "It forces me to the conclusion that we have been visited by a band of grown men, from whom our own groups of squabbling schoolboys can do well to take example."[14]

However, there were those who struck a more cautionary note. Ex-Kenton trombonist Bill Russo wrote a revealing article for *Melody Maker* shortly before the tour began, disabusing those "schoolboys" who thought New York was a jazz Mecca and which concluded with the notion that learning at a remove, largely from records, was actually far more valuable to the local jazzmen.[15] But even then there existed a paradox. Ever since the reinstatement of the transatlantic liner runs to New York in the late 1940s, musicians employed on ships like the *Queen Mary* had realized that there was a profitable sideline to be had by bringing back American records. With the UK record industry still lagging behind its American counterpart, this informal import route had been the only way to truly keep up with what was happening in New York, but it wasn't available to just anyone. Whereas the major UK labels might only release a handful of jazz albums per year, often two or three years out of date, the newer American independent imprints – Blue Note and Prestige chief among them – operated on a much smaller scale, producing regular product in order to survive. Recordings rarely sat on the shelf and it was by no means uncommon for a Blue Note album to reach the shops within a couple of months of being recorded. Ironically, these independents had much in common with Tony Hall's *modus operandi* at Tempo, but whereas Vogue-Decca, Tempo's parent company, had already struck licence deals with key American labels including Pacific Jazz and Contemporary, Blue Note's catalogue remained largely untapped (the direct import of Blue Note albums into the UK didn't start until 1961). Laying your hands on the originals was tantamount to finding a gold nugget: Tony Hall vividly remembers meeting his transatlantic connection in Archer Street, paying a then astronomical £4.00 per LP. The music on these latest albums by Art Blakey, Horace Silver, Sonny Rollins and others was highly prized – like hearing the words of a prophet – but even the packaging spoke of a level of affluence unimaginable in the austere circumstances of post-war Britain: the thick cardboard covers and bold cover art of these originals made the flimsy British equivalents look like cheap imitations. It was hard not to extend the comparison to the music; in early 1956, it looked as if these fragments of a jazz fan's pipe dream were all that was ever to reach the shores of the UK.

Nevertheless, Tony Hall remained determined to reverse the fortunes of the local product. He had recently brokered another deal with an American record label, Imperial Records, who had licensed the quartet tracks Tubby Hayes had recorded the previous summer and now required further titles to boost the playlist to LP length. For Hall, the news was actually something of a mixed blessing. Time and again on the Tempo sessions his enthusiasm for the task in hand had come up against an odd mixture of reluctance, lack of interest and nervous inferiority from the local players. Years later he painted a decidedly disobliging picture of what went on behind the scenes:

> More often than not, I had to struggle to get local musicians to record and once I'd got them in the studio, struggle to get some of them in a fit state to actually do the job at hand. Some lacked concentration, finding it difficult to complete a three hour session. They just didn't seem to know how to enjoy themselves in the studio. In retrospect, some of those sessions could have been infinitely better if the musicians had approached them with a healthier attitude.[16]

The musicians weren't entirely to blame. Saddled with Decca's choice of recording engineers (including Bert Steffens, an individual who pooh-poohed Hall's playing of Rudy Van Gelder's Blue Note albums as a suggestion of what sound he was after) and working in a studio that frequently had the same amount of creative atmosphere as a mortuary, sometimes they were simply thrown together and left to get on with it. Unlike Blue Note, Decca's budget didn't allow for paid rehearsals, and only a few of Tempo's regulars thought out and rehearsed their programme in advance. Fortunately, Tubby Hayes's quintet session on July 17th was among the label's early successes, largely thanks to the close association of its members, all of whom were regulars in Hayes's larger band.

Appalled at Decca's disregard of the ephemeral niceties of recording an album, Hall was now taking it upon himself to provide sandwiches and refreshments in the studio in order to get his musicians to relax, but the July 17th date marked something of a departure for all concerned. After Hall had called a halt for a refreshment break, Hayes, Dickie Hawdon, Harry South, Bill Eyden and bassist Pete Elderfield piled into the pub across the road and, upon their return, decided that a more conducive atmosphere would be established if the studio lighting were turned off and only the light from the control booth remained. The idea wasn't strictly original: Miles Davis's masterful *Blue Haze* had been recorded the previous year in identical circumstances; but, be it plagiarism or a tribute, Hall found that the effect upon his players was immediate. Hayes even felt so relaxed that he also kicked off his shoes. The net result was the session's highlight, a lengthy, improvised twelve-bar blues titled 'Hall Hears The Blues'.

However, even with the new 12" format, there were still limits as to how far the musicians could extend themselves, as Hall was well aware. To this end, he arrived at every Tempo session armed with a stopwatch, hardly a creative incentive, but such was the atmosphere in the darkened studio on this evening that he quickly abandoned any notion of calling time. Accordingly the performance of 'Hall Hears The Blues' nudges the quarter of an hour mark – close to an LP's maximum side length in 1956. Nevertheless, the producer was delighted. The performance had made a fitting climax to a session that had shown an overall relaxation rare in British jazz circles. Well satisfied with the results, Hall duly handed over tapes to Imperial Records, as well as selling the surplus material, including the marathon blues, to another US label, Savoy. All six titles would also be issued in the UK by Tempo as *After Lights Out*, Hayes's first 12" LP release. Reviewing the album in *Jazz Monthly*, Alun Morgan – hitherto somewhat undecided as to Hayes's merits – now praised the saxophonist unstintingly: "Hayes is now our most consistent musician playing in this particular style. [He] is less prone to clichés than some of his contemporaries: his tone is full and his solos have a welcome individuality." Drawing imaginary lines of battle, Morgan saved his most partisan thought to close: "This LP contains jazz of more lasting interest than some of Ronnie Scott's quintet records."[17]

The success of the Tempo recording was a welcome distraction for Hayes. Despite now sounding better than ever, his road band continued to meet a mixed response. But whilst it may have failed as a commercial concern, the group had actually succeeded in doing something far more valuable. In taking its leader across the length and breadth of the UK, it had made him a highly visible musical personality. Already the name Tubby Hayes was beginning to mean something to young jazz fans. Wrote Benny Green in the *NME*,

> In some weird way that defies explanation, Edward Brian "Tubby" Hayes has, over the past two or three years become something of a legendary character to the teenagers of the provinces. He has somehow captured the imagination of the younger fans

possibly because he is no older than they are and they can identify themselves with him and enjoy a sort of vicarious self-pride when he does something special, perhaps because the boisterous happy spirit is there for everyone to see.[18]

One such teenager, Jack Massarik, later a prominent jazz critic but then a budding saxophonist, was among those who followed Hayes from venue to venue in suburban London and was stunned by the seemingly effortless brilliance of one so young:

> Studying his magnificent technique in action, I noticed that his fingers hardly seemed to move, the fingertips never leaving the pearl-buttons, just fluttering imperceptibly against them as if in a light epileptic tremor as the notes poured out. I also became familiar with Tubby's invariable warm-up routine – one clean, fast semi-tone run from the top of the instrument to the bottom, just to make sure everything worked. Then would come a quick pint of IPA bitter, a bit of banter with the publican and the purposeful call to action "let's do it."[19]

There is no better document of Tubby Hayes's in-person power – the ability to sunder listeners which fans like Jack Massarik recall so vividly – than that recorded by Tempo on the last day of July 1956, released on the album *Jazz At The Flamingo*. Tony Hall was again the mastermind and once more his ties with London's clubland had proved crucial to the venture. The Flamingo's regular band, the Tony Kinsey Quintet, had taken a month's engagement entertaining British troops in Cyprus and in their absence Tony Crombie had assembled an ad-hoc unit featuring Ronnie Scott, Harry Klein, Terry Shannon and Lennie Bush. The popularity of the new unit was instantaneous and Hall wasted no time in persuading the powers-that-be at Decca that it should be recorded, preferably live at the club. The only problem lay in the actual logistics. For such a shoestring effort, Decca weren't about to lug expensive recording equipment down the stairs of the Mapleton Hotel. Thinking on his feet, Hall hit upon the novel idea of staging the band live in the Railway Arms pub, adjacent to the company's West Hampstead studios, and running the necessary recording cables across the street, thus simulating a live session at the club. Finally, Decca gave the green light and, after suitable publicity in *Melody Maker*, a capacity audience of two hundred and fifty duly turned up on the night of July 31st.

Hall had another trump card. The front-line of Klein and Scott were virile enough in their own right, but adding Tubby Hayes, he reasoned, could only up the excitement. Guesting on 'Night in Tunisia' and 'Laker's Day' – a steaming blues titled in honour of cricketer Jim Laker's nineteen-wicket toll on Australia that same day – Hayes responded with two of his most energized solos to date. Although the crowd roared their delight on the night, when the resulting album was released early the following year, the saxophonist found himself crucified on the same old critical altar. He was taken to task for "typical unsubtle" solos by *Melody Maker*,[20] with *Jazz Monthly*'s reviewer describing the recording as "quite worthless musically. All I can see in [these] offerings are technical fluency and the ability to go on for a long time. Certainly they have no melodic invention."[21] Daring to display a confidence almost unique in British jazz circles, Hayes was finally beginning to realize just what he was up against. Indeed, the reception given his playing on the *Jazz At The Flamingo* album was a precursor of the sort of critique he'd fitfully receive throughout the remainder of his career.

The final months of the Tubby Hayes orchestra's existence were blighted by the same problems that had beset its entire lifespan, but now the lack of suitable work, surfeit of unscrupulous promoters and an ever-decreasing jazz content were squeezing any enthusiasm there was left from its members. Just a short while earlier it had been possible to laugh off these tribulations: after all, they were still a relatively new band making their way, with much still to prove. But after a year and a half on the road these topsy-turvy fortunes were beginning to breed a deep cynicism, much the same as that which had spelled the end of the Ronnie Scott band the previous year. Hayes's outfit, however, had to face something Scott's group never had to, and, in the opinion of one of its number, Jackie Sharpe, it was this new musical threat that finally sounded the band's death knell.

With the entry of Bill Haley and the Comets' recording of 'Shake, Rattle And Roll' into the UK charts in December 1954, rock and roll arrived in Britain. The very notion of a chart was itself relatively new. The American magazine *Billboard* had been the first to publish a table of best-selling records during the 1930s, but the idea had only begun in the UK as late as 1952, when *New Musical Express* decided to incorporate a new way of gauging what was capturing the public's imagination. Prior to this, the popularity of a song was judged the traditional way, by sheet-music sales. With the advent of both the record chart and the introduction of the new vinyl format of the 45 rpm single in the early 1950s, conditions were ripe for a new kind of transient fame. Indeed, much of what is now commonplace in music jargon has its roots in this revolution – the hit single, the chart-topper, the No. 1 artist.

Rock and roll had come along at just the right time to capitalize on these new inventions but the genesis of the music had started much earlier in the rhythm and blues and jump bands of men such as saxophonist Louis Jordan, whose cheerful eight-to-the-bar rhythms offered a new wrinkle on the concept of swing. Even Bill Haley himself had begun his career in another idiom, western swing, but his shift to the new style was so successful that not only did it lift his own career onto a whole new level, it effectively launched an entire cultural movement. When the Comets' single 'Rock Around The Clock' was featured over the opening credits of the movie *The Blackboard Jungle* in 1955 it provoked rioting at some cinemas, prompting the press to issue stern warnings about the subversive nature of the new craze. It was nothing new. Since the dawn of the twentieth century popular music had always been aligned with some sort of corruption of youth – the flappers of the twenties and the Bobby-Soxers who'd screamed for Frank Sinatra are just two examples – but to those in authority rock and roll looked likely to open a whole new post-war Pandora's Box.

Unsurprisingly, America experienced a tough time coming to terms with the new music. While its forthright rhythmic content may have provided the kind of ready excitement not heard since the earliest days of jazz, rock and roll's apparent lack of lyrical sophistication left many of the day's established musical stars high and dry. There was no room in this new revolution for the exactitude of a Frank Sinatra, a Doris Day or a Nat King Cole and, as the music took hold, almost overnight, what had originally amounted to an amusing diversion turned into a serious threat. Wholesome didn't enter into the equation: the new rebellion was aimed at, and appealed exclusively to, a youthful audience, and, almost as an instantaneous by-product, the teenager was born, unwilling to be a pattern-perfect miniature of their elders and betters.

Although a personality like Bill Haley was unlikely to upset anyone – not exactly svelte and the wrong side of thirty, he made an unlikely teen hero – the line of performers, both black and white, that followed in his wake was a distinctly different proposition. Emerging from a gospel background, pianist and vocalist Little Richard had a penchant for make-up, becoming what might be termed the first truly "modern" rock star, equally attuned to the importance of physical imagery as he was to musical vibrancy. Soon to become the very stock in trade for any rock artist, controversial private lives also seemed to come with the territory: another pianist, Jerry Lee Lewis, had come from a similar church background to Richard, but had upped the rock star stakes by first marrying bigamously and then tying the knot with his thirteen-year-old cousin.

Ironically, by far the most controversial of the first wave of rock and roll musicians was Tupelo-born Elvis Aaron Presley, a man on the face of it as beatifically handsome as any crooner and as American as apple pie. In Presley the new music had found its own mass-marketable king, and, as if confirming this coronation, he was one of the first rock and roll stars to be signed by a major label, RCA-Victor, with his debut recording for the company, 'Heartbreak Hotel', selling over a million copies during the first four months of 1956. Suddenly, the singer found himself commercial hot property. Nationwide television appearances followed but finally – after wooing both record label executives and teenage girls alike – Presley found himself in hot water. The new star's provocative image proved simply too much for the censors. Not content to cosset and caress the microphone, as Frank Sinatra had done, instead Presley thrust its rigid stand around the stage like some overblown aluminium phallus. Inevitably, America's mainstream critics attacked his act for being permissive, obscene and indicative of the general post-war decay of moral fibre, and even the FBI cast its eye over the singer, earmarking him as a serious danger to the country's security. No popular artist had previously been accorded such status and it was clear for all to see that rock and roll was ushering in a very different kind of fame and fortune.

Anglicizing the new style was no easy matter but Flamingo club boss Jeff Kruger wasted no time getting in on the act. Suggesting to Tony Crombie a group built on Bill Haley's model, he initially received a rebuff, but, having experienced immense difficulty in keeping his own ambitious bands together, the drummer realized the idea might afford him a possible way out of the small-time finances of the jazz scene. Thinking big, he demanded £100 a week, a figure Kruger thought was astronomical, but which he eventually agreed to. Thus Tony Crombie and The Rockets, Britain's first rock and roll band, were born. Their success was instantaneous. The band's opening night at Portsmouth in September 1956 had sold out within hours of tickets going on sale and soon Crombie and Kruger were raking in money. Within a further three weeks Kruger had bought a Rolls Royce. Both men knew that percentage jazz gigs in far-flung village halls would never have earned this.

Soon others were following Crombie's prototypical example, including Tommy Steele, the Bermondsey-born guitarist and vocalist whose band The Steelmen had a hit with 'Rock With The Caveman', a record featuring a cameo by none other than Ronnie Scott. In no time at all, Steele had gone from being a modestly paid merchant seaman to earning £200 per appearance. The message was clear: rock and roll could catapult you straight to the top of show business without the need for a lengthy apprenticeship as you worked your way up the career ladder. It made for an intoxicating prospect.

Rock and roll's impact upon the UK jazz scene wasn't immediate. Even Tony Crombie's defection wasn't taken too seriously: two years earlier he'd taken a stab at leading the UK's first rhythm and blues outfit, a fad that had quickly passed. Indeed, the majority of modernists considered the new music little more than a joke. To some, it was just part and parcel of the myriad of American styles that now comprised a commercial dance band's repertoire. Featuring 'Shake, Rattle And Roll', 'See You Later Alligator', 'Hound Dog' and 'Rock Around The Clock', the pad of the Tubby Hayes band even had its share of nods towards the new trend, but by the autumn of 1956 accommodating yet another fashion became one concession too many for a group already weighed down by compromise. The final weeks of the band's life were decidedly anticlimactic. On September 28th they performed at Butlin's in Clacton as part of the holiday camp's ill-fated Jazz Festival Weekend, before playing their final engagement at Ealing Town Hall on October 3rd. When it came, the end was as undignified as it was anticlimactic. Dealing with duplicitous promoters out on the road was one thing, but as the year had worn on it had become apparent that even Tito Burns wasn't playing entirely fair and square. Jack Sharpe never forgot the reaction the band received after it returned from a Scottish tour shortly before the break-up.

> We were tired, hungry and demoralized and decided to confront Tito, the aim to ask him for financial assistance. As the coach pulled up outside Tito's residence in plush Maida Vale, Tubby and I were elected the spokesmen. The door opened to reveal Tito resplendent in a silk dressing gown. He listened to our tale of woe, nodded as we protested that we were totally skint. He beamed us a consolatory smile "Well, that makes all of us, doesn't it?"[22]

Hayes was uncertain exactly which direction his career would take next, but he was far from worried. "Tubby sat drinking tea and beaming all over his face," reported *Beat* magazine's Carl Carter after encountering him at Archer Street's Harmony Inn that autumn. "No-one could detect that this young man had just received a blow that would have made most men of 21 give up. After a couple of years' hard work he had wound up with no band, no money, no nothing – just for trying to give pleasure to the thousands of fans throughout Great Britain."[23] A year and a half of the inconsistent fortunes of commercial bandleading had been quite enough and he relished his new-found freedom. That autumn he became part of the touring entourage of Bix Curtis's Jazz From London (JFL), an English equivalent of Jazz at the Philharmonic (JATP), which mixed and matched some of the leading local players in staged jam sessions. Like JATP's mastermind Norman Granz, Curtis had aims far loftier than simply putting jazzmen on stage to make a buck, as he explained in the JFL tour programme:

> We feel that Jazz from London has an important function. Apart from youngsters, there are many Mums and Dads who hold rhythmic interest [sic]. Should we be successful in obtaining their patronage to our concerts, they will see that jazz is on a decent footing. Not only will they come again but they will feel no qualms about encouraging the presence of their sons and daughters. This will spread the growth of our music and do it decently.

There was no mention of the moral threat of rock and roll but the implication was clear: modern jazz might suddenly, and ironically, find itself lifted from subversive to saviour, providing an antidote to the new generation of hip-swivelling, surly teenagers. The truth was less clear-cut. Stories of the hedonistic antics of Tony Crombie and his Rockets were already beginning to filter through the business but even those on-stage with Jazz from London weren't exactly squeaky-clean. They included a compulsive gambler, several heavy drinkers, a clique of casual drug users and, as one surviving musician

Tubby Hayes and
Ronnie Scott, The
Downbeat Club,
late 1956. Author's
collection.

remembers from a wild weekend during the band's stay over in Manchester, at least one sexual deviant.

The JFL troupe touched its home base that winter with an appearance at the Jazz Jamboree at Hammersmith, an annual event guaranteed to get the critics' pens twitching, but for the music press by far the biggest story as 1956 closed was the return of Victor Feldman. The previous autumn, after months of niggling indecision, Feldman had finally come to a decision about his musical future. Tired of the constraints of the parochial jazz scene, tethered by memories of his "Kid Krupa" past and desperate to improve his musicianship, he had realized the ultimate dream by emigrating to the US. Although it was a fantasy shared by many of his colleagues, including Tubby Hayes, few had been brave enough to see it through. The unprecedented success of George Shearing had provided all the evidence needed to argue that a British passport needn't be a musical handicap and the select number of English players who'd dared follow him – pianists Ronnie Ball and Ralph Sharon most notably – had never looked back. Feldman didn't buck the trend. After an uncertain start, he had fallen on his feet with a job offer from Woody Herman. The gig took him across the United States, providing a cultural as well as musical education, and convinced him that the transatlantic move had been worthwhile.

Inevitably, Feldman's return to the UK in December 1956 ended up having something of the air of a reunion about it. Working with erstwhile colleagues like Hayes, Ronnie Scott, Dizzy Reece and Phil Seamen, he spent most of his month-long vacation on stage at the Mapleton, Club Basie and Star clubs, or shuttling between TV and recording studios. Ever enterprising, Tony Hall hastily organized several sessions for Tempo, using Feldman's new-found international status as leverage with Decca's normally reluctant bosses. The resulting albums were impressive not only for Feldman's contributions, as big band leader, composer and instrumentalist, but for how he had drawn the best out of his old confrères, including Tubby Hayes. On two sextet and ninetet sets, Hayes had switched to the baritone saxophone, an instrument he later expressed a dislike for, but which he played with the same ineluctable drive as his customary tenor.

Along with the baritone, Hayes was also looking elsewhere for a new instrumental challenge. Watching Feldman night after night, he'd grown increasingly fascinated by the vibraphone, openly wondering whether the instrument might make a suitable double. After all, he was well versed in keyboard harmony and had already begun to write and arrange his own compositions. He was also, by his own admission, a frustrated drummer. The potential of playing percussive single-line improvisation or rich chord voicing using several mallets made the vibraphone the ideal outlet for all of these ambitions. However, if this makes Hayes's decision to play the vibes seem like the result of careful planning and deliberation, the truth is somewhat more romantic. Indeed, like that of his initial meeting with Ronnie Scott, the story has been recounted many times, often in distorted from, and has been cited as taking place in varying locations. It appears that Hayes first played his new instrument on Boxing Day 1956, at a session held at the Flamingo club in the Mapleton restaurant. Yet again, there is a near Hollywood-like simplicity to this story, and it certainly makes for a far more interesting narrative than discovering that Hayes had studied painstakingly for months prior to this debut. But, as with the earlier meeting with Scott, the truth appears to go hand in hand with the legend. For reasons that are not clear, Victor Feldman had not arrived but had left his vibraphone set up on stage. Having eyed the instrument eagerly over the preceding nights, Hayes then took it upon himself to play an impromptu version of Milt Jackson's 'Bag's Groove' with the assembled group. "Admittedly, it was a nice easy tempo and everybody seemed to like it," he modestly recalled in 1960.[24]

The first recorded example of Hayes's vibes work comes barely six weeks later. In 2012, a recording of one of the Jazz From London shows from the winter of 1956–57 was released on CD by the Acrobat label, on which, as part of a group also including Jimmy Skidmore, Hank Shaw and Ken Wray, Hayes plays both tenor and vibes. The precocious aptitude he displayed on his new instrumental double is revealed on two numbers, 'Salute To The Bandbox' and 'Birks' Works'.

One can hear a slightly incredulous note in Bix Curtis's voice as he introduces the first item on which Hayes picks up his mallets, but the sheer assurance of the performance that follows counters any suggestion of gimmickry. 'Birks' Works' is even more relaxed and, although Hayes's improvised lines lack the total fluency that had already marked his saxophone work, one cannot help but be impressed by his surprising confidence.[25]

Alongside the two vibraphone features, the highlight of the JFL tape is a Hayes/Skidmore duel on 'Caravan', giving a taste of what the semi-regular club combo the two men co-led at the time must have sounded like. Despite some grandiose predictions from writers such as Tony Hall, the brief two-tenor hook-up didn't last, probably because the two men's attitudes to the job in hand differed so wildly. Skidmore was a fine player, but his work ethic hardly matched that of his young partner. Not all that long beforehand, Hayes might have concurred with the older man's blow-and-go outlook, but he was now looking to present something with far more polish.

Finding just the right band was not proving easy. As winter edged towards spring, he tried out a variety of line-ups, including a quintet featuring trumpeter Bert Courtley, trombonist Eddie Harvey, bassist Phil Bates and drummer Bill Eyden. Following Gerry Mulligan's example, the piano-less concept was highly fashionable, but, as Eddie Harvey remembered, Hayes was after something quite different to Mulligan's easygoing swing: "I used to think 'how on earth am I supposed to play trombone at these ridiculous fast tempos?' Good fun though!"[26]

Tubby's symbiotic partnership with Jimmy Deuchar was also about to be curtailed, following the trumpeter's decision to live and work in Germany. A valedictory recording by the pairing for Tempo on March 29th, 1957, and released in scattered fashion over various LPs and EPs, gives a good indication of both the players' and the producer's aims. The closing track from the session, another sprawling fifteen-minute blues improvisation titled 'Swingin' In Studio Two', features one of Hayes's best solos to date, one bursting with authenticity yet without sounding particularly in hock to any one American influence. "Tempo jazz *wasn't* Hard Bop," Tony Hall remembered. "We used to call it Hard Swing."[27] This distinction is borne out in listening to the varying musical styles on offer: altoist Derek Humble sounds close to West Coast players like Herb Geller, whereas Phil Seamen's playing calls to mind that of Philly Joe Jones, and, whilst the music undoubtedly swings, what it lacks is any sort of true defining direction. However, by the time he appeared on the Deuchar recording, Tubby Hayes was already rehearsing a new collaborative band, one promising a very distinct musical identity, and which would set the proverbial jazz cat amongst the critical pigeons: the Jazz Couriers.

Ironically, for a project that had the indelible imprint of his genius stamped all over it, the germ of the idea for the Jazz Couriers came not from Tubby Hayes but from Ronnie Scott. Like Hayes, Scott had grown weary of the ad-hoc nature of much of his work and thought he and Hayes "could work fairly regularly, rather than just gigging around with any rhythm section that happened along."[28] The two men had already done the occasional gig together in a quintet setting (there are photographs from Club 20 in Leeds the previous year) but what Scott now had in mind was something altogether more formal and saleable. Above all, it had to avoid anything trite or musically substandard. Both men knew all too well the dangers of pursuing a musical policy that tried to encompass the latest pop and dance crazes. Any genuine and lasting success, Scott argued, would only come from doing what they did best – playing modern jazz. The two men also had much more going for them than just musical talent: smart, stylish, charismatic and accomplished, they made excellent salesmen for any band they fronted, and had both already attracted something of a cult following among British jazz fans. Pooling these resources seemed, to Scott at least, to be almost inevitable.

Hayes was more pragmatic: with only two tenor saxophones, plus his vibraphone and a rhythm section, the greatest challenge would clearly be one of avoiding a limited group identity. "I was a bit doubtful at first," he later told John Martin of *Jazz News*. "I thought the sound would be too monotonous."[29]

Scott also knew how to be persuasive. Listening to Hayes's reservations, he realized he'd found the perfect carrot and stick. Why didn't the younger man use the opportunity to exercise his growing fascination with composing and arranging, something he hadn't yet been able to do to any real extent? Surely that would give the band all the variety it needed? This proposition swung the deal for Hayes and, in March 1957, the two men set about the practicalities of their forthcoming collaboration.

Settling the personnel was relatively easy. The co-leaders had both been happy with the rhythm section of Terry Shannon, Bill Eyden and a new young bassist Malcolm Cecil (soon replaced by Phil Bates) which had appeared on recent club dates. The selection wasn't simply convenient: all five men enjoyed the same kind of jazz. Indeed, as more moderate tastes held sway over the majority of British jazz fans, there seemed to be an overdue need to reassert some of the music's base excitement. The co-operative American band the Jazz Messengers, formed by pianist Horace Silver and drummer Art Blakey, had tied their colours to the mast a few years earlier and, as Hayes and Scott cast about for a name that would avoid any doubt as to the music on offer, someone suggested the Jazz Couriers. Instantly it stuck.

Hayes and Scott had been among the first British jazz musicians to appreciate the full-on drive of the Jazz Messengers' music. Earthy, intense and relentlessly swinging, the band's work may have captured something of the steaming, pressure-cooker intensity of life in New York, but elsewhere reaction to its message was mixed. The Messengers' first UK release – licensed from Columbia Records by the Philips label – was issued at the beginning of 1957, just ahead of the formation of the Jazz Couriers, and had registered an odd reaction from local critics. In the edition of *Melody Maker* in which it was reviewed, more column inches were devoted to new albums by the

Avon Cities Jazz Band and Joe Turner than to the Messengers record and, rather than being transformed by the group's music, the paper's Bob Dawbarn appeared mystified, describing how the band "specialize in the use of Latin-American and off-tempo rhythms [and] curious staccato ensemble links between solos."[30] Hard bop, it seemed, might just translate into hard to sell.

In later years, much was to be made of the lack of availability of Blue Note albums in the UK during the formative stages of hard bop, with the general consensus being that the style had taken far longer to take root in Britain due to its lack of representation in local record shops. Although the label was without doubt the major player in documenting the development of the new music, by no means did it hold the monopoly. Nor was hard bop completely absent from the catalogues of UK labels. All the musicians in the Jazz Messengers' original line-up had recorded for other companies, many of whom licensed product to Britain. Indeed, rather than revealing a dearth of records in the new style, a cursory glance at domestic jazz releases in the UK for 1957 shows a surprisingly healthy number of albums in the hard bop vein. Besides the Messengers' eponymous Philips album, these included *Byrd's Eye View* by Donald Byrd (with Horace Silver, Hank Mobley and Art Blakey), Hank Mobley's *Jazz Message No. 2* (alongside the young Lee Morgan), Horace Silver's *Silver's Blue* (with Mobley and Donald Byrd), Hank Mobley's *Mobley's Message* (again with Byrd) and two albums in the hard bop style by the new Miles Davis quintet with the then largely unknown saxophonist John Coltrane, *Miles* and *Round About Midnight*.

The ubiquity of Hank Mobley's presence throughout these discs wasn't simply a coincidence. Since his emergence from Max Roach's quartet in the early 1950s the saxophonist had become one of the most consistent jazzmen of his generation, and one who was to have a peculiarly insidious influence. Mobley's key achievement was the marriage of the harmonic and rhythmic language of Charlie Parker with a tone that showed neither allegiance to the heavier attack of Sonny Rollins nor to the more opaque playing of the post-Lester Young "Brothers." The saxophonist himself later famously described his as "not a big sound or a small sound but a round sound."[31] Combining this asset with a canny rhythmic subtlety, he delivered his improvisations like a velvet-gloved punch, a method that held an especial appeal to European musicians. By the time they formed the Jazz Couriers, the American's records were highly prized by both Tubby Hayes and Ronnie Scott, as Tony Hall remembers:

> It's funny because everyone now talks of Rollins and Coltrane as influences but at the time Hank Mobley was a far more important influence for Ronnie and Tubby. He was more influential over here than in the States, something I've never been able to work out. Of course, they listened to Rollins but no-one really knew much about

Coltrane. He certainly didn't loom large like he did a few years later, so it was Hank Mobley that they loved.[32]

If Hayes and Scott had plenty of on-record source material from which to draw their inspiration, they nevertheless still faced an uphill struggle in finding a suitable venue in which to preach the new gospel. Jazz promotion in London hadn't really progressed from the days of Club XI, with the *modus operandi* remaining largely that of hiring a room, hiring some players, placing an ad in the back pages of the *Melody Maker* and hoping for the best. At the beginning of 1957, even the best-known of the capital's clubs – Jazz at the Flamingo – was still occupying someone else's premises, having moved from a successful run at the Mapleton Hotel to the famous Pigalle restaurant. However, in a remarkably fortuitous piece of timing, the Courier's formation coincided with the opening of a brand new club to permanently house the Flamingo presentations in Wardour Street. The Flamingo's bosses – father and son Sam and Jeff Kruger – were among the very few promoters who thought jazz deserved better presentation. Jeff Kruger was also willing to put his money where his mouth was. The new Flamingo venue cost a lavish £12,000 to fit out and although this figure was soon to be dwarfed by the kind of money Kruger would earn from a crossover to rhythm and blues and soul in the coming years, it was still no mean amount to throw at a non-mainstream music. Kruger's ambition impressed both Tubby Hayes and Ronnie Scott – if anyone would back the Jazz Couriers, they thought, it would be him, and they were right. The impresario had instantly recognized market potential in having two of the UK's most popular modern jazzmen under his wing and he wasted no time in signing the new band as one of his club's resident acts. A few weeks later, on Sunday April 7th, 1957, the Flamingo's new premises finally opened for business: the Jazz Couriers were up and running.

Despite all the publicity puff and an opening party attended by members of the visiting Count Basie band, the Flamingo wasn't quite the quality establishment Kruger might have liked the press to believe. Surviving musicians still remember the spartan amenities of its band room but, even for the paying customers, the club had a charm that was little more than basic. *Jazz Journal's* Brian Nicholls wrote a damning appraisal of the new premises during the summer of 1957, describing how the venue "had the atmosphere of a damp oven. Condensation was streaming down the walls and one part of the club bore a close resemblance to a swamp, with pools of dirty water forming on the floor."[33]

But whereas the Flamingo itself may have been largely an old idea in novel dress, Hayes and Scott's resident band were clearly offering something genuinely new, not least in the winning way in which both front men sold themselves and their fellow players to the public. It didn't take long for the local press to realize that there was a revolution taking place in Wardour Street, and when Benny Green wrote an extensive piece on the new band

"The End of the Old Order." The Jazz Couriers on-stage at the Flamingo, summer 1957. Bill Eyden (drums), Phil Bates (bass), Terry Shannon (piano) with Scott and Hayes. Courtesy Maureen Eyden.

for *Jazz News*, he was quick to praise its casual and yet polished approach. With typical perception, he also identified the painstaking preparation that lay behind the band's music:

> The apparent thoughtless liaison between the five Couriers can only have been the fruits of arduous labours in rehearsal. In fact, as far as musical discipline is concerned the Couriers approach their technical problems with the concentration one often mistakenly associates with a commercial band. If the truth be known, the Couriers make most commercial orchestras sound like a leaderless rabble.[34]

If the Jazz Couriers' music was not ultimately to prove as gritty as genuine hard bop, and lacked the style's intrinsically sanctified message, it was certainly far harder-hitting than anything yet encountered by London jazz audiences. With Jeff Kruger organizing a revolving residency at both the Flamingo and Florida clubs, for five months they had the band virtually to themselves.

Along with the impression the band was making on its audience, it had also begun to affect the ambitions of a younger generation of up-and-coming musicians, including teenaged saxophonists Alan Skidmore, Peter King and Dick Morrissey, all of whom made regular pilgrimages to the Couriers' gigs.

It was easy to understand why. Hayes and Scott had it all – the super-slick presentation, the musical nous, the uncanny ability to think as one.

However, there were those close to the two co-leaders who saw a less even balance to their relationship. Fellow tenorist Tommy Whittle even made the shrewd suggestion that Scott had enticed Hayes into the fold in order to exercise some control on the competition, a gambit as old as jazz itself.[35] Bassist Pete Blannin thought that Hayes had actually brought the best out of Scott, but at a price. "He apparently had a bit of a complex about playing with Tubby. Tubby was such a whirlwind that Ronnie sometimes felt uncomfortable with this ball of energy next to him."[36] Although Hayes had tremendous respect for Scott, he made no secret of the fact that everyone in the Couriers was expected to work hard, his co-leader being no exception. "[Tubby] was the real organizer in the Couriers," recalls Tony Hall, "making sure they rehearsed, and he really dominated the group."[37] Indeed, it's difficult to imagine just what kind of outfit the band would have become had Hayes's persona not been so hard-driving.

Ronnie Scott's lifelong business partner – and at one point the Jazz Couriers' manager – Pete King preferred to spread the plaudits equally and believed that the success of the band wasn't simply due to the contribution of one man: "Tubby had the technique, Ronnie had the power and the way they spurred each other on was fabulous. They were both incredibly good players and had a flair for selling the music as well as playing it."[38]

It was this flair that instantly marked the Jazz Couriers out from their contemporaries. Five handsome young men, in sharp-lined Cecil Gee suits, negotiating the trickiest of music with an almost off-hand nonchalance, they were bound to make an impression on everyone who encountered them, from the paying public to up-and-coming musicians and journalists alike. Benny Green's *Jazz News* piece on the band was subtitled "The End of the Old Order and Beginning of the New," as if the arrival of the band heralded a genuine local sea change. Along with the group's novel stage presence, there was a concerted effort to make their music differ from that of previous two-sax line-ups. Indeed, the band's approach featured surprisingly little in the way of the twin-tenor fisticuffs made famous by the pairings of Gene Ammons and Sonny Stitt and Wardell Gray and Dexter Gordon. Instead, it had soon become apparent that much of its appeal lay in Hayes's ever-growing compositional and arranging skills. Incredibly, for one so inexperienced at writing, Hayes had taken it upon himself to assemble the Couriers' entire library and, however fearful he may have initially been of the potential limitations of two tenor saxophones and a rhythm section, he was soon able to provide the band with a surprisingly varied number of tone colours: when the sax-led instrumentation was in danger of becoming routine, they could utilize the sound of tenor and vibes, something Hayes liked to employ in equal measure on slow and fast tunes, each showing an increasing mastery of his new instrumental double. Whatever approach they chose, the Jazz Couriers consistently offered a rare blend of head and heart, delivered with genuine co-operation between the front men.

Where the two co-leaders differed was in their off-stage personas. Hayes had already learned how to enjoy a good time at the bar between sets, indulging to ever more extravagant levels, and boisterously dominating whatever company he kept with his roaring laughter. Scott was cooler, calmer, and an altogether less outgoing personality, whose fun was more often had at the bookies' expense rather than in gregarious rabble-rousing: "We were never really that close," he confessed after his co-leader's death. "Our personalities were too disparate for that. Tubby was an extrovert, ebullient character who burnt any and every available candle at both ends. I couldn't keep up with him and I never felt the inclination to do so."[39]

For the first few months of the band's existence, the Couriers' reputation rested solely on word of mouth, a few favourable press reviews and a single TV appearance. It was therefore clearly a matter of some urgency to record an album. That summer, Jeff Kruger negotiated a deal enabling the group to record under Tony Hall's watchful eye for Tempo, with the two dates scheduled at Decca Studios – August 8th and 15th, 1957 – resulting in the band's debut LP, *Tubby Hayes And The Jazz Couriers Featuring Ronnie Scott*.

The album's opening track, Hayes's 'Through The Night Roared The Overland Express', effectively defined their approach, sounding for all the world as it could have been lifted off a record by the Jazz Messengers. With its undulating 64-bar structure and lyrical Latin bridge, the theme closely echoes the work of Horace Silver, whilst the two front men's solos – with Jimmy Deuchar appearing as an added starter – channel the spirit of players such as Hank Mobley and Sonny Rollins. Behind them Terry Shannon is Horace Silver to the letter and Bill Eyden's metronomic ride cymbal faithfully echoes Art Blakey.

Just how up-to-date the Couriers were is shown in the album's next theme, Tadd Dameron's pretty 'On A Misty Night'. The composer had recorded his original version less than a year earlier in November 1956 for the Prestige LP *Mating Call*, which had yet to receive a UK release. The Couriers had presumably taken their arrangement from a copy brought back from the US by one of their ocean-going colleagues, transforming the piece into a vehicle for Hayes's limpid vibraphone work.

The recording date ended with what was to become the band's signature arrangement, Hayes's score of Irving Berlin's 'Cheek To Cheek'. With its steaming two-tenor theme statement, tear-arse tempo and hairpin accuracy, in a little over four minutes the track outlines everything the band stood for and remains among its most impressive achievements. And yet there is something of a paradox to the performance: although the music is superficially cut from the same cloth as contemporary American jazz, it somehow lacks the relaxation of the original. Indeed, this was to be a contention voiced frequently about the work of the band, with critics zoning in on Hayes and

Scott's propensity to cram their solos with endless streams of notes and the group's general preoccupation with appearing hip. Regardless of these reservations, there can be little doubt that the bustling energy of the Couriers' music came as a refreshing wake-up call to those who had grown used to the more reserved charms of other local jazz units.

Recording the Jazz Couriers thankfully proved less of a headache for Tony Hall than documenting many of his other Tempo artists:

> The Couriers' first date was one of the first things I ever did at Tempo intended for a 12" LP. Part of the reason that so many of the other Tempo sessions only ever appeared on EPs and 10" albums wasn't simply money. But because it was a working band, with the Couriers everything was rehearsed in advance. They were keen to present their music well and it showed and working with a regular band helped time-wise. As they were playing music they knew well you didn't need lots of re-takes.[40]

The band completed their first LP on August 15th, recording four further tracks which are, if anything, even more representative of their approach. A cover of Hank Mobley's 'Reunion' is yet another rapid appropriation of a recently recorded American jazz composition, having featured on the Blue Note album *Hank Mobley and His All Stars*, recorded only eight months prior to the Couriers' version. The track also gives an early indication of Hayes's hyperactive desire to do it all, playing not only his most virtuosic vibraphone improvisation to date – clearly in thrall to Milt Jackson – but also an equally assured tenor solo. The closing score of 'A Foggy Day', however, lowers the temperature to present a distinctly mellow slice of modern jazz, perhaps closer in spirit to Hammersmith Palais than Birdland.

What strikes those coming to the Jazz Couriers' music after the passage of over half a century is not simply the band's overblown youthful enthusiasm, but the very real understanding of the materials at their disposal. Indeed, it can be argued convincingly that the unit's first album is one of the very few genuinely world-class recordings made by British jazzmen during the 1950s. It's therefore somewhat ironic to find that the contemporary critical reaction given the record upon its initial release was no more partisan or enthusiastic than it had been for Hayes's earlier efforts. Jazz critics can't realistically be pilloried for lacking prescience, but when *Jazz Journal*'s Brian Nicholls delivered a pricelessly downbeat appraisal of the album in 1958, he seemed to have missed the point entirely; the band's finely honed style, he wrote, was "only a short step away from the scribble movement"[41] (one assumes he meant the common practice of hurriedly writing themes out on the spot in the studio) and he concluded with the rather condescending observation that Hayes and Scott were "moving in the right direction."

In fact, as 1957 progressed, the band's popularity continued to soar. The results of the annual readers' poll in *Melody Maker* that October found the Couriers at number four in the Small Combo section, with Hayes and Scott at numbers three and five respectively in the tenor ratings. Hayes had also arrived at third place in the vibraphone category, a remarkable achievement considering he had been playing the instrument for barely ten months. The group's message spread further still that same month when they at last broke their London curfew and headed out on the road. Making a lightning tour of the UK with a somewhat unlikely touring package sponsored by the *Daily Express* titled "Rhythm With The Stars," they found themselves on an otherwise decidedly light-entertainment-oriented bill, accompanying the now-forgotten singer Yana. It made for a highly incongruous national debut. Scott remembered playing a Belfast venue on the tour

> that had a revolving stage. And there were a lot of very big name artists on the bill. And I remember when we started our set all the lights went up and about six guys came out selling ice creams and programmes and this revolving stage we were on speeded up and never stopped revolving for the whole half hour we were on.[42]

There were other commercial concessions besides the *Daily Express* package: throughout late 1957 into the following spring Hayes made regular broadcast appearances on bandleader Tommy Watt's BBC radio shows *The Band Waggon* and *Time For Watt* (on which, billed as "Tubby the Tenor," he worked alongside the young Matt Monro) and, at the peak of the Jazz Couriers' success, both he and Ronnie Scott were recruited to the house band on BBC TV's *Six Five Special*, alongside musicians such as Harry Klein, Johnny Hawksworth and Ronnie Verrell.[43] Hayes also continued to guest on recordings by other leaders, including a session with pianist Eddie Thompson in January 1958 – *Midnight In London* – made for export to the USA, on which he played vibraphone.

With all its titles pertaining to London and even including such fare as 'Underneath The Arches', Thompson's recording was hopelessly gimmick-laden – marketing British jazz with such heavy-handed pastiche that it was at times almost embarrassing. Even Tony Hall's earlier export productions (such as *Pub Crawling With Jimmy Deuchar*) hadn't stooped quite so low to get themselves noticed, but whilst there remained some merit in organizing and recording albums solely for the US market, the steady influx of visiting American musicians that had followed the lifting of the union ban now made it possible for local jazzmen to impress their opposite numbers in person. Saxophonist Frank Foster had been highly complimentary when he caught the Jazz Couriers in London during a tour with Count Basie in 1957 and word was clearly beginning to spread. Another union stipulation also now aided the locals: visiting American bands were required to appear with a British support group, and while warming up an expectant crowd wasn't always

Hayes on vibes with Phil Bates and Bill Eyden, circa late 1957. Courtesy Maureen Eyden.

the easiest job in the world for the English players, the tours did provide an opportunity to meet and get to know their heroes. When the National Jazz Federation announced that the Jazz Couriers had been chosen to share the bill on the first UK tour by the Dave Brubeck Quartet in early 1958, Hayes and Scott knew they had the chance to showcase their music opposite one of the biggest draws in the business. It was an opportunity they were to seize with eager hands.

4 The End of the Old Order (1958–59)

The best of our boys can hold their own with the majority of the Americans. I don't worry what the so-called critics say. They don't know, anyhow.

Ronnie Scott, *Melody Maker*, 1958

If not quite at the heady heights to which chart success would take him in the early 1960s, by the time of his arrival in Britain in January 1958 Dave Brubeck was already well on the way to stardom. Although he'd nailed his colours to the mast of modernism early on (some of the recorded output of his late 1940s octet still sounds bewildering), the pianist's career had only really taken off with the formation of his quartet in 1951. Featuring the alto saxophonist Paul Desmond – an urbane and lyrical performer who had done the then-unimaginable in formulating an alto style that sounded a world away from Charlie Parker – the band became big news almost overnight, forging a strong following on US college campuses. It was easy to understand the appeal. For those who might only dabble in jazz, the music was wrought with enough serious cultural overtones to be deemed respectable. Brubeck himself could be a pretentious, even ponderous, performer, hammering out massively dense chords as if forcibly at odds with the delicacy displayed by Desmond, but therein lay the magnetism: the novel contrast between the altoist's witty eloquence and Brubeck's deliberation made for a group with a broad fan base and, alongside albums by the Modern Jazz Quartet (MJQ), records by Brubeck found their way into the collections of individuals who otherwise would have given modern jazz a wide berth. Jealousy of this success was rife, with musicians divided as to whether Brubeck was really onto something or merely milking a passing fad. Jazz critics were similarly polarized and, as it had in America, reaction to the pianist's oeuvre split the British music press into two quite distinct camps. Some, including Steve Race, adored the quartet;

others, like Benny Green, saw little merit in bands like Brubeck's and the MJQ trying to strangle the lifeblood out of jazz by making it "respectable." Ironically, these polemic disagreements helped business, so no one in the Brubeck camp really cared all that much when the critical brickbats flew.

With all the controversy, the Jazz Couriers knew that the Brubeck tour would be a guaranteed draw, and that it would put them in front of far greater numbers than could be squeezed into the Flamingo on a Saturday night. The itinerary was typically exhausting: sixteen venues in as many days, often performing two shows a night, taking in London, Coventry, Bristol, Bournemouth, Cardiff, Newcastle, Birmingham, Leicester, Sheffield, Glasgow, Bradford, Liverpool and Ipswich.

Immediately they set off, it was clear that the Brubeck clan were determined to make as much of their off-hours as possible, a viewpoint not wholly endorsed by their English counterparts. "It was like a family outing," Tubby Hayes recalled the following year. "There was Brubeck, his wife and two children, and [drummer] Joe Morello and his wife. They and the other boys used to stop the coach to take pictures of old ruins. The British boys used to run to the nearest pub."[1] As with all the tours Hayes had undertaken to date there were moments both mundane and hilarious, as well as those that were peculiar to a murky winter in austerity-ridden fifties Britain. Criss-crossing the UK in pre-motorway discomfort, everyone remained at the mercy of the Great British Transport Café, long familiar to the men of the Couriers but a new experience to the Americans. Ronnie Scott's dry humour in such circumstances instantly appealed to Paul Desmond. "Excuse me, can I see the wine list?" Scott would enquire in one dismal roadside establishment after another.[2]

As expected, Brubeck himself continued to divide opinion, even within the Couriers, and at close hand there was little in the way of Damascene conversion. The pianist, however, declared an unbridled enthusiasm for his support act, famously remarking "They sound more like an American band than we do."[3] Over half a century on, it's easy to be somewhat cynical about Brubeck's patronage. With its quasi-classical flavours and considered rationale, his music was much more than just a geographical ocean away from that of the Couriers, but during the 1950s an American jazzman's endorsement – almost regardless of *who* the American was – meant everything, and accordingly the Couriers wore their Brubeck prize with pride.

Brubeck's words of praise were also as much politic as passionate. On American groups' previous tours, the balance had been tipped so firmly in the visitors' favour that the presence of a local support band had been little more than cosmetic. But, as the tour with the Jazz Couriers progressed, it became clear that for once it was the home team who were in the lead. Writing in *Jazz Journal* after hearing the package at the Royal Festival Hall, Brian Nicholls observed that the contribution of the Jazz Couriers was the surprising part of the show. The balance of fast ones, and of slow ones, and of ballads and originals was just right. The extent to which the crowd responded can be gauged by the fact that only one person clapped at the announcement of the last number – a point traditionally reserved for the cries of "about time too" and thunderous applause.[4]

Such a phenomenon deserved to be captured in perpetuity and so, halfway through the tour, it was decided to record the band's second Tempo album live at one of the Brubeck shows. The very idea of a live recording was itself highly novel. Unlike in America, where within the few short years since the introduction of the LP format live albums had been released by everyone from Sonny Rollins to Erroll Garner, in-person recordings by British jazzmen were still something of a rarity. Recorded over two houses at London's Dominion Theatre of February 16th, 1958, *The Jazz Couriers In Concert* finally provided a UK entry that could sit, without qualification, alongside such classics as *Stan Getz At Storyville*, *Sonny Rollins At The Village Vanguard* and *The Jazz Messengers At The Café Bohemia*.

For a time the album was the Tempo label's biggest seller and it has remained the band's best-known recording, a situation helped considerably by the fact that it was reissued by EMI's budget-line imprint Music For Pleasure during the mid-sixties, one of the few Tempo sessions to ever receive a vinyl re-press.

From the nervy opening riff to 'What Is This Thing Called Love' to the super-charged rerun of 'Cheek To Cheek' which concludes the set, all five players perform at the top of their game, with the emphasis very much on hard, relentless swing. Indeed, the two ballads, 'Speak Low' and 'Time Was', are the briefest items on the album, dispatched rather like palate cleansers between courses of meaty tenor. However, given the limits of their allotted time on stage, and with a tough local audience to convince, one can forgive the Couriers' enthusiasm in throwing their hardest punches in succession.

The recording also boasts two performances that have etched their way into the subconscious of a generation of British jazz listeners. Hayes's original composition 'The Serpent' (dedicated to Bix Curtis's outsized manhood) is a perfect slice of hard bop, which could easily pass for the work of Horace Silver, whilst the arrangement of Frank Loesser's 'Guys And Dolls' which opens the album's second side, remains one of the most fondly remembered of all the band's pieces. With its tumbling tag-team exchanges between the two front men and unexpectedly witty ending, it still serves as the perfect summary of the Couriers' approach – sophisticated yet direct, nonchalant but technically demanding.

Much of the album's in-person ambience comes from Tempo's decision to include Ronnie Scott's dry announcements, always a key part of the Jazz Couriers' presentations. "And now, from an LP which you may have seen in the shops, titled Elvis Presley sings Thelonious Monk," he quips ahead of one tune but, in introducing Hayes, Scott put aside the frivolity to describe his partner as "someone who I sincerely believe is one of the finest jazz musicians that Britain has ever produced."

It wasn't mere flattery. Although by the time he'd recorded the *Dominion* album, Tubby Hayes was already close to becoming the ultimate saxophone athlete, he would breast even further ahead in the year to come, prompted by what was a seemingly prosaic technical change: during 1958 he acquired a new saxophone mouthpiece, an alteration that may look merely cosmetic to the casual observer but which to the player in question can prove seismic. Indeed, Hayes's tone – the saxophonist's equivalent of a fingerprint – was to undergo a radical transformation during the next few months. It may well prove instructive to pause and examine exactly how and why this occurred.

The majority of the photographs taken of Tubby Hayes during the first seven years of his professional career show him using either an ebonite or plastic mouthpiece, including the fashionable white-coloured models built by the Brillhart and Selmer companies. By the middle of 1958, however, he had begun using a metal Otto Link mouthpiece. Virtually every name American saxophonist from Coleman Hawkins onwards had at one time played a Link, each of them drawn to its projecting power and consistency of tone. Arguably harder to control and yet more rewarding if persisted with, the Link mouthpiece provides a more "open" tone and it was this quality that enabled Hayes to build the expressive, broad and rounded sound that was to become his musical signature into the next decade.

It seems highly probable that he may have also had to change the strength of the reeds he was then using. It is notoriously difficult to find reeds that "speak" well on Link mouthpieces and simply transferring a player's usual brand and strength from their old mouthpiece doesn't always work. A period of experimentation is normally required – how protracted and how thorough depends entirely on the individual – but given Hayes's later protestation that "I just put a reed on and if I don't like it, I try another"[5] one can't imagine he took long to sort out his preferences. No one is exactly certain when Hayes changed his "set-up" (saxophone player speak for describing their mouthpiece and reed combination) but it seems he may well have been using it on a special recording project for Tempo taped some time in March 1958, utilizing overdubbed tape recording, a technique then in its pre-Beatles infancy.

Overdubbing wasn't altogether an unknown process in jazz – even early jazzmen such as Sidney Bechet had experimented with it – but by the middle-1950s, with the need to expand recording techniques to keep pace with the demands of the long-playing record, it had begun to become more commonplace. Although its biggest advantage was ultimately to be practical – a performer could simply drop in his or her contribution onto an existing recording – it had also made a good A&R hook for record companies looking to highlight the versatility of their artists. In 1956 Zoot Sims had recorded an album in which he comprised a one-man saxophone section, just one example of the many American recording projects now dabbling with overdubbing, while UK musicians who had embraced the new technology to varying degrees of success had included Humphrey Lyttelton, Victor Feldman and Art Ellefson.

Tubby Hayes's decision to explore the process arose not only from the need for an A&R gimmick, but also by a very real musical frustration. On casual pick-up gigs he often found himself fighting unsympathetic accompaniment. In the sleeve notes for the original Tempo issue of his multi-track performance he explained that "if I played the piano behind my own solos, I should be able to play the correct backings." Exploding the idea by overdubbing a full saxophone section and additional vibes, he continued, "sounds logical, but to put the idea into practice was not so easy."[6]

As always, despite realizing the marketing potential of such a coup, Tony Hall found himself up against both the clock and the intractable Bert Steffens, Decca's less than sympathetic engineer. For Steffens, recording one of Hall's ordinary jazz dates was trial enough, but working with no less than nine tape machines very nearly proved too much. At one point he inadvertently binned a key section of tape, but given the stress involved, the end results were surprisingly effective.

By far the best of the three performances taped that day is Hayes's original 'Blues For Those Who Thus Desire', created by the leader initially laying down an alto part alongside Phil Bates's bass and Bill Eyden's drums, before adding on vibes, baritone and tenor. The highlight is an impressive saxophone soli in which Hayes's accuracy and attack is all the more impressive for being extended five-fold. "Some people will no doubt say the contents of this recording are not jazz because they are not spontaneous," he wrote in his accompanying sleeve notes,[7] effectively giving critics carte blanche to steam in. Indeed, the general reaction to the issued EP – titled appropriately enough *The Eighth Wonder* – was one of complacency rather than awe, with some critics finding the overdub idea unashamedly self-indulgent. Max Harrison delivered an especially damning appraisal in *Jazz Monthly*, calling the leader's solos "rather pointless doodles." The journalist may have also made an intentional *double entendre* when he concluded that Hayes "plays very well with himself."[8]

After their jaunt across the UK with the Dave Brubeck quartet, the Jazz Couriers had settled back into the routine round of London club gigs. Apart from the odd sortie to the heady suburbs of Southall and Hendon, the band's workload during March consisted almost entirely of engagements at the Flamingo and Florida clubs. Early the following month, they were out on the road again, making a thirteen-day tour across England, Wales and Scotland supporting vocalist Sarah Vaughan. Business was good and Vaughan's enthusiastic endorsement of her support band was another healthy sign. Yet, despite this transatlantic recognition, the Couriers continued to meet with

The Couriers' front-line on-stage at the Flamingo, summer 1958. Courtesy Geoff Buller.

qualified rather than wholesale success, praised for being the best the country could offer one moment, then finding their music derided as derivative and insecure the next.

Answering these criticisms in an interview for *Melody Maker* during July 1958, Ronnie Scott was emphatic: "The best of our boys can hold their own with the majority of the Americans. I don't worry what the so-called critics say. They don't know, anyhow."[9] The following month, the paper challenged Scott to elaborate, raising the old argument that British jazzmen had only ever offered surface gloss. "These days, I think, you and Tubby Hayes are putting technique before jazz feeling," Maurice Burman accused the saxophonist. "I don't see that," Scott replied. "If you have any jazz feeling, acquiring more technique isn't going to lessen it. In fact, the more technique the better you can play. One can't acquire more jazz feeling but one can and should acquire more technique."[10]

Both men's arguments held some water. Burman had been correct in identifying the Achilles heel that would continue to plague many British modernists in the years ahead – the perpetual emphasis on high-energy feats of musical daring at the expense of all else – but Scott also had a point. By the middle of 1958, the Jazz Couriers were clearly streets ahead of any other British modern jazz group. This surge forwards had been made principally through bloody-minded determination – neither Scott nor Tubby Hayes had got their technical expertise for nothing – and in parading the results of this hard graft so obviously they were helping raise the bar for all British jazz musicians. Not only did it seem nonsensical to knock them, it seemed like nothing so much as an attempt to keep British jazzmen down at heel. How *dare* they get *this good*!

The band picked up a new bassist during June 1958, the only personnel change within the group in over a year. Phil Bates had been a solid if not exactly inspired contributor but, to some ears, his close friendship with Hayes signalled that the appointment was made more for social reasons than musical ones. When he chose to leave, word was soon out that the best jazz outfit in the country was recruiting. Those who the band's manager Pete King alerted included twenty-two-year-old Jeff Clyne, then a member of the Vic Ash Sextet. Just two years younger than Hayes, Clyne was also closer to the saxophonist's age than the other members of the band, something he saw as an enormous contribution to their friendship. "Although Tubby had been around for quite a while he was still really young. Guys like Ronnie and Bill Eyden were quite a bit older than us, so I think he liked having someone nearer his own age in the band at last."[11] To the astrologically minded Hayes, Clyne's recruitment was much more than a quirk of fate.[12] The band now boasted three Aquarians: Scott, born on January 28th, Clyne on the 29th and Hayes himself on the 30th. "This was always a source of amazement to us all," the bassist remembered. "Tubby really thought it mattered!"

What mattered most though was the music. In Jeff Clyne the Jazz Couriers now had a player whose general sense of musicianship was representative of the fast-improving standard of British jazzmen. Clyne had enjoyed a formal musical education and it showed, although even he found the prospects of joining a band so famed for its exacting standards more than a little daunting:

> I always felt a bit out of my depth in the whole proceedings. One minute I was just coming out of National Service and the next I'm in the top band in the country. It was a demanding situation. You made sure you knew your stuff and in that respect I think Tubby was – in inverted commas – the "taskmaster" because he did demand that kind of commitment to the band, to the music. There were different work ethics, I think, but any kind of personal differences never spilt on stage though. Everyone knew the value of the band.[13]

By 1958 Tony Hall's dream of getting musicians like Tubby Hayes heard in the US had become something tantamount to an obsession. Alongside his enthusiasm for Hayes, he had also been an ardent champion of the Jamaican trumpeter Dizzy Reece, frequently citing him as his favourite UK-based jazzman. Reece had had a hard time establishing himself in London. The issue lay not with his colour, but moreover with his testy attitude. Quixotic, mercurial and supremely intellectual, he often came across as blunt and intolerant and had already enjoyed his share of run-ins with promoters and fellow musicians. Although his playing was notoriously inconsistent – his early recordings in London have alternating moments of brilliance and bluster – he was nevertheless patently sincere: all he wanted was to be given the chance to show what he could do. Tony Hall was one of the few who recognized that Reece's problem was as much to do with his environment as with his character, and he sympathized with the frustration of a gifted individual who seemed unable to find an ideal context or suitable playing partners.

The few recordings by Reece that had been issued in the US had started something of an underground cult. Miles Davis was even rumoured to be a fan, but lip service was one thing – what Hall wanted was practical assistance. In August 1958, following two years of dogged correspondence, his indefatigable determination finally paid off. Blue Note Records had at last agreed to finance a date headed by Reece. However, along with the invitation came a caveat. "Alfred [Lion, Blue Note's producer] liked Dizzy's anarchic approach," Hall said later, "but pointed out that he was unknown [in the USA] and therefore nobody would buy it in the States. The only way a Dizzy Reece album would make commercial sense was to involve some big name American players."[14] Hall's meagre budget didn't stretch to flying British musicians to the US and so he began to think more creatively.

Fortunately for the producer, the answer lay almost on the doorstep. Whilst making one of his periodic visits to Paris, Reece had befriended fellow trumpeter Donald Byrd, whose band including drummer Art Taylor were making an extended European tour. A former member of the Jazz Messengers, Byrd was one of the best-known names in hard bop, and had already appeared on several Blue Note sessions. Surely his was as big a name as was needed to give the project some kudos? Hall cabled Alfred Lion who instantly recognized the opportunity and gave the Englishman the green light. "[He] sent me some money to bring them over and we did [the album] in four and a half hours at Broadhurst Gardens one Saturday afternoon."[15]

For the time being it was to remain a coup that no one involved in could shout about. Neither the American Federation of Musicians nor the British Musicians' Union had been informed and neither had the necessary Ministry of Labour permits been secured, but Hall's practicality ensured that nothing, not even highbrow bureaucracy, was going to frustrate his plans. Just hours away from realizing his dream he resorted to the simple expedient of bribery to keep a lid on events, giving the caretaker at Decca Studios a fiver to go down the pub. Officially, the August 24th sessions were supposed to have taken place in Paris with the English musicians "on vacation," but few believed the ruse.

Hall and Reece had settled upon a personnel that featured – almost inevitably – Tubby Hayes and Terry Shannon, two players bespoke for such an occasion, together with bassist Lloyd Thompson, a Canadian who had recorded with Sidney Bechet in Paris the year before and who had only recently decamped to Britain. Hayes was the trump card. Donald Byrd had already heard the saxophonist on an earlier stop-over in London and was deeply impressed, as he remarked to Hall in the original album sleeve notes: "Man, he can play. I'd like to have thrown some real fast tempos at him, just to get him mad. But he'd have made them."[16] Indeed, Hayes's playing throughout the August 24th, 1958 session is among the best of his career, as well as a testament to his steady nerve in such fast company. "Tubby did a blues on it which I think is his best solo on record," Hall remarked some years later.[17]

In the brief biographical resumes on the back of the original LP, Hayes's favourites are listed as "Parker, Stitt, Getz, Rollins, Mobley, Coltrane and Griffin" and echoes of all these influences can be felt throughout the session, from the omniscient sound of Rollins to the terrifying dexterity of Griffin. The latter in particular had become a new hero. Not only did the two men share a nickname in The Little Giant, there were other similarities: both had lightning-fast techniques and both could conjure and execute logical musical ideas at extremely fast tempos. Indeed, what strikes one most about Hayes's contribution to the Reece session is not simply the urgent, unbridled passion he brings to the recording but the sheer accuracy of his playing.

The opening Reece composition which gave the album its title, 'Blues In Trinity', makes a truly astonishing introduction. A triple-time blues, wherein the soloists could choose one of three tempos to solo at, it clearly reveals Reece to be a musician with ambitions beyond the rote and the formulaic requirements of hard bop. After the composer's opening solo, Hayes enters, in Hall's liner note description, "snorting fire and fury." If not quite as belligerent-sounding as that, he certainly matches Art Taylor's stoking drums. Much the same occurs on Reece's 'Color Blind', featuring an exchange between the front-line players that is little short of electrifying. If the session showed off Hayes's robust side far better than any of his recordings to date, it also contained further evidence of his maturity as a ballad player, an aspect of his playing few critics had yet fully acknowledged. He is the only soloist on 'Round About Midnight', offering a full-toned, surprisingly direct and soulful reading of the theme. Tony Hall found the track "very moving"[18] and there is indeed something genuinely affecting about Hayes's striking use of sustained notes and vibrato.

There is also no indication whatsoever that any of the London players felt inferior to their American counterparts. Reece undercuts the more mellifluous Donald Byrd at every turn and one can hear a rhythmic under-standing between Terry Shannon and Art Taylor that the pianist was sadly never to experience again. But, throughout the album, it is Hayes who most catches the ear. During the 1980s two further pieces from the session were unearthed, including the first track taped that afternoon, a theme-less blow on the changes of the standard 'Indiana', titled 'Just A Penny', in honour of Tempo's regular photographic contributor, Bill Penny. It shows the saxophonist hitting the ground running – there were clearly no nerves, nor any sort of musical bedding-in required. Right up until last piece taped that day, Reece's 'Shepherd's Serenade', boasting another full-to-the-brim tenor solo, he continued to play with unabated energy.

Apparently, the good spirits persisted after the session had ended, with Byrd and Taylor heading to the Flamingo for the Jazz Couriers' evening gig. Despite all the camaraderie, drummer Colin Barnes remembers it was not an edifying night for Taylor. The American sat in but far from receiving the awe-struck reception he'd expected, Barnes remembers seeing him thoroughly demolished in a series of exchanges with Hayes before Bill Eyden was hauled back on-stage. Given the music Hayes and Taylor had made earlier that day, it was an odd sort of encore.[19]

Tidying up the loose ends in the wake of the *Blues In Trinity* session, Tony Hall experienced a surreal mix of pride and embarrassment. Alfred Lion had cabled that the balance on the Decca tapes was not acceptable and that his regular engineer Rudy Van Gelder had been forced to do more than his share of remastering. However, along with the criticism, there was also some more welcome news, which fully justified Hall's faith: "Alfred Lion played [the album] to Art Blakey and Blakey seriously thought about getting Tubby and Dizzy Reece as a [Jazz] Messengers front-line – I've heard that from more than one person."[20]

As tempting as the offer may have sounded, there were lessons to be learnt for those involved: a year after taping *Blues In Trinity*, Reece emigrated to the United States, a move that soon proved to be anticlimactic. Indeed, his contract with Blue Note lasted for only three years and his discography never again yielded anything quite as impressive as *Blues In Trinity* (Hayes and Reece's final on-record meeting, taped later in 1958, is the effective but rather piecemeal soundtrack music to the film noir thriller *Nowhere To Go*). Hayes's manager Pete King once offered a considered opinion that had Hayes followed suit and taken up Art Blakey's mooted offer, his career may well have gone much the same way. King also asserted that whatever prestige there would have been attached to such a move wouldn't have compensated for the potential boredom. Hayes it seemed had his own clearly mapped-out trajectory and, not for the last time in his career, he had discovered that playing the Americans at their own game was far, far easier on his home turf.

Three months after the *Blues In Trinity* session, Tony Hall again used his powers of transatlantic persuasion to finally enable the Jazz Couriers to record for an US record company. Getting an American lawyer friend Mannie Greenfield to lobby Joe Carlton, boss of the Carlton label, Hall had one thought in mind:

> I just wanted to get the Couriers out on an American record label, and get them heard in the States, which I could see wasn't going to happen through Decca. I didn't specifically think of Carlton. I would have rather it had been Blue Note, of course. Carlton were

far from an ideal label, but somehow they agreed and I was sent a princely sum of £500 to get a session together.[21]

The eight tracks recorded for Carlton during November 1958 represent the Jazz Couriers' collective peak and are, in Tony Hall's opinion, the best music the band ever recorded. As with the recent Blue Note set, the occasion was another of those all-too-rare moments when inspiration coincided with a scheduled recording session, but there are two other contributing factors that make the *Couriers Of Jazz* (as Carlton marketed the LP in order to avoid confusion with an American band called the Jazz Couriers, led by vibraphonist Dave Pike) a signal success.

Firstly, the recording balance is astounding, especially so when one considers that the session was recorded in the very same Decca studio as every other contemporary Tempo set. The reason, Tony Hall later revealed, was that a new young engineer Michael Mailes had been recruited for the job in place of the usual incumbent, Bert Steffens. Second, the recent appointment of Jeff Clyne had given the Couriers' rhythm section much more flexibility than on the band's two previous sets. The album also comprises the group's most interesting recorded programme, mixing Hayes's originals with choice pieces from the Great American Songbook. There is also far more of a sense of relaxation to the music, as if the band were now so comfortably in advance of their counterparts that they no longer needed to prove themselves quite so relentlessly.

Tony Hall's sleeve notes on the subsequent British issue on the London label declared the set to be "the easiest-going, most relaxed disc dates I can remember"[22] whilst celebrated critic Ralph J. Gleason's annotation on the US release made much of the ascending standard of the Couriers' music, stating "They cook along as though Piccadilly Circus was only a block and a half from Birdland."[23] If the tone was somewhat patronising, the sentiment was certainly accurate. Gleason even compared the band to the quintet of Al Cohn and Zoot Sims.

The album drives from the outset. Hayes's 'Mirage' is yet another Silveresque outing, offering further confirmation of his ease within the hard bop vernacular. The mood of authenticity is maintained on 'After Tea', a grooving minor blues whose economic relaxed solos make nonsense of the "too many notes" critiques often thrown at the band. In 'The Monk', Hayes even feels comfortable enough to chance his arm at a little pastiche, a mood further enhanced by Terry Shannon and Bill Eyden playing celeste and timpani drum, as Thelonious Monk and Max Roach had done on the album *Brilliant Corners*.[24] As well as all the allusions to the latest American trends, the album also contains music displaying a distinctly local flavour. Complete with its verse voiced in doomy medieval harmony, Hayes's score of 'My Funny Valentine' is a performance that reveals both the aspirations and apprenticeships of the band – halfway between a classic jazz ballad and a dance-hall bum clutcher. Even more representative of the general impression the band was making out on the road is the final number, Hayes's score of the standard, 'Day In, Day Out', a pell-mell exercise in the 'Cheek To Cheek' tradition, the effect of which is almost mind-numbing. Indeed, Hayes's solo on this track has the dual distinction of being both one of his most characteristic – a perfectly executed example of the marriage of musical intellect and improvisational skill – and also one of his most easily assailable.

Full of finely detailed decorous lines, dovetailing perfectly with the harmony beneath them, Hayes's ideas are so well formulated as to run the risk of making the man behind the music appear more like a machine. Jazz critics had long loathed this sort of thing, but, occasionally, such consistency could leave even Hayes's admirers nonplussed. Despite having tremendous respect for his partner, Ronnie Scott later admitted to holding a deep-seated reservation about Hayes's technical skills: "There was always a but with me, with Tubby. I don't know what you'd call it. It was like you turned a switch and bang, it was always there, a bit – mechanical."[25] A performance like 'Day In, Day Out' had also begun to show the potential cracks in the Couriers *en masse*. Immaculately played, and without doubt as technically sound as anything then being recorded in America, it was certainly impressive, but, with such feats remaining largely unmatched by any other British jazzmen, the band now faced the dangerously ironic situation of leading in a one-horse race.

This impression was compounded when *Melody Maker* announced its 1958–59 poll winners on January 3rd, 1959, bringing the news that Hayes had at last won the tenor saxophone category, a position that he would go on to hold for a further eleven years. The Jazz Couriers had also done well, topping the small band votes, with Hayes making further showings in the vibes, composing and arranging categories. He had also come fourth on baritone and sixth for his "miscellaneous instrument" skill as a flautist, not yet heard on record, and there was a portentous showing at number five in the Musician of the Year category.

"When you start in the business you have that kind of ambition," Hayes remarked of his tenor victory, "and frankly it's a nice feeling. Especially when you know there are guys like Ronnie, Don, Tommy, Art and Skid, and they're all such great players. Of course, working with Ronnie has been wonderful for me . . . he has always been tops over here."[26]

Work for the Couriers continued unabated as 1959 got under way, but with ever-increasing demand for the group, Jeff Kruger was taking liberties that had begun to rankle its members. Although still centred in London, the band were now making more and more appearances across the length of the UK, with lightning trips to Liverpool and Manchester slipped between dates in the home counties. One-nighters were generally not a problem: after all, they had been grist to the mill of all five men's careers more or less since day one. But things came to head in late February when Kruger offered the band what they thought was a three-night-a-week residency at the Flamingo: "It turned out that it was not three nights at the club at all but three nights working for Kruger wherever he liked to book us," Hayes told *Melody Maker* on March 7th. Already used to an itinerary that had on occasion looked like it had been assembled during a game of blind man's bluff, Kruger's contract seemed like a blueprint for logistical disaster. "When we turned it down, he gave us five days' notice. In that time it was impossible to fix other work. The result was that I blew my top."[27]

It was a very public explosion, with an enraged Hayes using the forum of the band's Flamingo gig to attack what he saw as Kruger's unscrupulous managerial conduct. According to *Melody Maker*, "[He] harangued 100-odd members [of the audience] over the microphone," with one witness describing the outburst as "the most sordid business I have witnessed in any club." Kruger's immediate response to such outspoken criticism was to sack Hayes and bar him from the club, adding in a press statement that he considered his conduct "unbecoming to a band leader."[28]

Although Kruger had to act fast, and had absolute justification in criticizing Hayes's on-stage conduct, one can wholly sympathize with the saxophonist's feelings. Life on the road with the Jazz Couriers was the same old triumph of practicality and youthful vigour over daunting odds as it had been in all of Hayes's previous bands. It needn't be made worse by unsympathetic management.

The group had two preferred modes of transport for out-of-town gigs: either they took the overnight train, or Scott drove. "Ronnie had one of those cars you'd see in old French films and we'd all pile into that, bass and drums strapped to the top," Jeff Clyne remembered. "You'd really get to know each other travelling for hours like that." The bassist also recalled the band making several visits to a venue soon to be associated with a very different brand of musical intensity: "We used to do the Cavern in Liverpool – this was pre-Beatles. Going up on the train, doing the gig, and then getting the sleeper back. It was as easy as that in those days."[29]

On Wednesday March 25th the band visited the north-west for an engagement at the Tivoli Bar in Morecambe, Lancashire. The gig itself was a routine affair – the kind of thing that the band's members had been doing for the entirety of their professional lives: an out-of-town club date, run by a local enthusiast, with a ready audience starved of regular access to the best jazz groups of the day. The promoter was Peter Bould, then owner of a record shop in Chorley but already well on his way to becoming an outstanding recording engineer (he would later go on to record albums by, among others, Gil Evans and Art Pepper). Getting the Jazz Couriers this far north was something of a coup and, as Bould later confessed, both he and the management of the Tivoli had somewhat underestimated the attendance figures. Those fans not lucky enough to get inside were forced to watch the gig from the street, pressed tight against a window which looked like it might not take the strain.[30] Bould had also made the decision to record the gig for his own private use, with four of the evening's performances eventually appearing on a limited-edition vinyl pressing in 2012.[31]

What makes the Morecambe recording so special is that, unlike the Jazz Couriers' commercial albums, or even the small clutch of their surviving BBC broadcast appearances, it documents the band stretching out on a typical club set, in some cases to extraordinary lengths. Most of the performances clock in over ten minutes in length, with several nudging a quarter of an hour. Familiar items receive new twists and turns, and the addition of some new material gives a fresh understanding of the Couriers' creative peak. Further endorsement might be added by saying that the band even top the outstanding form heard on the previous autumn's session for Carlton, but above all the tapes finally give twenty-first-century listeners a chance to hear just how impressive the band was in a club setting.

All of the virtues – and some of the occasional drawbacks – of the group's music are on display: there is Hayes's Herculean ability to play solos which, whilst expansive in length, are both consistently engaging and chock-full of invention, and his tone, varying from a purr to a roar, is magnificently captured. Scott's sometime over-eagerness to keep pace with his young partner is in evidence too, whilst the rhythm section – Bill Eyden especially – prod and prompt the front-line like never before. The music snaps and sparkles throughout and highlights come thick and fast: the opening version of Horace Silver's 'Tippin'' has a Hayes solo over the ubiquitous "rhythm changes" that is definitive. No harmonic wrinkle is left unexplored and at times he hints, surely by coincidence, at some of the substitutions that John Coltrane was to examine on his album *Giant Steps*. There is also a superlative version of his own ballad 'Embers' (re-recorded later that year by his quartet). But perhaps the most revealing of all of the baker's dozen of tracks taped that night is a mid-tempo version of 'For All We Know', where the intricate arrangement, with its fill-all-gaps fussiness, betrays the ever-present ghost of the Palais band.

The closing performance of the evening, 'Cherokee', is way off the speedometer, but both horn men devour it, with Hayes in particular playing with a startling command of both time and tone. One cannot help but smile at the youthful bellicosity of it all.

Hayes and Jeff Kruger settled their differences within a few weeks of the saxophonist's public outburst. It was senseless to persist with the feud: the British jazz scene was still too small and too insular to endure such enmity and, despite Kruger's rather empirical manner, he was a highly useful professional contact. Not only was the impresario promoting music, he had now begun to extend his business into film and television production. Though not exactly Oscar-winning material, and often made to the tightest of deadlines, Kruger's celluloid efforts nevertheless still required a musical score and, once again, he preferred to keep things in-house, hiring Tony Crombie to compose the scores and assemble the bands. Crombie in turn would often recruit Tubby Hayes.

With typically shrewd business acumen, Kruger realized that the resulting recordings from his film and library music endeavours could in effect be recycled as commercially available albums. The first to be released – licensed to Tempo – was *London Jazz Quartet*, a 1959 recording in which Tubby Hayes had made full use of his multi-instrumental skills, playing not only tenor and vibraphone, but also alto saxophone and flute.

Originally intended for use on the dead-air Test Card TV slot, inevitably the session is the weakest entry in Hayes's 1950s discography, full of superficially impressive doubling but little else. Arguably the best thing about the album is the appearance of the young Alan Branscombe, a pianist, saxophonist and vibraphonist with the same frighteningly accomplished multi-instrumental skills as Hayes. To judge the album on purely jazz terms is unfair. In fact, despite its impressive cast, *London Jazz Quartet* represents one of the lowest blows in British modernism: a sort of palatable muzak expediently peddled as jazz, as *Jazz Journal*'s reviewer noted: "For anyone who is content to take bits and pieces it is a pleasant record. There are no weak spots – nor is there anything extraordinary."[32]

But there *were* extraordinary things happening in British jazz at this time – things outside even the ambitions of a front-rank player like Tubby Hayes.

As it entered the last year of the 1950s, Great Britain remained much the same country as it had been as the decade had dawned. Post-war hopes had swiftly given way to Cold War realism and although it had led the way in several technological, sporting and cultural achievements – the Comet airliner, the four-minute mile, the ascent of Everest – the UK was primarily a nation hidebound by its past, a tatty lion presiding over a crumbling empire. Clement Attlee's pioneering Labour administration hadn't delivered the Welfare State utopia promised by its landslide victory in 1945, and since 1951 the UK's government had wobbled rather awkwardly in the hands of the Conservatives. Although the country had eventually steadied under Harold Macmillan, in turn leading to greater prosperity and the first real signs of a post-war consumer society in which the standard of everyday living kept pace with affordable new technology, little had really changed. Indeed, as the nation continued to struggle to rebuild itself after the titanic effort of World War II, there was even a deep cynicism that the true victor hadn't been the British people but the American economy.

Across the Atlantic, however, progress seemed to be everywhere – in film, in music, in fashion, even in the everyday home. Even though all these break-throughs were being made in a country that still hadn't yet come to terms with such basic issues as civil rights, for many English onlookers the United States continued to be regarded as a land of wide-open opportunity. But, beneath its surface, a revolution was taking place, radically transforming the art form that had long been thought of by Europeans as one of America's greatest cultural gifts: jazz.

The notions of using music as a political barometer or as a tool to express social outrage hadn't yet touched British jazz, but by 1959 there was a clear corollary between the work of several leading American jazzmen and the state of their nation. The United States was a troubled place: a nuclear superpower effectively policing one half of the globe, but full of fractious insecurity within its own borders – equally disquieted by the threat of Reds under the bed and black faces at a bus stop. Indeed, the land of the free was still inextricably bound up in outdated ideas of civil liberty. During the summer of 1959, Miles Davis was beaten over the head by a white policeman outside the New York nightclub where he was working, simply for refusing to move along: all the proof that was needed to show that, despite the freedom of their art, young black musicians continued to face the same inhumane hurdles that had confronted their parents' and grandparents' generations. While some sought to sidestep the issue, doing so by intellectualizing their music on European terms, as did the Modern Jazz Quartet, others simply chose to leave the US never to return. Those that were unafraid to remain and deal with these provocations head on – including figures such as Davis, Charles Mingus and Max Roach – faced a tough time, even with those who ostensibly supported them. The record business in America was still primarily white-run and, as much as it may have irked their maverick tendencies, players such as Mingus and Davis couldn't escape its established infrastructure. The only place for effective reaction was in the music itself. As the 1950s ended, American jazz suddenly exploded into a purple patch of immense creativity, fuelled by a new attitude best described as a volatile passion for asking "why?" The questions were as much social as musical: black American jazzmen knew there was a freedom in music which as yet eluded them as citizens. Why, if it was possible to play jazz for a white or mixed audience, did it remain impossible in some states to share a bus with white Americans, or a restaurant, or even a classroom?

However, whilst the theme of socio-political commentary lay at the very heart of the music of a performer such as Charles Mingus – a reminder that jazz was as much a social force as an artistic one – it was an attitude that struck few chords in British jazzmen. The UK was only just shaking off the "mustn't grumble, make do and mend" yoke of World War II and the work of even the most creative local jazzmen had precious little to do with the pursuit of any kind of wider political or social freedom. Indeed, so little had changed in over a decade that the British jazz players who continued to receive the best press were those who persisted in following fashion rather than abandoning it. Not for nothing did Tubby Hayes and the Jazz Couriers top the polls and receive warm accolades from the likes of Dave Brubeck. Copying the latest American licks was one thing, but English jazzmen didn't really have much in the way of anything social to rebel against – the fierce demonstrative undertow that had fuelled much of the music's progress in America simply had no UK counterpart. Charles Mingus could happily lampoon and demolish a figure like Governor Faubus (central to the Rosa Parks and Little Rock Nine incidents) but what did London's jazzmen have to protest about at the end of the 1950s: early closing time on Sunday nights? Blue Boar Services?

Lacking these dark demons, much of the British modern jazz recorded in the late 1950s now sounds rather carefree and lightweight. The music of Tony Kinsey, Don Rendell, Tommy Whittle, Ronnie Ross and others may well have been technically first-rate, but it somehow lacked the pressured intensity of its American counterpart. Even contemporary observers couldn't fail to spot the absence of the intrinsic factor. "It is as British as Chris Barber or tea and cakes," wrote *Melody Maker*'s Bob Dawbarn when reviewing an LP by Whittle around this time, "but I am darned if I know why." The truth remained that British jazzmen were operating in ever-decreasing circles, forced to work in less than conducive circumstances, and prisoners of the game of catch-up. Although a notable exception, the success of the Jazz Couriers was still largely a triumph of emulation over innovation, but alongside all the mimicry, there existed a brave few willing to try and break the mould, the most prominent among them being Joe Harriott.

Harriott's playing had always sat somewhat at odds with the polite sound of the local product, but when tuberculosis floored him in 1958, the altoist had spent the long weeks recuperating in hospital dreaming up new ideas that might take his music forward. To this end, he formulated an unprecedented method for what he termed painting pictures in music, inspired by the work of artists such as Picasso and Paul Klee. The notions of rhythm, instrumental function and accompanying harmony were to be randomized, so that what emerged was a democratic performance more akin to a musical discussion than a series of individual monologues on a set subject. Looking to each other for inspiration, Harriott boldly proposed, there would no longer be the need to follow any role models – American or otherwise. Although impressed by what was undoubtedly a highly ambitious idea, it was instantly clear that the members of the saxophonist's regular quintet were far from convinced. Harry South and Hank Shaw couldn't see the point in abandoning what they already did so well to chase down what may well prove to be a musical blind alley and eventually the disagreement split the band. Undeterred, and with new and more sympathetic personnel, including trumpeter Shake Keane, Harriott began to include his "free-form" experiments on club dates during 1959. The effect was immediately divisive. The leader initially dealt with the controversy with characteristic strong will, joking in the press that "so far, nobody has thrown anything at us,"[33] but privately he knew that it was not only bemused audiences who were scoffing. Tubby Hayes was apparently amongst the doubters, allegedly greeting one of Harriott's early abstract performances with the words "If that's fucking jazz, give me trad!"[34] By suddenly making the unprecedented decision to turn to his fellow musicians for a creative springboard, Harriott had embarrassingly highlighted the insecurities of the local scene: free-form had turned into the Modern Jazz Elephant in The Room. Few at the time realized that the concept had actually unlocked the shackles that had for so long inhibited British jazz, and for musicians like Hayes, inextricably bound by the terms of American jazz, such experiments seemed little more than a rebellious tantrum.

Hayes now found chaos in his personal life too. The arguments at home had finally tipped Maggie over the edge and she had walked out for good, refusing point blank to listen to any more of her husband's excuses. Estranged and bitter, he now lived a bachelor existence at a flat in Carlton Vale shared with Phil Seamen and the young Scottish tenorist Bobby Wellins. A year younger than Hayes, and just beginning to make an underground reputation for himself, Wellins was already a saxophonist of startling individuality, having successfully cultivated a sound unlike that of any other player, American or English. To begin with there was his slow, wavering vibrato, to which he added a decidedly quirky sense of phrasing, which snaked in and out the beat without any reference to fashionable strings of bebop semi-quavers. For the younger man though, it was Hayes who was the real hero, a player who "always reminded me of champagne, he was bubbling over all the time and his music was like that."[35]

The three-way relationship at Carlton Vale had a more practical side too. As Hayes and Phil Seamen's daily session duties meant they were rarely at home during daylight hours, Wellins became, in effect, his flat-mates' general factotum – washing up, cleaning the flat, taking phone calls, ordering taxis. "My job was to take care of the house and then be able to practice – a marvellous arrangement," Wellins recalled.[36] But there were downsides too. Seamen's dog Billie, a formidable Alsatian with an aggressive temper, had begun to see far more of Wellins than its owner, meaning that whenever Seamen arrived home from a day in the studios it would duly go berserk. Then there was Seamen's drug habit to be dealt with. Sharing a room with the drummer, Wellins would often be woken up by Seamen's convulsions, and he was also fond of "fixing" at the kitchen table, sometimes inadvertently splattering his flat-mates' meals with blood.[37]

Wellins was also forging a close relationship with pianist Stan Tracey, Hayes's old band mate from the Kenny Baker days. Like Wellins, Tracey was earning his keep playing in a commercial dance band, in this instance that of Ted Heath. The music was often tedious but the lucrative wage helped compensate for the boredom. The gig had also put the pianist at something of a remove from his jazz colleagues, a situation that ironically enabled him to work out the direction in which he wanted his music to go. Weary of the fashions of the day, Tracey soon boiled down his influences to two key figures: the maverick Thelonious Monk and the perennially modern Duke Ellington. But in the days before transcriptions and epic tomes of analysis, dismantling the former's complex cipher took the patience of a saint, as Tracey's neighbour at the time Cleo Laine would later attest. Not everyone was so keen, and when Ted Heath asked the young pianist to play the written solos of his predecessor Frank Horrox and Tracey refused, the band enjoyed the bizarre spectacle of having its polite dance charts prised open by a two-fisted piano assault. It was a situation that couldn't last. Asked later what he had learned from Heath, Tracey quipped "I learned how to leave."

In the spring of 1959, around the time that Tubby Hayes alighted at Carlton Vale, Tracey recorded a formidable album with Phil Seamen and bassist Kenny Napper, *Little Klunk*, a record that more or less set out his stylistic stall and which reeked of unalloyed authenticity. Even the generally nonplussed Seamen glowed at the results, describing the recording as "the first time we've done anything as good as them"[38] – "them" meaning the Americans. Occasionally, Hayes would augment the band, but whenever and wherever players like Tracey, Wellins, Seamen and Hayes got together their focus would be on the same thing – escaping the tired old restrictions of the local jazz scene.

Once in a while, they did: Tracey and Wellins both travelled to America under the band-for-band agreement, whilst Hayes, one of the very few British jazzmen to have a reputation in continental Europe, made his first solo tour of Germany in June 1959. Following a recommendation from Jimmy Deuchar, together with Cleo Laine he ventured to Cologne to play a week of concert appearances with Kurt Edelhagen's band. Surviving tapes from the trip find him playing with a new brilliance, as if being freed from his usual confines had energized him even further. How much longer could he remain a purely European phenomenon? Surely such skill now needed a truly international forum?

Although the Jazz Couriers continued to be enormously popular, they were now in very real danger of becoming a self-perpetuating pastiche. During the early summer of 1959, with it clear that the band was running low on both incentive and creative steam, Jeff Clyne decided it was time to head to pastures new. Bill Eyden was the next to go, feeling that he'd seen the band pass its peak. For the time being, Kenny Napper and Phil Seamen filled the gaps, but Tubby Hayes was now less concerned about the group's personnel than its overall direction. Only Ronnie Scott was really content to keep the Couriers together, reluctant to let the successful format go.

The band taped *The Last Word*, its fourth and final LP, over two sessions in June and July. The results support Hayes's and Scott's subsequent observations about a closed circuit of mutual influence, and on the opening arrangement of 'If This Isn't Love' (one of Hayes's finest scores) it is remarkably hard to tell the front-liners apart. Although the record has other notable assets – including Hayes's debut on flute on 'Yesterdays' – and everything swings expertly under Phil Seamen's influence, there is something slightly under-ambitious and disappointing in its atmosphere, as if for the first time the band were going through the motions of ticking off a contractual obligation.

Critical reaction to the album was also mixed. *Jazz Journal* thought it a "worthy tribute to the Jazz Couriers" and "if some of the ideas are second-hand and inspired by the top modernists of America, this is amply compensated for by the impeccable playing throughout."[39] Jack Cooke of *Jazz Monthly*, however, had less endearing things to say, picking up on a "dispirited air about the session, and a feeling of contrivance which was not evident for much of the group's life."[40]

Matching these diverse opinions, the final few weeks of the Jazz Couriers' existence were an odd mix of the routine and the exceptional. Gigs at the Flamingo, one-nighters in Hastings and Chichester and a valedictory appearance on BBC's *Jazz Club* on August 13th all contrasted strongly with the band's first – and long overdue – overseas trip, comprising a week of concert appearances with guest altoist Bruce Turner in Vienna, under the auspices of the World Youth Festival.[41] (It remains unfathomable why the Jazz Couriers were never involved in any of the Anglo-American tour exchanges.) The Austrian sojourn was among the Couriers' last major engagements and the end came shortly afterwards, on Sunday August 30th, 1959, when a badly advertised and poorly attended concert at Cork City Hall marked their inglorious final bow. Shortly afterwards, Hayes remarked that the disbanding of the group had been inevitable – they'd achieved as much as they ever would – and that, after much deliberation, it had been a collective decision to swallow things: "Frankly, I think the split-up was mainly due to the fact we all needed a change and that some enthusiasm had gone from the group," Ronnie Scott told Tony Hall. "Because the jazz scene in this country is so restricted, we found ourselves just going round the same old circle of clubs and one-nighters and a certain amount of the original impetus was lost. But this seems inevitable over here."[42] There were other considerations too. "We had a ball for two years," Hayes told *Jazz News* the following year. "Then I began to run out of ideas for the two tenors. Apart from that Ronnie was playing two-thirds of the lead tenor work and I was on the harmonies. After a while I thought I was beginning to sound too much like him."[43]

Nevertheless, as the Couriers went their not entirely separate ways, there remained an unspoken pride in the band's collective achievements. They had certainly done more than any other local ensemble to raise the benchmark of British jazz. Indeed, the generation of British jazzmen that followed in the 1960s would have found their path a much harder one to travel had Hayes, Scott, Shannon and co. not pushed and elbowed their way into the front ranks of international recognition.

5 Now It's Who Have *They* Got? (1959–61)

I was back in the States and I was listening and I heard a thing, a tune, a very pretty tune that we used to play back in the late Forties and early Fifties called 'Cherokee' and I didn't hear the beginning of the song and so I didn't hear the announcement and I heard this tenor saxophone and he was playing something marvellous and I said "Jeezus. John Coltrane?" I thought it was an American, I said "Jeez, who is this?" And when it finished they said "And that was Tubby Hayes, a wonderful British tenor saxophonist" and that was the first time I heard the name. Then I heard the name more and more and I got a chance to meet Tubby and I admire him very much and I love the way he plays the saxophone.

Benny Golson, *Hear Me Talkin',* BBC radio, 1964

Ronnie Scott's remarks about the restrictions of the British jazz scene weren't just peevish digs, but had been made with a very real concern and dissatisfaction about the limited playing opportunities available to Britain's modernists. The situation was nothing new – that was the point. The modern jazz scene in the UK had survived for over a decade, but its infrastructure hadn't really changed since the late 1940s. The NJF-run Marquee Club, which opened in 1957, had seemed like a positive step in the right direction, but little had followed in its wake. Outside of this, the Flamingo remained the principal London venue, but mindful of Jeff Kruger's sensationally insensitive handling of the Jazz Couriers' interests earlier in the year, Scott was now keener than ever to escape from the hands of club owners who seemed big on lip service but short on respect. During the final weeks of the band, he'd begun to openly wonder if he couldn't do a better job of running a club himself.

A jazz musician running his own venue wasn't entirely unheard of. Humphrey Lyttelton had tried his hand in the early 1950s, although the exercise consisted of nothing more radical than annexing the existing premises at 100 Oxford Street, while, at the other end of the spectrum, John Dankworth had used several West End venues to present his own club nights. As a former member of the ill-fated Club XI co-operative, Ronnie Scott had also experienced the headaches of attempting this do-it-yourself brand of promotion, but as he mulled over what to do after the Couriers' demise in the autumn of 1959, the sudden availability of the basement of 39 Gerrard Street in Soho reignited an idea he'd held since his first visits to New York in the late 1940s.

Scott knew number 39 well, as did most of London's modernists. For a time during the early 1950s it had been the Zan-Zeba club, which had presented the odd night of jazz in a very insalubrious atmosphere. The premises had also variously operated as a near-beer joint (where prostitutes promised ever more lascivious favours if their unsuspecting punter bought just one more drink) and a cab driver's nocturnal hang-out. Sharing the same off-beat hours as the cabbies, men like Scott, Tubby Hayes and Benny Green would often call in to say hello, play cards and, given the availability of the basement's dilapidated piano, occasionally jam or rehearse. Sympathetic to their aims, in late summer 1959 the club's landlord Jack Fordham (owner of the first ever London burger bar in nearby Berwick Street) offered Scott and the Couriers' erstwhile manager Pete King the opportunity to take on the premises at a bargain rent. Chewing it over didn't take long. Scott didn't really relish the idea of heading out on the road again with yet another new band and King – already skilled in the sometimes tricky art of management through his involvement with the Harold Davison office – had exactly the sort of instinctive business savvy necessary to make the idea fly.

Although a cheap rent and a willing partner were crucial incentives, Benny Green saw Scott's frustration with the other London promoters as the clincher in the deal: "Ronnie decided that if he could form a club then he would be independent of these people. It was simply an escape from these wretched small time entrepreneurs that ran the clubs."[1]

That autumn, Scott and King began to realize their dream, and, as with virtually every enterprise the saxophonist had headed in his career to date, idealism outweighed both practicality and finance. There were second-hand chairs bought at a snip from an East End warehouse, a coffee machine that sometimes burbled louder than the music and a decorating plan that consisted of roping in whoever dropped by to see what was happening and arming them with a paintbrush. Ronnie Scott's finally opened its doors on October 30th, 1959, offering a bill featuring Tubby Hayes and Jack Parnell, among others, and instantly it piqued the interest of local fans and musicians alike. Despite the favourable press reaction, Scott now faced the same dilemma as every other British jazz club promoter – how to survive while promoting parochial players only. The odds were already heavily stacked against him, and, while he applauded the proprietor's enthusiasm, Benny Green was among those privately doubting whether the venture would ever get past infancy: "I felt that if he was still operating on New Year's Eve, he would be doing better than he could have ever hoped."[2] Nor had the established club owners taken kindly to Scott's intervention into their domain, although even they realized there was little they could do, other than wish him well and hope for the best – theirs not his.

Despite all the fiscal uncertainty, for Scott the new venue's musical aim was clear-cut: "I'd always felt that the jazz clubs, such as they were in those days, really catered to kids who wanted to come down and dance, and I thought that it would be nice if there was a place where the music was primary and there wasn't any dancing."[3] And, without any of the selfishness one might expect from a man opening a club in which he could have featured himself exclusively, Scott thought the venture should also serve as a forum for some of the more promising younger modernists who'd emerged on the heels of the Jazz Couriers.

Although British modern jazz had enjoyed a somewhat shaky existence for a decade or so, it had thrown up very little in the way of new talent along the way. The top men in 1950 – Dankworth, Scott, Jimmy Deuchar, Tony Kinsey *et al.* – were still the top men as the 1960s drew near. To those who were outside the music – the critics, the reviewers and even the fans – this dearth of new blood may have been worrying, but to those at the centre of things it provided the peculiar circumstance of being able to remain comfortably at the top of a tree that no one else appeared capable of climbing. Benny Green even went so far as to describe the situation as a "closed shop." But at the very tail end of the 1950s the shop was about to be burst into by a small group of extraordinarily talented young players.

The alto saxophonist Peter King was perhaps the most outstanding of the new breed. Tubby Hayes and Ronnie Scott had both had encounters with the shy, acne-ridden teenager which had left a deep impression. Although he'd been playing the alto for barely a few months, King was already performing with a technical facility close to virtuoso standard and with a harmonic understanding that took bebop as read in a way far removed from the sometimes hit-or-miss efforts of the earlier local modernists. Nevertheless, he found his first gig with Hayes, playing a guest spot at a club in Acton, a nerve-wracking experience.[4] Afterwards Hayes had complimented the youngster on his cool reserve, something King thought ironic given how terrified he'd been. A few weeks later, Ronnie Scott heard King during a jam session at the infamous Mandrake in Soho's Meard Street, an after-hours drinking den that ran ostensibly as a chess club, and had been so impressed that he asked the then unknown altoist to play opposite Hayes at the opening night of his new venue.

For a time King had been part of a band that also included Dick Morrissey, a tenor saxophonist who had made an almost overnight transition to modern jazz from playing traditional-style clarinet. Born in 1940, the same year as King, Morrissey was also alarmingly young, but like the altoist he displayed a precocious grasp of the mechanics of modern jazz. Within a couple of months of first picking up the tenor, he was already beginning to demonstrate the same energized musical clout that Tubby Hayes had done a decade earlier. Indeed, there are moments on his first album *It's Morrissey, Man!*, recorded in 1961, just shy of his twenty-first birthday, when he comes remarkably close to biting the older man's heels.

King and Morrissey made no secret of their debt to Hayes and, in turn, they found the older man positively encouraging. Whilst they may have attracted his endorsement on-stage, they soon realized that there was more to fitting in than mere musical compatibility. The tight clique of Hayes, Scott, Keith Christie, Ian Hamer, Harry Klein and the other leading British jazz names might have regarded itself as a meritocracy based upon acceptance of an individual player's skills, but in reality it operated more like a private members' club, with entry only considered if a new boy proved he had the "right stuff" to go along with his musical contribution. "We were all a bit hung up on that macho shit then," Peter King remembers. "I think I was accepted as a good player but there was the feeling that I still had to pay my dues in other ways. I really had no problem with any of the guys once I had proved I could play and 'talk the talk' so to speak. I had to earn their respect for the way I handled myself."[5] Handling yourself seemed to consist of being able to whoop it up before a gig and still deliver the goods musically. Recalls King:

> All this sounds terribly hedonistic in today's politically correct climate, but it helped to produce great, powerful and soulful music. The important thing was to take risks and push the limits in music and life. I think we were all feeling the after effect of the Battle of Britain spirit. Most of us learned how to keep the highest musical standards no matter how spaced-out we were! If you didn't, you felt you were not made of the right stuff.[6]

But whereas King took this sort of behaviour as his initiation rite, there were others who realized it simply wasn't for them. Indeed, these fast-track routes into the in-crowd could prove both compromising and tragic, as pianist Brian Dee remembers:

> There were the guys who'd got into the drug thing because it meant it would get them closer to someone they either idolized or wanted to work with. If you were fixing with someone, you had an in with them. That was pretty sick, because even before I really got into the session world, I used to think it was quite possible to be an ordinary bloke and still play good jazz. You didn't have to fall to pieces to do it. I was never into the drug thing and so consequently if you didn't do something there would be a whole scene in which your face didn't fit. It was quite sad really.[7]

In the weeks after the Jazz Couriers' demise Tubby Hayes was far from idle. He had launched a new quartet by the simple expedient of retaining the Couriers' rhythm section, and unencumbered by another front-line instrument, his music was now looser and less formal, with yet more space into which he could expand. Work at the Flamingo and the Marquee continued, with the quartet beginning an epic run opposite the quintet of Joe Harriott, a residency that etched its way into the consciousness of a generation of London jazz listeners. He also briefly tried his hand at club promotion, using his old stamping ground The White Hart at Acton as "Tubby's Place" for a few weeks towards the end of 1959.

As well as appearing at the new Scott club with the quartet, Tubby was using the premises to rehearse with the revived Downbeat Big Band, the collaborative unit he'd inherited from Jimmy Deuchar in 1957, and which was now serving as a useful forum for his nascent arranging talents (the band recorded an unissued acetate at Scott's on November 14th the purpose of which has never been ascertained). He also took a few jobs on vibes with Stan Tracey's quartet, the instrumentation of which mirrored the MJQ, but both this and the Downbeat project were only sidebars to the main action. His real preoccupation remained his own quartet, which he was keen to record as soon as possible. The opportunity finally came in December 1959, when the band taped two sessions at Decca Studios yielding what was indisputably his best album to date – and a recording that ranks among his finest work – *Tubby's Groove*.

Once again, the mastermind was Tony Hall, who made the intentions of the album crystal clear in the original sleeve notes. Post-Jazz Couriers Hayes was being let off the leash:

> To work with just the support of a swinging rhythm section is obviously the goal of any ambitious, serious-minded jazz horn man. There is nothing to equal the resulting freedom, and freedom is particularly important to someone with the drive and vigour of Tubby Hayes. In the quartet he has taken advantage of it in every possible way.[8]

Although Hayes hadn't recorded a session of his own in a quartet setting since the splendid *Swinging Giant* EPs back in 1955, it was a format that held a special appeal not only for him but for all of his tenor-playing heroes. Stan Getz later called the line-up of tenor saxophone, piano, double bass and drums the jazz equivalent of the string quartet in classical music, and by the time Hayes got around to creating the performances for *Tubby's Groove*, each of his key saxophone influences had created definitive records using the horn-plus-rhythm instrumentation: Getz himself had taped two outstanding sets for Verve a few years previously, *The Steamer* and *Award Winner*, whilst Sonny Rollins's *Saxophone Colossus* from 1956 was seen by many as the tenorist's finest hour to date, with the album *Newk's Time* from the following year not far behind. Johnny Griffin's blistering Blue Note debut, *Introducing Johnny Griffin*, from 1956, was another notable quartet set and around the time Hayes entered the studios for his Tempo effort, John Coltrane was in the final stages of completing his landmark statement, *Giant Steps.*

Each of these recordings made clear their leaders' style, sound and direction, and although the rationales were as varied as methodical (Coltrane), hell-for-leather (Griffin) and informal (Getz) each demonstrated that the player in question had musical personality enough to pull off forty minutes or so without the listener lamenting the absence of another front-line instrument. Following suit, Tony Hall agreed that the new album should primarily be a feature for the leader. Even so, this didn't prevent Jeff Clyne from feeling distinctly apprehensive. The bassist later recalled being more nervous about the quartet sessions than he had been for his recording debut with the Couriers a year before, a feeling not helped by the presence in the control booth of Kenny Napper, one of his heroes. Apart from this vignette, Clyne remembered little else from the two days that produced such a memorable recording.[9] Even the producer has only vague recollections. "You don't think of something as a classic album when you're taping it. It's just what you're doing at the time," Tony Hall remarks. "You certainly don't think of what people will make of it in fifty years' time. All I *do* remember is that the sessions went well and that everyone was happy with what was recorded."[10]

The opening version of Dizzy Gillespie and Chano Pozo's 'Tin Tin Deo' was, according to Hall, intended as the leader's big showcase: "I wanted Tubby to do one tune with just him soloing all the way through – no other solos – and we settled on Tin Tin Deo. I thought it was a success, one reason being that Phil Seamen had a good day. Well, most of it was good!"[11]

'Tin Tin Deo' is indeed something of a marathon. At nearly ten minutes in duration, Hayes's soloing was now edging into Coltrane-like lengths, but with a general sense of well-thought-out architecture to his improvisation the impression he creates is quite different. In particular, he utilizes the change from a minor to a major key during the song's bridge to such good effect that the overall impact, whilst somewhat mesmeric, is not merely that of virtuosity for its own sake. The basic tonality of F minor also suits the tenor's range, whilst the composition's relatively simple sequence made it a good place for Hayes to exercise his increasing fascination with the extended harmony, as he described on the album's sleeve: "I'm trying to get round the changes rather than go for the conventional 7th. I'm trying to utilize the 13ths, 11ths and the notes that go with them. I'm trying to find melodies on the top parts of these chords, to glide through the changes."[12] 'Tin Tin Deo' is full of such devices; however, to his credit, not once does Hayes sound as if he is struggling to incorporate these more oblique choices.

His tone on 'Tin Tin Deo' is also magnificent. Big as a barn door and yet still flexible, able to both smoothly caress and boom out, and edged with an unaffected gorgeous vibrato that greatly enhances the emotional impact of his lines, as on the following ballad, 'Like Someone In Love', a performance also notable for its mature use of dynamics, an area of musical deportment not then paid much attention in British jazz circles.

Richard Rodgers's 'The Surrey With The Fringe On Top' is the album's up-tempo flag-waver, although Hayes's solo, winding its way across the entire range of the tenor, never once sounds rushed. The almost nerveless relaxation displayed by Phil Seamen at this tempo is also astonishing and, as on the Jazz Couriers' final album, the drummer demonstrates an uncanny ability to make even the most rampant speeds seem airy and controlled. The track's half-tempo coda, built on the round-and-round tag beloved by players such as Dexter Gordon and Sonny Stitt, gives another chance to catch Hayes's tactical use of vibrato.

Tony Hall remembers that it was Hayes's interest in the work of Johnny Griffin that led him to cover 'Sunny Monday', a pretty and lyrical theme from the pen of little-known Chicago tenorman John Hines. Griffin had taped a version for his recent Riverside album, *Way Out!* but, if anything, the Englishman's cover is even more accomplished than the original. The construction of the performance is somewhat unusual: the theme's eight-bar A sections, reminiscent in harmonic content to Charlie Parker's 'Confirmation' (and Hayes's own 'Royal Ascot') are played in waltz tempo but are bridged by a middle-eight B section written in four. The band makes an excellent job of handling these changes, with Seamen in particular capturing the genteel mood of pastiche in the ¾ sections. However, the real highlight occurs in Hayes's three-chorus solo, which includes a device new to him – unaccompanied improvisation.

In his sleeve notes Tony Hall made much of Hayes's skill at such feats, citing Sonny Rollins's previous efforts as a solo horn as the only precedent, but whereas Rollins had favoured the idea of recording entirely solo pieces, Hayes saw the device as a useful way to stave off the potential monotony of a single horn and an accompanying rhythm section: "We started doing this not as a sort of gimmick, but as a way of giving the group a different sound. I find it a tremendous challenge, too, as an instrumentalist, to be able to swing on my own. And here again there's unlimited freedom in my choice of changes."[13] In the pocket, never rushed, and sounding neither lazy and uncertain nor pushy and overexcited, perhaps what is most remarkable about the solo exposition on 'Sunny Monday' is the saxophonist's beautiful sense of time.

The album's closer is a wholly improvised blues, subsequently titled 'Blue Hayes', with which Hayes declared his desire to get back to the roots: "No-one here has ever recorded a really slow blues. We tried it as a tribute to all the many great coloured musicians, whose blues playing has knocked us out."[14] Following Shannon's Sonny Clark-like set-up, the leader outlines a solo full of direct emotional impact, subtle dynamics, and a telling use of superimposed chord substitutions. His stop-time chorus, as Tony Hall notes, takes things right back to the dawn of jazz. Indeed, so effective is Hayes's exploration of one of the basic tenets of jazz – the slow blues – it makes his decision never to repeat the exercise all the more lamentable. The performance had also delivered the best answer to those critics who saw the tenorist as all flash and no substance, closing an outstanding album not with a bang, but with something far subtler.

The six tracks that comprised the original Tempo release of *Tubby's Groove* marked, in the words of Tony Hall, "the most completely representative album yet recorded by an extremely talented musician, whose best is yet to come."[15] With the emphasis so strongly upon Hayes the heavyweight tenorist (a single vibes feature, 'Embers', was placed as something of a palate cleanser after the epic feast that was 'Tin Tin Deo') it is all too easy to overlook and underestimate the contributions of his sidemen Terry Shannon, Jeff Clyne and Phil Seamen to the proceedings. Shannon in particular is superb, prompting the leader one minute and the next laying back as the saxophonist runs the assault course of altered harmonies.

Throughout the entire album the rhythm section illustrates that relaxation and drive – the magic combination that had eluded many British jazzmen to date – was not only possible but sustainable. Whether the tempo is the helter-skelter of 'The Surrey With The Fringe On Top' or the deep groove of 'Blue Hayes', each is played with a conviction and cohesion that sounds every bit as authentic as that heard on American releases of the time, making *Tubby's Groove* as much a collective triumph as a signal victory for its headliner.

In fact, there had never been a British jazz album quite like it. Whereas critical reaction to Hayes's previous releases had generally been uneven, this time it was uniformly positive: Bob Dawbarn of *Melody Maker* spoke for many when he called the set the best jazz record ever made in the UK, and accordingly the album became the first British recording to be voted the paper's LP of the Month, beating off stiff competition from Sonny Rollins and Dave Brubeck. "Hayes is a complete musician with both a remarkable technical control and, much rarer, a wide emotional spectrum," Dawbarn declared with undisguised partisan enthusiasm.[16] *Jazz News*'s John Martin thought the album had proved the saxophonist's determination to "explore new territory on his own without waiting to hear what the latest Americans are up to." Martin also identified an affinity with John Coltrane ("although he has a better tone") before going into effusive overdrive in an attempt to capture the essence of Hayes's approach:

> He uses his technique to overlap the changes with little coda-like phrases that dove-tail into the next sequence. The result is that there is a continuity in his playing that is never broken. It is as though he is playing the dual role of soloist and accompanist. Technique is an inextricable part of Tubby's style. His is a broad, robust and eager approach. He sounds as if he was permanently

switched on yet, what at first is ostensibly mechanical, is really only a superficial gloss behind which is a hard thinking mind. He employs a wonderful variety of unpredictable phrases to make this album interesting. Of course, he has his clichés like most musicians, but what sets Tubby apart from most of the other British musicians is that he seldom uses them. The only reason I do not give this album the full five stars is that I believe Tubby has even more to say in the future.[17]

Tubby's Groove also impressed American listeners, with celebrated critic Nat Hentoff praising Hayes in *DownBeat* magazine as

an intelligent and sensitive performer who is fast welding elements from Johnny Griffin and Sonny Rollins into a personal style. His magnificent technique enables him to interpret the most involved phrases with confidence. His tone, bold and caressing by turns, is invariably well suited to his melodic substance. The emotional compass of his music is a good deal wider than is general with jazzmen of his generation.

Tubby's Groove was the last monumental achievement of Hayes's first decade as a jazz musician and appropriately enough its contents serve as something of a summary of all he had achieved to date. To many observers, taken together with 1967's *Mexican Green*, the album brackets the years during which the saxophonist reached his career apex, an argument that continues to hold water. There had been earlier triumphs of course, such as the *Blues In Trinity* and *The Couriers Of Jazz* sessions, but with *Tubby's Groove* Hayes had delivered the first completely mature example of his talent on record.

Marvellously paced, without any weak tracks or substandard performances, the album is a tribute to both Hayes's immense consistency and his ability to inspire those around him. It also marks the juncture at which he settled into place some of the devices that would feature effectively in his work throughout the 1960s: lengthy solos, unaccompanied choruses and the general relegation of the vibraphone to the role of a set-breaking relief for ballad themes. The record also continues to stand up remarkably well alongside its American counterparts. If not quite having the genre-defining impact of *Giant Steps* or *Saxophone Colossus*, its solid celebration of the *lingua franca* of hard bop makes it more akin to albums such as Hank Mobley's *Soul Station* or Stanley Turrentine's *Look Out!*

Above all, it is a recording that has stood the biggest test of all, that of time. Its sheer élan communicates just as well in the new millennia as it did in the "never had it so good" days of Harold Macmillan.

There is also a postscript to its success: when Jasmine Records reissued *Tubby's Groove* on CD in 2000, its contents were augmented by three further "out-takes" from a single-sided acetate that Hayes had entrusted to drummer Spike Wells. These performances – two of which initially went unidentified – included an alternative take of 'Tin Tin Deo', slightly shorter but with Hayes offering a fresh-minted solo, and two new themes, Charlie Parker's 'Visa' and Hayes's own composition 'Supper At Phil's'. The former includes a blistering thirteen-chorus improvisation from the saxophonist, which, with its popping energy, slippery double-time runs and a joyous authority, serves admirably as a summary of his style at the close of the 1950s.

'Supper At Phil's' is another performance taken at the kind of grooving medium-up tempo at which Johnny Griffin excelled. The influence here is clear, and if one hears 'Hot Sausage' from Griffin's Riverside album *Way Out!* it's possible to even sense a little déjà vu.

Intriguingly, in late 2008, three further unreleased tracks from the sessions also came to light. Given an almost total absence of additional material from Hayes's years at Tempo, this discovery constituted not only a major coup but the culmination of a fascinating story that had begun in 1960, centred once again on Tony Hall.

The success of organizing Dizzy Reece's Blue Note contract had given the producer renewed confidence. "I knew there was only so much that could be done with Tempo," he later confessed, "so when I hung out with Alfred Lion, it was my intention to get him to sign Dizzy *and* Tubby because they were the best we had over here and were truly of an international calibre. I was doing everything possible to alert Alfred to how good they were."[18]

To this end the producer sent Lion two tape reels comprising six performances from the sessions that had produced *Tubby's Groove*. What Lion did with the recordings next is not exactly clear, but having never been slated for release it appears that by the 1970s they had disappeared into the enormous archive of Blue Note tapes held by United Artists. They remained lost and unheard until Michael Cuscuna, head of the new Blue Note operation and the reissue market's equivalent of Indiana Jones, succeeded in finally locating them again among Lion's personal effects. What they contain is the Holy Grail of Tubby Hayes artefacts.

Interestingly, the tapes appeared to be sequenced together for an album and, although three of the performances were those already familiar from Spike Well's worn acetate, they also included material that was wholly new. Delivered at medium tempo, the wartime popular song 'Symphony' is a revelation and, like its session mate 'Sunny Monday', is completed by a dazzling unaccompanied chorus from the leader's tenor, full of well-paced lines that curve their way through the harmony and never lose sight of the lyrical qualities of the original melody. Hayes's original 'Hook's Way' turns out to be a retitling of 'After Tea' from the Jazz Couriers library and has a gripping series of blues choruses from the leader, several of which dispense with piano accompaniment. The final number is an unlikely appropriation of 'The Trolley Song', of Judy Garland fame, dispatched at a suitably locomotive tempo and with Phil Seamen's Blakey-like ride cymbal well to the fore. Like 'Surrey With A Fringe On Top' from *Tubby's Groove* (with which it shares some classic Hayesian licks), the speedy tempo never defeats Hayes nor any of his hand-in-glove sidemen. Indeed, the performance is among the best the saxophonist ever delivered in a recording studio, all the more remarkable for being shelved for over half a century.

With such excellence on display, one is forced to ask exactly why Alfred Lion simply did nothing with these recordings. The answer is surprisingly prosaic: Lion's earlier signing of Dizzy Reece had proved irrefutably that selling a UK-associated jazz artist in the USA continued to be no easy task.[19] Taking on another foreign player – and one who, unlike Reece, wasn't even resident on the same continent – would have most likely struck Lion as far too risky. For all its kudos, Blue Note was still a small label in 1960 and even though the company was faithful to artists who never promised much in the way of sales figures, most notably Hank Mobley, the bottom line nevertheless still had to be met. In addition to this, at the point when Lion received Hall's tapes he had just signed two promising new tenor saxophonists, Stanley Turrentine and Tina Brooks. With a catalogue already boasting albums by Sonny Rollins, John Coltrane and Johnny Griffin, the label – to put it bluntly – simply didn't need Tubby Hayes. Interestingly, Tony Hall also hints at something deeper: "How many white artists were there on Blue Note? There were exceptions like J. R. Monterose, who was a terrific musician, but they only made one or two albums for that label."[20]

However, there is one more twist in the tale. Under the title *Tubby's New Groove*, the Blue Note tapes were eventually released on CD by the Candid label in 2011, meeting with universal critical acclaim. Although not strictly a re-release, the album won Reissue of the Year in *Jazzwise* magazine soon after, but for Tony Hall the long-deferred sense of satisfaction was also tinged with irony: Candid had once been an American record label but was now owned and run by an Englishman. Finally, the tail was wagging the dog.

As the 1960s began, Tubby Hayes stood head and shoulders above virtually every other British jazzman. Others may well have achieved goals he had yet to meet – in particular that of working in the United States – but there was no doubting his stature as the identifiable face of British modernism. Confirmation of his popularity came in January 1960 when he was once more crowned in the *Melody Maker* poll, retaining the tenor saxophone title he had won the previous year. As welcome as the victory was, it also came with a sense of frustration. Even to casual observers, there seemed little that Hayes hadn't already done and many wondered openly if there were any more local mountains left to climb.

As the reviews of *Tubby's Groove* had made clear, Hayes's music remained firmly within the remit of hard bop, but whilst the majority of English modern

The Downbeat Big Band, Manor House, summer 1960. Saxophones: Ronnie Scott, Tubby Hayes, Alan Branscombe and Jackie Sharpe. Trombone: Keith Christie. Trumpets: Les Condon, Eddie Blair (soloing), Bobby Pratt, Jimmy Deuchar. Bass: Jeff Clyne. Drums: Bobby Orr (pianist Terry Shannon is out of shot). Courtesy Bobby Orr.

jazz musicians continued to be content to work inside the parameters that had been established by bebop a decade or so earlier, there were those in America who were now trying to find new ways out of the formula. Bored of playing music crammed with ever more chord changes, Miles Davis had begun to experiment with simple scales – or modes – as the basis for improvisation during the late 1950s. The first album to fully document this approach was 1959's *Kind Of Blue*, a record of elegant and austere beauty, and an LP apparently adored by the members of the Tubby Hayes quartet. Jeff Clyne later remembered writing out Davis's 'So What' for the band.[21] Davis's album had also featured John Coltrane, one of Hayes's principal inspirations, who that same year recorded *Giant Steps*, a set that was the very antithesis of what his boss was attempting. Rather than escaping the maze of harmony, Coltrane sought to make it ever more complex, creating complex systems of superimposed chords that required a virtuoso technique to negotiate. Tubby Hayes found the American's approach intoxicating, as he told *Jazz Journal*:

> Coltrane is my favourite of all the modern tenor players – he is so original and creative. So much more creative than even the other good ones. Like Sonny Stitt for instance – Stitt plays beautifully but he has those little runs and things which have almost become

clichés. Coltrane is never like that: he is always, and particularly on the freedom of his own record dates, he is always striving for something new, something original. Sometimes, he doesn't always make it – he may fluff a note here and there or play a run that doesn't quite come off – but he is always trying something new. I heard a record the other day on which he plays two or even three notes that are hard for the human ear to hear. I am sure some people will condemn it as a horrible row, but who knows to what it might lead? Some of those chord sequences he uses, such as those on *Giant Steps* are far in advance of anything anyone else has ever attempted. How he can play like that, at that tempo, amazes me. He explores the harmonics of the saxophone and produces those high notes which, who knows, may add another octave to the range of the tenor – and that would be an advantage.[22]

Supporting these claims, when asked on the BBC's *Jazz Session* during 1960 which record he would nominate as an outstanding example of the direction in which he saw jazz progressing, Hayes unhesitatingly recommended *Giant Steps*. It was easy to understand the endorsement. The title track represented the ultimate destination of bebop's ideals: the music was intensely complex and utterly intellectual, a super-extension of all the aspects of modern jazz that had captured Hayes's imagination since the late 1940s. However, even with a player as excitingly intense as Coltrane executing it, it wasn't impossible to escape the nagging suspicion that the theory would ultimately prove to be a stylistic cul-de-sac. Bebop had put in more chords than swing musicians used. Coltrane had doubled the equation. What else could there be left to do, other than repeat the formula until jazz became a genuine harmonic maze? Coltrane himself would draw similar conclusions soon after but, for the time being, Tubby Hayes had found a performer who offered the ultimate in comparative musical benchmarks.

Alongside Coltrane and Miles Davis's innovations, other ways of broadening the language of jazz were just beginning to open up. During the late 1950s Dave Brubeck had begun to incorporate unusual time signatures in order to break the dominance of regular 4/4 swing, whilst the band of Charles Mingus explored the textural qualities of the jazz ensemble in a way that was nothing short of Ellingtonian. But by far the most radical of those trying to find new freedoms was Ornette Coleman, the Texas-born alto saxophonist whose music simply abandoned the notions of pre-set harmony altogether, taking jazz back to its roots in unfettered field hollers and unconventional melodic lines.

Coleman set the jazz world on its head with this concept, with critics soon labelling his music 'free jazz'. Some thought him a charlatan, others a new messiah (with titles like *Tomorrow Is The Question* and *The Shape Of Jazz To Come*, the saxophonist's albums were big on marketing polemics), but where he had indisputably proved his worth was as a composer and bandleader. Coleman had a natural feel for melody and his early compositions, such as 'Lonely Woman' and 'Peace', were strong enough to attract even those who found his squawky playing too much to bear, including Modern Jazz Quartet leader John Lewis, who went on record as describing the altoist's break-throughs as the most important made in jazz since Charlie Parker. Above all, Coleman's music continued to swing, often joyously so. Indeed, once the listener had got past all the hype and the outrageously prophetic album titles, they quickly found it possessed all the most basic ingredients of jazz. Never-theless, the battle lines had been drawn.

The ramifications of Ornette Coleman's innovations would rock the jazz world well into the 1960s, opening up the field for equal numbers of genuinely able improvisers and chancers. At its best, the approach would fuel some of the finest jazz of the decade, including the output of the 1964–68 Miles Davis quintet; at its worse it would spawn the idea of the free-blowing improvising collective, creating the kind of music that one observer described, rather cruelly, as sounding like "a fire in a pet shop." Perhaps even more crucially, with its emphasis on democratic dialogue, the concept of free jazz had suddenly rendered obsolete the old idea of the soloist as a musical He-Man. Machismo had been part and parcel of jazz since the very beginning and the music was full of players known for their stamina and strength – from Roy Eldridge to Sonny Rollins and beyond. It was certainly Tubby Hayes's way too, something easily confirmed by looking at the names of those with whom he was being compared in the early 1960s: Johnny Griffin, Benny Golson, Rollins and Coltrane, each highly muscular performers.

Like many British jazzmen, Hayes initially regarded Ornette Coleman as a joke, although he did mellow towards the altoist's music when Jeff Clyne began to express an interest. Coltrane may well have been Hayes's idol at this point, but Clyne found his boss possessed an almost barometric ability to pick up on any musical trend:

> It's funny, because Tubby would get really into the personality of whoever he was into. When it was Miles he wouldn't say much on the microphone. When Cannonball [Adderley] came over, he'd get into the chat. With Coltrane, it would be the long solos, stretching out very earnestly. He was always him, but you'd notice these little things as he got into something.[23]

If in his fascination with Coltrane Hayes now felt he was getting ever closer to the cutting edge, he need only have looked at the local record industry to blunt his optimism. "If the record company had stuck a John Coltrane Quartet label on Tubby Hayes's LP, *Tubby's Groove*, no doubt it would be in the best-selling charts by now," wrote one reader to *Melody Maker* during the summer of 1960, but when the paper published Tony Hall's sad tale about not

At the Concorde Club, Southampton, circa 1960. Author's collection.

being able to raise the £19.00 necessary to record a further Tempo session that year, everything was put into stark perspective. The small-beer figure said it all: British jazz had often been seen as the poor relation in musical terms, but financially it was virtually a pauper. When Coltrane had signed with Atlantic Records in 1959, the deal had been $7000 for a one-year contract, with an option to extend if both parties were happy.[24] The saxophonist had also received a Lincoln Continental. British musicians were lucky to get the bus fare home.

Understandably, Hayes was now keener than ever to escape the petty-mindedness of the local scene and as 1960 began he and his manager Pete King discussed how best to bring his music to a wider audience: "I remember vividly that we went out to dinner, with his wife and my wife, and [then] we sat down on the floor of his flat over in Notting Hill, and we worked out a schedule for the way forward for Tubby."

King's "schedule" was anything but cast in stone but, blessed with a typical Londoner's gift of the gab, he soon began to cajole and bluff his way into the offices of the mighty. "I went out looking for anything that Tubby could possibly get into," he remembered, "and one of the things was a BBC [TV] series."[25]

King's entry into the world of television came from producer Stewart Morris and he couldn't have talked to anyone better. Young and headstrong, Morris had fought a stiff battle to penetrate the ranks of the BBC but, once inside, he ensured that the old establishment fully embraced the new youth culture, eventually rising to the position of the corporation's Head of Variety during the 1970s (he was to be responsible for several light entertainment staples including *Juke Box Jury*). In early 1960, Morris saw sense in a show that could cater for the potential audience that lay between teenaged fans of rock and roll on one hand and their parents' generation on the other. He quickly sketched up the idea for a new programme, *Tempo 60*, which would in his own words "put jazz over in the commercial sense – to please the general public and also the fans."[26] Amazingly the BBC took the bait but, despite the producer's iron-clad faith, to some the idea of a jazz-slanted programme going out at the prime-time slot of 7.30 pm on a Friday evening bordered on scheduling lunacy. As preparations for the series began, Pete King saw his chance, however, and threw Tubby Hayes's name into the hat for the position of musical director. It was a gamble that worked and, when Morris eventually agreed to Hayes's taking up the role, no one felt the surprise more keenly than King.

The core of *Tempo 60*'s musical output would come from a six-piece line-up, effectively the Hayes quartet with Ronnie Scott and Jimmy Deuchar added, and with a guest list that included Stéphane Grappelli, Matt Monro, Kenny Baker and Swedish singer Monica Zetterlund, among others, it looked like the series would be a healthily mature antidote to the teen culture that had so dominated previous shows like *Oh, Boy!* The first programme aired on May 13th, but almost straight away it drew criticism. The letters page of *Melody Maker* bristled with pointed questions about why the resident group hadn't received more space and suspicion that the programme was nothing more than a variety show in jazz clothing. Unsurprisingly, it couldn't last and, despite Stewart Morris's vocal attempts to call off the chop, after seven weeks *Tempo 60* was axed.

Outside of music, Hayes's personal life also continued to wax and wane. Although still married to Maggie, he now had a new girlfriend, the exotically named Alexandra Souriya Rose Khan, whom he had met at a London theatre. As the new relationship blossomed both parties took it upon themselves to enlighten the other: Tubby brought Rose LPs of classical music – "on some sort of mission to educate my mother in musical theory," recalls the couple's eldest son Richard – whilst Rose introduced her new man to the world of the theatrical party.[27] Initially, there was no urgent need for a divorce as Tubby and Maggie rarely saw each other and this distant but civil situation persisted until the spring of 1960 when Rose discovered she was pregnant. She was intent on keeping the child and Tubby knew what he needed to do. A divorce from Maggie was duly granted on July 1st, 1960.

Hayes's band was also headed for a split. Despite the group being among the most popular attractions of the UK jazz scene – as their well-attended residency at the Marquee confirmed – there remained the ever-present issue of Phil Seamen's unreliability. By the late summer of 1960, after the politic turning of many blind eyes to the drummer's antics, Hayes decided enough was enough. Jeff Clyne remembered the difficulty of the decision.

> Phil was arriving late and it just wasn't happening on the stand. He was very unpredictable. He could be as nice as pie or totally mean. You could never tell with Phil. Sometimes there'd be more anxiety than anything else: "Is he gonna make it?" kind of thing. He was creating headaches for Tubby. They were great, great mates but in the end he just wasn't taking care of business.[28]

These contentions came to a head in epic fashion, and in public, on the quartet's appearance at the Beaulieu Jazz Festival in August 1960. Echoing the disaster of the recent Newport Jazz Festival, the weekend eventually ended in a riot after drunken fans had clambered onto the roof of the stage. Hayes's set the previous day also had its own brand of anarchy. "Just before we went on Tubby told us he was going to have to let Phil go," Jeff Clyne recalled. "Well, you can imagine what followed. There was this tremendous row which then spilled on stage. I remember we were doing this blues where I had a walking bass solo. This solo went on *forever* whilst Tubby and Phil had an argument on stage."[29]

Despite the loss of Seamen, Hayes remained on track. A few weeks after the Beaulieu debacle, *Jazz News* magazine published an interview with the saxophonist conducted by John Martin, during which he delivered both an effective summary of his career to date and an outline of his future goals. "My style has come gradually," he remarked. "The group has helped a lot." When Martin broached the subject of the recent comparisons with Coltrane and Sonny Stitt, Hayes was unequivocal in his response: "I think the tenor sound should be a full sound. After all, the tenor players before Lester played with a full sound, like Coleman Hawkins." He also appended a note of caution to those critics who still considered him a musical circus act. "I don't play to show off. I just try to play a little different. People associate me with fast numbers but I like to play all types." Martin also posed the inevitable question of where he was headed next. Hayes was quick to mention a projected new sextet with Jimmy Deuchar and Keith Christie, adding "I'm not bored. Of course, I would like to go to the States but just for a look around first. I suppose the only way I can do that is in an exchange. I hope something might come off this winter."[30]

As with virtually all of Hayes's published interviews there is a note of serenity to the *Jazz News* profile. Indeed, he sounds perfectly at home with his career success, although something of this self-satisfaction may have also been attributable to his personal circumstances: Rose was barely two weeks from giving birth to their first child. However, any thoughts on impending fatherhood were not appended in Martin's interview, probably a discreet nod to the couple's out-of-wedlock status.

Fifteen days after the publication of the *Jazz News* cover story, on Sunday September 25th, 1960, Rose gave birth to a baby boy, named Richard Terence Hayes, the first born of Tubby's two sons. By all accounts, the saxophonist wasn't a naturally instinctive father. In a superb example of understatement, Stan Tracey, whose son Clark was born shortly after, remembers him as "not exactly a stay-at-home guy."[31] In fact, there was precious little time for Hayes to bond with his new child as barely a month later he was off on the road again, with the quartet operating as a support group for the American vocalist Carmen McRae. A few days after the close of the tour, on November 9th, Tubby and Rose finally wed, a ceremony that once more had to be squeezed between his professional commitments: that same day he made an understandably breathless contribution to a BBC *Jazz Club* broadcast by Harry South's big band.

Unsurprisingly, as the year drew to a close, Hayes was keen to record again. It had been close to a year since he'd recorded an album and with the healthy critical reaction given *Tubby's Groove* surely there was no better time to tape an encore? However, he now found Tony Hall's enthusiasm at its lowest ebb. Decca had recently turned away Hall's suggestion to record two of the new wave of British jazzmen, Peter King and Bobby Wellins, and only after the success of a recent tour opposite Miles Davis had they sanctioned a session by the Vic Ash–Harry Klein Jazz Five. The album would be the final British jazz release on Tempo. After five years of dogged determination, and exhausted by the objections of his seniors, Hall had finally conceded defeat:

> It had been the ultimate labour of love, when I think back. If you look at how hard I had to push the people at Decca to record Tubby, or the Jazz Couriers, you'd think I was asking them to record something dreadfully substandard. Even after the success of *Tubby's Groove* and the Jazz Five album, which I still think is one of the best things ever done over here, things didn't improve. There was supposed to have been a follow-up to *Tubby's Groove* but that never happened. I began to realize that Decca didn't really appreciate how good the music was. I can see their point now. After all, business is business and they wanted sales. One of the last things I did with Tempo was to push for the [American] Riverside

label to take the Jazz Couriers, which they did. I considered going it alone for a while and did produce one session by Bogey Gaynair, which waited forty-five years to be released, but as things began to change in the music, the avant-garde came up. I saw nothing that really appealed to me. It had been a labour of love but had I gone on, I think it would have just got tiresome.[32]

New recording or not, 1960 had been very much a year of progress for Hayes; there had been the, admittedly short-lived, TV coup with *Tempo 60* and the unprecedented success of *Tubby's Groove*, but one nagging question remained – when *would* he finally get to America? Holidaying in Paris that December, Zoot Sims had asked *Melody Maker* "How's Tubby Hayes? He'd be a knockout in the States."[33] He couldn't know it, but the opportunity for Hayes to deliver that international sucker punch was now only months away.

The European part of Hayes's international vision had begun in the late summer of 1960, with a solo visit to Sweden, and it continued early in the New Year, with the quartet playing a short season at the Storyville clubs in Frankfurt and Cologne. Barely sixteen years after the end of World War II, it was all too easy to expect a certain amount of anti-British sentiment to exist, but Hayes and his musicians quickly discovered that music was a language able to surmount historical as well as national boundaries. Indeed, when compared to that in England, the German jazz scene was remarkably healthy and notably broad-minded; throughout their engagement in Cologne, the quartet had appeared opposite a traditional jazz band, a situation that would have been unthinkable back in London.

Ever since its arrival in the UK in the late 1940s, bebop had attracted a certain amount of musical enmity from those preferring older forms of jazz and within a short time British jazz fans had divided themselves neatly into two camps – traditional and modern. The traditionalists – and more specifically the *revivalists* – thought they were preserving a music that had been all but swept away by the commercial notions of the Swing Era and considered bebop nothing more than a hideous abomination of the post-Atomic age. The modernists thought the "mouldy fygge" fans of traditional jazz were nothing less than musical Luddites, trying to hold back the natural progression of the idiom. Much of the invective on this subject published by the jazz press during the 1950s and early 1960s now reads rather embarrassingly – almost like peering into a time capsule in which relics from an old family argument have been frozen in perpetuity – but at the time those defending either camp were both openly hostile and deadly serious.

Part of the problem lay in the unavoidable fact that traditional jazz – or, more specifically, a highly Anglicized variant of the music – had caught the ear of the wider public, something that even a well-known modern jazz musician like Tubby Hayes had failed to do. By 1961, the bands of Chris Barber, Acker Bilk and Kenny Ball had all done the improbable by putting jazz at the top of the popular music charts, thus beginning a short but intense surge of public interest that soon became known simply as the Trad Boom. If anyone had been paying close attention, they would have spotted that the "hits" scored by Barber, Bilk and Ball were more easy-listening than strictly jazz – 'Petite Fleur', 'Stranger On The Shore' and 'Midnight In Moscow' had never been staples in turn-of-the-century New Orleans – but nobody much cared. The music was sunny, breezy and a welcome antidote to both the morbid political outlook of the time and the increasingly solemn efforts made in the name of jazz modernism. Inevitably, it didn't take long for hungry publicists to throw themselves at the fast-moving bandwagon.

Apart from musical differences, the fans of the respective Trad and Modern camps even had their own sartorial codes. Ivy league ties, Italian bum-freezer suits and winkle-picker shoes had become all but a uniform for British modern jazzmen, making the musicians in a group like the Tubby Hayes quartet virtually indistinguishable from those in, say, Allan Ganley's or Ronnie Scott's bands. This smart anonymity seemed to say "music first," and laid the foundation stone of the Mod movement. But, for many of the Trad bands, a strongly individual visual presence ensured something else altogether. Occasionally the dividing lines were blurred: with their contemporary suits Chris Barber and Kenny Ball's sidemen wouldn't have looked out of place in a modern jazz unit, but when Acker Bilk's Paramount Jazzband opted to ape the style of the Edwardian era, with its pin-striped waistcoats and the leader's signature bowler hat, they unwittingly launched the search for ever more gimmick-ridden band identities.

It was all very innocent at first, but as time wore on band attire began to range freely into the realms of the absurd, from the military uniform of the Confederacy to gamblers' frock coats, stockbrokers' three-piece suits and bowlers and beyond. However, the real trouble started when these increasingly outrageous outfits began to obscure the sincerity of the musicians wearing them. It was difficult not to get caught up in the bickering: "I absolutely abhor the dressing up and the comic stuff with not much music coming out," Tubby Hayes told *TV Times* at the height of the boom,[34] and when Jimmy Deuchar was asked to put the case for the modernists in *Melody Maker*, his disdain was clear:

> Most of the Trad players probably don't have the technique to sound individual. If they learned their instruments properly they might stand a chance. To tell you the truth, I don't know one Trad band from the other until I see what they're dressed in. I hate to see people who can play not making it when people who can't are working seven days a week, perhaps making small fortunes.[35]

As if in answer to Deuchar's attack, elsewhere in the same issue Acker Bilk had penned an article titled "Is it a Crime to be Successful?"

The quick and easy answer was yes, especially when that success involved substantial commercial gain. Perhaps the biggest irony was that, smack in the middle of the Trad Boom, British modern jazz had also scored an unlikely commercial bullseye. In February 1961, John Dankworth's version of 'African Waltz' reached number nine in the UK singles chart and, infectious and groovy, the record proved that a good strong beat and a catchy hook could always capture the public, regardless of the idiom from which it emerged. Dankworth had also benefited enormously from the backing of a major record label, EMI, something that the majority of his contemporaries, including Tubby Hayes, still lacked.

With Tony Hall's negotiations with Decca having got nowhere, in the spring of 1961, finally exhausted by this impasse, Hayes decided to bypass Hall altogether to look elsewhere for a recording opportunity. As originally conceived, his plan was to record a big band album: the Downbeat Big Band still hadn't reached the wider public and, as an initial salvo for a new label, the impression of Tubby Hayes the orchestrator coupled with Tubby Hayes the multi-instrumental virtuoso seemed to make perfect sense. Hayes and manager Pete King also thought they knew exactly who to pitch the idea to.

Jack Baverstock was among the giants of the UK record industry and as A&R manager at Fontana Records (one arm of the Dutch Philips label) he had already made his mark. The label was a relatively new player on the local scene, having only been established in 1958, but Baverstock had soon worked wonders in creating a rich catalogue incorporating jazz, folk and pop music. A suave and striking figure, he had all the gravitas of Tony Hall, but unlike Hall he didn't have to fight too many executives to reach a decision – the final say rested with him. Spurred on by the enthusiasm of a fellow Philips producer, former trumpeter Terry Brown, an erstwhile employer of Hayes, it took Baverstock very little time at all to make up his mind. Hayes, it was decided, would form the backbone of an unprecedented campaign to reach a new audience for British modern jazz and his first album for the label would present him as never before. Crucially, Fontana had both the money and the faith to back up its promise. Even so the saxophonist was unprepared for the generosity of the label's remit, as Benny Green recalled in his sleeve notes for the resulting LP: "This album represents the first occasion I can remember when one of our major instrumentalists was let loose, so to speak, in a recording studio, told he could play what he liked, with as many musicians as he liked, on as protracted a session as he liked."[36] At last, after five years of mixed results at the hands of Decca, Hayes was getting the chance to record *his* music the way *he wanted*.

Planning for this epic undertaking occupied much of early 1961, with Hayes and Benny Green initially sitting down to consider a set of standards suitable for inclusion. Hayes also wanted to contribute some of his own compositions and to make as varied a use of his arranging skills as was possible. Three differing instrumental line-ups were finally decided upon: the regular quartet,

Recording *Tubbs* at Philips Studios, London, Tuesday March 21st, 1961. Trumpets: Jimmy Deuchar, Stan Roderick, Bobby Pratt and Eddie Blair. Trombones: Jim Wilson, Keith Christie and Don Lusher (Ray Premru is out of shot). Bass: Jeff Clyne. Piccolo: Johnny Scott. Courtesy Liz Grönlund.

a woodwind-based group and a brass-only big band. According to the label's release sheets four separate sessions were scheduled for the making of the new album, Tuesday 21st, Wednesday 22nd, Thursday 23rd and Tuesday 28th of March 1961, with the recording taking place at Philips Studios at Stanhope Place, near Marble Arch.

The big band that Hayes assembled for the first session was a virtual who's-who of the London jazz and session world of the time, including, among others, trumpeters Bobby Pratt and Jimmy Deuchar, trombonists Don Lusher and Keith Christie and tuba specialist Alfie Rees. This all-brass instrumentation creates a sound at once powerful and iron-clad, leavened only by the leader's soloing and the rather twee contributions of Johnny Scott's piccolo. What prompted Tubby to include the occasionally distracting sound of Scott's instrument doubling the lead trumpet lines is moot (although Tommy Watt was also fond of the effect, as Hayes knew well) but his decision to concentrate on a reed-less line-up may have been inspired by hearing the 1958 Metrojazz album, *Sonny Rollins And The Big Brass*, an oft-overlooked gem in the American tenorist's pre-Bridge sabbatical discography. The Metrojazz recording placed Rollins's tenor saxophone front and centre in the mix and Hayes's session follows suit, with the first title recorded, 'Love Walked In', offering the best example thus far of the sheer lustre of his tone. Comparing the depth and clarity of his sound here with that on his Tempo recordings is like being asked to express a preference over an original Rembrandt or a duplication on a drinks coaster.

The next track, Hayes's composition 'Tubbsville', is, in the words of Benny Green, "full of overtones of the neo-gospel school of jazz composition perhaps best exemplified in the writing of people like Bobby Timmons and the Adderley brothers."[37] With its waltzing 6/4 lilt, it's not unlike a faster-paced 'African Waltz' and Hayes's tenor cries out across the call-and-response backings in a manner that might make it difficult for a blindfold test victim to ascertain the land of his birth.

The last of the big band scores is Hayes's setting of 'Cherokee', the shibboleth of fast-fingered saxophonists everywhere. As if to invigorate what was already by then a hackneyed choice, the arrangement begins in Ab rather than the more commonly used key of Bb. The point of this exercise is realized during Hayes's unaccompanied break, which takes the tune up a whole tone into the regular key. The stunning outpouring of a solo that follows is the work of a musician clearly familiar with every aspect of his source material. By the time of this recording Hayes would have been playing 'Cherokee' for something like a dozen years, and his knowledge of its ever harmonic contour is conveyed by the ease with which he negotiates the perilous middle sixteen bars, with its fast succession of modulations through the keys of B, A and G. Were this not enough, he then plays an unaccompanied half-chorus solo passage which is a truly blistering example of his combination of technical expertise and musical architecture. Indeed, there are few examples of Hayes on record that better capture his formidable artistic temperament, and for that reason the recording quickly became a firm favourite with the saxophonist's existing fans, as well as winning over new listeners.

Hayes's vibraphone playing was the focus of the following day's recording, for which he'd assembled a five-man woodwind ensemble together with guitarist Dave Goldberg and his regular trio of Shannon, Clyne and Eyden. Two tracks from this session were slated for release (it is highly possible that more titles, including a version of 'The Thrill Is Gone', were also taped but do not survive): a gentle ballad setting of the Peggy Lee associated 'The Folks Who Live On The Hill' and 'S'posin'', a one-time finger-snapping vehicle for Frank Sinatra. The mood is understandably lighter with occasional nods towards easy listening, as if Hayes were determined to show the breadth of his arranging skills.

At the opposite end of the spectrum are the four quartet tracks recorded on the final day of the sessions. Although 'The Late One' – a torrential Hayes original that sounds like an overdriven union of 'Tickletoe' and 'Airegin' – is probably the best example to date of the leader's immaculate technique at speed, sleeve-note writer Benny Green chose the tenor solo on Rodgers and Hart's 'Falling In Love With Love' to highlight "the facet of Tubby's complete mastery of his instrument which came to him last of all, the ability to produce without any sense of strain, a full, majestic sound" going on to praise the "richness of tone which could have only been produced by a born musician."[38]

Indeed, away from all the speedy grandstanding, Hayes creates a performance every bit as graceful as those of Stan Getz.

On 'R.T.H.' (a dedication to his son Richard Terence Hayes), the saxophonist digs into his soul-jazz bag for a performance which, like the earlier 'Tubbsville', reveals his appetite for contemporary trends, whilst 'Wonderful! Wonderful!' perhaps comes closest to the approach of the poll-winning Hayes quartet on its live appearances. Hayes had borrowed the theme – originally a hit for Johnny Mathis – from the repertoire of Sonny Rollins, who found its unusually elongated and semi-modal structure ideal for improvisation. Hayes clearly thought the same and the beautifully constructed solo he offers caps what had been a fruitful few days in the studio.

The only thing left to do was to choose a title for the new album, and for a piece of work so wholly representative of the man who'd made it, Fontana elected to call the album simply *Tubbs*.[39]

Further confirmation that Hayes was well ahead of most of his contemporaries came a few weeks later on May 4th when he returned to BBC's *Jazz Club* to participate in a reunion with Victor Feldman. Appearing as a guest artist with the rhythm section of the Ronnie Scott–Jimmy Deuchar quintet, he chose to play John Coltrane's 'A Moment's Notice', a composition so formidably complex that few jazzmen besides its composer – on either side of the Atlantic – had dared tackle it. Hayes positively charges through the piece, never once appearing to be foxed by its unusually rapid series of modulations. Playing fast and complicated music was by no means new to him, but what makes this performance of 'A Moment's Notice' all the more impressive is the likelihood that Hayes had transcribed it directly from the original LP. Long before formal education helped fill in the gaps in jazz musicians' knowledge, this method of learning was vital to virtually every British modernist. Few, however, would have dreamt of attempting something so inherently difficult. Fewer still could have pulled off the kind of performance Hayes does. The audience roars its approval and over half a century later, it's still enough to make a saxophonist weep.[40]

Jazz Club's producer Terry Henebery had also graciously allowed Hayes to book the entire nineteen-man line-up from his recent Fontana album for a further broadcast on June 8th, a luxury that cost the corporation the lavish outlay of £127. 15s. 6d. Seated in the studio audience was no less a figure than arranger Nelson Riddle, who responded to being buttonholed by compere Alan Dell by revealing that he had "great admiration" for Hayes. The warmth of the audience's applause for Riddle's words spoke volumes: the one-time wunderkind of the tenor had suddenly blossomed into a world-class orchestrator as well. Who else on the British jazz scene could top that? Indeed, during the week following the broadcast, *Melody Maker* published a letter by one N. R. Sommers, a fan who'd heard the broadcast, which perfectly captures this moment of jingoistic pride. Under the headline "Now it's who have *they* got?" Sommers wrote:

We are continually hearing about the obvious supremacy of the American jazzman and, with monotonous regularity, the question is posed: "Who have we got in the same street as . . . ?" I have just listened to *Jazz Club* and in one respect it seems the boot is on the other foot. "Who have they got in the same street as Tubby Hayes?" After his astonishing virtuoso performance, I am more than ever convinced that here is a home-grown jazzman of unbeatable class.[41]

The *Tubbs* album was released that same week, and amid a flurry of publicity virtually unheard of surrounding a British jazz release, the critical reaction it met was uniformly favourable. *Melody Maker*'s Bob Dawbarn thought "[the record] deserves the highest possible praise. If anyone doubts that Tubby is a jazzman of international importance then this record should dispel such thoughts once and for all."[42] The paper then duly voted the recording its LP of the Month, Hayes's second such honour in twelve months.

Writing in *Jazz News*, Kitty Grime found delight in a record that had at last captured Hayes's true spirit: "Man and boy, Tubby Hayes has always had (above all his other considerable gifts) the gift of communicating sheer relish in the physical act of playing his instrument. He's an overwhelmingly exuberant player, firmly rooted in the bop tradition, which leaves no change unexplored and no tempo undoubled. This record is far and away the best demonstration of his skills that I have heard."

"The only carp I can find," she continued, "is something we all notice in British accompanists – lack of real involvement in the moment, so that those well-known inhibitions seem to get in the way of spontaneous response to the soloist . . . there is a steep drop in the temperature when [Hayes] finishes his solos [but] this is, in all, a record of which everyone can be proud – and one which you can stack in any modern jazz library."[43]

6 Down in the Village (1961–62)

Tubby's ebullient personality as well as his unequalled instrumental dazzle, makes him one of the most exciting and likeable musicians in British jazz. He has a natural and appropriate showmanship on the stand, the only genuine showmanship in jazz, and that is intensity. Perhaps in the beginning there was something of what the ad-man call "teenage identification" in the warmth of the audience reaction Tubbs has always achieved. Few could say that now. Tubby is probably the busiest modern jazzman in Britain and, in this writer's opinion, as far as talent is concerned, there is plenty more where that came from.

Chris Godfrey, *Jazz News*, January 17th, 1962

The success of *Tubbs* had many ramifications, not least of which was upon Pete King's attempts at brokering a deal enabling American soloists to visit Ronnie Scott's club. Although it had survived for close to two years, by the summer of 1961, the club was in dire need of something to pep up its financial fortunes. The only solution was to import US musicians, but overcoming the prejudice and protectionism that stood against the proposal required not only patience and gall: it required Britain to offer something in return. In principle, the deal was simple: King was mooting a literal reduction of the band-for-band exchange that had operated since 1956, and argued that a man-for-man swap meant that neither side lost out. In practice, however, the idea was fraught with difficulties for both parties. From the off it had been inevitable that Tubby Hayes would be the most likely candidate for export, but getting through all the red tape necessary to make the offer was taking its toll. In an attempt to hasten the process King planted the rumour that Hayes would be holidaying in New York at some point later that year – while he was there why shouldn't he be allowed to play a gig or two?

As the negotiations went back and forth that summer, together with several other leading British modernists, Hayes was involved in a transatlantic exchange of another kind, participating in the filming of the Rank feature film *All Night Long* at Pinewood Studios. A modern-day update of Shakespeare's *Othello*, starring Richard Attenborough and Patrick McGoohan, the plot had been transplanted to a jam session at an East-End warehouse, an improbability that required not only a jazz score but a bevy of jazz musicians to both play and act on-screen. Drummer Allan Ganley had been recruited to hire the British musicians for the project and quickly realized the "jobs for the boys" nature of the work. The prospect of big-screen exposure and a fee to match was incentive enough to lure Hayes, Keith Christie, Bert Courtley, Johnny Scott and others away for a few weeks, but the filming itself was agonisingly slow, with the hours of boredom occasionally punctuated by one of guest star Charles Mingus's epic tantrums.[1] Ultimately, the film was to prove something of a flop. Despite a cast that also included Dave Brubeck, then riding the pop charts with 'Take Five', the project failed lamentably in creating the kind of impression its producers had intended, and like other similar jazz-based movies its neither fish-nor-fowl nature made it almost impossible to market effectively. Jazz fans hated its cliché-ridden dialogue and phoney mimed solos, while mainstream audiences were simultaneously put off by the heavy emphasis on modern jazz.

Hayes spent much of his time between scenes hanging out with Richard Attenborough or writing (he completed part of a suite co-composed with John Dankworth, Dave Lindup and Dudley Moore at this time[2]), but everyone knew what he was really waiting for was news from New York.

Interviewed in *Melody Maker* soon after principal photography for *All Night Long* had ended, he spoke candidly about how he envisaged his future. "The ideal would be to work in London for a few months of the year, then go to the Continent and America. I don't see that I have to give up everything and live in another country in order to broaden things."[3] Yet again, he was well ahead of the game, looking forward to the kind of global careers enjoyed by later generations of British jazzmen. In the meantime, his fledgling plans to play in New York were still struggling to get off the ground.

Pete King began the shuttle diplomacy necessary in striking the deal during August. On paper, the task was easy: all he had to do was get the say-so of the AFM president, James C. Petrillo. The British Musicians' Union had already given its consent to an American soloist playing a short run in London, but proving to the Americans that one of New York's clubs needed a British player in return was an entirely different ball game. Nicknamed Little Caesar, and notorious for his intractability, Petrillo might as well have come straight from central casting for a Hollywood gangster movie. To his surprise King found him remarkably amenable, and far less intimidating than had been imagined, something the Englishman later attributed to his having dealt with similarly heavy characters within the London underworld. King also found the New

York jazz community more than helpful. "Just as we're always searching for something fresh here, so are they," he told *Disc* magazine. "And they want our guys. I was amazed how many people knew of Tubby. I guess the word's got around. Zoot Sims and Al Cohn have all the Jazz Couriers records and were very impressed with Ronnie and Tubby. Everyone wanted to hear Tubbs' latest on Fontana. They were knocked out when they heard it."[4]

On the musical side, King's corner was also being fought by Zoot Sims, who already knew both Hayes and Ronnie Scott from his earlier visits to the UK. Sims had even suggested a venue for Hayes to play, the Half Note on Hudson and Spring, a small club popular with the cognoscenti, not unlike Ronnie Scott's, in fact. The Half Note's owners, the Italian-American Cantorinos, liked Sims and trusted his judgement and when played Hayes's albums realized that the English player offered much more than mere novelty value.[5] Securing the American tenorist's agreement to make the reciprocal appearance in London, King called home to confirm that the exchange was finally in place. Tubby Hayes was going to America, at long last.

Ahead of his Stateside debut, Hayes remained as feverishly busy as ever, packing in quartet engagements, festival sets, TV recordings and two album sessions, both of which sat somewhat outside the realms of his usual work.[6] Over three days in August he was involved in a peculiar project for Fontana, in which the celebrated American percussionist Jack Costanzo (regarded for his work with Nat King Cole and Stan Kenton) collaborated with some of the local talent, including Harold McNair, Shake Keane and Phil Seamen, for an album titled *Equation In Rhythm*. To describe this record as a curate's egg is to seriously understate its inconsistent nature. The majority of the music occupies a curious no-man's-land half way between a serious attempt at fusing African rhythms and jazz, and music that may as well come from a Tarzan movie, so heavy-handed is its sense of pastiche.

In amongst all the drums and chanting are Hayes's 'Southern Suite Part One: Penitentiary Breakout' and 'Part Two: Chase and Capture', a mini-masterpiece of big band scoring that reassembles parts of the 'Suite for Woodwind and Brass' Hayes had written for a BBC broadcast earlier that summer. The second of the curios taped just prior to his US debut was a set recorded under drummer Tony Kinsey's leadership for Jeff Kruger's Ember label, *An Evening With Tony Kinsey*. Although the drummer's choice of players, including Jimmy Deuchar, Bill Le Sage and Lennie Bush, were all top-drawer, the music – a palatable brand of light-bop – rarely catches light.

As the jazz press sounded jingoistic bells over his forthcoming American debut, Hayes realized full well the weight of responsibility that now sat solely on his shoulders. Just hours before his departure, he recorded his thoughts in a letter to his wife Rose:

> The greatest adventure so far of my life is about to begin in just a few hours. I feel I have a huge responsibility going with me for the

whole cause of jazz music in this country. I promise dearly that for the sake of yourself, Richard and all the sincere musicians of our scene that I will do my utmost to create a favourable impression musically and socially.

Believe me, my Darling that if it weren't for your help, encouragement and understanding I would not have got through the last two years to see this dream of mine coming so close to reality ... you and Richard and I must stand together even though 3000 miles apart because this can be the decisive weeks of the future of my career, our whole way of life together and can pave the way for better deals all round for the chaps (the shrewd ones).[7]

Hayes flew to New York three days ahead of his opening at the Half Note and immediately hooked up with Zoot Sims, who acted as an unofficial tour guide round the city's clubs. Some of the music he heard on these sorties was heartening, such as the Miles Davis sextet with Hank Mobley and J. J. Johnson, though other groups including Ornette Coleman's quartet proved just as bewildering in the flesh as they had on record.[8] Amid wild predictions in the English press from Tony Hall and others, he also discovered that the rhythm section that had been assembled to accompany him at the Half Note didn't contain any of the currently fashionable New York names: pianist Walter Bishop Jr was a bop veteran whose previous experience included stints with Charlie Parker, bassist Julian Euells had appeared on record with John Coltrane and drummer Wilbert Hogan was a journeyman player whom he had met previously during a London visit by the Lionel Hampton band. There had been no time for rehearsal, but that was probably the least of Hayes's worries as he stepped up onto the Half Note's tiny bandstand on the evening of September 19th, 1961. As he looked out across the club, the audience included Miles Davis, Al Cohn and Zoot Sims. If ever there was a time to create the impact that Pete King, Ronnie Scott, Tony Hall and all the other partisan supporters had so hoped he would, it was now. With typical self-assurance, he smiled, turned around and clicked off the first number. Waiting impatiently for Bishop's piano introduction to conclude, he then put the saxophone to his lips, closed his eyes and began to play.

No tape recording of this historic debut appearance is thought to exist but the reactions contained in both the English and American music press immediately afterward convey almost as much. Zoot Sims was first out the blocks, telling *Melody Maker* "Send him right back home! He is the end!" Fellow tenor Al Cohn added, "He is great. The guy never gives up, just blows hard all the time and never fluffs a note."[9]

Covering Hayes's opening night for *Metronome*, Dan Morgenstern delivered a rather more expansive assessment of the new arrival:

Tubby Hayes, 1961. Author's collection.

Radiating confidence (but never arrogantly so), Tubby showed that he meant business just by the way he handled his horn. He swings, has beautiful instrumental control, and is fully conversant with the contemporary jazz language. Though not a startlingly original stylist, his playing cannot be put down as mere copying. He shows the influence of Rollins in attack and phrasing and of Stan Getz in the fluidity of his lines. His sound lies somewhere in between the two and is perhaps the most personal of his attributes. Still young (twenty-six), his style is not yet fully matured and he has a youthful tendency to play at greater length than necessary. All in all we were most happy to make the acquaintance of this swinging ambassador from Britain, who can definitely hold his own in fast company.[10]

"The musicians couldn't do enough for me," Hayes reported back to *Melody Maker*. "Most New York jazzmen have great enthusiasm for playing."[11] But for those Hayes had left behind, pride in his historic achievement was mixed with a certain cynicism, as Peter King remembered: "[He] was always a great musician but I remember when he first went to America and recorded and he came back to England and all of a sudden he was on the front page of the *Melody Maker*, he was musician of the year and everything. And nobody knew who he was before that!"[12]

Whilst Hayes found himself accorded tremendous respect from the majority of the New York players he encountered, he also experienced isolated incidents of suspicion and outright hostility. One prominent American saxophonist (several names have been suggested, none of which has ever been confirmed) allegedly told him that "If you come here stealing our jobs, I'm gonna make you swim the Atlantic back home to England"[13] and, according to Peter King, he found himself in an embarrassing situation when he called in on drummer Art Taylor. Taylor, with whom Hayes had recorded the *Blues In Trinity* album three years earlier, simply froze the Englishman out.[14]

Happier memories included finally meeting Sonny Rollins, then close to the end of his two-year "Bridge" sabbatical.[15] The American saxophone god had apparently heard the latest Fontana album and complimented Hayes on his version of 'The Folks Who Live On The Hill'. There was also an impromptu "sit-in" with the Al Cohn–Zoot Sims quintet, a roast-up only adding to the overwhelming impression he was making on the locals: "He made us feel real sluggish," Cohn dryly remarked afterwards.[16]

Always keenly aware of the environment in which he was working, Hayes instantly noticed the vast difference between the kind of audiences he was now playing to and those at home in London, finding a far less buttoned-up attitude to what constituted a night's work. He told *Jazz News*'s John Merrydown:

> It's an older crowd and a drinking crowd. People come and go all night. We worked at the Half Note from 9.30 pm to 3.30 am playing about five sets of no more than forty-five minutes each. So you play about three tunes a set and then take twenty minutes off. It's very much more relaxed as you don't have the feeling that you've got to knock people out. In Britain, you tend to have the situation whereby the first set nobody is there and in the second set everybody is going home.[17]

Before the triumphant fortnight in New York was over, there were a few more mountains left to climb. A one-off gig at Birdland was followed by a guest appearance with the Slide Hampton octet in Washington, an engagement that appears to mark the only occasion when Hayes and fellow fast-fingered tenorist George Coleman occupied the stand together. More importantly, as part of the reciprocal deal organized by Pete King, he was also scheduled to record an album for Epic Records.

The label's parent company, Columbia, were all for the idea, but the American Federation of Musicians quickly stepped in to offer their objections. It was fine for Epic to license a British-made album, as they'd already done with *Tubbs*, but recording Hayes in America was a step too far – nothing less than the blatant hijacking of a work opportunity that should rightfully go to a local player. Once again, Pete King found himself frantically cabling New York, trying to persuade the powers that be that far from taking the bread out of an American musician's mouth, a recording would provide further work for the local accompanists and studio staff. Finally, the AFM relented, but it had been an eleventh-hour decision. The first recording date had been scheduled for October 3rd, but just days before Hayes was still none the wiser as to who else would be taking part.

Finally, after much speculation, producer Mike Berniker organized two sessions with slight variations in personnel, based around the rhythm section of Horace Parlan on piano, George Duvivier on bass and drummer Dave Bailey. As a guest star, Berniker had been unable to get his and Hayes's first choice Donald Byrd and so had opted for Clark Terry as a replacement. There would also be a further ad-hoc contribution from vibraphonist Eddie Costa.

Even more so than the Half Note appearance, Hayes knew the recording would illustrate his gifts to a wider world. News of his giant-slaying Big Apple debut may well have already reached London, but here was the chance to take back audible proof. As such, his preparation for the album was characteristically meticulous. On the days leading up to the first session he made his way across town to Columbia's studio at 799 7th Avenue to spend several hours alone in a practice room, examining every nuance of the pieces he'd chosen to record. It was a situation that could hardly have been more different to that he had grown used to back in London, wherein record sessions had frequently been shoehorned in without any adequate allotment of rehearsal time. Hayes's calmness in the face of what might have seemed an intimidating task deeply impressed those involved in the sessions, including veteran jazz author and producer Stanley Dance, who wrote of a "stiff upper lip" attitude in the sleeve notes of the resulting album:

> The "unflappable" individual, the person who retains his wits while the heavens fall, is always esteemed in Tubby's homeland. Recording for the first time with such proven masters like Clark Terry and George Duvivier might, with some, have brought on a *crise de nerfs*, but nothing of the sort occurred.[18]

The first session was set for midnight on October 3rd, during which Hayes, Parlan, Duvivier and Bailey intended to record several quartet tracks. News of the recording had spread like wildfire and adding to the sense of occasion the studio's control room was full of visitors, including saxophonist Gene Quill, arrangers Manny Albam and Bill Potts, jazz writer Baron Timme Rosenkrantz and London record-store owner Doug Dobell. In between his own sets at Birdland, Eddie Costa had also wandered in, setting up his vibes whilst still in his raincoat before making an impromptu contribution to two tracks. Despite the slight changes of plan and the crowd of onlookers, the session went off without a hitch, with Hayes registering a deep impression on his sidemen. After one particularly spirited take, Stanley Dance recalled Dave Bailey looking up at the Englishman and stating, "You're cruel!"[19] Years later, Bailey remembered why: "I was shocked at how good he was. I think he was the very best of the non-American jazz musicians, closely followed by Niels-Henning Ørsted Pedersen and that is an opinion shared particularly among Afro-American players."[20]

Indeed, if anyone were to be blindfold tested with the *Tubbs In NY* album and asked whether they suspected any one of the performers to be non-American, the answer could only be a negative one. There is absolutely nothing in Hayes's soloing to suggest that his was a musical language learned largely by rote, several thousand miles away from its source – authenticity and relaxation reek from every bar. It also speaks volumes that Clark Terry, who had already participated in a number of classic jazz recordings by Thelonious Monk, Duke Ellington and Gerry Mulligan, later reported that the LP he made with Hayes was his own favourite recording. For his part, Hayes was delighted to find that in two and a half hours, he had completed enough material for an entire album. All but one of the tracks recorded at this initial session were included on the original release, and each contains superlative playing by the leader.

Hayes had thoughtfully included two themes by one of his heroes, Sonny Rollins's 'Doxy' and 'Airegin', the readings of which effectively outline the parameters of his style. 'Doxy' is a slice of pure New York jazz funk, with Hayes's time and tone – leaner than on the recent *Tubbs* album – displaying a marked affinity with Stanley Turrentine. There is nothing hurried or uncertain about anything he plays and he locks down superbly into the deep groove set-up by Parlan, Duvivier and Bailey. 'Airegin' occupies the other extreme and displays his virtuoso instrumental command over a formidable set of changes. Hayes's preparation over the preceding few days had clearly paid off and his improvisations on both tracks are enough to put even a scene-stealing player such as Eddie Costa in the shade.

The vibraphonist is absent from the remaining three titles recorded on October 3rd, 'Soho Soul', 'Soon' and 'You For Me'. The first, an original composition with a fashionable call-and-response opening, is marred by a ragged ending, ensuring that it went unreleased until the 1980s, but Hayes's versions of 'Soon' and 'You For Me' both made it onto the original album.

Programmed as the album's opening track, 'You For Me' begins appropriately with a stunning unaccompanied introduction – a clarion call that has seared its way into the subconscious of a generation of British jazz listeners – and continues through a performance that displays Hayes's methodical harmonic understanding like nothing before. The song's structure is anything but conventional, moving quickly through a series of modulations which, whilst logical, are nevertheless highly unpredictable and which could easily unseat a lesser player. Hayes has no such difficulty, offering an improvisation as detailed as it is forthright, the perfect encapsulation of his virtuoso approach.

The following evening's session added Clark Terry and began with the trumpeter's ultra-fast blues-with-a-bridge 'Opus Ocean', containing another definitive tenor solo, followed by a contribution from Terry which is only marginally less inspired. The two men's exchanges towards the close of the performance ramp up the feeling of joyous abandon to almost intoxicating levels. Indeed, the entire track is an example of those truly transcendent jazz moments when a musician's willpower, creativity and feeling are spontaneously allied. One can only imagine how things must have felt in the studio!

Another Terry composition, 'A Pint Of Bitter' – dedicated by its composer to Hayes and his fondness for London ales – is a funky down groove of the type from which Horace Silver had carved a whole movement, containing a suitably relaxed and evenly paced tenor solo (again hinting at Stanley Turrentine), more puckish trumpet (this time with Terry's trademark conversational plunger mute) and a dancing Costa vibraphone outing.

Like its predecessor, the October 4th session also produced a surplus of material, with three tracks failing to be included on the scheduled album release. A further Terry original 'A Simple Waltz' echoes another fashion of the time, the 6/4 jazz waltz, while an early attempt at Hayes's own 'Half A Sawbuck' is a hard bop exercise that fails to truly gel. The best of these off-cuts is a simple, elegant reading of the ballad 'You're My Everything', so beautifully played that one wonders why it didn't make it onto the original LP release.[21]

Hayes was delighted with the results of the two nights of recording and by the time he flew home from New York on October 6th, the masters were already winging their way to Fontana in London. The recordings were released in both the UK and America during the following spring, to a generally favourable press. Benny Green's review of *Tubbs In NY* (Epic's American equivalent received the title of *Tubby The Tenor*[22]) in *The Observer* described the album as "one of great importance" and singled out Hayes's reading of 'Soon' as the highlight, calling it "one of the greatest saxophone performances ever made by a local musician. Even judged by world standards it is a highly impressive exhibition of superlative technique, harmonic shrewdness and, above all, fiery attack and spirit."[23]

Green had also written the sleeve notes for the Fontana issue, an encomium which included the last word on Hayes's success in America:

Just as brilliant and from a historical point of view perhaps more significant, [the album] is concrete proof at last that one of our musicians is fit to play in any company anywhere. Even five years ago 'Tubbs in N.Y.' would have seemed like wishful thinking. Even after hearing the six tracks I find it all a little difficult to grasp.[24]

The most immediate problem that now confronted Hayes was dealing with the anticlimax of a return home. After the pace and pressure of New York, inevitably everything back in Britain seemed hackneyed and less ambitious.[25] BBC TV's *Tonight* had seen fit to welcome him back but otherwise his working life reverted instantly and disappointingly to the same bland old routine. Almost immediately after his arrival home, the quartet headed out on a hastily organized provincial tour, taking in the Cavern in Liverpool, Edinburgh, Glasgow, Leeds, Coventry and Birmingham, punctuated by a round of incongruous regional TV appearances.[26] Behind the scenes, though, Pete King remained determined to capitalize on Hayes's recent US triumph. Television, King argued, was now the best way to bigger *national* exposure. *Tempo 60* had proved to be a failure, not because of the contributions of Hayes and co. but in spite of them. Too much had been sacrificed in order to draw in an audience and so when King approached ATV in the autumn of 1961, he suggested a new tack. Tubby Hayes was now a significant musical personality in his own right – one need only look at his American success, his recent poll wins and his new album deal to see that – so why not base a programme upon these assets rather than masking them under the guise of diluted variety? Surprisingly, ATV liked the idea and, at the end of October 1961, the company announced it had commissioned a thirteen-episode series to be titled *Tubby Plays Hayes*.

Such a proposition now seems like commercial suicide: Hayes was to present a weekly, half-hour show featuring his own quartet and singer Elaine Delmar with added guest stars including Ronnie Scott, Vic Ash and Harold McNair. There was no pandering to pop trends, no punches pulled and seemingly no questions asked. Described in *Melody Maker* as "the most uncompromising jazz ... that has yet appeared on British TV,"[27] the first episode aired on November 9th and the series continued into the New Year, but, sadly, gauging exactly how much of a success the programme was is now impossible. No episodes appear to have survived, and no soundtrack tapes have ever surfaced, so that all we are left with is a deep curiosity as to how the show might have looked and sounded, as well as the vain hope that someday some remnant may turn up.

Soon after Hayes returned from New York, Zoot Sims inaugurated the US side of the exchange deal by appearing at Ronnie Scott's club. Up close, the American star proved a delight, offering up unpretentious, no-nonsense music which reaffirmed that not everything going on under the banner of "modern" jazz need be mind-numbingly difficult to comprehend. However,

The Tubby Hayes Quartet on-stage at Rivington Barn, Lancashire, Wednesday December 13th, 1961. Courtesy Rod Hamer.

despite its portentous significance Sims's visit was somewhat overshadowed by that made by another American saxophonist – and Tubby Hayes's favourite US jazzman – playing exactly the kind of music that made modern jazz appear to be running headlong into anarchy: John Coltrane.

The tenorist's group was touring the UK opposite the band of Dizzy Gillespie but while the package made sense business-wise – a solid draw alongside a new star – the music it offered showed just how far jazz had now progressed. Gillespie was his usual bon-vivant self, putting his music across with an enthusiasm that could even communicate to non-specialist listeners. Coltrane and his band, on the other hand, did nothing so much as befuddle British audiences.

A week before the UK visit the saxophonist had recorded at New York's Village Vanguard, producing an album which included a performance that came to be seen as emblematic, 'Chasin' The Trane'. A boiling, seething and, at points, agonized exploration of the twelve-bar blues, taking in equal moments of simple folk-like beauty and downright ugliness, it occupied an entire fifteen-minute side of an LP, making it as much of a test of endurance for the listener as a musical breakthrough for its performer.

No one in the UK had yet been exposed to music offering this kind of emotional intensity. Unsurprisingly, the reaction to Coltrane's opening concert in Kilburn on November 11th was almost wholly dismissive. What on earth was Coltrane doing? Could someone please explain why he'd hired Eric Dolphy? Why did Elvin Jones have to play so loud? The questions went on. *Melody Maker*'s Bob Dawbarn led the assault with a review titled "What Happened?" "An afternoon preparing myself with Coltrane records – all of which I like and admire – proved no preparation at all," confessed Dawbarn, who compared the saxophonist's improvisations to higher mathematics. "Frankly the Coltrane Quintet was so far out it made Gillespie sound as formal and easy to follow as Acker Bilk."[28] Others, however, found the new approach positively refreshing. *Jazz News*'s columnist Danny Halperin was among the few writers to come out in Coltrane's favour, praising the Kilburn concert as "the most exciting, the most delightfully demanding music ever heard on the British jazz stage."[29]

Coltrane's appearance understandably attracted great scrutiny from London's jazz establishment. The opening concert had been attended by Tubby Hayes, Peter King, Don Rendell and other leading lights and their reactions varied from Damascene conversion to total confusion. Much of the controversy centred on the thirty-minute version of 'My Favourite Things'. Serving as a vehicle for his soprano saxophone, an instrument he'd almost single-handedly restored from obscurity, the theme had provided Coltrane with an unlikely commercial hit in the US but had not yet been released in the UK, resulting in a compounded shock. The recorded version had edged close to quarter of an hour, which to many listeners already seemed like glutinous indulgence, but in concert things were apt to extend even further. British musicians were no strangers to the practice of stretching out in clubs (with Tubby Hayes the leading local offender) but Coltrane's mammoth improvisation was something else, something almost indecipherable. Some, like Don Rendell, found it transformational. Others, including Hayes, were less convinced. Tommy Whittle remembered meeting him on the way back from the Kilburn gig: "I asked him had he enjoyed Coltrane and he said 'I think so, only he played My Favourite Things for forty minutes!' He couldn't get over the length of the thing."[30] Indeed, Hayes's respect for the American saxophonist now wobbled on the axis of taste. He openly wondered what had happened to the "old" Coltrane, the harmonic dynamo with the lightning-fast technical skills in whom he had recognized something of a kindred spirit. He knew he was hearing something new and undoubtedly unique, but he was none the wiser as to what that something was.[31] Nor had he any real idea yet what he could possibly extrapolate from it.

Coltrane's visit had left many questions in its wake, not only for Hayes. As well as providing a genuine piece of avant-garde action, the tour had reawakened the old argument about the effectiveness of Britain's modern jazz movement. Hayes's recent trip to the US may well have been an ambassadorial triumph, but when set beside the music of American players such as Coltrane, Rollins and Ornette Coleman, did the country's greatest jazz export really have the bona-fide qualifications to be a truly outstanding modern innovator? Was Hayes's popularity based solely on his technical ability? Was it a victory of smoke and mirrors over genuine musical substance? Had his eminence blinded many to the fact that other British jazzmen were now making far more creative music? Those who had grown heartily sick of Hayes's monopolizing ubiquity included Danny Halperin of *Jazz News*. Astute, assiduous and outspoken, Halperin was one of the few local journalists bold enough to suggest that, when all was said and done, Hayes was in fact little more than a highly effective musical synthesizer. "Tubby has everything in abundance," he opined in the magazine's December 13th issue, "except the kind of restraint that might keep him from indulging in endless strings of meaningless, repetitive choruses."[32] This was by no means the last time Halperin would single out Hayes for criticism, but he had a point: British modern jazz was in danger of becoming almost a parody, not only of American styles, but of itself.

Despite his vaunted position, by the beginning of 1962, Tubby Hayes had reached a turning point. Although he was busier than most other modern jazzmen, and was generally regarded with more public affection than were any of his peers, he now found himself at the helm of a group that appeared to have run its course. Indeed, there was a sense of déjà vu to it all, reminiscent of the final days of the Jazz Couriers. Had he not been so ambitious, things could have probably carried on indefinitely, but Hayes's appetite for change was too strong to ignore.

As he thought long and hard about his dilemma, the quartet's work maintained the same incessant pace, although both musically and socially the band now provided more disenchantment than satisfaction. He also continued to be in demand as a guest artist, work that included making several appearances with the Scott–Deuchar quintet at Ronnie Scott's. It may well have been the backstage conversation with Deuchar at these gigs that prompted Hayes's next musical move. Tired of the formula of his band with Scott, the trumpeter was also looking for a change and suggested he and Hayes pool their resources.

Jazz News broke the story on January 24th, while Hayes's own comments about the break-up of the quartet appeared in *Disc* magazine six days later. He told Tony Hall:

> I guess everyone needs a change. We've been together a long time now. Except for one year, Bill's been my drummer since 1955 and Terry's been with me since April 1957. But I'm looking forward eagerly to the new quintet. I've always dug Jimmy's playing and as we both arrange and compose we should be able to get a lot more things going. And I want mature musicians in the band so that we can tackle anything.[33]

Hall also reported that the existing Shannon–Clyne–Eyden trio were to continue as a unit in their own right and that they wished Hayes well, but beneath all the cheery sentiment lay a less than happy atmosphere. As the quartet had honoured its final engagements, the relationship between Hayes and his sidemen had grown ever more tense. Among the band's last bookings was an exchange for Belgian tenorist Bobby Jaspar, who had visited Ronnie Scott's club in January 1962. Jaspar had recently returned home after five years in the United States and consequently the exchange required the Hayes group to play at a Belgian jazz club, the Blue Note in Brussels.[34] Instantly, a situation arose that blighted the success of the trip. In company of long-time friend Tony Ketley, Hayes decided to fly to Belgium, whilst the rhythm section travelled by cross-channel ferry. During the flight, Hayes began to express his misgivings about the quartet, telling Ketley that Jeff Clyne's increasing habit of substituting other players if he received a better offer was the last straw.[35] Off the stand the three rhythm-section men were now all but ignoring their leader, deeply peeved at how little money they were earning by comparison. Although the Blue Note gig was a musical success, by the time the band returned to London, Hayes had made his decision.[36]

Pete King had already ensured there was a steady influx of work for the new quintet: the group would be resident at Ronnie Scott's for five nights a week, a BBC broadcast had been booked for early March, and a television appearance scheduled for AR-TV's *Here And Now* was barely two weeks away. King had also secured an appearance for Hayes on the BBC's new transcription-based World Service programme *Jazz for Moderns*. However, settling the personnel of the new unit by no means proved easy. Dismissing three of the best players on the local jazz scene may have been a necessary act but it had left a depleted field, and, in the little time left before the new unit made its debut, Deuchar and Hayes drew up a combined shortlist, made shorter still by the non-availability of several likely candidates. After failing to reach an agreement about hiring Brian Dee on piano, they settled for a genuine outsider. At twenty-two, Gordon Beck was certainly young, but having already played with bands led by Tony Crombie, Bobby Wellins, Vic Ash and Harry Klein, he appeared to have the required experience. Indeed, those that had employed him had found Beck's forward-thinking playing a decided plus. His attitude, however, perhaps best described as dilated pessimism, was less welcome, as Hayes would soon discover.

If Beck's engagement raised more than a few eyebrows, then the appointment of Allan Ganley as the quintet's drummer caused both jazz fans and critics alike to choke aloud. "The big question mark about the band," Hayes told *Disc*, "has been how Allan Ganley would fit in on drums. We've always thought of Allan in terms of the more – what shall I say – cool musicians. Well, in actual fact he tells me his ambition has always been to play with guys like Jimmy and myself."[37] Years later, Ganley recalled how Hayes would have rather booked Phil Seamen but that he had been put off by Seamen's inconsistency.

The leader was also keen to secure a similarly solid bassist and turned, much to Ganley's relief, to Freddy Logan, a musician whose international pedigree had ironically done more to dissipate his reputation than widen it.[38] Logan had been born in Amsterdam, but such were his worldwide connections that sometimes audiences weren't entirely sure of his provenance. He had worked in London briefly during the 1950s before playing in Germany, Holland and Australia. Consequently, when the Three-Out trio arrived in London from down under in late 1961, many listeners assumed Logan was Australian. At six foot three, the bassist towered over the remainder of his colleagues in the Hayes quintet, including his diminutive leader and, fittingly for an individual who was to become very much the workhorse of the unit, Logan was more of a team player than a prima donna. Allan Ganley recalled:

> Some bass players, all they want to do is be a soloist. They're not really interested in being a member of the rhythm section. Freddy wasn't like that. When you get three guys that really listen to one another and to what they are accompanying then that's when it really gels and things happen. Because of that, Tubby's was one of the nicest rhythm sections I've worked in.[39]

On the back of his regular TV appearances, Hayes was now coming as close to a popular figure as was possible in British modern jazz, so much so that even the mainstream press were now taking an interest. On February 23rd David Ash of the *Daily Express* offered a colourful portrait of the saxophonist. Buttonholing him at Ronnie Scott's, Ash found his subject "an incredibly boyish 27, in rumpled slacks and casual sweater."[40] He confessed to the journalist that he found little time to practise, or spend time with his wife and child, but expressed great enthusiasm about his latest project, "[a] new 15-piece orchestra [which] includes a French horn player from the Philharmonia and a harpist from the Covent Garden Orchestra" which, according to Ash, was about to get "the egg-head treatment" on the BBC.

In reality, Hayes's recording session for BBC *Jazz for Moderns* was a somewhat rushed affair. Held at Maida Vale on February 21st, just two days ahead of his new quintet's opening night, there was little preparation, evidenced by both the choice of material, which exactly duplicates that heard on a previous *Jazz Session* broadcast the year before, and the time involved. According to the BBC files, the entire programme, some half an hour of music, was rehearsed and recorded in three hours. As an interesting footnote to what had been a somewhat expedient and quickly forgotten exercise, when the original BBC tapes were discovered in 2009, the broadcast was issued on a limited-edition LP by the enterprising Gearbox Records label, thus making it one of the few radio performances by Hayes to have received an official commercial release. Its contents include at least one neglected masterpiece in Hayes's full-blown arrangement of 'Down In The Village', a theme apparently taken from a projected suite based on his recent experiences in New York. With its whooping French horn cries and afro rhythms, it suggests a link to John Coltrane's *Africa/Brass* album, showing how the saxophonist was beginning to deal with the avant-garde on his own terms.

The quintet's first tour proper began on March 10th in Margate, before taking in appearances in Leicester, Coventry, Birmingham, Liverpool, Bangor and Hampton Court, each gig ensuring that the band's reputation wasn't simply confined within the four walls of the Scott club. They also made their first domestic BBC radio appearance on March 7th on the Third Programme's *Jazz Session*, the highlight of which was a new composition titled 'In The Night', on which Hayes used the soprano saxophone for the first time, clearly inspired by his recent brush with Coltrane.[41]

The music press didn't publish its first reviews of the new band until early March: in a short article titled "Tubby's Quintet May be Britain's Greatest Ever," *Melody Maker*'s Bob Dawbarn bubbled with enthusiasm, finding the leader rejuvenated by the turnover in personnel:

> Tubby himself seems to have altered his style to help the group sound. His playing now strikes me as gentler and more melodic than it was with the quartet. There is less of the dazzling virtuoso, perhaps, but, a new-found lyricism. His vibes blend beautifully with Deuchar's muted trumpet. One last, but important, point: I can't remember a band with such good internal balance and dynamics.[42]

In one of the most candid critiques Hayes had yet received, *Jazz Journal*'s John Howes also profiled the new band. Less brutal than Danny Halperin, but no less honest, Howes began by praising the variety of approaches the group offered, but went on to highlight what he saw as a very real dichotomy between the saxophonist's ambitions and abilities:

> It is obvious that TH has been listening very carefully to Coltrane recently. In trying to investigate the rhythmic and harmonic advances Coltrane has made over the past two or three years, he has set himself a formidable task and perhaps unwittingly undermined his own purpose. His tone is not suited to the stark and fragmented line implicit in modern musical thinking, having still a good deal in common with the gentler and more verbose style of his earliest influences. It is in swinging bop numbers of less adventurous structure that TH really comes into his own, when he can relax and let his fluent line and virile tone do the work; no progress being made here, fewer surprises, and who wants them if the alternative is such a joy to listen to? And it is in these relaxed moments, when he is really blowing and not concentrating on producing unfamiliar music, that TH sometimes sounds almost like Coltrane for a phrase or two; here and there he begins a chorus with a phrase of piercing attack very much in the Coltrane idiom, only to revert after a few notes to his normal '50s bop style.[43]

Jimmy Deuchar and Allan Ganley also found themselves caught by Howes's critical searchlight; the trumpeter was labelled "a diffident soloist, sometimes to the point of flippancy," while Ganley's playing was criticized as "too rigid and inflexible for the more ambitious numbers."

The rather negative assessment of Deuchar actually had its basis in an unspoken truth. The trumpeter had never been an assiduous practiser and his ideas and execution didn't always match up. But there were other factors contributing to his inconsistency that weren't the kind of thing any jazz critic dare put in print, as Allan Ganley remembered: "Jimmy played great but when he had a drink it was a different thing completely, unfortunately. There was a chair on the stage at Ronnie's and you'd suddenly look round and see Jimmy sitting there and he's nodding off."[44] Indeed, as the band's music grew ever more cohesive, it was accompanied by the ironic realization that socially things were not always quite as well matched. Gordon Beck felt particularly ill at ease alongside his more hedonistic colleagues. "[Tubby] did everything excessively," the pianist once recalled. "I remember we were coming back from a gig up north in Freddy Logan's old Mercedes and we pulled off the road to listen to the [Oxford and Cambridge] boat race commentary on the radio. In the space of about 20 minutes Tubby and Jimmy Deuchar knocked off a bottle of vodka and a bottle of Cointreau." It was impossible to not feel admiration for Hayes, though, and Beck's horror at his leader's off-stage habits was offset by his astonishment at his musical stamina. "Tubby would come on the stand for a Saturday-night session full of beans and say 'OK here we go!' and he was off at a million-miles-an-hour – but we were all shattered."[45]

Eager to capitalize on the success of the quintet, in early May Fontana announced that the band were to record live at Ronnie Scott's club. Two evenings were set aside for the project, Thursday 17th and Friday 18th, a decision that yielded rich dividends. Live jazz recording was growing ever more commonplace in the early 1960s, and the previous year had seen the landmark albums recorded by Miles Davis (*In Person: Friday and Saturday Night at The Blackhawk*), John Coltrane (*Live at The Village Vanguard*) and Bill Evans (*Sunday At The Village Vanguard*), each an acknowledged classic of its kind. The addition of something similar to Hayes's canon made sense to everyone concerned, doubly so as several jazz critics had already noted that the clout of hearing the saxophonist live had never really conveyed itself on his studio sets. Released as *Down In The Village* and *Late Spot At Scott's*, the two albums taped at Gerrard Street that spring have since become two of the best known, and best loved, of all of Hayes's output and, five decades after they were first released, their impact is still immediate. Those lucky enough to have been in on the action as it happened were even more fortunate. Jazz writer Brian Davis remembered that there were high spirits both on and off the bandstand. Fontana had arranged that a photographer be present on one of the nights – "one of those old-fashioned photographers with tripod and a black sheet over his head," recalled Davis – but Hayes and his musicians had refused to take the situation seriously: "The guys, of course, were taking the unholy mickey, striking exaggerated Edwardian poses and generally falling about. This hilarious mood persisted until the music started, undoubtedly contributing to the general good feeling and high musical fare."[46]

Both albums abound in great jazz, and, as with Miles Davis's Blackhawk sets, hearing one without the other is unimaginable. *Down In The Village* is the more varied in content, and therefore more indicative of Hayes at his diverse multi-instrumental best. Among the highlights is Jimmy Deuchar's opening tear-arse arrangement of 'Johnny One Note', with the leader's tenor successfully contriving to marry mobility with a lustrous tone, something he again achieves on the fiendishly complex Deuchar original 'First Eleven' which concludes the album. Between these two performances, there is a subtle vibraphone reading of 'But Beautiful', the waltzing 'The Most Beautiful Girl In The World', with another sing-song lyrical improvisation from the leader, a reprise of the soprano saxophone vehicle 'In The Night', this time sounding more overtly Coltrane-like than the previous BBC recording, and the modal title track, containing, in its hard-hitting vibes solo and Allan Ganley's snapping rim shots, the dance-friendly elements that have ensured its continued popularity as one of Hayes's best-known recordings.[47]

Late Spot At Scott's focuses more directly upon Hayes's tenor saxophone skills, with only a single vibraphone piece, a simple and relatively brief account of the ballad 'Angel Eyes', arranged by Allan Ganley. The remaining four items are even more unrelenting than those heard on *Down In the Village*: the opener 'Half A Sawbuck' – perhaps a reply to 'Half a Sixpence'? – had been among the rejected items recorded for Hayes's New York album the previous year, but which this time is truly bedazzling. The leader's bustling tenor solo (one of the first pieces by Hayes that the author heard) is almost superhuman in its confidence and accuracy, never more so than at the point in which he executes a spectacularly articulated double-time phrase across the descending whole-tone harmony.

Similarly authoritative are the versions of Hayes's colourfully named composition 'The Sausage Scraper', a strutting minor-keyed theme which sleeve-note writer Terry Brown aligned to the contemporary work of the Cannonball Adderley quintet, and an arrangement of Gershwin's 'My Man's Gone Now', with a tenor solo that over its course grows in both complexity and emotional candour. The album's final piece is a cover of Horace Silver's 'Yeah!' with Allan Ganley's crisp drumming even outdoing the groove of the composer's original recording.

Alongside the leader's top-form performance, *Down In The Village* and *Late Spot At Scott's* also give ample evidence of how well assimilated the entire quintet had become in just a little over two months. Deuchar's trumpet playing is at its most consistent (a fact highlighted by Ronnie Scott in his sleeve notes to *Down In The Village*) and, whilst not registering particularly strongly as a solo voice, Logan's bass is – appropriate to his height – a tower of strength. Allan Ganley's drumming, especially on the supercharged tempos of 'Johnny One Note' and 'First Eleven', also controverts any potential criticism of a lack of fire. Even Gordon Beck, already beginning to question his place in the group, plays with a relaxation and appropriateness to the idiom which makes nonsense of his self-doubt.

Although the albums were released at very different points in the quintet's lifespan, the critical reaction they met was largely positive. *Down In The Village* was particularly well received by *Melody Maker*'s Bob Dawbarn in December 1962,[48] a reception matched by Mark Gardner's review in *Jazz Journal* a month later which, despite containing the priceless line "Hayes has not, as yet, forged a recognizable tenor sax style" (an opinion Gardner would soon retract), gave definite approval.[49]

Nine days after the recordings at Ronnie Scott's, Tubby Hayes flew to the United States to begin his second round of American engagements. The previous year's visit had been something of a trial run but this time the itinerary was more extensive: besides the two weeks at the Half Note there would be two additional weekend slots at the Jazz Gallery as a guest with the Art Farmer–Benny Golson Jazztet, an appearance at a festival in Washington and a recording date for Mercury Records. Exciting as it all sounded, as Hayes stepped onto the plane he still had no idea about who he would be working with. Things became a lot clearer upon arrival. He learned that his accompanying trio would comprise Walter Bishop Jr on piano, a hold-over from his previous visit; bassist Butch Warren, a young up-and-coming player soon to make a sterling contribution to the band of Thelonious Monk; and drummer Roy Brooks, recently with Horace Silver's quintet. This time around, their opening engagement was not made in the low-key, relaxed atmosphere of the Half Note but at the First International Jazz Festival in Washington, where on the afternoon of June 3rd, much to his amazement, Hayes found himself following Duke Ellington on-stage. As with his festival appearances back in the UK, the pressured circumstances were less than ideal. "It was a place like Wembley Pool, holding around eight or ten thousand people. It was stifling hot and the acoustics were dreadful," he told *Melody Maker*.[50] Nevertheless he was able to deliver a sterling thirty-minute set, broadcast on *Voice of America*. One title from this session, a suitably steaming version of Sonny Rollins's 'Oleo', was commercially released in 2013, revealing Hayes to be in overflowing form and clearly untroubled about the prestigious nature of the gig.[51]

Indeed, the telegrams and phone calls that filtered back to the offices of the UK's press during early June indicated that the saxophonist had yet again dazzled the hardest of all jazz audiences – the musicians – with the Half Note playing host to sitters-in including Dexter Gordon, Gerry Mulligan and Philly Joe Jones, all eager to jam with the club's guest artist. As flattering as the attention was, Hayes knew full well that he was receiving a tourist's welcome. Digging a little deeper into the local scene, he'd soon discovered that ex-pats like Dizzy Reece – who had once believed that the move to New York would solve his problems – were hardly working at all and that New York had more than its share of outstanding straight-ahead musicians being pushed out of work by the burgeoning avant-garde movement. The music he heard on his time off – everything from Ornette Coleman to Harry James – only added to the sense of being at the centre of a jazz scene a world away from that he knew in the UK: fast-moving, complex, hard to pin down and with one night's star struggling to find work the following morning. "The difference with the situation in the States," he told writer Val Wilmer the following year, "is that although it's a terrible rat-race, if you have a commodity to sell, you can get it in there and sell it. I got the feeling in New York that even the guys who aren't working are dying to play because there is so much competition."[52]

Hayes's US trip coincided with a holiday package offered by the Ronnie Scott club, enabling twenty-five of its members – at a price of £115. 10s., inclusive of air fares and hotels – to soak up the New York jazz scene for a few intoxicating days. Young jazz fan Peter Rowan was one of the Scott club tourists and remembers an encounter with Hayes at a Birdland jam session: "The buzz went round about Tubby's arrival, so a bunch of us headed up to the club. What a delight to see Tubby called up on stage! I believe he started with Confirmation. You could see he was enjoying the blow and it was a pleasure to see an Englishman holding his own in the esteemed company." However, there were less palatable aspects to the visit, as Rowan discovered when he bumped into Hayes at the bar. Missing his pints of bitter, the saxophonist remarked that "American beer tasted like piss!"[53]

As on his previous trip, there was also confusion over the mooted recording date, a situation that worryingly persisted almost up until the session itself. Finally, the evening before it was due to take place Mercury Records' producer Quincy Jones called with confirmation that everything had been set for 12 noon the following day, Saturday June 23rd. Jones had also settled the personnel quandary: Hayes would be joined by Walter Bishop Jr, bassist Sam Jones and drummer Louis Hayes, with two added front-line guests, saxophonist James Moody and multi-instrumentalist Roland Kirk. If the line-up didn't resemble any of the mouth-watering combinations rumoured by the British press – which had even mentioned a possible recording with Freddie Hubbard and Bill Evans, to be arranged by Oliver Nelson – it was still heavyweight enough to make Hayes feel more than a little trepidation, as he recounted in the sleeve notes to the resulting album: "As we drove up 6th avenue, my feelings were somewhat mixed, possibly apprehensive. I was about to record with great American jazzmen who knew nothing about the date until the day before and whom, apart from the piano player, I had never met; great jazz musicians who I had a deep respect for."[54]

Upon reaching the studio, Hayes immediately had the humbling experience of discovering that the respect didn't automatically run both ways. Moody, one-time star of the Dizzy Gillespie big band and a formidable musician

In New York, June 1962: Tubby and the Walter Bishop Jr Trio relax off-stage.
Courtesy Liz Grönlund.

equally adept on saxophone and flute, was surprised to see the Englishman carrying a tenor case. "When I asked him why," Hayes recounted, "he said 'Well man, I've heard your name and I thought you were a rock and roll singer!'"[55]

If working alongside Moody were not intimidating enough, Hayes also had to contend with Roland Kirk, a performer whose dynamism and verve outstripped even his own. Kirk was nothing short of a phenomenon. Blinded during childhood, he'd gone on to teach himself a variety of instruments including the saxophone and, despite his handicap, by his teens was touring extensively on the rhythm and blues circuit, building up his stamina and creative resolve to such a point that he was critically impervious. This resourcefulness had come in particularly handy when – apparently via a dream – he prophesied a future in which he played three saxophones at once. The dream became reality when Kirk began to utilize two ancient and obsolete variants of the saxophone, the Stritch and the Manzello, in tandem with his tenor and, in a remarkably short while, through a combination of sheer willpower and some DIY instrument doctoring, he was able to harmonize on all three horns simultaneously.

The sight which accompanied the sound was almost as spectacular: with his wraparound sunglasses and beret, superficially Kirk looked every inch the modern jazz hipster, but with three saxophones slung about his body, a flute stuck into the bell of his tenor, and accompanying whistles, sirens and percussion instruments to hand, he actually resembled nothing so much as a street busker, an analogy that sat rather well with the home-grown ethos of much of his music.

In the studio Hayes thought Kirk "seemed to be getting ready so many instruments that I had my doubts if he would be ready before the session was due to finish."[56] The musicians had only five hours in which to complete an album before Kirk, Jones and Hayes had to head to their respective evening engagements. Another indication of the last-minute nature of the recordings was that Moody had not been granted a contractual release by his record label and therefore appeared under the pseudonym of Jimmy Gloomy. Nevertheless, in these less than perfect circumstances, the six men threw together a surprisingly varied programme including a blues, 'Stitt's Tune' (once the theme of the Jazz Couriers), John Lewis's pretty 'Afternoon In Paris', two new Kirk compositions, 'Lady E' and 'I See With My Third "I"' and an obligatory ballad medley.

Although Kirk's reedless tenor solo on 'For Heaven's Sake' is arguably the record's most gripping performance (apparently Hayes tried practising the same effect in the band room at Ronnie Scott's, generally to the derision of his colleagues), Hayes's best moments come on the first track of the day 'Stitt's Tune', providing an ideal opportunity to compare and contrast the three saxophonists. Hayes solos first, bubbling away over the Jones–Hayes rhythmic axis before ceding to Kirk. Instantly one is struck by the difference in their respective approaches: Kirks's conversational and relaxed delivery betrays a far less contained musical dialect, altogether more personal. With its slightly slimmer tone and more emphatic articulation, Moody's solo also supports the argument that, for individuality within the given idiom, it was the Americans who were coming out on top.

As successful as the session was, Hayes felt it had been something of a missed opportunity. Unlike the fastidiously prepared for *Tubbs In NY* from the previous year, the results amounted to little more than a blowing session – admittedly a very attractive and enjoyable one – with little in the way of true co-operation among the front-line. Consequently, both the UK Fontana release – *Return Visit* – and its US counterpart – *Tubby's Back In Town* – received a far from unilateral critical reaction. Jack Cooke of *Jazz Monthly* described the album as a "partial failure," believing Hayes "deserved better than the off-hand session presented here."[57] Steve Voce in *Jazz Journal* was less dismissive, calling the album "an achievement for Hayes [because] for the first time we have the chance to evaluate his talent against those of some American top-liners." He concluded that *Return Visit*'s informal mood was "a nice change from some of the skull-crushing experiments which one is obliged to sit through these days."[58] Ironically enough, the American reviews of *Tubby's Back In Town* concentrated more upon the prowess of the foreign leader than upon that of the home team. Harvey Pekar of *DownBeat* accorded the record four and a half stars,[59] aligning Hayes to Sonny Stitt and Sonny

Rollins and describing him as "a musician capable of giving many well-regarded U.S. tenor players a run for their money."[60]

A reporter from *Melody Maker* greeted Hayes on his arrival back at London Airport on June 27th, eager to hear whether he had finally made up his mind about a permanent move to New York. He remained non-committal.[61] To some observers, the situation was a no-brainer: having proved he could clearly do more than merely hold his own in the fastest of company, and having virtually exhausted his opportunities in Britain, why didn't he just make the move?

Those closer to the saxophonist saw the situation as less clear-cut: Hayes was now in an unprecedented position for a British musician, that of being a genuinely international jazz commuter, able to work with equal success in the US and Europe.[62] Therefore, why bother to emigrate? Others thought the lack of a wholesale commitment to the American dream was symptomatic of Hayes's vain desire to remain top dog, something that he undoubtedly would not have been had he moved to a city inhabited by men such as John Coltrane and Sonny Rollins.

He had certainly returned to a full diary, with the quintet now a mandatory inclusion at all the major UK jazz festivals.[63] During the summer of 1962, alongside honouring their residency at Ronnie Scott's, the band played at the National Jazz Festival in Richmond, the East Coast Jazz Festival in Cleethorpes and the Redcar Jazz Festival in Yorkshire, although, as the group made its way between its engagements, it was becoming clear that Gordon Beck's worries hadn't gone away. Everyone had grown used to the pianist's gloomy outlook, but he was now protesting a little too vigorously about his incompatibility with the rest of the band for it to be ignored much longer. Backstage at gigs, Hayes was quietly predicting to Allan Ganley that Beck's days with the group were numbered.[64]

Terry Shannon finally rejoined Hayes during September, just in time for the quintet's run opposite Dexter Gordon at Ronnie Scott's. The club's import policy was now running like clockwork, affording local musicians the opportunity to show their idols just what they were made of. "The atmosphere down there was amazing," recalled Allan Ganley. "We'd get really good crowds, even if we weren't on with an American guest. The band was really popular and people used to come from all over to hear us. I can remember the Oscar Peterson trio coming in and Ed Thigpen sitting in the front row watching me. That gees you up a bit!"[65]

Another international visitor was making a more personal impact on Tubby Hayes. Solweig Elizabeth "Liz" Grönlund was a Finnish jazz fan who had come to London to work as an interpreter. The minuscule jazz scene she'd known in Helsinki paled into insignificance once she discovered Ronnie Scott's club and she soon became a frequent visitor, drawn as much to Hayes the man as his music. "I had an eye for Tubby," she remembered. "It was such

Liz Grönlund circa 1962. Courtesy Liz Grönlund.

a small club that I couldn't avoid meeting him. He went to play and I had to go to the loo and pass him so contact was unavoidable."[66]

Five years Hayes's senior, blonde, striking and, with a strong foreign accent, Grönlund had an air of being vaguely unobtainable but nevertheless the attraction was instant and mutual. Although, at thirteen stone, Hayes's weight had now ballooned to match his nickname, there remained something utterly captivating in his manner. His broad, friendly smile lit up a face which, for all its chubbiness, had a boyish charm, and he had a positive air of confidence and success about him, two facets well acknowledged as aphrodisiacs. Grönlund couldn't help but be impressed by him, and despite the couple's fling lasting barely a few weeks, it was time enough for her to become thoroughly fascinated with her beau. She soon discovered a warmer side to his nature, one he kept hidden from the tough circle of his day-to-day professional life. But it was impossible: Hayes was a married man, with a ridiculously overcrowded set of responsibilities, and so they took the mutual decision to call off the affair. They did, however, agree to keep in touch.

Tubby had been married to Rose for close to two years, and their son Richard was now a toddler, but for the saxophonist the normalities of home life hardly registered. Indeed, Richard Hayes has only hazy memories of his father's presence at the family's Kensington Park Gardens apartment during this time. As they had during his previous marriage to Maggie, musical demands came first, leaving Hayes little time for anything else, fatherhood included. An account of his lifestyle published in *TV Times* in March 1962 noted a daily workload that began "when the alarm goes at 8 am."

For a couple of hours he writes music for himself and the new recently formed quintet. Then it's rehearsing with the boys. Sometimes there is a recording session in the afternoon and then, if there is time, Tubby goes home for a couple of hours to relax with his wife Rose and their one-year-old son Richard. But mostly there is no time and he will slip into one of the London jazz clubs, have a quiet drink, listen to records, then play from 7.30 till midnight. At weekends Tubby and his boys often play until 5 am then sleep the clock around.[67]

The article does not append any commentary from Rose, and the wholesome impression it creates is a little too picture-perfect to ring true. In reality, by the end of 1962, Hayes's marriage was already beginning to show signs of strain. There were those who thought Rose's "matronly"[68] persona was good for the saxophonist, but when Hayes cast a considered eye over their relationship in an interview some years later, he revealed an all-too-familiar story: "[Rose] liked the social side, but the rest was too much. When I had to play at the club every night and came home wringing wet with sweat and then sat writing my arrangements for the next day – well, that was too much."[69]

Even the couple's tastes in music differed: Hayes later revealed that Rose had liked to listen to vocalists at home whilst he preferred to keep pace with the latest American jazz albums.

There were also inconsistencies in the saxophonist's professional life. The contract with Fontana had at last enabled him to build a profile with the record-buying public but, at the same time as this breakthrough, Hayes found himself in conflict with the BBC. Negotiating the draconian orthodoxies of the corporation had always constituted one of the great headaches of the British jazz scene, but in the spring of 1962 the *Light Programme* banned what it considered extreme modern jazz, declaring that certain musicians were now taking their art form a little too far for it to fall into the category of "entertainment."[70] Hayes was among those who were told, in no uncertain terms, to toe the line, but despite outrage in the press – with John Dankworth even comparing the BBC's attitude to the apartheid regime in South Africa – there was little the musicians could do. For much of the following twelve months *Jazz Club* remained largely the preserve of Trad bands, with the odd palatable modernist relegated to its *Late Jazz* slot, aired at a time that even the BBC conceded was a tad nocturnal for rousing New Orleans music. There remained limited opportunities for airplay over on Network Three's *Jazz Session* and, on December 12th, the Tubby Hayes Quintet, with guests Leon Calvert, Eddie Blair and Keith Christie, made its first appearance on the airwaves since March.

Away from the BBC, the band was faring far better having been contracted for another five-part ATV series, to be recorded at Ronnie Scott's club and transmitted under the title *Tubby Hayes Plays*. News of this coup was

The Anglo-American Four Brothers: Al Cohn, Tubby Hayes, Zoot Sims and Ronnie Scott, December 1962. Author's collection.

somewhat overshadowed by persistent rumours that Hayes was to join Woody Herman, an offer the American bandleader had previously extended to Ronnie Scott. Hayes told the press that, although he was naturally flattered by the invitation, the money being offered was an issue. This response was undoubtedly a smokescreen – Herman's invitation was even less attractive than Art Blakey's had been at the height of the Jazz Couriers. Hayes now had a solid career of his own – why on earth would he forgo it to return to being a sideman? However, 1962 closed without any definite answer as to whether he would emigrate to the US and, overall, the year had been one of consolidation rather than rocketing progress.[71] Crucially, despite the odd impasses like the BBC ban, he had retained his high-profile visibility as the UK's best-known modern jazz figure – both to specialist and non-specialist listeners alike – and with the news of the launch of his new television series it was likely that there would be further opportunities to capitalize on his mainstream media success. If Stan Getz could do the improbable and catch the public's ear, why couldn't Tubby Hayes? What could possibly stand in his way?

It was more a question of who rather than what. Had any British modern jazzmen been paying attention to the hit parade as the chimes struck midnight on December 31st, few would have recognized a threat from the oddly named band occupying the number 17 slot with a song called 'Love Me Do'.

The Beatles had arrived and for Tubby Hayes and his ilk their impact was to be seismic.

7 Tubby Hayes Loves You Madly (1963–64)

He goes at his music with such gusto, such confidence, that even those people who are unmoved by it or don't understand it can see that he knows exactly what he's doing and where he is going.

Peter Clayton, *Sunday Telegraph*, August 30th, 1964

Taking stock of his career to date, Hayes was interviewed by Les Tomkins for the magazine *Crescendo* in January 1963, and among the many aspects of the jazz business the resulting article touched upon was the saxophonist's pride in his band's increasing use of home-grown resources. The quintet was now playing more original music than ever – a two-fingered salute to the Luddites at the Beeb – and Hayes seemed keen to stress the idea that British jazz was now able to stand on its own feet.

> That's one of the best things about our group at the moment. There are one or two exceptions, but the majority of the library is either originals by Jimmy, myself, or whoever else has written them, or standards. We don't play very many American jazz compositions. I've nothing against them, of course – some are marvellous. I just think it's about time we did some things of our own.[1]

Two months later, when he took part in *Crescendo*'s informal "Disc Discussion" alongside Duke Ellington trombonists Buster Cooper and Chuck Connors, he was even more dismissive, having surprisingly little to say in favour of the majority of what he heard.[2] He wondered openly about the thinking behind records by the MJQ and Bob Brookmeyer and reserved his only effusive endorsements for tracks by Dexter Gordon and Lockjaw Davis,[3] as if he at last felt comfortable enough to abandon the notion that American jazz was automatically superior to that played elsewhere in the world.

Proof of this had come in explosive form that February, when Johnny Griffin arrived in London to play a season at Ronnie Scott's, appearing opposite Hayes's quintet. The pocket-sized Chicagoan's reputation for blistering tempos and technical infallibility was close to Hayes's own; as he wore down the Scott club's rhythm section over a series of marathon sets, there was at last the chance to see how the local speed merchant fared when set beside the American original. The answer was very well indeed, with Griffin showing genuine enthusiasm for his opposite number. By and large the two men got along splendidly, with mutual respect in evidence at all times, except when the American drank too much. On one especially riotous evening Griffin sought to remind his English counterpart that it was he who was still the fastest gun. "And don't you forget it, Fatso!"[4] Despite the odd flash of egocentricity, Griffin's playing made a refreshing change from the pretentiousness of much of what was going on within the avant-garde. Although men like Coltrane and Rollins were making far more challenging music, like Hayes's, Griffin's style retained the most basic elements of the idiom. Indeed, the saxophonist's recent albums on the Riverside label had even shown a distinct preoccupation with taking music back to its roots rather than to the outer limits, reflecting a new wave of interest in what critics were calling soul-jazz.[5] But it was to be a boom of a quite different kind that was to most affect British jazzmen in the coming months.

Across the winter of 1962–63, after a decade or so of finding themselves almost automatically guaranteed the monopoly of the local clubs, London's small community of modern jazzmen had suddenly found themselves fighting for space. Centred upon Blues Incorporated, the band of guitarist Alexis Korner, a sudden surge in interest in rhythm and blues was beginning to squeeze out the work opportunities to be had at the Flamingo and the Marquee. Whereas local modern jazz, as typified by Tubby Hayes's example, was all about sophisticated harmonic and technical expertise, Korner's credo was that everything was based in the appealing rootsy simplicity of the blues. However, he was also a man of surprisingly eclectic tastes, just as happy covering the gambolling folky themes of Ornette Coleman as he was playing Muddy Waters, keen to remind anyone who'd listen that jazz and blues shared the same basic language. For a generation of younger British musicians trying to break into the jazz scene Korner's band – with regular work aplenty – provided something of a finishing school. "It was my university, my music college, if you like," recalls saxophonist Alan Skidmore, who spent two years in Blues Incorporated during the mid-1960s, "because after years of playing in these crap little dance bands, you got a chance to play the blues, which, after all, is the basis of it all."[6]

Rhythm and blues also provided a welcome home for those who found their faces just hadn't fitted into the tight Gerrard Street clique, including organist Graham Bond, saxophonist Dick Heckstall-Smith, bassist Jack Bruce and drummer Ginger Baker,[7] who would all pass through Korner's band before uniting as the Graham Bond Organization, a sort of proto-R&B supergroup. Simultaneously the music was also serving as a starting point for those with more mainstream pop ambitions, including Mick Jagger and Charlie Watts, who had both spent time working with Blues Incorporated; Rod Stewart, who sang with Long John Baldry; and the guitarist Eric Clapton, a member of John Mayall's Bluesbreakers. Although the enormous importance of the R&B movement in shaping both British jazz and popular music in the 1960s and beyond cannot be overemphasized, during the early 1960s many established jazzmen treated it with the same mix of suspicion and contempt as they had rock and roll a few years earlier. It was a fad, a passing trend, a boom that would soon bust. The more perspicacious promoters, however, could already see the writing on the wall: the crowds that jam-packed Jeff Kruger's Flamingo club were now not coming to listen to modern jazzmen like Tubby Hayes but to *dance* to R&B. It was the old art-versus-entertainment conundrum, but if anyone were looking for confirmation of who was winning, the signing of Blues Incorporated by the Harold Davison agency in early 1963 said it all. No one could doubt the music's importance any longer – Davison didn't back anything but winners.[8]

There nevertheless remained those who continued to believe that popular acceptance needn't mean pandering to less sophisticated tastes. In February 1963, Davison's old friend Vic Lewis assembled an all-star group, including Tubby Hayes, Ronnie Scott and Jimmy Deuchar, to record the English half of an album he'd begun in America, *Bossa-Nova At Home And Away*, the latest in a veritable glut of records in the new Brazilian style. The bossa-nova had been launched upon the listening public a year before, with the release of the Stan Getz–Charlie Byrd album *Jazz Samba* and, when one of the tracks from the LP 'Desafinado' had been lifted for release as a single, almost overnight it had transformed the career of Stan Getz. The tenor saxophonist now found himself in a position few jazzmen had ever enjoyed: topping the popular charts with a recording that hadn't sacrificed one iota of his musicality.

Thinking along similar lines, Jack Baverstock believed Tubby Hayes could also make a bid for the singles charts and in February 1963 hastily organized the recording of a handful of likely items at Philips Studios. "We picked some pretty unusual material," Hayes told *Melody Maker*, " 'I Believe In You' and the title song from *How to Succeed in Business Without Really Trying*, 'I'm An Old Cowhand', 'Sally' and an original bossa-nova called 'Ricardo'."[9] But while Baverstock decided exactly which of these pieces should be offered up to the British pop charts, the quintet's eyes were fixed further afield.

The band had been booked to play a two-week engagement at Oslo's Big Chief Jazz Club beginning on February 27th. On paper, there couldn't have been a more opportune time to take their message to a new audience: the quintet had won the *Melody Maker* poll as top small group ten days earlier, with Hayes topping the tenor saxophone section and Jimmy Deuchar and Allan Ganley both coming second in their respective instrumental categories.

The Big Chief Jazz Club, Oslo, Norway, March 1963: Allan Ganley, Freddy Logan and Tubby (Terry Shannon is out of shot). Courtesy Liz Grönlund.

However, from the moment the musicians stepped onto the plane it was obvious there were tensions. "The seeds of a split were definitely there," confirmed Allan Ganley. "It wasn't like it was before. Tubby and Jimmy had sort of gone off together and there was Terry and I. He was moaning a lot about Tubby's flash way of playing."[10] The Big Chief gig itself was an unqualified success, but the band's off hours revealed yet more fractiousness. "They all wanted to do different things," Hayes's friend Tony Ketley noted. "Allan and I went off to see the Kon-Tiki exhibition, but Tubby just wanted to party."[11]

For the time being the Tubby Hayes Quintet's differences remained personal rather than professional, and collectively the band continued to represent all that was good in British modern jazz. The jazz scene may have still been relatively confined, but its members enjoyed a musical solidarity that was useful in overcoming all manner of obstacles. Rock and roll hadn't wiped them out, nor, despite its encroachment into the hallowed ground of venues like the Marquee and the Flamingo, had rhythm and blues. But, by the spring of 1963, there was an altogether more worrying threat to contend with.

Scoring their first number one, 'Please Please Me', that February, and rush-releasing their debut LP a month later, The Beatles had ushered in the initial phase of the Beat Boom, a sea change which, although not directly connected with jazz, would soon have a tsunami-like effect on players like Tubby Hayes.

The band's short but eventful journey from obscurity to at first national and then worldwide fame quickly became the stuff of legend. As John, Paul, George and Ringo charmed their way into public consciousness that spring

Jimmy Deuchar and Tubby, Oslo, March 1963. Courtesy Liz Grönlund.

(a victory attributable in large part to the shrewd and tenacious management of Brian Epstein), the marketing machine had gathered pace at an alarming rate. Suddenly The Beatles were everywhere: on television, on the radio, on magazine covers (making the prestigious and coveted front page of *Melody Maker* on March 23rd), all the while lodging themselves immovably in the public's ear.

In the early twenty-first century, it is tantamount to critical suicide to downgrade The Beatles, and there are few who could argue with the fact that the fortuitous blend of John Lennon's lyrical cynicism and Paul McCartney's sunny sense of melody resulted in some of the finest popular songs ever written. But, in the early 1960s, suddenly awash with Beat music, the London jazz community could be forgiven for thinking that a catastrophic flood of sub-talented, carefully marketed and gimmick-ridden guitar bands was about to engulf them. As critical brickbats got hurled at Gerry and the Pacemakers, The Searchers, The Hollies and all the other groups who emerged in The Beatles' wake, few had stopped to notice that Lennon and McCartney had been born barely a few years after musicians like Tubby Hayes. Although still young, British modern jazz was about to age overnight.

At the time The Beatles began injecting a refreshing and youthful originality into the popular charts, Hayes was beginning to toy with his own ideas about the input of new musical blood. When he was featured on the BBC's *Hear Me Talkin'* programme in February he had discussed a tentative plan to form a new rehearsal band, similar in approach to the now defunct Downbeat Big Band. Although the idea had been nothing more than a casual postulation, the avalanche of letters from young players wishing to be included that arrived at Broadcasting House and the offices of the *Melody Maker* in the following weeks convinced him that a student orchestra might make a worthy cause. After sorting through the ninety or so applications with journalist Bob Dawbarn, the first rehearsal was scheduled to be held at Ronnie Scott's on Sunday March 31st. Across the UK, eager hands opened their invitation to work with Britain's top modern jazzman, amongst them bassist Danny Thompson and drummer John Marshall, both to emerge as key figures in the UK jazz scene in the decade ahead.[12]

The formation of the student orchestra had also reignited Hayes's desire to lead his own working big band. The BBC *Jazz Session* and *Jazz for Moderns* broadcasts from the previous year had proved tremendously popular. However, whereas the bands on these programmes had been specially convened for the purpose, Hayes thought it was now time for something a little more permanent. The age-old consideration of money remained a headache, but there seemed to be a workable compromise in keeping the band as small as possible: thirteen men in number, rather like the contemporary American outfits led by Maynard Ferguson and Gerry Mulligan. Conveniently, he had chosen to build the band around the players in his quintet, upping the numbers with the addition of trumpeters Ian Hamer and Les Condon, trombonists Keith Christie and Ken Wray and saxophonists Alan Branscombe, Jackie Sharpe, Bobby Wellins and Peter King. Hayes's invitation was not to be taken lightly and for some, including King, being chosen for the band had something of the air of being picked to play for England. He later wrote:

> With Tubby, you knew you were there because you were the best guy for the job and you were privileged to be at the cutting edge of what was happening. It was a genuine all-star band. We knew it was a unique organization and everyone pulled out all the stops when we played. It was a kind of pride in being the best at that time.[13]

The formation of the big band immediately fulfilled several of Hayes's ambitions, chief of which was that of having a ready forum for his writing. He also remained keen to project his arranging talents into more commercial spheres, but overcoming prejudice was proving tricky. The previous autumn Pete King had opened the batting with the BBC, trying to convince the powers-that-be that a modern jazzman like Hayes could also create music suitable for an easy-listening audience. Discussions went to and fro throughout the winter of 1962–63, but only with the extension of the *Light Programme*'s broadcasting hours in April 1963 did the BBC sanction a "trial" session, intended for late-night transmission the following month. Despite his delight that all the persistence had paid off, King nevertheless found Hayes's brief daunting:

> He had to front a large orchestra and I mean a large orchestra, not just trumpets and trombones but French horns and strings. And

I said to Tubby "Who's going to do all the writing?" And he said "I am!" I said "That's fantastic – I hadn't thought you would undertake such a thing." And he got a book out of the library or bought it or something: it was all about the ranges of all the instruments.[14]

King's memory may be a little fanciful where the last point is concerned, as Hayes was already capable of arranging for all manner of instrumentations, but he was correct about how ambitious the project was. Featuring a sixteen-piece string orchestra, four French horns, harpist David Snell and the entire quintet, with, on some titles, the addition of vocalist Joy Marshall (an appointment made perhaps with more than just an eye on the music), no recording to date had better illustrated how copious and precocious was Tubby Hayes's grasp of orchestration. The most impressive arrangement was a set-piece medley of 'I Believe In You' and the title song from *How to Succeed in Business*, on which Hayes's writing veered from romantic to virile in quick succession, incorporating an introduction stolen verbatim from 'I'm Late, I'm Late' on the Stan Getz/Eddie Sauter album *Focus*, but ironically, for an exercise that had proved to be largely successful, the *Light Programme* session with strings appears to have never been repeated. It was a bitter blow.

Worse still, the saxophonist's new single release on Fontana – 'Sally' – was also getting the bird. Lost in a chart topped by The Beatles, Billy J. Kramer and Gerry and the Pacemakers, the record sank with barely a trace, not so much panned for being an over-ambitious idea (the music itself is actually rather innocuous) as simply overlooked.[15] The closest it had come to public recognition had been a couple of in-person TV airings and Dusty Springfield probably spoke for many when she was played the single in *Melody Maker*'s "Blind Date" spot that June: "For what I know about this sort of music it could be from a Stoke-on-Trent dance hall or the Ray Charles band! This one doesn't stand an earthly. It's probably well done but I don't like it. It doesn't get anywhere."[16]

The lesson of these commercial experiments was that too much compromise didn't work. Hayes had always fared far better when he stuck to his guns – he wasn't meant to be a pop star or an easy-listening doyen – he was meant to be a world-class jazzman. Although there would be no American trip during 1963, the debut of his big band on May 24th would at least ensure that the critics had something new to write about.

The location for the band's first gig was an unexpected one: Fishbourne in West Sussex, home of a popular provincial club run by Don Norman. In the weeks ahead of the gig, the leader offered enough titbits to the press to guarantee a healthy turnout, including the news that no lesser figure than John Dankworth had offered his services to play lead alto for the night.

Bob Dawbarn of *Melody Maker* offered some explanation as to how a band comprised entirely of London musicians – effectively a microcosm of jazz in the capital – had come to play its first engagement in the provinces:

"If you think Chichester an unlikely place for such an event, then you don't know Don Norman – surely the most dedicated of jazz club promoters."[17] Amongst the many out-of-town jazz club organizers Hayes knew and worked for, Norman was a genuine rarity. Having gained high regard among both audiences and musicians alike, his enthusiasm for the big band project was a tremendous boost. He was also prepared to put in the legwork necessary to ensure a good attendance, as Dawbarn discovered when he "arrived some two hours before the session to find the two notices on the door of the club's premises. One read: 'Tonight, the Big Ben Big Band'. The other announced that all tickets had been sold out."

There had been only one slight alteration to the plans: John Dankworth (billed on Norman's hand-out adverts under the pseudonym "Johnny Laine") was unable to make the gig and was replaced by Ronnie Ross. The loss, however, was momentary: "If anyone was still feeling slightly disappointed, those thoughts quickly evaporated when Hayes, nervous energy almost visible, drove his group through an excellent selection, many written by members of the band."

A local newspaper also reported:

> Hayes was a study in himself at the concert. Gesturing wildly, pursing his lips at the saxophone section one moment, waving a frantic right arm the next, and hands shooting into the air like a basketball player reaching for the net to bring the band to a high-note climax together, he coaxed his talent-laden team. Occasionally, he looked slightly comic; usually, he resembled the demanding perfectionist.[18]

The audience roared its approval, with Bob Dawbarn concluding that the night had marked "the birth of the most exciting big band ever to hit the British jazz scene." The success, the journalist observed, was attributable in no small part to Hayes's own inexhaustible enthusiasm. "When it comes to energy, nuclear power stations have nothing on Tubby Hayes. If they could harness Hayes-power for just 24 hours we'd be able to light our homes for the next twenty years."[19]

The transformational power of Hayes's energy was never better illustrated than by the story of a young trumpeter who'd arrived in London from his native Leicester earlier that spring: Henry Lowther. Attempting to make his musical mark in the capital wasn't proving easy, but when a bassist friend who was studying with Freddy Logan recommended the twenty-one-year-old Lowther try the Tubby Hayes rehearsal band, he duly did, only to find the nominal leader absent. Staying on at Ronnie Scott's after the rehearsal, and hoping to catch the Hayes quintet in action, he was surprised to find himself suddenly co-opted into its ranks as a replacement for Jimmy Deuchar:

[I] was just sitting there waiting for him to go back on to do the second set, and Tubby suddenly taps me on the shoulder and said to me "Fancy a blow?" And I was both delighted and terrified at the same time. I was terrified but I was not going to let the opportunity go. So I sat in with Tubby. And I'd only been in London two months, and had never played with musicians of that standard, ever. I sat in, and we only played three tunes and I can still remember what we played: Straight No Chaser, Yesterdays and – for me or for anybody – an unbelievably fast What Is This Thing Called Love. Tubby was well known for his fast tempos and he put me on the spot in a way: "See what you can do?" sort of thing. I got through it and I'll always remember how nice they were to me, including Tubby, but especially Allan Ganley, who was absolutely wonderful.[20]

By the summer of 1963, after a year working with Hayes, Ganley at last thought he'd got the measure of his leader. The musical fireworks the saxophonist offered were occasionally just a front:

Sometimes on the stand it was like "look how fast I can play and for how long" which is open-mouthed stuff but not always as musical as he could play when he just relaxed and didn't bother about creating an impression. He was a showman, a natural showman, but when you'd get him in a situation where it was just a few guys hanging around and someone would just start playing, he could be much more relaxed. The best I'd ever hear him play would be at a party, an after-hours thing where he wasn't trying to impress.[21]

Ganley also continued to marvel at his leader's brinkmanship. Copious amounts of alcohol before a performance – be it a gig, a TV show or a broadcast – were the norm, with no apparent negative effect on his playing. Trying to keep up with Hayes was foolhardy, to say the least. As a consequence, Jimmy Deuchar was often too drunk to play coherently and, as Peter King discovered after joining Hayes's big band, the leader's pre-gig routine of heading to the nearest public house could have disastrous results:

You would regularly find yourself in the bar before a gig being urged by Tubby to "Go on, have another double" only to stagger on stage hardly able to control your legs let alone your fingers. Tubby would be as stoned as everyone else but would yell out at a breakneck tempo "One, two, one, two, three, four!" into the fastest damned tune in the library. He would storm through the chart and solo as if he were stone-cold sober, while everyone else struggled to keep up.[22]

The ridiculous demands of Hayes's workload continued to render his home life almost non-existent. Dividing time between the quintet's residency at Scott's, sundry recording studios and travelling to and from engagements across the UK and Europe, he'd seen all too little of Rose and Richard in 1963. Indeed, there exists a touching photograph from August of that year, taken backstage at the Richmond festival, showing the young Richard eagerly eyeing up Allan Ganley's drums: Tubby is not in the picture, itself almost an allegory of his input into his family's life. Nevertheless, when Rose fell pregnant again that summer, he at last appeared to take some stock of the situation. In August, *Jazz News and Review* published a candid interview with Hayes conducted by Val Wilmer – a writer always able to conjure interesting responses from those she profiled – revealing that the prospect of moving to America was now less engrossing than ever. Hayes observed:

> I've got so much work now that I think I may as well stay in Europe. My name seems to be getting better known on the continent and also I've got a wife and child and another on the way to consider. If I was on my own I might go, but I'd be silly to risk going there and maybe not working for a while when I've got plenty here.[23]

International reputation or not, Hayes was still open to a mauling by the local jazz critics. When *Melody Maker* delivered an indictment of the state of the local product during the autumn of 1963, the verdict was damning. The scene was full of the same stale contentions: too few gigs, the monopoly of a handful of established names, the shortcomings of the BBC and the failure of the London modernists in grasping that their art was a branch of the entertainment industry. "How much are the musicians to blame for their own circumstance?" Bob Dawbarn asked. "I, personally, am heartily bored by the same old routines – numbers that go on for twenty minutes or more, with long solos all round, then everybody swapping eight-bar exchanges, then fours, then twos. And bass and drum solos on every number."[24]

For many, Tubby Hayes was above such criticism, but to others he continued to embody all the very worst attributes of British jazz: flashy, superficially impressive and tediously long-winded, he had succeeded in reducing the music to little more than a routine display of virtuoso chops. Hayes had already been given an opportunity to answer most of these charges when interviewed earlier that year by Les Tomkins, telling the journalist succinctly that "a set is a set."

> I don't go on and say: "Right – we're going to play a slow one, a fast one, a medium one, a ballad and a tear-up." That's not jazz. That's more like show-band business. We go on the stand and we may

feel like playing something down – or we may feel like playing fast ones all night.[25]

Hayes continued:

> I read these things where people say "too many notes," and quite honestly I couldn't give a damn. I play as I want to play. It's purely self-expression. Maybe you could fault me there for not really catering for the public. But if I was catering for the public I wouldn't be playing what I'm playing. I'd be playing the old twang-twang, wouldn't I?[26]

The rapid success of the Beat Boom had provided the best ammunition for those seeking to attack the hermetic nature of British jazz. In the same issue of *Melody Maker* as Bob Dawbarn's critique of the local jazz scene, The Beatles' manager Brian Epstein discussed the burgeoning success of his NEMS enterprise, which was fast turning a stable of unknowns into a galaxy of stars. The contrast could not have been more pronounced. Next to the overnight rise of The Beatles and all the other exponents of "the old twang-twang," the progress of British modern jazz seemed to be taking place at a snail's pace. "I try not to listen to it. I think it's a row. I think it's bad for youngsters to be brought up on this kind of music," Hayes was quoted as saying of the new music but it was a statement made of equal parts jealousy and contempt.[27] Such polemics dominated the music press of the time, with the ongoing debates in the letters pages of *Melody Maker* and other magazines taking on the same tone of partisan hostility that had characterized the Trad Boom barely two years earlier. Jazz, some believed, had had its day and the sooner its devotees realized this the better. A typical example is the attack made on Hayes by the ever so earnest Miss J. Stokes of Ilford in *Melody Maker* during August 1963: "I think HIS music is a row and it is bad for youngsters to be brought up on his kind of music. He has a cheek to criticize The Beatles and The Rolling Stones when he plays rubbish himself."[28]

Nevertheless, he continued to be a solid draw in clubland and, as 1963 drew to a close, the Tubby Hayes Quintet remained one of the busiest jazz acts on the circuit, taking in engagements across the length and breadth of the UK. Bringing modern jazz to the provinces that lay outside of London had been part and parcel of Hayes's work from the off, but exactly how he might have sounded on an out-of-town engagement, or indeed away from any controlled recorded environment, had, up to this point, gone largely undocumented. Indeed, prior to 1963 only a handful of tapes of Hayes outside a recording studio exist, a somewhat scanty trawl for over a decade's worth of cross-country music making. But by the early 1960s the situation was beginning to change. The wider availability of hire-purchase agreements now meant that expensive electrical items, including home tape recorders, were within easy reach for the first time. Models by Grundig, Elizabethan and Ferrograph quickly became popular, with the latter company hand-building a hundred machines a week at its early-sixties height. It was easy to understand the boom in interest: portable and simple to use, these new recorders meant freedom from the monopoly of the record deck. Although tape was still relatively expensive, it enabled a new kind of enthusiast to flourish: the amateur recordist. It had now become possible not only to record a band at home, or rehearsing informally, but also out on a gig. American jazz fans had long grown used to this practice, but no one on the London jazz scene seized upon the notion more eagerly during the 1960s than Les Tomkins.

Since the days of the T and H Modern Rhythm Club, Tomkins had progressed into journalism, writing features for *Melody Maker* and *Crescendo*, and, through a fortuitous combination of circumstances, late in 1963 he was apparently given carte blanche to tape-record whatever – and *whenever* – he wanted at Ronnie Scott's club. Tomkins was already using his Ferrograph machine to record interviews, but in a backstage conversation with Scott he had expressed regret that the hours of jazz that took place on the tiny Gerrard Street bandstand were simply being lost to the club's four walls. According to Tomkins, Scott's response was "Well, look – you've got the machine right there. Bring it down any time you like and see what you can get."[29]

He began his recording efforts soon after, during Roland Kirk's October residency at the club.

> Ronnie and Pete supplied me with a special lead to connect to the PA system. I was out of sight with my machine on a disused staircase behind the bar. At the time they were using a microphone identical to mine – a Reslo ribbon. As time went on, there were nights when the socket my lead went into was in use; so I would place my mic on the corner of the bar, where it would get as balanced as possible a sound.[30]

As these recordings had a somewhat covert origin, there has been some doubt expressed as to whether Tomkins ever consulted any of the participants, especially after a variety of labels began releasing the results from the 1990s onwards. Countering with the claim that at no time did he consider what he was recording to have any commercial implications, Tomkins maintains "the important thing was that, although people would see me arriving and leaving and chat to me, they never knew for sure whether I was recording at any given time, or whether I was recording them. So their spontaneity was not inhibited."[31]

This rather opaque *modus operandi* meant that, whilst some musicians who took part in these sessions wanted to hear the results, others later vociferously protested that Tomkins had never asked them for permission to record and was in effect "bootlegging." The truth is probably balanced equally between the two extremes. Few musicians at the time would have really considered that a recording made through a PA microphone onto a portable tape machine could potentially constitute a real infringement of their rights: only thirty years later, with the advent of sophisticated digital sound restoration equipment, did Tomkins's tapes begin to yield anything of commercial usability.[32]

Discussion of Tomkins's variable but always revealing recordings will thread through the narrative of the following chapters, but in examining his first efforts from 1963 it is possible to address more closely both the advantages and drawbacks of the process of covert recording. Tubby Hayes appears three times on tapes made during November and December of 1963, and excerpts from all of the sessions have been commercially released on CD. Given Tomkins's admission that he made no declarations as to when he set his recorder running, one can assume that Hayes was unaware of being taped, and, consequently, what one hears is wholly representative of the quintet's typical in-person appearances at that time. The first recording from November 7th begins with a vibraphone account of the Fran Landesman/ Tommy Wolf's ballad 'Spring Can Really Hang You Up The Most', a song to which Hayes would return several times in the ensuing years. The up-close nature of the recording lends a distinct physicality to Hayes's playing, an effect that is only reinforced on a version of his own composition 'Don't Fall Off The Bridge' which follows, on which he plays tenor.

On the December 3rd session, which produced versions of Jimmy Deuchar's 'If You Knew', Hayes's own 'As Close As You Are' and a blistering cover of 'Two Bass Hit', the saxophonist's tone takes on a chewy and rubbery quality which, whilst not unattractive, at times makes listeners feel as if they are sitting directly *inside* the bell of the instrument. A single track, 'Half A Sawbuck', survives from an all-nighter session held on December 16th, during which Hayes's tone is different again, sounding rough and unfocused during the solo passages as if he were moving the horn in and out of range of the microphone. Some critical reviews of the CDs taken from Tomkins's archive have been dismissive of this inconsistency, and it's all too easy to get hung up on the sonic impression of the music rather than concentrating on its content. Hayes and his sidemen are in uniformly excellent form across all three nights, especially Deuchar who, on the December 3rd titles, appears very much in control, clearly enjoying one of those occasions when, in the words of Ronnie Scott, his lip was "in."

According to Allan Ganley the combination of a consistent personnel and a conducive workplace was the key factor in the Hayes quintet's ongoing success, with the drummer identifying Scott's club as a sort of spiritual home for the band. However, acting as emissaries out on the road, the group's fortunes were often somewhat less starry. Whereas a venue like Ronnie Scott's made a concerted effort to create a favourable atmosphere for both the clientele and the musicians, some provincial clubs offered little in the way of either ambience or comfort.[33] Nevertheless, Hayes often found his music better received outside the capital than in it, as he told Brian Blain:

> These people have paid a lot to hear us – they can't take a tube to town any time they like to hear a professional jazz group. They deserve the best we can give. There's too much jazz centred on London. It's inevitable, I suppose, but it's a pity – and one of the results is that London audiences are often quite blasé about what you are doing, and difficult to move. On the other hand, this doesn't mean that we play down to [provincial listeners]. Once I've created an atmosphere by introducing the tune, it's up to the people to make some effort to meet the musicians as well.[34]

On December 4th the Tubby Hayes Quintet visited the elegantly named Dancing Slipper ballroom in West Bridgford, Nottingham, a familiar stop-off to many touring bands. The Slipper's jazz presentations were run by an enterprising one-armed fan named Bill "Foo" Kinnell, who did his best to lure the good and the great to what was to all intents and purposes a highly unlikely outpost for the music, a dance hall situated above a row of shops in the suburbs. Through little more than single-handed enthusiasm (no pun intended), Kinnell had built up an enthusiastic fan following for his club nights at the "Hobbling Clogs," as the locals referred to the venue; among those who could be found attending these gigs was future Conservative MP Kenneth Clarke.[35]

Like Ronnie Scott's, the Dancing Slipper also boasted its own amateur recording enthusiast, Allan Gilmour, who would go on to record hundreds of hours of music from the club's gigs over the following few years, the majority of which remains unheard. Occasionally Gilmour would give out tapes to those musicians he'd recorded, some of which would later surface on commercial issues.[36] In the early 1980s, Spotlite Records acquired a copy of the Hayes quintet's performance from December 4th, 1963 and released four selections on an LP titled *A Tribute: Tubbs*, packaged with an affectionate sleeve note by Ronnie Scott. These four tracks, 'All Of You', 'Don't Fall Off The Bridge', 'Modes And Blues' and 'Blue Flues', comprised the first ever archive release by Tubby Hayes, thus beginning the rediscovery of his genius which has continued into the digital age. As such, the LP was warmly received and, although it is not generally the author's practice to quote *posthumous* reviews of Hayes's recorded output in this study, one appraisal of the album sums up both the atmosphere and the music of that December night so well that it is worthy of a repeat in full. Clearly impressed by the windfall, *NME*'s Brian Case wrote:

> "You catch jazz, you don't learn it," said Johnny Griffin, and like Griffin or Dexter, Tubbs was a contagious knees-up. [This] live

club session from the Dancing Slipper, Nottingham, gives a vivid reminder of just how lucky the audience of flat barnets, bumfreezers and winkle pickers were.

After a typically hardboiled announcement by the leader – albumen nightclub complexion and unblinking hare's eyes – the quintet leans into an easy, practised arrangement of All Of You. Deuchar's solo is shapely and nimble, with catapulted climaxes from Ganley, and it unfolds in a clear narrative. Tubbs' entry is typically dramatic, a knot of contorted rhythms which the tenorman palms with Houdini ease to noodle awhile before shaken by a fit of flashing runs. As with Griffin, speed was a central element in his aesthetic, adrenaline stammers overtaking each other on the inside, risers overlapping, abrupt cable-car descents to the honking bottom register – in short the rocketing confidence in modernism of the second generation prodigy. Not easy to follow, but Terry Shannon's touch is distinctive as Wynton Kelly's blues and beauty, and the crowding chorus-swapping conclusion survives one awful yaw to batten onto a bouquet of Violets For Your Furs.

Throughout the album, these concluding interchanges pummel and press at the emotions, leaving the listener with the marks of the ropes across the back of his singlet.

Don't Fall opens on a Messenger's unison over mobile biff-bang drums, idles into Latin, adds a pinch of Arab, and triggers Tubbs' tenor. Spitting pebbles of sound at machine-gun speed brings out the lout in him, and up comes Jingle Bells at tempo, and a belligerent on-mic smack-up delivery of blues familiarities. His energy centre has that unpredictable sense of swerve and jitter that sometimes surfaces in great basketball around the net.

Deuchar follows, balancing a row of sagging smears with another of fast-tongued exactitudes, before handing over to the piano which swings relentlessly deeper in the Silver manner with stubby blues conjugations.

Modes and Blues startles with its change of mood from reflective flute and padding bass to furious drums, boppish horn unison and tenor blast-off.

Blue Flues has a brooding spaciousness in which walking bass registers, and superb unaccompanied horn cadenzas.[37]

If Case sometimes gets into a terrible knot of metaphors, his overflowing enthusiasm is fully justified, leaving little to add to his assessment. However, it is worth adding that, within the four performances chosen from December 4th, there is a perfect microcosm of the band's approach, from the lyrical and compact opening of 'All Of You'[38] through to the ambitious and almost Mingus-like 'Blue Flues', itself an indication of the leader's ever-growing compositional prowess. And, even if the somewhat veiled audio fails to capture the sound of the band with the clarity of an "official" recording, the cohesion of the group shines through.[39]

The remainder of 1963 was dominated by the big band. On November 24th they returned to Don Norman's club in Chichester for a one-off mini-festival appearance opposite Annie Ross and the Tony Kinsey quintet, and on December 16th they made their debut at a London jazz hostelry soon to become a regular part of Hayes's musical activities, the Bull's Head at Barnes. Squeezing the thirteen musicians onto the Bull's small stage required an act of co-operative contortion, but the audience cheered its approval, echoing the reaction to the band's first outing on BBC's *Jazz Club* the previous week, during which they'd faced stiff competition from The Beatles' appearance on *Juke Box Jury*.[40]

For those who had been faithful to the big band game, the early 1960s were a challenge. The financial conditions for regular touring bands were now more parlous than lucrative and few were willing to brave the challenge full-time. Vic Lewis had retired from the road to run a promotions agency (eventually absorbed by Brian Epstein's NEMS enterprise), whilst John Dankworth was devoting ever-increasing time to film and TV commissions.[41] In an odd example of the artistic tail wagging the commercial dog, film score duties had only served to make Dankworth's jazz writing more adventurous and, over the summer and autumn of 1963, he assembled an all-star cast to record the first of his many themed suites, in this instance based on the works of Charles Dickens. A more ambitious concept required a more ambitious record label, and the bandleader was in no doubt as to whom to turn. After disappointing affiliations with Parlophone, Top Rank and Roulette, he preferred the idea of working with Jack Baverstock. "I went to Philips because [Baverstock] was doing so well with Tubby Hayes," he told *Melody Maker*. "He was recording British modern jazz when most people didn't want to know about it."[42] Consequently, *What The Dickens* became the first of a series of excellent albums Dankworth recorded for Fontana, and with a guest list featuring Tubby Hayes, Jimmy Deuchar, Bobby Wellins, Ronnie Ross, Peter King, Dick Morrissey, Tony Coe and Ronnie Scott, it was a tribute to the leader's organizational skills that the record retained a sense of structure, rather than becoming a series of disjointed cameo appearances. Hayes's presence in particular proved transformational, never more so than on the duet shared with the leader's alto, 'Dodson and Fogg'.[43]

1964 began with Mr and Mrs Hayes awaiting the imminent birth of their second child. Lewis Alexander Hayes duly arrived on Sunday January 26th, a few days ahead of his father's twenty-ninth birthday, doubtless confirming Hayes's faith in all things Aquarius. The couple's eldest son Richard was not yet four and the demands that two young children now placed upon Rose were doubly compounded by her husband's continued absence from their home life. Indeed, in the weeks surrounding Lewis's birth his workload refused to let up. The quintet's residency at Ronnie Scott's continued apace (with Les Tomkins capturing the band on tape on January 3rd) and there were also recording dates with chanteuse Caterina Valente, a return to BBC's *Jazz Club*, a one-off resuscitation of the octet at the Bull's Head and a brief northern jaunt to Sunderland and Newcastle. On January 31st Les Tomkins once again recorded Hayes at Scott's, with the set's closer, Clark Terry's 'Opus Ocean', providing an almost ridiculously over-accelerated display of the leader's up-tempo skills. The performance all but defeats Jimmy Deuchar, but Hayes has no such problem; his unaccompanied solo is a staggering example of both his technical skill and his creativity. Chorus upon chorus goes by in a flash, and he piles in virtually every device in the book: vocalization, feverish double-time and bluesy smears all combine in a statement that is definitive Hayes, and one that, in a single performance, vindicates Les Tomkins's controversial efforts.[44]

A performance such as 'Opus Ocean' also reveals an ongoing dilemma in Hayes's music – that of his constant ability to outstrip the efforts of his colleagues. As Kitty Grime had noted three years earlier, there was often a "steep drop in temperature" in Hayes's bands once the leader had finished soloing, even with players as forthright as Jimmy Deuchar present. The quintet had undoubtedly been the most evenly matched of his groups so far but, by the beginning of 1964, it was becoming apparent that Hayes was aiming for something beyond the confines of hard bop. A further recording made by Les Tomkins early in February reveals this in spades. On his adventurous composition 'Modes And Blues' the saxophonist plays a solo of extraordinary length – around twenty minutes – during which he seems fitfully at odds with almost everything around him.

By 1964, the very nature of the small jazz unit – and in particular the role of the rhythm section – was rapidly changing, with the equation being radically altered by the examples of McCoy Tyner, Jimmy Garrison and Elvin Jones with John Coltrane's quartet and Herbie Hancock, Ron Carter and Tony Williams with Miles Davis's band. Whereas hard bop had freed up the rules regarding interaction with the front-line soloist, the rhythm sections in Coltrane's and Davis's band were now freely independent units, operating with a democratic understanding that had made the music a truly open dialogue. With such equality, even the most conventional of material could be newly transformed – as can be witnessed in the recordings made by the Davis quintet during the course of 1964[45] – and with typical perspicacity Tubby Hayes now saw this approach as a useful tool in escaping the formulaic delivery that had come to characterize his music. However, discussions between the members of the quintet soon revealed a reluctance to attempt "some different types of material."[46] "He wanted to go the sort of Coltrane route," Allan Ganley remembered, "and that wasn't my thing at all."[47]

A far more balanced account of the quintet's music is that taped on February 12th during a return visit to the Dancing Slipper ballroom in West Bridgford.

In 2011 a CD containing five of the evening's performances was released, revealing the band at close to its collective peak.[48] Crucially, rather than concentrating on experimental originals, the choice of material is far wider than of yore, bringing in transformations of standard songs that demonstrate yet another alter ego of the hard bop approach heard elsewhere. There is a coolly melodic 'Younger Than Springtime', a feature for the leader's lithesome vibraphone variations, and an elegant reading of Rodgers and Hart's 'With The Wind And The Rain In Your Hair', including a tenor solo from Hayes which alternates bursts of Rollins-like invention with Getzian vibrato. By far the most impressive performance is that of 'Dancing In The Dark', tackled helter-skelter and boasting another staggeringly accomplished unaccompanied solo from Hayes, which even succeeds in outdoing the one on the earlier 'Opus Ocean'. Countering all the claims that he was too cool a drummer for a player like Hayes, Allan Ganley matches his boss's near superhuman stamina blow for blow on the final item of the night, Jimmy Deuchar's steaming 'Suddenly Last Tuesday', into which Hayes interjects themes as disconnected as 'Baby It's Cold Outside' and Thelonious Monk's 'Rhythm-A-Ning'.

Two nights after their appearance at the Dancing Slipper, the quintet were back in London to begin their regular Friday/Saturday night stint at Ronnie Scott's, as they'd done for virtually every weekend of the preceding two years. However, Friday February 14th also marked the arrival of the Duke Ellington band in the capital for the beginning of their annual UK tour. Many of the Ellington band already had friends and connections in London: as soon as they had decamped to their hotel, a small contingent including trumpeters Rolf Ericsson and Cat Anderson decided to make their way to Soho, joining the Hayes quintet on stage for a friendly jam session captured by Les Tomkins's tape recorder. The resulting recording finds the saxophonist enthusiastically refereeing between the two Ellingtonians, with Jimmy Deuchar also clearly out to prove his mettle. But the session was merely the beginning of a long, long night.[49]

The partying that had started at Gerrard Street went on well into the small hours, with a loose gaggle of local musicians and assorted hangers-on moving on to Jack Sharpe's Downbeat Club in Old Compton Street, an establishment whose casual observance of licensing hours made it a magnet for players seeking an after-hours blow. The ensuing session pitted Hayes and the locals against fellow tenorist Paul Gonsalves, a long-standing Ellingtonian, whose epic work on the 1956 Newport Jazz Festival recording of 'Diminuendo And Crescendo In Blue' had done so much to reignite his leader's fortunes.[50] Gonsalves had long been a favourite of Hayes's[51] and the two men's mutual appreciation was also matched in their equal capacity for drink. By the time the party at the Downbeat finally finished at around eight in the morning, the American was hopelessly drunk, However, Hayes – his hollow-legged consti-tution intact – simply went back home to bed to sleep it off.

What happened next has been told and retold with varying degrees of accuracy, distortion and embellishment ever since. Separating the folklore from the fact is made a great deal easier when consulting Hayes's own memories of the incident, which he recounted several times over the remainder of his career. Aside from the immediate accounts he gave the press at the time, we know that he spoke about the events of Saturday February 15th, 1964 on BBC radio on at least three occasions and wrote at least once about his experience that night for *Melody Maker*. Nevertheless, despite this comprehensive contemporary documentation, hindsight does still have its uses, as several key facts about the night were only revealed some years after Hayes's death. The following composite account is drawn from Hayes's recollections on the BBC's *The Jazz Scene* programme in 1966, from *Crescendo* magazine in March 1964 and from an article published in *Melody Maker* five years later in 1969.

The cycle of events began late on the Saturday afternoon, with Hayes anticipating nothing more than his usual weekend stint at Scott's:

> Jimmy [Deuchar] had arranged to call me so we could go to the [Royal Festival] Hall and take in part of the first show before going to Ronnie's to do the gig. But when he called I was so tired that I said I thought I'd leave it and catch the band later. Luckily Jimmy talked me into going. To add to the drama – though I didn't guess it then – I dropped my horn off at Ronnie's on the way to the concert. Anyway, we got to the hall and went in the dressing room to talk to the guys. I hadn't seen Paul [Gonsalves] but didn't think about it particularly. Suddenly in came dear old Dougie Tobutt of the [Harold] Davison office to say that Duke wanted to see me. I went into Duke's room and he told me Paul was unwell. He asked straight out: could I and would I do the show? I can't explain the feeling but I was overwhelmed. I agreed to have a go.
>
> Harold Davison phoned Ronnie Scott and got permission for me to do it and Ronnie kindly sent my tenor down by taxi. I had no sort of preparation, but perhaps that was best. While I waited for my tenor, Billy Strayhorn put the music in order for me. The band went on and started the programme without Paul or me. Then the horn arrived and I just crept out on stage, feeling pretty terrible. The first thing I had in my music file was Far East Suite and I was looking at that while Duke made his announcement. Then he called Perdido which didn't exactly help. And Jimmy Hamilton said "Don't worry looking, there's no part for that."[52] So I sort of played along where I could and laid out when need be, you know, and I also remember Duke giving me a little solo to play and it was a wonderful thrill. And then, of course, another number came up and Jimmy Hamilton said "Right, we all go down the front for

this one." And once again there was no music. So the five saxes – we go out front and fortunately it was a number that I'm sort of reasonably familiar with and it's one where Harry Carney plays the lead on the clarinet. I had the sort of fourth tenor part which doubles the lead an octave down or something, so I was able to play it I'm very pleased to say. It was one of my favourite pieces of Ellington music, 'Rockin' in Rhythm'.[53] And so it went on. I followed the rule of when in doubt, lay out. As I said at the time: how about me up there miming?[54] The hardest piece was the 'Harlem Suite'. I had the original tenor part from, when was it, 1950? I knew the record and remembered there was a tenor solo. And then it came up, every note written. Well, I played it somehow.[55]

When Duke asked me to do the second concert as well, I was completely knocked out. One thing I'll never forget is sitting down at the end of the band and looking back along the line of saxophones: Hamilton, Hodges, Carney, Procope. Man, it was beautiful.[56] Playing in that section was wonderful. The quality of sound was quite frightening at times. And they didn't seem to be blowing over-loud. And as for the band as a whole, most of the time I was concentrating on looking for the music and playing, but I particularly noticed [trombonist] Lawrence Brown's terrific sound behind me.[57]

Hayes's own account tells us much about his feelings towards the concert itself, but the recollections of others are useful in rounding out the fore and aft of this remarkable occasion. Writing in 1998, Hayes's former manager, Pete King, revealed that on the Saturday afternoon he had received a call at his home from the Harold Davison office enquiring "if Ronnie Scott was available to play with Duke that very night as Paul Gonsalves had gone missing. I can't recall if Ronnie was working or I couldn't reach him. Whatever, I suggested Tubby."[58]

The Englishman's stoic display of grit had mightily impressed the Ellington players. "[Tubby is] a first class musician. I did what I could to help him the first time. You don't have to show him twice," Jimmy Hamilton told Max Jones of *Melody Maker*.[59] Jones also recorded that even the normally undemonstrative Johnny Hodges had called Hayes "terrific."[60] Les Tomkins had solicited similar praise from both Harry Carney and Russell Procope in *Crescendo*, with Carney stating:

[Tubby] knows what he's doing because to sit in with the band and do such a commendable job he had to be excellent. We have about the worst book, so far as explaining how to play the arrangements. We don't have anything cut and dried, that follows from the left hand corner to the right hand corner. As a matter of fact, I think he played the new music better than we played it![61]

Procope agreed: "It takes guts to get up there and do that sort of thing."[62]

Alongside the favourable reaction of the musicians involved, the press also had a field day. Hayes had rarely made the national papers, but now he found his name in the *Sunday Times*, with a review titled "Tubby Hayes Rides High on the Duke's Bandwagon." In an effusive account of the evening, Derek Jewell described the saxophonist's last-minute inclusion as a "coup de théâtre rarely paralleled."[63] *Jazz Journal*'s Sinclair Traill thought that "[Hayes] can have known no prouder moment than when he received a warm handshake from the 'boss' and the 'thumbs-up' and congratulatory grins from the Ellington bandmen,"[64] whilst Bob Houston delivered a characteristically colourful version of events in *Melody Maker*:

> If Tubby looked a bit apprehensive as he scanned the music for Perdido, it didn't show. And after two storming solo choruses on The Opener, everything was swinging. Sam Woodyard leaned across from behind the drum kit to shake Tubby's hand. Jimmy Hamilton smiled his approval and even the impassive Hodges was seen to be moved. Duke added his approval by stomping into the blues for another round of the Tubby tenor and the audience went wild. For a moment, patriotism reigned and Tubby was the hero of the hour.[65]

Stating that Hayes had been "yanked from his comfortable seat in the audience" in order to play the gig, Houston's well-meaning article was also the unwitting source of much of the subsequent myth about the evening of February 15th. Despite adequate contemporary evidence countering his claim, Houston's version of events quickly entered British jazz folklore, and was even repeated in the sleeve notes to the album Hayes and Gonsalves recorded together shortly afterward.[66] One can easily understand the appeal of the story, which sounds far more in keeping with Hayes's "giant-slaying legend" than the rather more prosaic truth. Indeed, it sits neatly alongside other such legendary triumphs for Hayes – his first joust with Ronnie Scott, his impromptu debut on the vibraphone and so on. And, as Pete King later remembered, the myth had been a useful tool in burying a bit of bad news that might have otherwise stolen Hayes's thunder: "I was very proud of him and many of the audience were ecstatic. But, and I can understand this, there were some mumblings about his appearance from some musicians and critics. After all, the punters had paid to see Paul Gonsalves with the Duke, not a local boy, however brilliant he was."[67]

"Tubby Hayes wants you to know that he too loves you madly."
Tubby at the microphone, Duke Ellington in the foreground.
The Royal Festival Hall, Saturday February 15th, 1964.
Courtesy Liz Grönlund.

8 The Best of Both Worlds (1964–65)

Tubby Hayes comes out of this evening like Roland Kirk suffering from multiple schizophrenia.

George Melly introducing the Tubby Hayes big band,
BBC Jazz Club, May 1965

For London's jazz community Ellington's visit had been a welcome reminder that musical sanity hadn't been totally swamped in a post-Beatles backlash.[1] Elsewhere, however, it was difficult to escape the impression that with little more than a guitar and a Liverpool accent you could now find the world at your feet. By the spring of 1964, The Beatles were no longer simply a band; they were a way of life, a cult transforming the lives of those who followed them in the same catalytic way that Charlie Parker had once transformed young jazz musicians. Whether you were a jobbing musician at the local Palais tottering through Jimmy Lalley's arrangement of 'All My Loving' or a top London session man drafted in to make something credible of a piece of teenage hokum, the impact of their music had become inescapable. For those against the revolution, opportunities for spleen venting came almost daily: when they won the Variety Club Show Business Personality of the Year Awards in March 1964, the band were handed their "purple hearts" (as John Lennon put it) by Prime Minister Harold Wilson, who seemed perfectly happy to go along with all the chummy Northern badinage. Harold and The Beatles? Politicians and pop stars? What on earth was going on? But for those in favour opportunity knocked, and as never before the road from obscurity to stardom appeared to require not much more than a good break. The same month as The Beatles received their Variety Club gongs, Cilla Black, former hat check girl at the Cavern in Liverpool, topped the UK charts with the Bacharach–David song 'Anyone Who Had A Heart'. It didn't matter that Black had barely served any sort of musical apprenticeship: she had been brushed by the providential hand of Brian Epstein and that was enough.

Having broken America, Epstein's plans for The Beatles grew more lavishly ambitious. Early in 1964, riding the crest of what the press now dubbed Beatlemania, the group began filming its first feature film, *A Hard Day's Night*. When it was announced that advance sales of the band's latest single 'Can't Buy Me Love' numbered over 865,000, anyone listening over the incessant din of adoring pubescent female fans would have heard the well-oiled machinations of a fast-expanding business empire. Epstein's NEMS stable was now in effect turning out immediate stars, many with frankly meagre talents, a few with far deeper aspirations. That spring, when Macmillan published John Lennon's *In His Own Write*, a surreal collection of poetry and line drawings, some perceptive critics thought they saw a troubled genius beneath the flippancy and laddish attitude. But for every Lennon there was a horde of lesser talents, making fast bucks out of not much more than luck. Via Epstein's influence, EMI's Parlophone label signed its share of duds alongside the genuine article and when *Melody Maker* described the label's producer George Martin – who had previously worked on records by comedy artists and jazz musicians – as a "hit-maker" there were early signs that the critics knew who was really pulling the musical strings. As producer for The Beatles, Martin was to become an icon, but not all of the work foisted on him by default proved to be as agreeable: Billy J. Kramer had topped the charts with Lennon and McCartney's composition 'Little Children' during early 1964, a recording that Martin had to mix as diplomatically as possible to ensure he hid the singer's patently bad pitching. Ironically, the record became Kramer's only US number one, a supreme case of sending not coals but nutty slack to Newcastle.

Fortunately America's jazz exports didn't pull the same stunt in reverse. On March 6th, 1964, Stan Getz, a lifelong hero for a whole generation of British jazz saxophonists including Tubby Hayes, finally opened at Ronnie Scott's. The rapturous welcome afforded the club's guest was matched only by his own disregard for the whole endeavour. Booked at a snip of his usual fee, Getz became more truculent as the engagement wore on, arguing spectacularly with Scott and King and at one point forcing his hosts to consider replacing him with Zoot Sims. But, despite all the testiness, Hayes and his colleagues were delighted to hear this idol up close.[2] Appearing opposite Getz every night was a revelation: the American's signature sound was more gorgeous in real life than on record, his formidable technical skill exercised with nerveless, unblinking passivity. One night the mystery of his otherworldly tone looked like it might be cracked. The saxophonist had left his tenor in the club's tiny office to step outside for a cigarette and, seated around the instrument, curiosity got the better of Hayes, Ronnie Scott, Stan Robinson and several others, who all took turns to play the horn and found it disappointingly ordinary.[3] However, the American's example could still transform those who'd heard it in person. When Hayes travelled to Cologne to record a radio session with bandleader Kurt Edelhagen the week after Getz had opened at Ronnie's, the effect was immediately apparent.[4]

Carrying Tubby Hayes's music to a wider audience was still a concern for Pete King. Although the managerial plan he'd sketched out four years previously now had all its boxes ticked, King argued that there was still too little exposure for Hayes on mainstream television. ITV had shown the last episode of *Tubby Hayes Plays* on March 18th – a staggering two years after it was recorded! – and was now featuring the Hayes quintet on the short-lived series *Jazz Girl*,[5] but both programmes had a piecemeal, compromised air to them, as if dumbing the music down to bite-size chunks were the only way to put its message across. What was needed was a TV producer with the same faith and vision that Jack Baverstock had at Fontana. Luckily, a televisual equivalent *did* exist, although ironically he was not to be found in the moneyed quarters of commercial broadcasting but inside the ranks of the BBC.

Terry Henebery had previously worked wonders on the corporation's *Jazz Club* radio series. When BBC2 launched in April 1964, with the bold declaration of providing ample space for the arts, he found himself hastily seconded to the helm of a new TV series, *Jazz 625*, a move that required him to undertake a crash-course in the new medium. "Our aim is to let the music speak for itself, to show jazz musicians thinking and working," he told *Melody Maker*.[6] It was a goal that the series was to achieve with consistent success.

The timing of the new venture, Henebery later noted, was especially apt. Securing American musicians to perform on the programme was made far easier by the "British Invasion" that had followed The Beatles' initial US visit in February 1964. Sometimes these exchanges had an air of surrealism to them, such as when the producer booked the Oscar Peterson trio in a swap for the Dave Clark Five – a balance that meant that technically it took three of Clark's band to equal Peterson – but as useful as the import policy was, Henebery also maintained an equal commitment to local musicians, many of whom he'd unwittingly earmarked whilst producing *Jazz Club*. Tubby Hayes had been a mandatory choice and on March 22nd the quintet recorded two *Jazz 625* episodes at the Marquee, with added guest vocalists Mark Murphy and Betty Bennett.[7] Sadly, neither has been re-screened since their initial airing in 1964.

Hayes had also written several arrangements for an album recorded by Murphy in London that spring[8] but although composing and arranging continued to be a preoccupation, gigs for his own big band remained thin on the ground.[9] Those that did occur had now taken on an almost bacchanalian air, with hordes of fans jammed sardine-tight into the back room of the Bull's Head in Barnes. Among the faithful was Fontana's Terry Brown and his experience of hearing the band live at the Bull that winter appears to have marked something of an epiphany.[10] Convinced that they deserved a better fate than a handful of pub gigs and the odd broadcast, Brown instantly lobbied Fontana to make a recording, reasoning that any group purporting to extend Hayes's musical example by doubling the equation looked likely to be a sure-fire winner. As usual, there were the considerations of marketing. The saxophonist's previous albums, such as *Return Visit* and *Late Spot At Scott's* were self-explanatory, but a record by a larger unit, Fontana's management argued, inevitably required a larger hook. Consequently, when the band finally assembled at Philips Studios in Marble Arch on April 20th and 26th it was to record an album representing an imagined musical travelogue, appropriately titled *Tubbs' Tours*.

It was all a gimmick, of course. If anyone had been expecting a sort of prototypical world-music from Hayes and co. they would have been disappointed to find each journey starting firmly from Gerrard Street. Indeed, some of the recording was devoted to reruns of popular items from the band's existing book, including 'Parisian Thorofare', 'In The Night' and 'The Killers', all of which had been effectively hijacked to fit the "concept album" idea. Where music was specially commissioned, such as Harry South's 'Raga' and Ian Hamer's 'Pedro's Walk', the sense of pastiche was noticeably heavy-handed. Only Peter King's 9/8 time composition 'Sasa Hivi' took the world concept seriously, inspiring a formidable tenor solo from the leader.[11]

Yet the album had delivered something new: a definitive Hayes flute performance on 'In The Night'. Having taken up the instrument in the late 1950s,[12] apparently after buying one purely on spec, Hayes had shown characteristically precocious ability – Peter King recalls he was playing his new double on gigs within a few days of purchasing it[13] – and it had also made a useful addition to his studio session armoury (one of his earliest flute solos is on Matt Monro's 'April Fool', from 1961[14]). For jazz improvisation, however, Hayes found the instrument a refreshing change, and rather than merely transferring his usual saxophone phrasing, he claimed the flute made him think "like a trumpet."[15] As the 1960s progressed it became his double of choice, eclipsing and then replacing the vibraphone, and, as with his work on tenor, he was quickly able to synthesize the approaches of other players – Harold McNair, James Moody, Roland Kirk and Charles Lloyd among them – into his existing style.[16]

Meeting a critical reaction that vindicated both Hayes's and Terry Brown's faith in the project, *Tubbs' Tours* was finally released late in 1964. "Throw those anti-British jazz prejudices out the window and get this album – it's magnificent big band jazz by anybody's standards," *Melody Maker* declared[17] whilst *Jazz Beat* named it their Record Of The Month. "Certainly, Woody Herman's latest Herd has made no finer LP than this," wrote the magazine's George Ellis.[18] But alongside the general mood of partisan praise, there were also several nay-sayers, including Jack Cooke, a critic who had never really warmed to Hayes's oeuvre. He now wrote in *Jazz Monthly* that although the saxophonist had "a lot of surface brilliance . . . underneath one is left with the uneasy feeling of having been exposed to nothing more than someone running on the spot."[19] Hayes's playing had become "static." "He seems to have found nothing to challenge him lately and this is beginning to show in his work," Cooke concluded perceptively, a criticism that Hayes himself might not have disagreed with.

The superficially glamorous world of film-work was one distraction. That spring, Hayes had recorded the soundtrack for the Hammer thriller *Hysteria*, in which his tenor saxophone threads through the plot as the principal instrumental voice. There had also been on-screen work alongside bassist Spike Heatley and drummer Bobby Orr in the forgettable comedy *The Beauty Jungle*. And, after convoluted negotiations, in May 1964 the quintet began filming for the Amicus horror portmanteau *Dr Terror's House of Horrors*.

As Allan Ganley later revealed, his leader's original remit was ambitious, to say the least.

> Tubby was asked to write the whole film score. In fact, we went in the studio to audition it. I remember it was a big studio and the producer and some hierarchy were sitting at a table listening to all this. We were a jazz quintet and this was a so-called horror film. What were we gonna do? So they threw it out![20]

The disappointment of failing to secure the commission was short-lived, however, as the entire quintet found themselves co-opted as actors in *Voodoo*, one of the film's five short stories, a task that they took to with a certain amount of amusement.

The plot was risible: played by Roy Castle, trumpeter "Biff" Bailey and his band – the Hayes quintet – visit the West Indies, a land of exotic tribal drums and imported cockney vocalists. When Bailey is caught transcribing some sacred ritual music, the voodoo god Dambala promises to exact a woeful revenge, which he eventually does, although not before wrecking the trumpeter's polite supper-club set featuring guest Kenny Lynch. Appearing in such hokum, the few weeks' filming at Shepperton were treated as one long and well-paid joke by the band, as Allan Ganley remembered. "We had a great time with Kenny. There was one scene round a table that was shot after lunch and Tubby was well away. And while we're filming he was falling asleep and leaning back, so someone had to hold him up. It was really funny."[21] The final nightclub sequence, in which a hurricane destroys Bailey's arrangements, also proved hilarious. "They had this huge wind machine and we're playing and we all have to make out we're falling over. The first time we did it we all burst out laughing. The director was going mad as we had to do all these retakes. It was a lot of fun!"[22] If *Dr Terror's House of Horrors* never quite added up to a cinematic masterpiece, its true value continues to lie in the wonderful colour footage of the Hayes quintet at close to the end of its life. Indeed, Hayes's participation in the project has even succeeded in elevating the film to cult level.[23]

Hayes's regular working itinerary had continued unabated throughout the filming, and on July 12th the quintet was joined by American tenorist Sal Nistico, visiting the UK with the Woody Herman band, for a friendly-fire jam session at Ronnie Scott's, captured by Les Tomkins's tape recorder. Bearing a remarkable physical similarity to Hayes, Nistico's predilection for hard and fast playing also made him something of a kindred spirit. Both men had been cursed by their fast-fingered reputation, dismissed by critics as superlative technicians and not superlative jazzmen. However, the two titles recorded by Tomkins at Scott's, 'Friends Blues' and 'Just Friends', make nonsense of any accusations of rote playing, with Nistico's blunt delivery contrasting with Hayes's darker-toned and far more conversational approach. Both saxophonists play at length, with stamina another shared attribute, but at no time does one sense the sort of probing soul-searching found in John Coltrane's extended improvisations of the period.[24] Nevertheless, Hayes had not given up on his desire to move his music forward, although by the late summer he had conceded that the quintet was no longer the format with which to push the envelope. Discussions as to what could be done to keep the band fresh had only revealed a marked disparity in ambitions. The approach of John Coltrane may have continued to fixate Hayes, but it was not an obsession shared by his sidemen: Jimmy Deuchar wanted to spend more time writing, Terry Shannon had grown bored with accompanying ever longer horn solos and Allan Ganley had realized that his leader's direction was branching incompatibly from his own. Added to this, Hayes was equally aware that it was he and not his band that were attracting international recognition. On August 13th he had featured in *DownBeat* magazine's "Talent Deserving Wider Recognition" category and when American saxophonist Benny Golson flew into London to conduct a specially assembled twenty-five piece British orchestra for the BBC's *Jazz 625* programme that same month, it was Hayes to whom Golson had turned to assemble the band.[25]

The quintet finally split in late August, with *Melody Maker*'s announcement of the decision having an especially bitter ring to it: "Obituary: Died in London, Britain's top jazz group – the Tubby Hayes Quintet. Cause of death: Old age and over-work. There will be no burial service but the corpse will be mourned by the vast majority of British jazz fans." "Nearly three years is a long time for any group to stay together," the band's manager Pete King told the paper. "The boys just decided it was time to do something different." "Like the Jazz Couriers, the Hayes Quintet is quitting while still at the top," the article concluded. "It will certainly take some replacing on the British scene. Perhaps other groups have learned the lesson it propounded – that there is a market for jazz if you can combine talent with good, original arrangements and a belief that your audience is made up of intelligent human beings."[26]

The month after the quintet folded, Hayes gave a lengthy interview to *Melody Maker*'s veteran writer Max Jones, during which he admitted that, in addition to all his other musical responsibilities, being the group's creative spark plug had very nearly exhausted him. Indeed, some aspects of the itinerary the saxophonist revealed to Jones now sound like lunacy, making one wonder how he had ever found time to lead his own band:

> A couple of months ago, I had nine short TV films to write for, and they were arrangements for a sixteen piece orchestra, at a few days' notice. In that time, I was playing every afternoon at Decca and every evening in the Midlands. One of the guys was waiting outside the studios each day to collect me and rush me up the M1 to Birmingham or Leicester or somewhere. Then back in the small hours and that was the only time I had for writing. A few hours' sleep and I was off to the studios again. I'm not complaining, it's wonderful to be busy, of course – but I feel I've not been able to do all these things to the best of my ability.[27]

Despite this feverish activity, Jones's profile presents Tubby Hayes as a man now very much in charge of his life: fundamentally secure, financially successful and with the rare luxury in jazz of being largely able to pick and choose his work. The real drama now lay outside his professional life. At the top of the article is a photograph of the quintet with Joy Marshall, the vocalist who had already figured in several of Hayes's more commercial projects and a woman to whom he felt increasingly attracted. Indeed, by the time the *Melody Maker* piece appeared in print, Hayes and Marshall had embarked on an affair. Not only would this relationship tear apart the saxophonist's home life, it would have an equally disastrous impact on his career.

At twenty-five, Marshall was already a formidably self-assured character. Born of mixed Afro-American and Cuban stock, she was the daughter of church-going parents who instilled in their offspring the values of a religious upbringing. Following service in the US Navy, at the age of twenty she turned professional. She had then spent two years traversing the United States before landing a residency at the Purple Onions club in San Francisco, where a New Zealand businessman named Royston Marker heard her and offered his managerial services, feeling "she had to be brought to England for a fresh start."[28] Soon after arriving in London in June 1962, Marshall found steady work guesting with the Tony Kinsey quintet at the Flamingo, before eventually replacing Cleo Laine with the John Dankworth Orchestra. At a time when in certain jazz circles having a black girlfriend was seen as the ultimate in hip achievement, Marshall also didn't go short on romantic offers. Glamorously attractive, she caught the attention of saxophonist Peter King, then a regular member of Tony Kinsey's band. Under pressure from her new manager, "Bee" Bram, the couple soon wed, principally to avoid the vocalist having to renew her work permit. It was to prove a marriage made in hell.[29] Marshall was far more streetwise than her husband and delighted in teasing his suburban English upbringing and financial insecurity, eventually pushing King to the brink of suicide. She also made no secret of her frequent affairs.

Exactly where and when Tubby Hayes first encountered Joy Marshall is not recorded. What is certain is that he found her instantly appealing. It's easy to see why. Marshall was hip, sexy and funny and understood the life of a professional musician in a way that no one outside the business ever could. Not only that, she had a feistiness that represented a genuine challenge. After the disappointments of Maggie and Rose, here at last was a woman who Hayes could look upon as an equal, capable of giving as good as she got.

Out of focus in every way: a rare shot of Joy Marshall and Tubby, circa summer 1965. Courtesy Tony Ketley.

Marshall had also arrived from the hub of jazz activity. She'd heard Coltrane and Rollins up close, knew the American jazz scene and had the kind of attitude that no amount of hipster pretence could match. It was a reminder that there remained a gap between Tubby Hayes's ambitions and achievements that was hard to bridge whilst still on British soil. Although he had all but abandoned the notion of emigrating, the opportunity of work in America continued to provide him with the kind of access to new developments largely denied his colleagues. His next visit – in exchange for Ben Webster – was scheduled for late November. After the inconsistent nature of his life and work since the break-up of the quintet, the trip couldn't come soon enough.

This time around Hayes's itinerary was far more widespread: a week at Boston's Jazz Workshop with a local trio, a guest spot at the Tavern in Toronto, a week at the Half Note and finally an appearance at the Kings and Queens Club in Providence, Rhode Island. Ahead of the gig in Boston, he spent an intoxicating few days in New York, sitting in with Al Cohn and Zoot Sims and encountering John Coltrane's quartet just days ahead of its landmark recording of *A Love Supreme*.[30] The music Hayes had once found so incomprehensibly difficult was now proving addictive, as he told *Melody Maker*:

> I heard [Coltrane] three times altogether and it knocked me out. I love Coltrane. The thing with [him] is that he's doing tremendously well now. He's really the hottest thing going on in New York. The Half-Note was jam-packed every night, filled with those kids – I suppose they're college boys – wearing big sweaters with COLTRANE embroidered on the back. Truthfully, I don't know if they understand what he's doing. But they get really excited, and that's fair enough. I used to stand among them and hear them shouting out encouragement and so on. Of course, it's an exciting group. They play very long numbers and the music builds and builds. Trane's rhythm section is great, really amazing. I must agree that Elvin Jones is a bit loud, though, I don't mind that myself, because I don't mind loud drummers as long as they're doing something. [Coltrane] played a couple of soprano things – one of them My Favourite Things – that must have lasted about five hours.[31]

Hayes was due to follow Coltrane into the Half Note, an unappealing prospect given the American's near cult-like association with the venue. The biggest boost, however, was the opportunity to perform with pianist Cedar Walton, bassist Reggie Workman and drummer Albert "Tootie" Heath, a rhythm section he was later to describe as the best he'd ever worked with and which was able to offer the kind of ambitious stimulus he so badly lacked back home.

Although there was no official recording of Hayes made during this trip, a tape of the soundtrack of his appearance on the Boston TV show *Jazz* on November 27th has circulated among collectors (and has now been issued on the Fresh Sound label). Its contents are as valuable for Hayes's comments as they are for his playing. After effectively demolishing the parochial rhythm section of pianist Ray Santisi, John Neves and Joe Cocuzzo, the saxophonist is interviewed by trumpeter Herb Pomeroy, who raises the thorny issue of whether jazz remained a solely American preserve. "Let's face it, jazz has come from here," Hayes responds, "[but] a lot of people have an interest in Europe in jazz music and we've learnt a lot from the guys coming over. And now, as the guys get a chance to play with American musicians I think gradually they're evolving styles of their own. It takes time." Pomeroy's sincere question as to whether Hayes had ever incorporated elements of his native folk music into his work brings forth an altogether less focused answer: "There's one or two things that we do use but not at all as much as we might."

One wonders how the question would have been answered by Hayes's contemporaries, such as Bobby Wellins, whose tender sound was so evocative of his native Scotland, or by pianist Michael Garrick, whose liturgical and poetic collaborations drew upon the most English of temperaments. Indeed, herein lays the greatest contention against Hayes's bona fide qualifications as a truly "English-styled" jazz musician. The argument that his eminence had only been achieved via direct and at times near-slavish emulation was not a new one. Hayes had often been called to task for wearing his latest American influences a little too readily on his sleeve, but that was simply his way – as it was the way of virtually every other British jazzman who came to prominence during the 1950s.

In exploring this argument further, the analogous examples of contemporary pop music and cinema are also useful. During the 1950s, when Cliff Richard, Tommy Steele and others had proffered an Anglicized variant of rock and roll, British popular music had hardly ever brushed the antenna of American listeners. Only after the arrival of The Beatles, with their brilliantly distinctive and charmingly unspoiled compositional gift, had the US been alerted to the fact that Britain could be a serious contender, rather than simply a pallid emulator. The discovery of a personal "British" way of doing things had occurred almost by default, fuelled by the inevitable certainty that American rock and roll was best left to Americans. Ironically, this was the same sentiment Ronnie Scott had expressed when he'd earlier stated that "America needs British bands like Damascus needs a synagogue."

A similar revelation had occurred within the new wave of British filmmakers of the early 1960s. Films such as *Saturday Night, Sunday Morning*, *A Taste Of Honey* and *This Sporting Life* embraced Britain's everyday culture rather than ignored it and, without false glamour, enabled a generation to find both inspiration and entertainment from within their own surroundings. This near cottage-industry rationale was to be the key to England's ascendancy as a cultural mecca during the Swinging Sixties, allowing creative genius to take on a much more low-key, quintessentially British reserve. British *jazz*, however, was slow to take this on board. Indeed, there is an almost perverse irony in the fact that Tubby Hayes enjoyed his greatest success in America at a time when the best-known English exports – from *The Avengers* and James Bond, to Michael Caine and Mary Quant – were so wholly *un*-American. This observation does not arbitrarily render the work of Tubby Hayes (nor George Shearing, Victor Feldman, Marian McPartland and Eddie Thompson for that matter) irrelevant or lacking in individuality, but rather it highlights how he, like many of his peers, had largely persisted in contriving to be a jazz musician on American terms, even after the goalposts had been so very obviously moved. Nevertheless, somewhere within the ostensibly gritty language of hard bop that he had assimilated so well by the early 1960s lay a Britain of post-war dreariness, rainy one-nighters and transport cafes, a world away from New York's searing hipness.[32]

On January 25th, 1965, Hayes broadcast on the BBC's new programme *It's Jazz* with a line-up comprising Terry Shannon, Jeff Clyne and drummer Benny Goodman, a group typical of the ad-hoc units he had fronted since the break-up of the quintet. All hands play with tangible enthusiasm throughout the programme but the music now lacks something of the sharply defined character of the saxophonist's previous bands. Above all, it reveals how local impasses continued to thwart the leader's ambitions, especially on the closing 'So What'. Beginning with a loose, out-of-tempo bass intro-duction from Jeff Clyne, there then follows a free flute solo over the theme's two alternating modes. Neither Goodman nor Shannon appear especially comfortable during this passage, and only when Hayes takes the tempo up to his customary light-speed do things really begin to grip. Goodman's splashy drums, however, sound only just barely able to cope; and when the free-form explorations return towards the end of the piece – with Hayes using growling multi-phonics – the drummer sounds completely bewildered. A few weeks after his trip to New York, the saxophonist's head may well have been full of Coltrane but his ears were full of the sound of a band struggling to keep pace.

Even more is revealed on a recording made by the same quartet at Ronnie Scott's the following month. Rediscovered by drummer Clark Tracey in 2007, and subsequently released on his Tentoten label under the highly appropriate title of *Intensity*, the set is one of the most potent examples of Hayes's Herculean stamina ever to be issued on record, with one title, the flute feature 'Sometime Ago', nudging close to half an hour. Yet again, over long stretches of static harmony, there is a clear disparity between what Hayes appears to be aiming for and what his rhythm section are able to offer. Although, with its trills and harmonic side-slipping, the performance superficially echoes the whirling trances of Coltrane, neither Shannon nor Goodman are really in on the act and one occasionally senses that Hayes is carrying far more of the musical weight than he might have liked. A verbal reproof to Goodman – who doesn't really seem to grasp what's required to sustain such an extended effort – is clearly audible at one point and there are moments when the only aspect of the performance worthy of praise is Hayes's staying power, as if jazz had now become a game of attrition rather than creation.

Ambiguities also continued to feature in Hayes's personal life. Quite why he chose to play 'Souriya', the ballad dedicated to his wife Rose, on the January *It's Jazz* broadcast is uncertain, especially when one considers what was then happening to the couple's marriage.

With their affair now in full swing, Joy Marshall had wasted no time in telling her husband that the new lover she'd taken was none other than his sometime boss. King was left reeling. Ignoring Phil Bates's advice to "do the macho thing" and beat Hayes up, he consulted with Les Condon, who persuaded him that the most level-headed reaction would be to seek a divorce, something that would only be possible if he could irrefutably prove that Marshall was the guilty party. To do so, King hired a private detective, with the intention of catching his wife and Hayes together. To make matters even more difficult, the ensuing denouement was close to farcical. King faced not only the surreal situation of having to stake out his own flat early one morning, but also the embarrassment of being discovered doing so by several close colleagues including Harry South and Jimmy Deuchar.[33] Hayes's initial reaction was to tell King to "Fuck off!" but, despite the awkward circumstances, neither man really wanted their musical association to end, and eventually agreed to a truce. "It was a terrible time for me, but the music was far too important for both of us to let shit like that get in the way," King later wrote. "He was a lot 'harder' than me about stuff like that but, although it hurt like hell, I wasn't going to leave the [big] band because of it and Tubby didn't want me to."[34]

The big band's next gig was a TV recording for *Jazz 625* at the Shepherd's Bush Empire on January 31st, an occasion King remembers with a mix of embarrassment and amusement. Seated in the audience alongside Jimmy Deuchar's girlfriend Moira was Joy Marshall, enthusiastically applauding her new man. "You can see me looking like thunder," King remembered in 2002, "whilst Joy is sitting in the front row with a big smile on her face, digging Tubby – just another example of the music coming before everything."[35]

Originally transmitted in April 1965, the *Jazz 625* episode featuring the Tubby Hayes big band has since become *the* iconic on-screen representation of the leader's talents, thanks largely to a piece of bureaucratic neglect on the part of the BBC. As with all the programmes in the series, the show was due a contracted repeat which, for some unspecified reason, it never received during the 1960s. Then, when BBC2 screened its ambitious *Jazz On A Summer's Day* weekend, nearly twenty years later in July 1984, the programme received a surprise dusting down. As a result, video recorders country-wide were set and running, including in the house where the author grew up, resulting in his introduction to the music of Tubby Hayes.[36] Nearly fifty years after it was first shown, the show is still having an impact; after the launch of the online video sharing network YouTube in 2005, it has since been seen by thousands more viewers.

The programme is outstanding on many levels, not least of which is Terry Henebery's typically artful but unpretentious direction. Unlike a great many jazz television shows, *Jazz 625* didn't go for in for silly let's-try-and-be-trendy camera effects. Instead, the producer ensured that bands were both well photographed and well recorded. Henebery's genius with the TV format was also revealed in his recruitment of Humphrey Lyttelton as the show's compere. Replacing the more stilted Steve Race, Lyttelton's run as *Jazz 625's* regular presenter actually commenced with the Hayes episode and, as with his introductory duties on radio's *Jazz Club*, his humour was intended as much for the musician's amusement as for the watching nation. Introducing Hayes, he remarked: "Somebody once came up to me after a number in fact where I'd just played clarinet and he said 'Do you play more than one instrument to show off your virility?' This was obviously a slip of the tongue but if versatility and virility are the same thing then Tubby Hayes is a positive He-man."

All of the music (which includes several reruns of material from *Tubbs' Tours*) is outstanding, and is delivered with an enthusiasm and technical grasp that gives no indication whatsoever that the band existed only sporadically. And given the rare chance to see Hayes and his colleagues in action, one is drawn equally to the personalities within the band as to the music they play. In their Italian suits, Ivy League ties and brylcreemed hair, they look immaculate, a deeply ironic image given how untidy were many of their personal lives. Indeed, when one looks at this baker's dozen of young, handsome musicians, it's difficult to comprehend that the line-up comprises several heavy-duty drug users, more than a handful of alcohol abusers and at least one convicted criminal. One is instantly transported back to an age where even hedonists wore suits, combed their hair and looked like they fitted in: in fact, Hayes and his band now look as about as dangerous to know as a team of middle managers.

The leader himself is charismatic to a fault, and when, during a brief interview, he sidles his chubby frame next to Lyttelton's imposing figure one cannot help but find it amusing: the tower of mainstream next to the modernistic pocket battleship. Watching Hayes's wide grin and happy friendly face, it's impossible not to smile back at the screen. Looking sharp, professional, and not at all troubled, one is reminded again of how young he was to have already achieved so much. The day before filming the *Jazz 625* episode, he had celebrated his thirtieth birthday, an age when many young men are still getting their life together.

On February 20th, Hayes once more topped the *Melody Maker* poll. In a special four-page pull-out titled "Tubby Does It Again," Bob Dawbarn began his analysis of the results by stating "Tubby Hayes bestrides the British jazz scene like a colossus. Once again his name dominates the British section of the Readers' Jazz Poll. If winning five sections outright was not enough, he also came second among the big bands, composers and arrangers."[37] Although Hayes's monopoly was now almost to be expected, his situation was by no means unique. The results in virtually every other category told largely an identical story, dominated by a mix of the same old familiar names – John Dankworth, Ronnie Ross, Cleo Laine, Stan Tracey, Allan Ganley, etc. Each victory only added to the argument that modern jazz in Britain had become little more than a revolving exchange between performers who had established themselves years ago. Where *was* the new blood?[38]

Getting inside the music was now far less of a guessing game for fledgling players than it had been when Tubby Hayes had begun (and in 1965 school-teacher Bill Ashton founded the embryonic version of what would become his National Youth Jazz Orchestra dynasty). But getting into the jazz scene itself was still as much about faces fitting as musical suitability. Interviewed in *Crescendo* later that year, Hayes sounded uncharacteristically pessimistic about the potential of some of the newer players he had come across:

> It's getting very sad. There's a certain lack of talent. There's some young guys who can play a certain amount; but the ones that can really play, as much as you really want or need or require to make the thing? It's very sad, I'm afraid. Maybe there aren't enough places for them to play. Maybe the competition isn't fierce enough?[39]

Some young players found Hayes instantly encouraging – drummers Trevor Tomkins and Johnny Butts were just two of the newer faces that he employed during this time – but for others the saxophonist's exacting standards proved far harder to satisfy. "In this country if you're looking for a drummer," Hayes told *Crescendo*, "you might go down to a club, stand at the back and think: 'He sounds good.' You get up on the stand with him – he sounds bloody awful. You can't tell, really, by listening off the stand."[40]

For a few nights at Ronnie Scott's in the spring of 1965, Hayes had used John Stevens, the ex-RAF drummer he had met whilst touring in Germany three years earlier. Already a musician of considerable dynamism, Stevens was nevertheless still experiencing difficulty in breaking into the business. Working with Hayes – a particular hero – was far less comfortable than he had imagined. Indeed, writer Brian Priestley later recalled seeing Stevens successfully grind one of Hayes's steaming up-tempo expositions to a halt one night, much to the tenorist's ire. "I really felt I wasn't together enough, because of his speed and strength," the drummer later wrote apologetically. Nevertheless, Hayes had recognized his sincere itch to play: "I tried in a way to ask him for support, to ask if he had any advice, and all he said, in the nicest way, was for me just to play. He was totally encouraging, and really he was giving me the freedom I wanted. At that time not too many leaders would do that."[41] Stevens would return the favour when he recruited Hayes for the band Splinters during the early 1970s.

Fronting unrehearsed line-ups at Ronnie Scott's was one thing, but there were other frustrations. Virtually all of Hayes's other work in the West End had dried up. The Flamingo and Marquee had now all but abandoned their jazz policy in favour of R&B and suddenly he found his diary disarmingly littered with gigs at suburban outposts such as Peckham Rye, Barnes or Wembley. With so much of their available work petering out, the rancour many jazzmen felt towards popular music only continued to deepen. Each faction continued to eye the other over with a sour blend of contempt, envy and suspicion. To the rockers, the jazzmen were old hat (John Lennon once pointedly told George Melly "you're standing in our way!"[42]), while to the jazzmen the young pop stars were nothing less than opportunistic chancers who were conning everyone but them. Whether the Beat Boom had really spelled the end of the old order of learning your craft and working your way up the ladder remained moot, but it had certainly robbed the British jazz scene of something far more valuable – a new young audience. As Ronnie Scott's brief and half-hearted stab at an R&B policy had proved a few years earlier, it was senseless trying to win them back on their own terms. Why go to Gerrard Street to hear musicians tickling at the idiom when the real thing was available a few streets away? What was required was some form of musical go-between capable of getting both parties to the negotiating table. As 1965 began, finally just such a figure emerged.

The Beatles had been shifted from their number one chart spot at the start of the year by a twenty-something organist and vocalist with the unlikely name of Georgie Fame, whose single 'Yeh, Yeh', a cover of a composition featured by jazz singer Jon Hendricks, suggested that a Beat-mesmerized public were now prepared to take something a little more sophisticated. Fame's was no overnight success. He had been born Clive Powell in Lancashire in 1943 and his musical ambitions started early, emulating his piano-playing heroes Jerry Lee Lewis, Fats Domino and Little Richard whilst still at school. In the late 1950s he had auditioned for the legendary Larry Parnes – *the* star maker of early British rock – and had so impressed the impresario that when he organized a backing band for Billy Fury, The Blue Flames, the teenaged Clive Powell was on piano under his new stage name, Georgie Fame.

After Fury sacked his sidemen, Fame elected to take on their leadership and in March 1962 the band began a three-year residency at the Flamingo, attracting large crowds which included both a healthy share of London's burgeoning West Indian population and large numbers of visiting black American servicemen eager to hear music redolent of home. Despite this popularity, Fame also attracted his share of prejudice, not only from the established jazzmen who played opposite him at the club, but even from the management itself, later revealing that the prevalent use of Hammond organ on the Blue Flames' Flamingo shows was originally prompted by Jeff Kruger's refusal to let anyone other than his jazz artists touch the club's piano![43]

Although his shows catered primarily for those who wanted to party the night away, often aided by the latest line in uppers, Fame had quickly proved he was much more than a one-trick pony. He'd always loved jazz and spent most of his spare time listening to it, patterning his vocal skills after those of Mose Allison and the king of vocalese (the art of setting lyrics to jazz improvisations) Jon Hendricks. When 'Yeh, Yeh' reached number one, and the royalties started flowing, Fame realized that at last he might have the chance to make good his long-held ambition to break into jazz and record with a big band. Toying with exactly who to approach about his idea, a friend suggested

Harry South. Fame duly made his introduction, initially receiving a less than enthusiastic reaction. South had seen it all before – the teen sensation who really wanted to be a jazz singer was nothing new – but the young man's sincerity won him over. As the two men began discussing the big band project, they quickly found they had much in common, so much so that when the Blue Flames needed a new drummer South wasted no time in recommending his old Tubby Hayes band mate Bill Eyden. The appointment of one of Britain's best jazz musicians to what was then one of Britain's busiest popular acts at first raised a few eyebrows, but crucially it marked the beginning of a far less blinkered outlook from both sides. As Fame and Harry South laid plans for their album collaboration during the spring of 1965, the irony of the situation was not lost on the arranger. Fame had wanted to use South's big band, an aggregation which, like Tubby Hayes's similar line-up, existed more on love and luck than hard cash, and he was willing to finance the entire exercise himself. For so long derided and ridiculed, the pop world was now offering a totally unprecedented helping hand. Even hard-bitten cynics like Hayes couldn't fail to be moved. "He loves jazz and you can have some interesting discussions with him," the saxophonist said of Fame in *Melody Maker*. "What I like specially about Georgie Fame is that I can talk to him in my musical language and he understands and can advise me about the contemporary pop scene. A lot of pop artists you couldn't get through to."[44]

Any opportunity to escape the same old narrow-mindedness was welcome, and early in June Hayes flew out to Los Angeles to begin his fourth US visit. Due to open his two-week engagement at Shelly's Manne-Hole on June 8th, 1965, problems awaited him the instant he stepped off the plane. Although the American Federation of Musicians had once more successfully facilitated the exchange deal and there appeared to have been no musical objections to the visit, before Hayes could officially begin work he came up against a trip wire of red tape laid down by the Department of Immigration, responsible for the issue of the necessary work permit. On his three previous visits there had been no such problem but now the department demanded that Hayes "prove his stature as a musician,"[45] a sharp reminder of the make-or-break power of protectionist bureaucracy. The Manne-Hole's management was even reduced to brandishing Hayes's entry in Leonard Feather's *Encyclopedia of Jazz* before the government men finally acquiesced, barely a few hours before his first set.

Feather himself was on hand to review the opening night, which had reunited Hayes with Victor Feldman, and offered his comments variously in *DownBeat* and *Melody Maker*, drawing a somewhat ambiguous conclusion:

> [Hayes's] main influences appear to be pre-John Coltrane; in his sense of continuity there is something of the 1957–58 Sonny Rollins in his up-tempo work. At this writing [he] does not seem to have a strongly individual sound or style, though repeated hearings might very well alter this reaction. Regardless of this point, he does

convey an urgently compelling rhythmic sense on medium and up numbers and on such ballads as Spring Can Really Hang You Up The Most, he achieves a warm mood, though the effect was weakened by an overlong series of cadenzas used as a finale.[46]

Another ex-pat, George Shearing, joined the band on its final set for lengthy explorations of 'Nardis' and 'Soon' and was less cautious than Feather, telling the press: "Tubby is one of the most exciting musicians to come along in years. He could make a very good living over here. In fact, I hope he'll return and never go home."[47]

Like those he'd made to New York in previous years, the Los Angeles trip gave Hayes a useful barometer reading of the US jazz scene. Although he found the West Coast, with its concentration on studio session work, far less appealing than New York, the local musical fraternity nevertheless welcomed him with open arms, and there were a series of lengthy radio and television interviews, a situation unheard of back home. There were also other revelations that couldn't have possibly been acquired from his vantage point thousands of miles away in London. Old heroes like the former Clifford Brown tenorman Harold Land were now beginning to reflect the trends of post-Coltrane jazz and there was a clamour of local interest in the avant-garde saxophonist John Handy, a player yet to really make an impression on European audiences. Even Shelly Manne's venue proved to be something of a disappointment, totally unlike the smart Hollywood supper club he'd expected.

Never one of Hayes's favourite drummers, Manne himself turned out to be far more impressive in person ("so alive and swinging and sensitive, listening to what's going on") but as the run progressed it was Victor Feldman who created the most profound impact.[48] Deeply impressed by the domestic comfort that his former colleague now enjoyed, Hayes was agog at the workload that went into its upkeep. Feldman was rarely out of the studios, working up to fifteen hours a day on TV, film and jingle sessions covering everything from harpsichord to glockenspiel. Sitting together in the Californian sunshine, Feldman proposed that Hayes could have the same kind of existence should he move over, a suggestion that his old friend found less than attractive. Travelling halfway across the globe to become a studio musician had never been an ambition, however lucrative it might prove.

Whilst at the Manne-Hole, Leonard Feather also took the opportunity to interview Hayes about the discoveries of his visit. The saxophonist was especially keen to stress the difference in attitude found in men like Feldman, Monty Budwig and Colin Bailey to that encountered in his London colleagues: "The atmosphere over here somehow encourages a more enthusiastic attitude among musicians than I find at home. They're always ready to get on the bandstand. There's never any panic about rounding up the men to start a set."[49]

The audience's rapt attention was also something novel: "Back home, especially when it's local musicians playing – and even sometimes with Americans – the audiences sit back with that 'show me' attitude, waiting for the drummer to come in on the wrong beat or the sax player to squeak, so they can turn to the guy next to them and say 'I told you so!'"[50]

During the interview Hayes also countered Feather's sixty-four-thousand-dollar question about his mooted emigration. To the surprise of some, he didn't exactly bite off the veteran writer's hand: "Well, I might if the right job came along," he answered, reminding Feather of the financial shortcomings of Woody Herman's earlier offer. "I do pretty well on my own in London."[51]

Those who knew Hayes well could see the reasoning behind the reluctance, as Peter King explains:

> He was doing very well in England at this time and he also had a big career as a studio musician. He did a lot of recording sessions for commercial things, films, that type of thing. He had a very good career here. And I think it might have been a little "unknown quantity" when he went to America. I just think he had a good career here and could go to the States when he wanted to. Tubby felt comfortable in England. His success in America had brought him a lot of success in Britain as well. I guess he had the best of both worlds.[52]

By the mid-1960s Hayes was also working regularly in continental Europe, a situation that greatly supported the impression that his was now a truly international career. Almost immediately after the run at Shelly's Manne-Hole ended, he flew to Germany for a week-long series of rehearsal, recordings and broadcast performances for the German radio station NDR's Jazz Workshop series. As on his two previous NDR sessions in 1963, the band was another multinational affair, and among its sprawling line-up were regular colleagues Keith Christie, Ronnie Ross, Johnny Scott and Ronnie Stephenson, American stars Benny Bailey, Jimmy Woode, Leo Wright and Stuff Smith, and several leading European jazzmen such as Roger Guerin, Ake Persson and Hans Koller. For his part, Hayes had been commissioned to contribute a new composition and arrangement, designed as a solo feature for his tenor playing. In the few short days between his return from Los Angeles and his arrival in Recklinghausen, he feverishly worked on something akin to a mini saxophone concerto. Not long before, trumpeter Ian Hamer had suggested that he'd like to write an extended showcase for his leader. Always better suited to cutting his own musical cloth, Hayes thought he could do a far more effective job, and, as usual, he was right.

Titled '100% Proof', Hayes's new concert work ranged across various tempos and moods, as well as embracing some prototypical free improvisation, and a surviving copy of its debut performance makes a useful prequel to the official recording made for Fontana a year later. Everything we now know of from that later version is essentially in place, albeit in somewhat embryonic form, with Hayes tying the disparate sections together with unaccompanied cadenzas that at times sound like a glorious head-on collision between Sonny Rollins and Stan Getz. Understandably for a new work, there are moments of confusion, but perhaps what is most noteworthy about the performance is how well Hayes had turned the drawback of a lack of suitable preparation time into a positive musical virtue. Indeed, '100% Proof' was a piece that relied almost entirely on the soloist's ability to extract the maximum of creative inspiration out of a limited harmonic sequence and do so over considerable length. Quite simply, it couldn't be done without a soloist of Hayes's stature; moreover, without a soloist of his creative ability, critical attention might have been drawn to the fact that the band *en masse* actually get very little to do. As such, it is impossible to describe the actual orchestration as among the greatest examples of Hayes's musical craftsmanship (it could be argued that it is the most overtly egocentric of all his creations); but, given that the effectiveness of the piece was almost wholly governed by whatever sort of creative mood the soloist was in at the time, the various versions Hayes recorded over the remainder of his life are highly useful in gauging his inspirations at the time. The version from Recklinghausen reveals a player almost in conflict with himself, striving to incorporate some of the latest musical trends but still adhering to the traditions of the bop idiom. Reconciling these approaches was to test both Hayes and his audience in the years immediately ahead.

After the wide-open opportunities of California and Germany, Hayes faced a disappointing return to the tired old closed shop. His affection for London itself remained as strong as ever – after all it was the jungle of which he remained the undisputed king – but it now hard for him to disguise his disgust at the disparity between home and abroad. In an interview with Les Tomkins published in *Crescendo* the following autumn, he spoke candidly about the after-effects of his visits to America:

> You come back with renewed enthusiasm because of the competition you've been faced with, especially in New York. It does gee you up a bit. You can't afford to coast. You've got to be on top form or try and be. I'm not putting England down, or London down, or any of the musicians down but I do think that the environment tends to make you a little complacent at times, and that includes myself when I'm here for too long.[53]

It was clear that Hayes's position as an international jazz commuter had now placed him once more in a one-horse race. No other British jazzman had his sort of career and accordingly no one could really empathize with the disappointment he felt returning to a jazz scene that remained so unhealthily insular. Musical inconsistency didn't help matters. His ad-hoc quartet with Terry Shannon, Jeff Clyne and Ronnie Stephenson continued its sporadic existence, but the reaction it met was now increasingly one of familiarity rather than awe.[54] When he enlisted Gordon Beck's trio for a series of gigs that August, two years on from their last appearances together, the pianist found his old boss a changed man, eaten up by frustration and unable to hide his feelings. "[He was] going from bad to worse, drinking more and more and becoming increasingly depressed. He became bitter and angry. He was a big star at 16 but when his popularity started to slip he couldn't handle it."[55]

Beck's trio were a luxury that wasn't always available. That same month yet another impromptu team comprising Brian Dee, Malcolm Cecil and Johnny Butts were pulled together for a brief northern tour, taking in Blackpool, Leeds and Manchester, the reviews of which reveal both the typical journalistic prejudices of the time and the saxophonist"s increasingly jaded attitude: Hayes had become formulaic, self-indulgent, even tedious. *Jazz Journal's* Steve Voce was in the audience for the quartet's gig at Manchester's Club 43 and, in a revealing account of the evening written for his regular "It Don't Mean a Thing" column, he described how Hayes had even resorted to a none-too-subtle method of hushing a blasé crowd: "During a long and boppy flute cadenza, [he] leant over to the mic and said 'I'm not boring you, am I?'"[56]

Hayes's itinerary over the first few weeks of the autumn of 1965 was hectic, but by no means unusually so. He flew to Munich on September 5th and began an eleven-day tour with Friedrich Gulda, with whom he'd worked the previous year, criss-crossing Germany and Austria with an all-star edition of the pianist's band featuring J. J. Johnson, Joe Zawinul, Freddie Hubbard, Ron Carter and Mel Lewis. Upon his return to the UK, the pace was no less frenetic. On the night of his arrival back from Austria he appeared at Ronnie Scott's club before boarding the train for Liverpool in order to play a Commonwealth Arts Festival concert opposite Cleo Laine and John Dankworth. Immediately after, he took the sleeper train to Glasgow for the next day's gruelling schedule: a whole day filming for a TV show with Dankworth before another Commonwealth-themed gig that same evening. He then took an overnight train back to London in order to rehearse his quartet ahead of a gig at the Bull's Head in Barnes. Added to this, he'd received a commission to write several orchestral arrangements for a planned trip to Stuttgart the following month. Although he approached the combined logistical and musical demands placed upon him cheerfully enough, inevitably something had to give. The week after his return from Scotland, Hayes suddenly collapsed.

The problem, of course, was simply one of over-work. Hayes's appetite for the job in hand was now having to combine with increasingly overstretched commitments. No longer able to rely on the UK jazz scene to make a living, he found himself – in his own words – "forced" to become a jazz commuter. As satisfying as the musical dividends were, they were clearly outweighed by the physical rigours. *Melody Maker* ran the story of the collapse under the headline "Tubby: Just How Much Work Can a Man Do?" and listed in full the overflowing itinerary he had honoured in the weeks leading up to the collapse. "It's hardly surprising that even someone with Tubby's iron constitution just flaked out," Bob Dawbarn wrote. "Most lumberjacks would collapse under the strain. Yet I've never heard Tubby give a substandard performance or even talk with anything less than enthusiasm about his work." The piece closed with the light-hearted but prophetic notion that "at this rate the MM Pollwinner for 1970 will be one Slim Hayes."[57]

Taking things easy was the only solution but for Hayes the suggestion that he should let up was laughably impractical. Nevertheless, some observers saw – or *thought* they saw – distinct signs of a public slowdown in the days following his collapse. On September 29th he played a further Commonwealth Arts Festival gig at the Royal Festival Hall, sharing the same bill as Joe Harriott's quintet, John Dankworth's big band and Maynard Ferguson. With typical festival timing, Harriott had over-run and Hayes's quartet was relegated to the task of mopping up whatever was left of the first half. As a contrast to the fiery outpourings of the preceding bands, the leader elected to play a ballad – "the longest version of Stella By Starlight ever heard – the lady really lingered," according to *Crescendo*[58] – but much to his disgust the decision to play something more thoughtful was reported as a musical cop-out.[59]

For the time being he retreated to the studio. That autumn, under the leadership of Sonny Rollins, he took part in the soundtrack to the Michael Caine film *Alfie*, a job far removed from the usual hack work of movie sessions, and he also participated in yet more recording for the still incomplete Georgie Fame/Harry South album. Even though the LP was still far from finished, news of Fame's big band collaboration had already begun to cause ripples. The Newcastle group The Animals, one of the earthiest of all the bands to have come up during the Beat Boom, had followed suit by launching their own big band venture at the Richmond Festival that summer. Key figures such as Kenny Wheeler, Dick Morrissey and Stan Robinson had been aboard and, rather than take it as a blow-and-go opportunity, even the jazzmen seemed eager for the project to succeed.[60] Purists, however, were outraged. When it was announced that the Spencer Davis Group and Georgie Fame[61] would be included at the annual Jazz Jamboree held at Hammersmith that November, the news proved too much for some jazz fans.

"Somebody has got his priorities mixed," wrote one irritable *Crescendo* reader after the concert. "After all, it is the Jazz Jamboree. Keep the Jamboree going, but let's have jazz, not rock groups."[62]

The letter also expressed alarm that Hayes had been allotted only two numbers in the closing set. Reaction had been polarized: *Crescendo*'s reviewer thought the Commonwealth Jazz Orchestra, a new and short-lived edition of Hayes's big band based around players from the dominions, "little more than a backdrop for ... all the usual virtuosity. Almost blasé, in fact,"[63] whereas *Melody Maker* printed a review titled "Tubby Takes the Honours at Jamboree": "Tubby's performance, as the show overran by half an hour, was a superb climax. His solo on 100% Proof was exciting, authoritative and brilliantly conceived."[64]

For some of those hearing '100% Proof' for the first time at Hammersmith the impression was lasting. Saxophonist Bob Sydor, then a member of the newly formed National Youth Jazz Orchestra, and soon to become one of Hayes's few pupils, remembers the performance as "even better" than the later studio recording, with Hayes "on fire."[65] The combustion didn't stop there. That same evening Hayes jammed with trumpeter Freddie Hubbard and pianist Jaki Byard at the Bull's Head. The two Americans had been stranded on their way back from Europe, and, as a surviving recording made by Ian Hamer reveals, Hayes wasn't content to let them take an easy night off. Indeed, the pace throughout the evening was blistering, culminating in a version of 'Cherokee' on which Peter King also vies for honours. Barely a few weeks after his collapse, Hayes was clearly not prepared to take things any easier.[66]

The sheer physicality of Hayes's music at this point is well documented on a recording made by Les Tomkins on December 11th, the closing night of the old Ronnie Scott's club in Gerrard Street. The mood was that of a party, with everyone celebrating the expansion of Scott's empire to encompass the bigger premises in nearby Frith Street.[67] Although the proprietor joins Hayes and the Gordon Beck trio for a lengthy impromptu blues which recalls the days of the Couriers, it is the quartet's set proper that includes the best performances of the night. One track from the session, Hayes's arrangement of the Schwartz–Dietz standard 'By Myself', was made commercially available in 2004, and its fierce, unbridled energy make it among the most potent of the saxophonist's recordings from the period.[68]

The arrangement itself gives away the key inspiration: maintaining an engrossing pattern of tension and release by using a whole-tone scale alternating with more conventional harmony, it closely shadows John Coltrane's transformation of 'Summertime' from the album *My Favourite Things*. Although Hayes makes the most of this dual approach, his exceedingly elongated improvisation contains little that directly echoes Coltrane. The tone is altogether rounder, and his marriage of songful lines and pecking rhythmic figures again makes it occasionally sound as if Stan Getz and Sonny Rollins have miraculously coalesced in one musical body. Underlining everything, however, whether Hayes is playing inside the harmony as only he could, or taking full advantage of the free-play available during the modal passages, is the sheer passion with which he plays. Informal though the recording is, it is almost as if Hayes unwittingly chose to close his 1965 discography with a taster of what was to come.

9 Addictive Tendencies (1966–67)

When I joined the band, he put his arm around me and said "Fantastic! At last I've got a drinking buddy!"

Ron Mathewson

The beginning of the New Year was surprisingly quiet. Quiet enough, in fact, for Hayes to take a breather, something his ridiculous itinerary now rarely allowed. Joy Marshall had just begun two weeks of cabaret work in Birmingham with pianist John Patrick's trio, and, with a few free days at his disposal, Hayes decided to tag along. Inactivity, however, rarely agreed with him and after a few days off he'd grown restless.[1] Looking for somewhere to blow, on the night of Friday January 14th Patrick took him along to the Aero club at Birmingham airport, where his itchy-fingered house guest was assured there was a group more than competent enough to allow him a satisfying sit-in.

The club's featured act that night was a local semi-professional outfit headed by a twenty-five-year-old drummer, Tony Levin. Born in January 1940, Levin had grown up in Birmingham, and had shown such impressive musical potential that by his late teens he was dividing his time between a day job in his father's home furnishing store, and work across the Midlands and the north of England in a quartet led by a formidable local saxophonist, Johnny Collins, often supporting visiting players including Ronnie Scott, Kathy Stobart and Ronnie Ross.

Although his first hero had been Louie Bellson, Levin had quickly moved on through the influences of Philly Joe Jones, Art Blakey and Roy Haynes up to Elvin Jones, becoming one of the first British players to pick up on the latter's singular message. He also knew Tubby Hayes's music well. "He was my favourite saxophone player in Britain," he later confessed. "I don't think I ever wanted to play with anyone [else on the British jazz scene] other than him"[2] and so when Hayes took to the stand at the Aero club that cold January night in 1966, Levin was "delighted, especially when he chose to play with us a very fast number called Cherokee."[3] But whilst the resident group probably thought there was nothing more to the night than an informal blow, Hayes himself quickly realized that it had transpired to be a covert audition: "Immediately I realized that the drummer was just the type of player that I was looking for," he wrote later. "We played for over an hour and I deliberately took him through all sorts of 'changes'."[4]

After months of headaches over rhythm section personnel, there was a certain irony in Hayes's discovery: he had at last found his ideal drummer a hundred miles away from London and with both a successful daytime career and a young family. Nevertheless, at the end of the night, he made a point of taking Levin's phone number, asking him whether he'd consider joining a new quartet he was planning. The drummer didn't need asking twice.

With Levin's recruitment, Hayes had finally realized that the solutions to his musical dilemmas might be found not in the "closed shop" of colleagues whose work he knew only too well, but in far less obvious places.

He next turned to the band of Alexis Korner in order to find the quartet's new bassist, Danny Thompson, a player who'd previously been a member of his own student orchestra. In fact, by 1966, Korner's band was operating as something of a finishing school for future Tubby Hayes sidemen, among them Mike and Chris Pyne, Ray Warleigh, Brian Smith and Alan Skidmore. Despite playing music that for all intents and purposes was the diametric opposite of Hayes's über-modernism, each of these younger players was well aware of the importance of their future employer. Brian Smith remembers Korner's band appearing opposite Hayes's group sometime around 1965, and recalls the saxophonist standing and listening whilst he played, perhaps earmarking him for future use. Danny Thompson's gifts had proved equally ear-grabbing. A remarkably robust-sounding performer, with a style pitched somewhere between Charles Mingus and Jimmy Garrison, Thompson's energy and drive made him an ideal candidate for a demanding horn player like Hayes. However, after the relaxed work ethic of Korner, Thompson found the saxophonist a formidable task master, demanding total physical and emotional commitment on the stand ("the rhythm section was his engine-room"[5]) and ready to openly chastize what he saw as weak performance. Indeed, the sheer energy necessary in keeping up with his new leader forced Thompson to develop his own wrist exercises in preparation for each gig.[6]

But whereas the bassist had been instantly pitched in with his new boss's London-centric workload, Tony Levin had simply sweated out his time awaiting Hayes's phone call: "I didn't hear anything more for about three weeks," he remembered. "Then he phoned me about a job in Swansea which started everything."[7] That first gig, early in March 1966, also marked the end of Terry Shannon's time as Hayes's regular accompanist. The ending of such a close partnership was never going to be easy. Ever since the days of the Brixton Hill parties, Shannon had been Hayes's piano player of choice and, even when his poor sight-reading abilities made him something of a liability, the saxophonist had stayed loyal. In the final weeks of their association, Danny Thompson recalled that Hayes had resorted to teaching the pianist new material by singing it to him,[8] but by the spring of 1966 the air of frustration between the two men could no longer be ignored. As creative as he may have been, Shannon remained a dyed-in-the-wool hard bopper and had not been quick to reflect the post-Evans/Tyner/Hancock shifts in his instrument's capabilities, something Hayes saw as necessary for any musical move forward. The pianist's burgeoning drink and drug problems were also now well out of hand[9] and on the morning of their departure for the gig at Swansea University – a journey that in the pre-M4 1960s necessitated leaving London at around ten o'clock – Shannon was nowhere to be seen. Hayes had little time to fix a replacement and the only solution appeared to be Danny Thompson's unlikely suggestion of Mike Pyne, a player who he had hitherto only encountered giving Tatumesque solo recitals in the intervals at Jackie Sharpe's Downbeat Club. One can imagine the journey down to Wales was full of anxiety: how on earth would a florid mainstream solo pianist sound within a post-bop line-up? Hayes needn't have worried. Pyne's natural ability – regardless of style – was then still something of an underground secret in London jazz circles, but the Swansea gig proved he was clearly capable of anything from the tightest of hard bop grooves to the fringes of the avant-garde. The leader was delighted and, by the time the band arrived back in London in the early hours of the following morning, Hayes had the final key piece of his musical jigsaw firmly in place.

Five years Hayes's junior, Mike Pyne had been born and raised in Yorkshire, alongside his jazz-loving brother Chris. As children both had started on piano, receiving tuition at a local convent school, but by their teens they had become fascinated with American revivalist jazz, with Mike quickly opting for the cornet and Chris favouring the trombone. As time wore on the siblings' musical tastes began to broaden into more mainstream and modern styles. Finally, the revelation of hearing a recording by Art Tatum convinced Mike that the piano was his true musical voice and at the very tail end of the 1950s he decided to make a go of things in London. He stayed only briefly, later describing the experience as "pretty terrible."[10] A return to Yorkshire for a period of intense practice followed.

By the time he arrived back in the capital in 1965, Bill Evans had become the guiding light for both Pyne's playing and composing, and his first trio gigs – played to small audiences and with fees to match – were with a unit aiming for something similar to the classic Evans–La Faro–Motian line-up. Despite working in virtual obscurity, Pyne nevertheless found himself in exactly the right environment to soak up new ideas: when a flat became available in the Sinclair Road block rented by his brother Chris, bassist Ron Mathewson and altoist Ray Warleigh, he moved in. Life in such a concentrated nucleus of musical experimentation meant that virtually everything else went by the wayside, including domestic niceties, as Ron Mathewson remembers: "It was incredible. Mike and Chris were totally unalike. Chris's room would be all neat and tidy, with everything in its place. Mike's was a tip, full of newspapers and magazines, records, music, everything. You couldn't move. He just lived for music."[11]

As the new quartet's engagements got under way, all three of the saxophonist's young sidemen realized the catalytic power of their leader. "Tubby has brought me out," Tony Levin told Mark Gardner in an interview for the *Birmingham Sunday Mercury* that spring. "I feel I'm playing cleaner and louder [as] Tubbs likes a loose beat behind him."[12] The drummer later remarked that he felt a thorough familiarity with Hayes on record had helped his quick integration into the new band, drawing a comparison between Tony Williams practising with Miles Davis's albums before joining the trumpeter's quintet.[13]

As had been the case with all his previous piano recruits, nightly exposure to Hayes's towering musical example had also begun to affect Mike Pyne: "When you play with someone like that regularly, it's bound to rub off on you,"[14] he later observed, adding that Hayes's high musical standards had provided an instant inspirational benchmark: "He imposed that 100 per cent and if you weren't up to it, then you weren't up to it and that was it, he would let you know. But if you were up to it, he would just give you free rein really."[15]

Until the discovery of live tapes from Nottingham's Dancing Slipper ballroom was made in 2005, exactly how the first edition of the 1966 Tubby Hayes quartet had sounded remained something of a mystery. Dating from

The new Tubby Hayes Quartet, The Ritz, Bournemouth, Friday April 22, 1966. Left to right: Tony Levin, Mike Pyne, Tubby, Danny Thompson. Courtesy Chris Bolton Levin.

the night of Monday March 28th, the recordings catch the band on what was one of its first out-of-town engagements, forming part of a short tour of the Midlands spanning into early April. As well as providing yet another unexpurgated example of Hayes's in-person impact, they also plug something of a gap in his existing discography.[16] At the time he appeared in Nottingham, Hayes's most recent album release was *Tubbs' Tours*, issued over a year before and featuring music a world away from what he was now playing. Indeed, one can imagine that the saxophonist's newly energized style may well have come as something of a surprise that night, even to his regular followers.

Throughout the recording (issued on CD by the Harkit label) the single domineering influence of John Coltrane looms large. Having all but the slenderest thread connecting it to the soulful ballad reading Hayes had recorded four years previously on *Return Visit*, the opening version of 'Alone Together' instantly sets the tone for the entire gig. The thundering D minor vamp sections, the leader's frequent movement outside the basic tonality of the piece, Pyne's powerful, Tyner-esque comping (despite being saddled with a badly out-of-tune club instrument) and Levin's bustling, Elvin Jones-like drum commentary are all pointers towards the Coltrane influence. Danny Thompson even echoes the patented unaccompanied introductions favoured by Jimmy Garrison on a marathon 'A Taste Of Honey', a performance that quickly turns into a swirling dervish-dance in the manner of 'My Favourite Things'. Intriguingly, Coltrane's inspiration even touches the one tenor saxophone ballad played that night, 'Spring Can Really Hang You Up The Most', containing a startling passage that directly echoes the saxophonist's famous "sheets of sound" approach from the late 1950s.[17]

The closing 'What Is This Thing Called Love' is taken as an absurdly fast feature for Levin, who plays superbly throughout; it is perhaps the only item wholly reminiscent of the "old" Hayes, although even this is appended with a thrashing freak-out ending drawing from the most potent parts of the avant-garde.

Oddly though, beneath the surface gloss of full-on American-styled authenticity there nevertheless remains something unquestionably British about the Nottingham session, a quality Phil Johnson picked up on when reviewing the CD release for the *Independent on Sunday*: "Had John Coltrane served his apprenticeship with Bert Ambrose rather than Dizzy Gillespie," Johnson perceptively observed, "this is what he might have sounded like."[18]

A good indication of Hayes's artistic thinking at this time – and of how he was attempting to balance his need for accountable musical accuracy with a new-found appetite for freedom – can be found in the joint interview he and his tenor-playing opposite number with Woody Herman, Sal Nistico, gave Les Tomkins for *Crescendo* on March 12th. His biggest concern was that his immense technical command and harmonic ear were seemingly of little use in unravelling the new wave of modern jazz. He told Nistico:

The way it's going towards playing "free" these days, I find that everything I've been practising over the years is no help to me. In the last year I've felt, not that I'm playing badly, but that, having played a certain way for fifteen years in the business, I've come to this wall now. I don't want to carry on coasting along the way I've been playing. I'm only thirty one – I see no reason to give in now. I'm young enough to keep on into something else. But, at the same time, I don't want to just go and play completely another way just for the sake of it. There seem to be a lot of younger musicians here who are trying to be different for the sake of being different, without actually knowing the roots. They think jazz started with Ornette Coleman, and anything that went before they don't know about.[19]

Coleman returned to the UK the following month to play a season at Ronnie Scott's. Whilst London hadn't quite got over the sensational concert the altoist had given at Croydon the previous summer, the prospect of seeing him unfurl his gifts night after night in a club setting looked like it might provide a better opportunity for a more balanced critique. The booking also spoke volumes about Scott's own lack of prejudice. Coleman was sharing the bill with Joy Marshall, consequently enabling Tubby Hayes to hear more of the new music than he'd ever done before. Nearly six years since the altoist's records had first appeared in Britain, he still found his playing largely unappealing: "A lot of it sounded pretty basic," he told *Melody Maker*. "Unfortunately, I found it a little boring at times. I think his earlier groups were more interesting than this one, but they did create some startling moods. Not happy moods though."[20]

Nevertheless, Hayes's own curiosity about new musical methods – the desire to break away from "coasting" he had expressed to Nistico – was now taking him down some unconventional paths. John Stevens, the drummer he had met in Cologne in 1961, and for whom Ornette Coleman represented a musical fountainhead, had recently opened a new venue, the Little Theatre Club in St Martins Lane, just off Trafalgar Square, with the emphasis strongly on musical adventure. At first no one knew exactly what to make of it all. "We were all a bit sceptical of the free guys back then," Peter King remembers. "I guess Tubby was not too keen on the British [avant-garde] guys at first but he was not the kind of guy to dismiss music if it developed into something important. He liked to keep up with anything new, if he considered it to be of value."[21] Indeed, word of Stevens's new venture had soon reached London's jazz establishment and, in the weeks following the Little Theatre's launch, intrigued visitors begun to drop by. Some, like Kenny Wheeler and Jeff Clyne, decided to stay, but even elder statesmen like Hayes and Phil Seamen also showed a passing interest. Saxophonist Trevor Watts recalls an inspirational visit the two men paid to the club soon after it opened: "Both he and Phil

[Seamen] came up to the Little Theatre Club and played. Not suddenly free music but standards in an open way. Just sax and drums, as I remember. And that was great to see and hear."[22]

All over London, there were other young players who, although they would eventually become regarded for music quite unlike that of Hayes and his peers, continued to find the older man's example inspirational. Elton Dean, like Trevor Watts another of the new wave of powerful young jazz saxophonists, remembered his first encounter with Hayes as a meeting engendering the deepest musical respect: "I had just bought my first saxophone – a tenor – and found myself in Ronnie's, Gerrard Street, listening to this dapper, portly gentleman who called himself Tubby. I had never heard such flawless fluency from anybody before this evening and I remember saying to my partner that I could never be as good as this guy."[23] Tenor and soprano saxophonist Evan Parker was another Little Theatre alumnus who had been tremendously moved by Hayes, as much for his off-stage attitude as for his "non-negotiable" playing. Meeting him after a concert at Birmingham University, Parker was "very impressed by Tubby taking his glove off to shake my hand when we said goodbye."[24]

But with clear idiomatic differences between the music of the newer jazzmen and those within Hayes's circle it was unsurprising that a certain amount of critical division arose. One of the most individual of the new wave of local jazzmen, pianist Howard Riley, summed up the situation thus:

> That generation of mine were the first to say "OK, we all acknowledge our debt to America but we've got to find our own voice" and I think that this was the big difference between my generation and what preceded it. Whereas before there had been a general accepted styling or way of playing jazz, like bebop. Tubby Hayes obviously added his own thing to it but he was the best at doing *that*.[25]

Escaping the dominant influence of America was by no means an easy or permanent achievement. As Tubby Hayes's playing entered another purple patch in mid-1966, there was a certain irony accompanying the renewed vigour. In a radio interview that summer, he spoke of his desire to play with a rhythm section that sounded like that of Herbie Hancock, Ron Carter and Tony Williams, then working with Miles Davis. It seemed an innocent enough remark[26] (and an ambition he would by and large realize with the continued employment of players such as Mike Pyne and Tony Levin); however, some perceptive observers thought otherwise: aged thirty-one, and with an independent professional career stretching back a decade and a half already behind him, shouldn't Hayes have stopped all the transatlantic tail-chasing by now? He was by no means the only British player to find it a difficult habit to shake off. Ronnie Scott's close proximity to the visiting American soloists at his club meant that, even as late as in his early forties, he was still passing through periods wherein it was possible to detect the latest first-hand influence. A saxophonist of similar age and experience nowadays might raise more than a few disapproving eyebrows. "It's about time people stopped pretending that British jazz is nearly as good as that played in the States," wrote *Melody Maker* reader John Bright around this time, bravely voicing concerns that many were turning a blind eye to. "There are at least fifty tenor players in America better than Tubby Hayes, Ronnie Scott and Dick Morrisey [sic]. Each of these musicians plays like a middle-aged man. Have they never heard of John Coltrane or Ornette Coleman?"[27]

Although there was a kernel of truth in Bright's argument, his outburst had failed to take account of the one crucial aspect in which players like Hayes and Scott differed from Coltrane and Coleman. By 1966 a leading light like Coltrane was in a position to make performing with his own group his sole musical outlet and no longer had to play on sessions by other leaders (something he'd done a great deal of in the 1950s) or under compromised circumstances of any kind. Indeed, that very same year he had announced his intention to abandon playing in club settings, preferring now to work only as a concert artist. The UK jazz scene, however, remained far more contained, with players far less able to stipulate their working conditions. Nor was there the amount of work available, or the proliferation of venues, for even the best of local talent, Tubby Hayes included, to sustain themselves on jazz alone. Although he had managed to ensure that his reputation as an improviser remained intact, by the mid-1960s Hayes's public visibility had already begun to decrease, contributing to an already fast-fermenting bitterness. "I'm forced to make my living in the recording studios," he told journalist Pauline Clark at this time[28] and, interviewed by Derek Jewell in the *Sunday Times* in November 1966, he spoke passionately of his reluctance to "settle for being a session man." "I want to play jazz, more than ever now."[29] The conflict of desire and opportunity was to all but demolish him in the years ahead.

For all his appetite for musical change, some of the conventions of the business still held their fascination for Hayes, and in early May 1966 he succeeded in pulling off something of a coup, securing five days of work for his revamped big band, including the recording of a new album.[30]

Boasting no fewer than eighteen players, the relaunched Tubby Hayes band which debuted that spring was actually a far more ambitious proposition than its predecessor. Although his previous big bands had always been built around those players in his regular small groups, Hayes's new quartet sidemen lacked the necessary experience and might have sat rather at odds with the cream of London's jazz-based session men. Consequently, the new unit's personnel was a mix of old familiar faces and the odd smattering of new blood: Kenny Baker, Greg Bowen, Ian Hamer, Les Condon and Kenny Wheeler comprised the trumpet section, the trombones featured Keith Christie, Johnny Marshall,

Nat Peck and Chris Smith and the saxophones (doubling woodwind) included Roy Willox, Ray Warleigh, Bob Efford, Ronnie Scott and Ronnie Ross. The line-up was completed by a failsafe rhythm section of Gordon Beck, Jeff Clyne and Ronnie Stephenson.

An appropriately overflowing crowd attended the band's first shake-down gig at the Bull's Head in Barnes[31] on the night of Monday May 9th, 1966 and the following morning the new unit assembled at Philips Studios to record the first of three sessions for a new Fontana album.

Producer Terry Brown intended the new LP to be a tribute to some of Hayes's favourite jazzmen, Sonny Rollins, Miles Davis, Milt Jackson, Thelonious Monk, Victor Feldman and Jimmy Deuchar amongst them. As with his previous big band album *Tubbs' Tours*, the leader had been democratic with the arranging duties, perhaps due in this instance as much to time pressures as to musical favouritism. Stan Tracey was an appropriate choice to arrange Thelonious Monk's 'Nutty' whilst Ian Hamer was asked to contribute scores of 'Night In Tunisia' and 'Sonnymoon For Two', the latter designed as a tenor joust for the leader and Ronnie Scott. Both men remembered their commissions as very eleventh-hour affairs. Indeed, the suggestion that the entire project was something of a collaborative dash for the finishing line can be felt when looking at the surviving manuscript covers of Hayes's own scores, bearing a bold signature in his own hand and the date May 1966.

In order to compile the best possible selection of material from the sessions, Hayes took home tape copies of the entire three days' worth of recordings at Philips, a decision favouring posterity. When the resulting album *100% Proof* was finally reissued on CD in 2005, no bonus material was included. However, during the research for this biography the author was privy to the complete batch of tapes from these sessions, including several alternate takes and three new pieces not included on the original LP. The sequence of these recordings also reveals the unique way in which the final album was assembled.

The first session on Tuesday May 10th began with three takes of Hayes's arrangement of Milt Jackson's 'Bluesology', intended as a feature for his vibraphone and Scott's tenor. The piece was to be Hayes's last recorded outing on his first instrumental double. While he was quite happy to incorporate the latest innovations into both his saxophone and flute playing, keeping pace with the work of the vibraphone's new stars such as Gary Burton and Bobby Hutcherson appears to have held little appeal to him. There were other, altogether more practical, considerations too. Studio session work had found Hayes increasingly being required to play all manner of tuned percussion – from glockenspiel and marimba – something he'd never envisaged nor particularly enjoyed ("Jeezus – you gotta hire a truck!" commented Sal Nistico on this absurd situation).[32] Tony Levin also remembered another reason for the cull: "He told me that every time he touched the vibes this metal stuff came off on his hands and when he picked up his horn his hands didn't feel right, so he decided he wasn't going to do it anymore."[33]

Next up on the first session was Hayes's score of Victor Feldman's composition for Miles Davis, 'Seven Steps To Heaven', written, according to its composer, in his car between sets at a Californian club. The arrangement was nailed in a single take, with a flowing tenor solo from the leader and a skittish flugelhorn contribution from Kenny Wheeler. Only time constraints can have necessitated the excising of what is an otherwise excellent performance from the original album release.

The penultimate number of the day was the master take of Ian Hamer's chart of 'Sonnymoon For Two', with the reunited Jazz Couriers front-line engaging in friendly-fire combat. The session closed with Ian Hamer's second score for the album, 'Night In Tunisia', recast as a flute feature. Yet again the leader delivers a virtuoso performance, broken only by the arranger's somewhat incoherent improvisation. Familiar to listeners to the original album, Hayes's incredible cadenza – with its use of Roland Kirk's singing-and-playing technique – apparently didn't satisfy his high standards and at the close of play he attempted an edit piece with the intention that it be spliced in ("I'll just do a little bit of tootling, babada babada, splosh"). However, as is so often the case on studio recordings, while the retake results are spirited enough they lack the freshness of the original, and consequently the edit was never used.

The following day, Wednesday May 11th, was spent at Queen Mary College in Mile End Road, rehearsing camera angles for the BBC's *Jazz Goes To College* programme, filmed that evening before an invited audience. The programme wasn't transmitted until December of that year, and, holidaying in America, Hayes himself missed it, having to content himself with soundtrack tapes sent to him by journalist Steve Voce.[34]

The band reconvened at Philips Studios on Thursday morning and immediately began by recording Hayes's own chart of Miles Davis's 'Milestones'. With a woodwind introduction that, for all its prettiness, sounds slightly out of place, almost as if it were incidental music for a radio play accidentally spliced in, the arrangement was one of the trickier items to be dealt with that week. Indeed, the chart was something of a tour de force, incorporating a terrifying saxophone soli ("the way that Benny Carter used to write and frighten saxophone players," wrote Terry Brown in the original sleeve notes[35]), together with solo contributions from Gordon Beck, Keith Christie and Jeff Clyne. The bassist later looked at the track as something of a period piece: "I think we hadn't really sussed the modal thing and we resolved [the harmony] at the end, but it turned out OK and, of course, Tubby was roaring."[36]

The "modal thing" also eludes Hayes in his solo – or rather he ignores it, instead offering an improvisation that contains fewer hints of the influence of John Coltrane than might be expected. If anything, the solo can be compared to the one by Coltrane's running mate on the original Miles Davis recording, Cannonball Adderley: there are no stark mode-based runs and the indelible spirit of bebop permeates, almost as if the improvisation just happens to find itself part of a modal performance rather than being dictated to by its strictures.

Once the problems with the introduction had been ironed out, Jeff Clyne recalled that 'Milestones' went in the can with relative ease (the session tape contains no alternate take). But the next title up that day proved far more problematic. A fast twelve-bar blues with an impossibly convoluted theme for the saxophones, Jimmy Deuchar's 'What's Blue?' took an age to get down and occupied the band for the rest of the session. After two attempts to repair the tail end of the arrangement with spliced edits, all further work on the chart was abandoned.

Rather ominously, the final day of recording fell on Friday the 13th but with nearly enough material already taped to comprise an entire album, there was little left to be done other than set down two unused retakes of 'Sonnymoon For Two', polish off a single take of 'Nutty' and record the leader's ballad feature on 'Spring Can Really Hang You Up The Most'. He delivers the latter's verse with only Beck's piano for accompaniment before unfurling a tender reading of the theme and a well-paced solo that reaches a dramatic trilling climax. The end result is simply stunning and certainly comes neck and neck with Stan Getz's celebrated version from the earlier Verve album *Reflections*. Nevertheless, the track was destined to remain on the shelf, nothing less than a tragedy when one realizes it was passed over to include 'Nutty', an unusually formulaic arrangement from Stan Tracey which gave its only solo space to Ray Warleigh and Les Condon.

With his ballad feature successfully in the can, it was time to call it a day. But, as Terry Brown's sleeve notes on the original LP revealed, Hayes decided to capitalize on the remaining hour of studio time by breaking out his arrangement of '100% Proof'. Although the BBC had twice broadcast the composition, the composer was keen to see if he could set something down for commercial issue. Watching the clock, Brown agreed, and after being informed that the piece was somewhat open-ended, a new tape was loaded. "We'd got through the bulk of the music and he wanted to do 100% Proof with the clock ticking round," recalled Jeff Clyne. "It was either we do it or not and it was take one. And it happened to be a historic thing because it worked straight out."[37] Although the story of the one-take taping of '100% Proof' has long been central to Tubby Hayes's legend, Clyne's memory, like Terry Brown's sleeve notes, somewhat fudges the facts. There were several scrapped false starts to the piece (probably down to the naked trumpet fanfare figure after Hayes's opening solo, which could prove even more hairy on live gigs) with the version familiar from the Fontana release in fact being the only surviving take, numbered three.

This minor revelation doesn't take anything away from the spectacular achievement that is Hayes's performance throughout '100% Proof'. Stretching for nearly a quarter of an hour, his tenor moves through jazz waltz grooves, fast bebop, balladry and some – albeit slightly tentative – free interplay with the rhythm section, and, as he reveals one facet after another, the effect is like that of listening to a musical dance of the seven veils. Over such lengths one might expect the saxophonist to touch upon the influence of Coltrane, whose extended forays he was then echoing on his club gigs, but there is surprisingly little indication of the American's influence. If Sonny Rollins is sometimes called to mind in the sheer audacity and gutsiness of Hayes's playing, once again there is nothing resembling direct plagiarism. In fact, with the taping of '100% Proof', Tubby Hayes had once more demonstrated his was a style that was singularly his own. In many ways, the performance threw down yet another formidable gauntlet to the emerging generation of younger local tenorists: The Little Giant remained a mighty hard act to follow.[38]

Hayes's new quartet finally made its debut on the BBC's *Jazz Club* in June 1966, and in August, with Phil Seamen replacing Tony Levin on drums, they played a support slot opposite Johnny Griffin at Ronnie Scott's, providing yet another opportunity to hear the two Little Giants in close proximity.[39] Les Tomkins was on hand to record part of the band's set on August 9th – his last recording of Hayes[40] – including a prolix but engrossing version of 'Night And Day', possibly inspired by American tenorist Joe Henderson's rendition on *Inner Urge*, an album then just released in the UK and a particular favourite within Hayes's circle.[41] After an abstracted Rollins-like opening, he goes on to play a loose ten-minute solo, which, like those on the recent BBC broadcast, sounds both relaxed and without any desperate straining for modern effects, and which draws a superlative performance from Seamen.

Whilst Hayes may have remained musically robust enough, the rigorous treadmill of too much studio work was clearly beginning to take a physical toll. The collapse of the previous autumn was an alarm bell that had not been heeded, and now, minus the weight that had given him his nickname and deeply disillusioned with his lack of jazz opportunities, he was turning increasingly from alcohol towards hard drugs, not so much as a creative stimulant but more as an escape from his professional frustrations.

During his tenure with the quartet Danny Thompson recalled seeing his leader using barbiturates prior to gigs and occasionally fixing heroin in one of the band cars during the interval, but like many of the saxophonist's colleagues he saw Hayes's relationship with hard drugs as tangential dabbling rather than die-hard addiction: "Tubby messed around with heroin," Thompson remembered. "Phil Seamen was the real junkie."[42] Living with a hardened addict certainly didn't help, with Joy Marshall's own drug habit only serving to make her already volatile temper even more explosive. The relationship between the couple had always been feisty, but it was generally balanced by a tenderness that could somehow redeem the periodic outbursts of jealousy and mistrust. However, when things got acrimonious, neither Marshall nor Hayes were in any position to put up much in the way of a measured and calm response – junkies can be evil people and Hayes was an outspoken drunk. There were also other, far more innocent casualties caught in the fallout of the couple's relationship.

Richard Hayes remembers his father continuing to be a fleeting presence in his life at this time. Some of their interactions were promisingly "normal" – Tubby slipping a packet of Rowntree's Fruit Gums beneath his son's pillow when he thought he was asleep, for example – whilst others showed that on occasion Hayes's professional and family life *could* co-exist. Richard recalls being taken with his younger brother Lewis to the Bull's Head at Barnes to watch his father on-stage, an exciting event made all the more enticing by "a glass of warm orange squash."[43] However, there were also other, far darker, moments. Although Rose was still immensely proud of her husband's career achievements, often pointing him out on the soundtrack to the television shows she watched with her young sons, Hayes was fast becoming, in Richard's words, "simply a face on a record cover." Barely six, he remembered "a lot of heated arguments,"[44] one of which involved his parents going for one another in front of a living room crowded with embarrassed musicians. "I had been asleep," he recounts, "but woke up because all the shouting was going on. I slipped into the living room to see my father raging uncontrollably at my mother and the two of them kicking an official letter across the floor at each other. I think that this is probably the same evening that my father scrawled 'I want a divorce' on the living room wall."[45] Occasionally, even Joy Marshall found Hayes too much to handle. Richard remembers her calling his mother, with the singer pleading that Rose take back a man who was becoming increasingly wayward.[46]

It was unsurprising that, surrounded by such pressure, Hayes's health began to falter. During the late summer of 1966 his legs had unexpectedly swollen, which had been followed by excruciating bouts of chest pain. As he'd done ever since his first collapse with the Kenny Baker band fifteen years previously, he soldiered on, ignoring all advice to get himself checked out by a doctor. Inevitably, something had to give. On the morning of Monday September 5th he awoke virtually unable to breathe. Rushed to the outpatients department of St Mary's Hospital in Paddington, he was diagnosed with a thrombosis affecting both the circulation in his legs and his lung function. Due to record a BBC session that evening, the doctors refused all requests to discharge him. He was ordered to rest and was expected to be out of action for several weeks. As news of his hospitalization broke out, friends, colleagues and fans rallied round, and there were soon floods of well-wishers making their way to St Mary's. Hayes was phlegmatic about his condition. Interviewed by Keith Harrison on the BBC's *Roundabout* programme, he maintained that he was treating the collapse as a blip and made it clear that a little rest was all he had needed.

Almost incredibly, though, he managed to stay focused on his band. Barely a few weeks after the leader's collapse, the Tubby Hayes quartet picked up a new bassist, Ron Mathewson. Born in the Shetland Isles in February 1944, Mathewson had undergone an unusual musical education. His older brother Matt was already an accomplished jazz pianist, but the younger Mathewson's introduction to improvisation had begun in a much less studied way, by grabbing a double bass to sub for a drunken musician in a local dance band ("I got fifty shillings and ten blisters," he later said.[47]). Amazingly, despite such an unpromising start, he quickly displayed an uncanny understanding of his instrument and when the chance came to join a Trad band in mainland Scotland soon after, Mathewson – all of seventeen – jumped at it. There then followed a manic period in which as a member of the Clyde Valley Stompers, Scotland's leading traditional group, he cleaned up during the Trad Boom.

Mathewson's musical horizons had also begun to broaden. By the mid-sixties he had made the sea-change discovery of Scott La Faro, the tragically short-lived bass virtuoso who had transformed the Bill Evans trio earlier in the decade. However, opportunities to play with other like-minded musicians were proving distinctly limited so for the time being he continued his musical footwork by moving to London to join the mainstream band of trumpeter Alex Welsh.

Mathewson had first heard Tubby Hayes when the Welsh band appeared opposite the saxophonist's quintet at the 1963 Cleethorpes jazz festival. And they had already played together in 1965, an initial meeting that had begun very awkwardly. Hayes had been booked to guest with Tommy Whittle's quartet at the Hopbine, the club Whittle ran in North Wembley. Mathewson had been hired as a deputy for the band's regular bassist Len Skeat. "I remember getting there and getting my bass out and in walks Tubby. He comes up to me and says 'Who the fuck are you?' So I reply 'I'm the bass player' and he says 'Well, we'll see about that!'"[48] Amazingly, forty years later Mathewson rediscovered a tape of the gig, recorded by the club's soundman Ted Lyons and, dusted down and remastered, it was issued on CD by the Harkit label in 2006, thus bringing to life a moment of genuine British jazz history.[49] With his vocal encouragements clearly captured on the tape, Hayes seemed happy enough with the young bassist's playing. Nevertheless, by the time Mike Pyne was recommending Mathewson for the quartet proper he had either forgotten him, or simply hadn't put two and two together. "Mike kept saying, 'look there's a bass player I play with who would love to do the gig' and Tubby was like 'Who?' Eventually though he called and that was it."[50]

The bassist's debut with the band in September 1966 was nothing less than a trial by fire:

> The first actual gig I did with Tubby was some TV show or something in the Midlands and Tubby turned round to me and said 'What Is This Thing Called Love?' You know that one, Ron?' I said yes and away Tubby went. Whee! I'd never played that fast in my life. Afterwards Tubby just said "You'll get the hang of it!"[51]

If the musical leap from Alex Welsh was titanic, some aspects of the social side of the new band required Mathewson to make no adjustment whatsoever.

"Mike Pyne used to drink tea in those days and TL [Tony Levin] was forever tearing back up the motorway to Birmingham and wasn't around much after the gigs. Tubby liked a drink. Vodka and tonic. So I can remember when I joined the band he put his arm round me and said 'Fantastic! At last I've got a drinking buddy!' And then we went off down the pub."[52]

For Tony Levin the arrival of Mathewson had been the final key in realizing the quartet's potential: "There was real understanding between the members of the band. I do think [this quartet] was a whole band rather than any other band that [Tubby] had. The contribution of the piano, bass and drums into the whole music was, I think, greater than all the earlier things he had done."[53] Other musicians had certainly noticed the difference, including Spike Wells, Levin's successor in the Hayes quartet:

> On the British scene Tony Levin was the drummer who had the biggest influence on me. He was the only one that could really swing in that style. You know 'There Is No Greater Love' on [the album] *Four And More* by Miles is the definition of a certain kind of swing, and I think that Mick, Ron and Tony had it down better than anyone else.[54]

Melody Maker printed its first review of the group in early November, following a gig at the Phoenix in Cavendish Square;[55] appropriately enough Bob Dawbarn spent three-quarters of the piece praising the new rhythm team: "In Mike Pyne, Ron Mathewson and Tony Levin, Tubby Hayes currently has the best rhythm section he has ever had. Levin, in particular, impressed me enormously. Not only does he swing like the clappers and possess a remarkable technique, but he listens to what is happening around him and complements the rest of the group most intelligently." Dawbarn also went on to highlight Pyne's "pleasing musical personality based on understatement" and Mathewson's "big tone and good rhythmic sense."[56]

The earliest known recorded documentation of the Pyne–Mathewson–Levin line-up came later that month, on November 18th, when promoter Peter Burman presented one of his Jazz *Tête-à-Tête* concerts at Bristol University. Appearing opposite the Tony Coe Quintet and local guitarist Frank Evans, the billing was slightly odd, as Hayes was listed as the guest artist of the Les Condon Quartet – effectively doing nothing more than adding the trumpeter to his regular band. Fortunately, Burman had the sense to record the concert, and two of Hayes's performances were issued the following year – in rather grainy and indistinct sound – on the 77 label. Nevertheless, despite their audio shortcomings, they make intriguing listening. The opening 'Freedom Monday', a Lee Morgan composition from the repertoire of Art Blakey's Jazz Messengers, hits a fashionably Blue Note-ish groove, halfway between Latin and boogaloo. Condon – a Morgan obsessive – solos with audible enthusiasm but ultimately fails to match his role model's creativity, whilst

Hayes on the other hand delivers an improvisation of immense invention, utilizing several devices reminiscent of those used by John Coltrane circa 1960.[57] There are multi-phonics, some "Giant Steps" chord superimposition and an effective use of the entire range of the horn. Pyne also solos well, with a certain Tyner-ish fluency, but his best moments come on the following track, a new Hayes ballad titled 'When My Baby Gets Mad – Everybody Split'. The dedicatee was none other than Joy Marshall, with the less than endearing – but wholly accurate – title commemorating her legendary temper. Getting past this humorous but functional tribute is easy: Pyne sets the performance up with a freely improvised, impressionistic piano solo, before Hayes delivers one of the finest ballad performances he ever committed to record, with a sense of pacing, grace and steely resolve that is nothing less than Getzian, and to which the rhythm section react magnificently, matching his dynamics, and moving in and out of the solo with tidal power.

With his health still to fully stabilize, and his lungs still recovering from the thrombosis, Hayes was advised that an escape to a warmer climate during the forthcoming winter might aid his recovery. So, late in November 1966, he arranged to take a Christmas holiday with Joy Marshall's family in California, a non-playing visit that would turn out to be his final trip to America. Ahead of his departure, there was a brief flurry of musical activity including a visit by the quartet to the Little Theatre in Rochester in Kent on the evening of December 4th. Tony Levin had the foresight to record the engagement on his portable reel-to-reel recorder, originally intending the tape to be a private memento for the band. However, during the years after Hayes's death Levin also played the recordings to his fellow musicians, among them Alan Skidmore, Evan Parker and Jeff Clyne, all of whom supported the drummer's opinion that not only were the performances among Hayes's finest but that they should be commercially released. For some years various stumbling blocks prevented this, but in 2005 they were finally issued, to immense critical acclaim, as a double CD named *Addictive Tendencies* on Levin's own label, Rare Music Recordings.[58]

The CD release may have brought the music alive for a new generation of listeners, but Levin had always retained very vivid memories of the evening. He recalled in 2007:

> I remember everything about that night. I got there and there was a row of wooden chairs on which Tubby was asleep. He had obviously had too much of something. He woke up and did one of his "wahey" shouts. He told me he'd been to the doctors that day and that he'd been told he had addictive tendencies. "That's all I need." He thought it was really funny.[59]

The band opened up on that wintry evening (in the unedited announcements on the original tapes Tubby can be heard remarking on how cold it is[60]) with a reprise of Hayes's composition 'Change Of Setting', recorded the previous year with Paul Gonsalves. Instantly, it's possible to hear just how much had changed within the saxophonist's world over the preceding few months. Ron Mathewson's impact is particular striking: the bassist's incredible sense of time locks together with Levin to create an undulating rollercoaster on which the leader rides with typically irrepressible energy. No group Hayes had ever led had swung quite like this. The band then move on to play 'Alone Together' which, when compared with the version from the Dancing Slipper eight months earlier, delivers potent evidence of the band's collective growth. Pyne offers up another lyrical introduction worthy of Bill Evans before Mathewson and Levin set up an interminable minor vamp. The ensuing improvisation Hayes unleashes over this churning intensity is as good a place as any to examine his musical ambitions at this time. There are signature licks, and several passages that are not too dissimilar to the cadenzas of '100% Proof' ('Alone Together' is in the relative minor) but there are also new tricks: an even greater emphasis of superimposed whole-tone harmony, extensive use of barking multi-phonics at the bottom of the horn and tonal distortion which on occasion touches on that being explored by Coltrane's new radical tenor-playing partner, Pharoah Sanders. An unaccompanied cadenza from the leader ties up twenty-five minutes of wondrous invention,. As the audience applaud, Hayes turns round to the band, and, in his raw London brogue – not the same, cool and considered voice in which we hear him announce – shouts out "Walkin'," cue for the well-known blues theme popularized by Miles Davis.

The trumpeter's original version, cut in 1954, was a masterpiece of medium-swung intensity, but, as with virtually every other piece Davis played with any regularity, the tempo crept ever upwards so that by the era of the Wayne Shorter–Herbie Hancock–Ron Carter–Tony Williams quintet things were apt to be decidedly rampant. Hayes had similar ideas on this night.

Playing a twelve-bar blues is a basic requirement for any jazz musician. Indeed, it is usually a blues that novice jazz performers first grapple with – no less a player than Dexter Gordon once cautioned "If you can't play the blues, you might as well forget it."[61] Despite the simplicity of the original basic form, with all its potential harmonic and rhythmic possibilities, the sequence has endeared itself to every generation of jazzmen, from Louis Armstrong, through Charlie Parker onto Coltrane, Ornette Coleman and beyond. Classic blues performances litter the discographies of all the major jazz soloists, including those of Tubby Hayes's heroes Sonny Rollins, John Coltrane and Stan Getz.[62] Hayes also had also made his own share of twelve-bar triumphs: 'Hall Hears The Blues', 'Swingin' in Studio Two' and 'Blues In Trinity' were among his best work from the mid-fifties, and the upstaging solo he let fly at James Moody and Roland Kirk on 'Stitt's Tune' from 1962's *Return Visit* album stands among the finest of his middle-period achievements. Inspired and captivating though all these earlier recordings are, they pale when set before the sundering power of the Rochester version of 'Walkin''.

Ultimately, as with all jazz critique, there is simply nothing more to be said than "go and hear the record," but there remains some merit in outlining some of the details of the solo. It lasts approximately six minutes and covers no less than forty-four choruses (by an amazing coincidence the same number as the medium-tempo 'No Blues' from the earlier Hopbine recording with Mathewson) at a tempo which, whilst not absurd by Hayes's standards, is certainly brisk enough. Crucially, there is nothing in evidence to support the saxophonist's own claim that it might take him several choruses to escape the web of his own clichés: in fact, quite the opposite occurs, as, from the off there are ideas literally gushing out in a sensational stream of consciousness.

Hayes calls for Pyne to "lay out" at the close of his first chorus, a request that the pianist eventually obeys with a resounding thunk. Clearly relishing the freedom of the piano-less accompaniment, by chorus four he is toying with a virtuosic descending motif, actually nothing more than a simple scalar exercise but played with such speed, ease and clarity that it makes the jaw drop. The characteristic triplet runs which appear in chorus five have much the same impact. Indeed, the solo is one of the best places in which to become acquainted with Hayes's skipping rhythmic feel, the time popping out within each note (witness the "laughing" phrase in chorus twelve). In chorus eighteen he makes the Coltrane-ish superimposition of the key of Ab, a minor third above the tonic, giving the solo a textural lift, just when the listener might be forgiven for thinking it could not become any more intense. The first quote – from Clifford Brown's 'Gertrude's Bounce' – appears during the same chorus. Mathewson does some Richard Davis-like double-stopping (playing two notes simultaneously) at chorus nineteen and Mike Pyne finally returns at chorus twenty-six, before a signature Hayes lick, starting in the altissimo register, dominates the following twelve bars. Hayes's joyous humour is again evident at chorus thirty, which features a further quote from 'Baby It's Cold Outside', a lightning-quick reference to the night's weather, and after a trilling figure at chorus thirty-two he leaps straight into several choruses of bebop chromatics, culminating in another quote, this time from 'I've Told Ev'ry Little Star'. The familiar 'Walkin'' shout chorus then appears before a wailing conclusion, forty-four choruses after take-off.

The immense stamina required to pull off these demanding marathon solos had long been stock in trade for Hayes. However, this being barely a few weeks after his thrombosis collapse, one wonders first at the prudence of continuing to punish himself so hard musically and, more pointedly, what stimulants – other than sheer adrenaline – may have been involved that night. When played the Rochester version of 'Walkin'' by the author during an interview, one leading British jazz saxophonist simply shook his head and remarked that he thought Hayes was "Charlie'd up to the eyeballs." Whether or not there was some sort of narcotic substance involved or not – and one suspects that given Hayes's earlier reference to "addictive tendencies" it is highly likely that the answer is yes – it does not lessen the impression of the solo. Cocaine could, in the words of the same saxophonist, "make you play all night, long, long intense solos," itself a good description of Hayes's performance throughout much of the Rochester recording.[63]

The following weekend, Hayes flew out to California for three weeks of recuperation. Whilst away he could relax, unwind and take things easy. Or at least that was what he was supposed to do. Provided a first-hand opportunity to check out new jazz artists who had yet to make it to Britain, slowing down was ironically proving more difficult in the US than it had ever been back home in London.[64] As he trawled the clubs of San Francisco, he even had occasion to augment the efforts of those he'd paid to hear, including participating in a memorable jam session with the ex-Mingus saxophonist John Handy.[65] However, despite the odd moments of musical revelry, this brief sojourn in America provided an opportunity to look ahead, clearly and without the petty parochial distractions that had so frustrated him of late: approaching his thirty-second birthday, he was still young enough to make a vital contribution to current jazz developments back in England. Although he had been a professional musician for over fifteen years, no one could possibly think of him as some vain, aging impostor. He had also now surrounded himself with a band of musicians disciplined and yet flexible enough to cope with his entire musical remit, arguably his best yet, and – in its creative ambitions if not in support and exposure – the London jazz scene to which he was about to return was remarkably robust. His recent health scares and personal tribulations were also now firmly behind him. Well rested, inspired and with a sheath-full of new compositions, he returned to the UK early in the New Year, fully intent on capitalizing on these combined fortunes.

The reignition of the Tubby Hayes quartet started almost straight away, with the band's packed itinerary for January culminating in a return to BBC's *Jazz Club* on the 28th. Including two of his new compositions, the broadcast provided instant, irrefutable proof that the leader was now more determined than ever to breast ahead. The show had opened with 'Dear Johnny B.', as crackling a hard bop exercise as Hayes had ever delivered, which offered a tribute to drummer Johnny Butts who had died following a road accident in Bermuda a few weeks earlier, and closed with 'Mexican Green', another new piece which, at over twelve minutes in length, was an extensive and explicit exploration of musical territory Hayes had previously only hinted at.[66]

Named after a powerful type of cannabis then popular in London jazz circles, similar to its predecessor '100% Proof', 'Mexican Green' was another long-form performance which took its main interest not from its compositional components, which are in fact slight and almost incidental, but rather from what Hayes and his musicians could find between these musical signposts. However, whereas '100% Proof' had placed Hayes in the familiar context of theme and solo improvisation over a predetermined harmonic chassis, 'Mexican Green' had only a brief written melody and little in the way of a pre-set harmonic sequence (clearly Hayes had heard Albert Ayler's 'Ghosts' by this point), concentrating solely upon a given key (rather unsurprisingly Bb concert, a safe home-ground for all jazz musicians). The musicians were then invited to take part in a freely interactive dialogue that contrived to depart further and further away from the basic tonality, as well as from any given time signature. Hayes himself described the intentions of this process thus:

> ['Mexican Green'] represents an approach to music that I haven't used before. I have always enjoyed the music of Machito and Tito Puente, especially the excitement that they create, usually with a very simple melodic line and a repetitive rhythm. The only written part of this composition is the theme which is played at a fast tempo near the beginning and again towards the end. We agree a key centre to begin the piece and every man listens carefully to the others, and follows whoever is playing the leading part at the time. One of the problems with this type of playing is that sometimes we may not get it together at all, and the end result can be disastrous. However, on the occasions when it really comes off, it can create a tremendous amount of excitement and a wonderful feeling of satisfaction.[67]

Since being licensed for commercial release by Miles Music in the 1990s, the version of 'Mexican Green' that concludes the January 1967 *Jazz Club* broadcast has become as familiar to Hayes fans as that recorded for Fontana shortly afterwards. While there are definite similarities between the two, the BBC recording serves much as an alternate take might in illustrating the subtle changes that the piece underwent during its development that winter. Perhaps what is most curious about 'Mexican Green' is that, even in its earliest extant version, it so successfully balances the extremes of Hayes's musical vision at the time. Its tight, strutting riff theme is shot through with the influence of sixties soul-jazz, almost to the point of kitsch parody, and yet barely moments later Hayes's playing exhibits the tonal distortions and extremes of register wholly appropriate to the "new thing." There is Coltrane-esque side-slipping away from the given key, and, as the component parts of the rhythm section break down, the tenorist's virtuoso runs are broken by a romantic, near-Eastern wailing. The contributions of Hayes's sidemen also move from structure to freedom with equal success, particularly during Ron Mathewson's startling unaccompanied arco passages, but, in line with Hayes's desire to create a work in which "every man listens carefully to the others," it is as a collective group statement rather than a series of individual solos that 'Mexican Green' most impresses.

If allowing his sidemen this amount of freedom constituted something new for Hayes, one element that continued to remain central to his ambitions was his reliance upon just the right drummer. As the January broadcast had made clear, Tony Levin had now blossomed into a sparring partner every bit as effective as his predecessors Bill Eyden and Phil Seamen had been. A few weeks after the BBC's *Jazz Club* recording, the Hayes quartet visited Levin's home town of Birmingham, in order to play a gig at the Station Inn. To the band's surprise, the evening received an appropriately effusive review in no less a publication than *DownBeat*. "With Levin [Hayes] has a particularly impressive rapport," reported the magazine's Mark Gardner. "Their constant dialogue in the Booker Ervin–Alan Dawson manner was articulate, humorous and joyful [and] as Hayes says, he is a rarity – a drummer with perfect dynamics."[68]

Long relishing the idea of "a whole band" in which every instrument made an equal contribution, Levin found Hayes's quartet a dream assignment, especially as its musical ethos grew ever more democratic.[69] However, his continued presence in the band required a never-ending exercise in career-juggling. Having already made the decision – both noble and practical – that he did not want to play music solely for money, and with both his continuing role in the family furniture business and a young family to support, Levin often faced long commutes to and from Birmingham. Making all this possible, the drummer's classic red Aston Martin soon became the envy of his colleagues – including the non-driving leader – with Levin quickly gaining the affectionate nickname of "The Second City Steamer." Indeed, in the days before speed cameras, he prided himself on the record he had set shortly after joining Hayes: London's Soho to Birmingham's Moseley in an hour and fifteen minutes. "It was great in those days," he remembered years later. "We'd finish at Ronnie's in the small hours and I'd pile my drums into the car and off I'd go. If it was summer, you'd drive as it was getting light and it was beautiful."[70]

Recording the quartet was the next logical step, but with one album (*100% Proof*) already in the can and the impending deletion of virtually his entire back catalogue, Fontana took some persuading. Despite his poll-winning stature, Hayes's records simply weren't shifting, as he revealed to Mark Gardner when the journalist caught the quartet at the Bull's Head that spring. "I mentioned that a number of his Fontana LPs were being remaindered, including his first recording made in the USA, [at] which point he withdrew a Fontana statement of royalties from his pocket showing his earnings from that source for the year amounted to £12. 8s. 6d!"[71]

Hayes's producer Terry Brown remained a useful conduit to Jack Baverstock's ear, but, whilst the label boss continued to be sympathetic to the cause of British jazz, his hands were now tied with corporate restrictions. Philips' pop sales were outstripping everything else, and although the possibility of bankrolling local jazz from the overspill of Fontana's big-selling artists such as Manfred Mann and the Spencer Davis Group existed, it didn't make Hayes an automatic shoo-in. Eventually, however, after what had seemed an age, Baverstock finally agreed to tape the saxophonist's band.

10 The Other Scene (1967–68)

In the end I just took the phone off the hook, locked the doors and didn't speak to a soul for about ten weeks.

Tubby Hayes, *Melody Maker*, 1968

The quartet entered Philips Studios over two days in February and March 1967. The gap between the initial date (February 2nd) and the latter (March 7th) may well be indicative both of how Hayes's musical aims altered during the course of the recordings and of his new sidemen's relative inexperience in a studio environment. Both Mike Pyne and Tony Levin were making their recording debut, a situation that could have conceivably called for many retakes and edits. Intriguingly, however, Levin remembered the album being taped in just *one* session, which may well be correct. Fontana's written archives are by no means a model of discographical order but what *is* certain is that the band recorded more music than was released on the final LP, including a quintet version of 'Mexican Green' which added Jeff Clyne's bass.[1] The absence of any further material on the CD re-release of the album is lamentable, as is the lack of information regarding which performances date from which session. Nevertheless, even without knowing its correct recorded chronology, *Mexican Green* is an album that tells a distinct story.[2]

In assessing any record about which there already exists extensive critique it is nigh-on impossible to avoid drawing at least some of the same conclusions as previous commentators. Just as it is hard not to describe Coltrane's *A Love Supreme* without reverting in some way to the transcendent and spiritual uplift of the music, nor to write about Ornette Coleman's *Free Jazz* without striking the analogy of a highly cryptic conversation, it remains difficult not to describe *Mexican Green* as a "manifesto statement." The boldness of this description isn't mere hyperbole, however. Although doubtless there *are* listeners who do not find it Hayes's greatest work, there can be few who fail to see it as a highly significant landmark in his musical journey. Indeed, as has again been written elsewhere, taken together with the earlier *Tubby's Groove*, the LP effectively bookends the saxophonist's most creative period.

One dictionary defines the word *manifesto* as "a public declaration of policy or principles." Although the saxophonist never made any sort of recorded verbal statement to support the notion, the album certainly covers enough musical ground to warrant the description: signature warp-speeds, lyrical balladry, a modal waltz, and a complex post-bop blues balance out the adventurous title track, with each item outlining a particular space in Hayes's musical territory. The repertoire also effectively mixes themes already established in live performance, together with items written specifically for the recording, such as 'Blues In Orbit', a composition which, according to Tony Levin, Hayes apparently never played again. What one hears therefore is music from a unit well integrated and practised, captured almost in passing between engagements, the very ideal of how a band should appear when recorded.

The opening 'Dear Johnny B.' registers even more strongly than on the earlier BBC broadcast, due in part to a recording balance that places Hayes front and centre, swathed in the period-style reverb. The richness of the tone comes as no surprise, but the position of the tenor in the mix gives it an even greater presence (Hayes had switched to a Berg Larsen mouthpiece with a much wider tip the previous year, resulting in a broader tone and, especially useful with Tony Levin, more volume). Indeed, the *sound* of the entire album provides an added attraction – saxophonist Theo Travis maintains that this is one of his principal reasons for naming the record as a seminal influence – just as the *sounds* of *Kind Of Blue* and John Coltrane's *Crescent* also create their own unique aura: this is music that would not have sounded anything like it does had it been recorded anywhere else.

Another of Hayes's recent compositions, 'Off The Wagon' – written following his collapse the previous September, and which the composer was fond of announcing as "our Country and Western, Rock and Roll, Avant-Garde, Rhythm and Blues, Bebop tune"[3] – also received its debut on the album. One can sense what Hayes was driving at in his poly-stylistic description, and the very idea clearly speaks of the influences – good and bad – then affecting him, but thankfully the performance itself contains only trace elements of other genres. In fact, like a great many of the most enduring and endearing jazz themes, 'Off The Wagon' is actually deceptively simple. Patterned around three sixteen-bar passages, and boasting an indelibly catchy melody, which had it been given wider exposure might had scored some popular success, the composition also utilizes harmonic devices which date back to the more complex bebop style of Hayes's youth. Indeed, with its archetypally boppish series of descending chords, the first sixteen bars occupy similar harmonic territory to a previous Hayes theme, 'Royal Ascot'.

Completing the album's first side, the modal waltz 'Trenton Place' strikes a rather more contemporary note, with the leader's flute at its most melancholy, whilst the ridiculously accelerated 'The Second City Steamer' offers not only a jaw-dropping display of Hayes's instrumental dexterity, but also a thunderous outing from Tony Levin, confirming his boss's skill as a talent spotter *par excellence*.

The original album's B-side begins with 'Blues In Orbit', a Hayes composition with more than a hint of Joe Henderson's methods in its construction, before 'A Dedication To Joy' – the final and permanent title for the saxophonist's tribute to his girlfriend – brings forth arguably the finest performance of the whole record. Mike Pyne's lush solo introduction ("I wish that we could have included his solo from every take. Each was completely different and equally enchanting," wrote Hayes on the album sleeve[4]) sets the leader's tenor up for an improvisation lyrical and muscular by turns and which contains, in bars fifteen and sixteen, a phrase of pure-spun Getzian beauty.

Throughout the album Pyne, Mathewson and Levin display their every musical virtue, proving irrefutably that the quartet was Hayes's most evenly matched band to date. Although Hayes remained very much the group's figurehead, he had at last found players who could extend and amplify his musical concepts. Almost inevitably, the band had begun to receive comparisons with the classic John Coltrane Quartet. "[It was] a breath-taking unit," recalled Brian Blain in a posthumously published article about Hayes, "rooted in harmony but always capable of reaching out into a glorious kind of free flight [and] if we hadn't been quite so preoccupied with all the excitement of the men who were orbiting [Ronnie Scott's] Old Place we would have realized where the centre of gravity really was."[5]

The "glorious kind of free flight" that was 'Mexican Green' itself proved hard to capture in the confines of Philips Studios, as Ron Mathewson remembers: "Tubby was in a box [*recording booth*]. I was in a box. Levin was out in the studio, I think. That can make it difficult to really play together."[6] There were also other constraints imposed by the practicalities of recording. All too aware that the performance had to fit onto an LP side, Hayes later wrote: "This type of playing can easily become contrived, especially if one is hampered by time limits, for there is no knowing how long – or how short for that matter – each individual is going to take to build to his logical climax, and if he is told he has to do it in fifteen seconds then the entire natural feeling is lost." The saxophonist also knew the dangers of indulging to the other extreme: "One night it lasted an hour and thirty-eight minutes which I will agree is a bit much!"[7]

The Fontana recording of 'Mexican Green' is one of the pivotal moments in Hayes's career, and continues to make for fascinating listening, not least because it represents such an explicit augmentation of his chosen methods. Never before had he loosened so many of his previously rigid musical ties. Nearly fifty years on, although the free-form sections may seem rather time-locked in their intent, the band's passion for co-operative exploration remains as convincing as ever, giving 'Mexican Green' – even now – a distinctly contemporary relevance. However, one question remains: how sincere was it all for Hayes? Did he really achieve a "wonderful feeling of satisfaction" from this new approach or was it, as some suspected, merely a fashion-conscious gesture?

The various reactions to the album's release given by the contemporary jazz press will be documented in a later chapter, placing them in context with Hayes's life at the time, but it is equally useful to cast an eye over how Tubby Hayes's great barrier-breaking experiment was viewed by his colleagues. Drummer Spike Wells – Tony Levin's successor in the quartet – considers the title track to be "pretty straightforward."[8]

> I feel it was something he was just doing for the sake of it. I think some of the older guys thought they ought to get in on the act if they were going to keep up with the times. I don't think his heart was in it and I don't really think it suited his style. There was too much there already. You've got to almost be ignorant in order to play that music convincingly. With Tubby, you found the usual phrases hidden in there somewhere.[9]

Wells's belief that Hayes had actually been hindered rather than helped by established disciplines is supported by Peter King. The altoist remembers Hayes using "semi-free passages" almost like a musical garnish and "always for a particular effect, not as an end in itself."[10] The example of Hayes's synthesizing various jazz styles threads throughout his story and is no less applicable during this period. Indeed, the notion of freedom "for a particular effect" is especially noteworthy, confirming that his use of certain avant-garde devices was simply to extend his musical language, rather than radically alter its dialect. The big difference between Hayes's interest in free improvisation and the interest he had shown in earlier styles like hard bop was that there was actually very little he could usefully extrapolate from it. By the time the avant-garde movement had shifted itself into the realms of politico-socio militancy on the one hand and quasi-exotic mysticism on the other, Hayes had had his fill. More importantly, his brief interest in the music hadn't substantially altered his existing style. In fact, a performance like 'Mexican Green' actually sounds more like a loose British response to the "time no changes" approach of Miles Davis's contemporary quintet than a wholesale avant-garde freak-out.[11] All the emphasis on the revolutionary title track has even occasionally obscured the fact that the finest moments on the *Mexican Green* album actually occur elsewhere. In fact, it's somewhat ironic that the track that best exemplifies Hayes's natural musical approach is not some barrier-breaking exercise in free-form but 'The Second City Steamer', the kind of tear-up performance that had long been his stock in trade.

A month after recording *Mexican Green*, on Sunday April 2nd the quartet returned to the Little Theatre in Rochester, the unlikely provincial venue that had been the scene of a triumphant gig the previous December. The performance was again recorded, and was among the tapes left in the possession of Hayes's mother when he died. In 2010, four excerpts from the gig were released on CD, each illustrating the "whole band" ethos spoken of so appreciably by Tony Levin.[12] Throughout the recording, there are many moments of brilliance from all hands, with the leader at his most prolix during a lengthy, tumbling improvisation on 'Lament'. At the opposite end of the emotional spectrum, a gentle, unfurling take of 'Nancy With The Laughing Face' confirms his often-overlooked gifts as an affecting balladeer. But in this instance it is the album's version of 'Mexican Green' that proves to be the most intriguing performance. Once again, there is a striking similarity to the elastic concepts of Miles Davis's quintet[13] and as the band embarks on a far more adventurous exploration than the one recorded for Fontana, Hayes sounds as if he's reached musical nirvana, trading off the energy of his young sidemen like never before.

Although an ocean apart, Hayes and Davis also now faced exactly the same dilemma. Having assembled one of the best rhythm sections in the business, everybody wanted to borrow them, *en masse* or individually. Ron Mathewson, who already had ties with several visiting American soloists, was by far the most frequent absentee during 1967, a situation that began to disenchant Tony Levin. The drummer also resented the commercial concessions the band occasionally had to make: when the quartet appeared on the *Light Programme*'s "Music Through Midnight" on April 20th the playlist had been a safe set of standards and bossa-novas suitable for a mainstream audience. "I wasn't too enthralled with the material he was playing," Levin remembered. "It was certainly less serious jazz music. He was into stuff like 'The Shadow Of Your Smile' – nothing wrong with that but I was into heavier stuff."[14]

Finding new audiences was now an increasing headache for musicians from all corners of the jazz business. The music no longer had the lure it once had in the heyday of the Flamingo and the Florida, and the conundrum of pleasing the purists or selling out confronted everyone. Tubby Hayes's diary that spring scarcely resembled the one from his West End domination a few years previously, it now included more and more grassroots venues such as the Bull's Head at Barnes, the Dog and Fox in Wimbledon, the Phoenix in Cavendish Square and the Greenman in Blackheath. Occasionally, under such circumstances, the band's "heavier stuff" could backfire spectacularly. When the quartet appeared at the fondly remembered Dopey Dick's Jazzhouse in West Hampstead shortly before it closed its doors for good in 1967, promoter Dick Jordan found the star's attitude unremittingly stubborn. "We booked a certain saxophonist and he made his first number last half-an-hour," Jordan ruefully told *Melody Maker*. "When I asked if he'd play with dancers in mind, his reply was 'If you wanted a ****ing dance band why didn't you book one?'"[15]

Paradoxically, the very appearance of Hayes's name could transform a club's fortunes, as Southend promoter Kenny Baxter discovered in the summer of 1967. Booking the Hayes quartet shortly after his venue had lost a substantial amount of money presenting the Don Rendell–Ian Carr quintet, Baxter was delighted with the overflowing crowd, rewarding Hayes with "an extra tenner – a small fortune then."[16]

Nevertheless, following his international triumphs, remuneration like this must have seemed like a paltry return for his skills. Wowing the good folk of places like Southend and Wimbledon just wasn't enough, financially or otherwise. As he became increasingly bitter about the marginalized nature of much of his work, Hayes found a new and unlikely target for his rancour – Ronnie Scott's club.

By 1967, the club's musical policy had begun to change. Whereas before an American headliner would alternate sets with a local band, Scott and King were now often booking an imported female vocalist as the support act. Although the double-header idea was good for business, it left very little room for local horn players. The situation was made doubly galling by the fact that were it not for Hayes's own brokering of the American market in 1961 all of this – the singers, the guest soloists, even the occasional big band – would never have been possible. Although those within his private circle were well aware of his feelings about the new policy, while giving a newspaper interview on the eve of a gig at yet another unlikely outpost for modernism – the Tropicana in Croydon – Hayes made a rare public attack on the club. "It's sour grapes to Britain and its total lack of recognition for British jazz bands," he told journalist Pauline Clark, who reported her subject "bewailing the 'total ignoring like we don't exist' British attitude." "There are no clubs for me to play at, except very few," Hayes continued. "Thank God for the Bull's Head at Barnes – that's where I play most with my band. The Ronnie Scott club in Soho takes on mainly American jazz bands. Even British jazz festivals are often completely monopolized by American bands. I think it's disgusting." Clark concluded with a somewhat forlorn portrait of her subject "[Music] has cost him two broken marriages, weeks in hospital through sheer fatigue, and four stone in weight. It's true, Tubby isn't tubby any more. He weighs just ten stone now and looks less."[17]

It was easy to see why British jazz had wound up in this cul-de-sac. The Beatles, Motown, psychedelic rock and other derivations of pop now had a far more immediate appeal, something easily gauged by the fact that the BBC – bastion of national rectitude and artistic standards – had by the end of 1967 relaunched its radio services to include Radio One, a station unashamedly based on the "pirate" concepts of Radios Caroline and London.

Up against what was to all intents and purposes a pop-based cultural revolution, British jazzmen simply looked and – in some instances – sounded like they were stuck in the past. Even the avant-gardists, whose music could loosely be lumped in with the day's freedom-oriented hippy ethos, couldn't

Way out! Tubby Hayes and Mike Pyne, the Club Octave, Southall, Friday April 21st, 1967
(Ron Mathewson and Tony Levin are out of shot). Courtesy Tony Fernley.

lure a new audience for jazz. The real issue was that modern jazz – an art form that increasingly required patience and a level of intellectualization – was going up against pop, a branch of entertainment that needed little more than a dance-floor. Although the accusations of artistic progress at the expense of mass appeal could also be levelled at some of the more experimental pop artists of the time, the vast majority of popular records released in the UK during 1967 were still aimed at the feet rather than the head. Indeed, singles like The Beatles' 'Penny Lane' or Sandie Shaw's 'Puppet On A String' had a catchiness to them that defied anyone to not smile, while Motown's energized bass riffs and nagging hooks were enough to reanimate a corpse.

Whereas many British jazzmen of Tubby Hayes's generation remained vociferously intolerant of pop music, in America it had been a somewhat different story, with several of the saxophonist's old heroes electing to find some sort of musical middle ground. Indeed, by 1967, the Blue Note label's celebrated roster of jazz stars, from Lee Morgan to Stanley Turrentine, were just as likely to feature covers of songs by Lennon and McCartney, Burt Bacharach or the Four Tops as they were scorching hard bop originals. This spirit of renegotiation didn't just affect younger players. Even older survivors like Buddy Rich and Woody Herman had been forced to concede that rock could yield something useful. The controversial defection of Miles Davis was also just around the corner, prompted by the trumpeter's horrified realization that his audience – once the hippest black cognoscenti on the planet – had abandoned him for the sounds of soul. The message was clear: too much self-indulgence, whether by a post-bop quintet or a free-jazz trio, wasn't winning the music any new friends.

With a press fanfare that looked decidedly puny next to the one for The Beatles' *Sergeant Pepper's Lonely Hearts Club Band*, released the same month, Fontana finally issued *100% Proof* in June 1967. Reactions to the album were generally favourable: those in the partisan camp included Steve Voce, who wrote in *Jazz Journal* that "this record is so good on so many counts that the critic finds himself stuck to avoid superlatives. As a big band record it is more exciting than any of Woody Herman's recent albums. As a tenor album it features better sax than any of Sonny Rollins or Stan Getz's last few issues."[18] The title track was hailed as "a tour de force" which "at times [echoes] Rollins, Coltrane and Getz, but always with the purposefulness we expect from [Hayes]." Voce had long been one of the party-faithful, and was typical of listeners who had already reached all of their critical conclusions about Hayes years before. But alongside the believers there remained those who failed to see the saxophonist as anything other than an overrated pretender. "I'm bound to admit that I find it almost impossible to write objectively about Hayes's solo work," wrote *Jazz Monthly*'s Brian Priestley of *100% Proof*, "simply because, after years of hearing him live and recorded, I seem to have acquired a built-in resistance to the Instant Boredom he usually offers. No sooner does he start one of his marathons than I find I'm concentrating on the rhythm section, or reading the menu, or studying my fingernails."[19]

Priestley had also been the only writer brave enough to raise the rather awkward truth that, for all its spit and polish, *100% Proof* was a record that largely smacked of another era. Indeed, by 1967 the entire notion of big band jazz itself had in some quarters become as "incredibly square" as Priestley had found the album's arrangements. Was this *really* the best Britain could offer in the way of modern jazz – a generic rerun of compositions that were already a decade out of date? Yet again a piece of spectacular tardiness on the part of a record label had succeeded in sabotaging the impact Hayes wished to make. Priestley couldn't have known that Fontana were sitting on a follow-up album by the quartet – a record that was without doubt among the finest British recordings of 1967 – and so his lukewarm reaction had some justification. For his part, Hayes began to experience a sense of déjà vu. It was like Tempo all over again – a reluctant parent label, album releases that were years out of date, and no real commitment to making further recordings. Nevertheless, through a combination of home-spun regard for Hayes's talents, and a love of the big band genre peculiar to British jazz audiences of all eras, *100% Proof* eventually won *Melody Maker*'s Jazz LP of the Year at the beginning of 1968.

The issues over *100% Proof* only added to the feelings of frustration that gripped Hayes at this point, and for the saxophonist the summer of 1967 was less a celebration of peace and love[20] and more an exercise in growing anger, a feeling leavened only by the odd glamorous gig with Georgie Fame or Matt Monro. His personal life continued to be a minefield. The relationship with Joy was now close to its peak, although things remained inconsistent, veering from tender to tumultuous and back with alarming rapidity. The couple's arguments were still as deadly serious as ever, but occasionally they could have a bizarrely comic edge to them, such as the time when, in the heat of a blazing tirade, Hayes had flushed Marshall's wig down the toilet. The relationship's real handicap, however, wasn't the rows: it was the shared addiction, which for both parties was fast deepening. Although he had begun regularly using heroin by this time, Hayes's primary vice remained alcohol. Marshall's tastes meanwhile now included a variety of narcotic substances, from uppers to cocaine, making her already inconsistent behaviour even more unpredictable. Every so often, having witnessed the singer's self-destructive streak in action, Hayes would have second thoughts, casting his mind back to the security and safety of life with his wife and children. During one drunken attempt at a reconciliation, the police had been called to Rose's flat, but refused to intervene until the saxophonist had left the premises.[21] There was also a particularly desperate attempt to win back his wife during which he had telephoned to say that he would kill himself if she didn't agree to meet.[22] Unmoved, Rose was content to call his bluff.

The wider jazz world also continued to trouble him: John Coltrane's death at the age of forty on July 17th, 1967 had marked the end of an era. Exhausted and spent, Coltrane's final years had been confusing for those who, like Hayes, had once regarded him as something of a messianic figure. Beating his chest and chanting, and surrounded by a battery of percussionists and horn players from the left field of the avant-garde, Coltrane's last live appearances had the spectacle of a tribal rite, with familiar material like 'My Favourite Things' now so transformed as to be largely unrecognizable.[23] Like Parker's death before it, the saxophonist's passing had robbed Tubby Hayes of not only a hero, but also of an all-important stylistic benchmark against which to measure his own music. At the dawn of the 1950s, he had dreamt of playing like Parker – the ultimate example of musical modernity. Ten years later it had been Coltrane's cutting-edge ideas that had captured his imagination. At some point between the deaths of these two heroes, Hayes had not only found his own voice, but also reached the peak of his career. The question now was: had he passed it?[24]

There were a handful of gigs that autumn that proved otherwise. He performed '100% Proof' with the Royal Philharmonic Orchestra at the Royal Festival Hall during September and there was even a rare outing for the big band at Ronnie Scott's, an evening all but sabotaged by an inebriated Philly Joe Jones. Peter Burman had also organized another nationwide tour for the quartet, accompanying the American vocalist Dakota Staton, but straight away things went wrong. Arriving in great discomfort for the opening night in Nottingham, Hayes had soldiered through the gig, but there was only one course of action: to concede defeat and return to London. The diagnosis was jaundice, with Peter Burman informing *Melody Maker* that the saxophonist "may be out of action for five or six weeks."[25]

It appears that even another health scare was not enough to curb Hayes's legendary addictive tendencies. As had followed his collapse with thrombosis the previous year, he was now under strict orders to lay off alcohol. It was a nigh-on impossible request: as a hardened social drinker, Hayes had been downing pints with the nonchalant ease of an expert since his teens, and being suddenly prohibited hit him harder than most. In addition to this, the physicians were insisting he now take total rest for three months. "I couldn't do it, for various reasons," he told *Melody Maker*. "I decided to do just the studio work and cut out the jazz dates and everything that involved travelling."[26] This reduced workload didn't sit easily with him, especially when he found that hour upon hour of bland session backing did nothing to improve what little jazz playing he was doing. Self-disgust was a natural by-product; for a musician who had always prided himself on the most exacting of standards, the impact was crushing. In a more abstemious and less driven soul, there would have been no such conflict, but for Hayes the disillusionment and the need to fill the gap left by alcohol led to only one choice, which he described euphemistically as "the other scene" – heroin.

Hayes was not alone in his compulsions. Several leading British jazzmen had already developed substantial heroin addictions, although in examining their differing circumstances there is surprisingly little to suggest a single root cause. Some had initially been fixated by the sheer indulgent nature of addiction, as was the case with Phil Seamen, who became a user, in the words of Stan Tracey, "because I rather fancy he liked the buzz."[27] Others had become addicts out of practical necessity. Tracey himself had turned to various stimulants a few years earlier – uppers at first but eventually progressing to cocaine and heroin – simply to keep on top of his outrageous workload at Ronnie Scott's. For the pianist's frequent musical partner, Bobby Wellins, escapism was the key. "There was no peer pressure," Wellins once tellingly remarked. Ironically enough, he had even had the surreal experience of being warned off of scoring by Phil Seamen. "He used to say to me 'If I ever catch you . . .'" Nevertheless, after years of abstinence, and in the face of what he saw as an insurmountable truth, the saxophonist's willpower eventually crumbled. "It was a general disillusionment that led me into using something to escape the reality of the fact that I wasn't going to be an internationally known jazz player."[28]

So why then would Tubby Hayes, as someone who *was* an internationally acknowledged jazz soloist, and who knew only too well the pitfalls of addiction from first-hand exposure to men such as Wellins and Seamen, allow himself to become an addict? The answers lay less in Hayes's naturally impulsive addictive tendencies than might be imagined. Indeed, it is noticeable that the deepest and most destructive period of his substance abuse occurred not at the peak of his career, during the early 1960s, when one might have expected him to require some sort of additional stimulus, as had Stan Tracey, but during a trough in which he was far less active than he'd ever been.

Inactivity and frustration were not the only contributory factors, though. Hayes was also bitter, a feeling he revealed unstintingly to Wellins. Whereas the younger man's pain came from having never been given the transatlantic breaks – doubly so following the success of Stan Tracey's landmark recording of *Under Milk Wood* – Hayes's ire came more from a feeling of being thwarted. The spade work he'd done as a musical ambassador to the United States earlier in the decade had not been built upon and, according to Wellins, the last straw came when Hayes was called into the office at Ronnie Scott's and summarily told that "his services would no longer be required as often as they had been."[29] Wellins later described the effect on Hayes as "shattering."

As they both slipped further into the trap of addiction, the two saxophonists sometimes found themselves carrying each other's burdens. Wellins remembers one particular incident – both tragic and amusing – during which the elder man had offered some practical assistance – at a price. Says Wellins:

> I was walking the streets, pretty far gone. It must have been two, three in the morning and I saw this little figure coming from the West End with a saxophone case. When he saw me he looked at me and said "What are you doing? What's going on? You're a tramp! And you stink!" And he took me back to [his flat in] Hans Road, which wasn't far away, ran me a bath and said "Get in that bath!" I wore a waistcoat then that was full of files of cocaine and bottles of heroin tablets. I still see it as funny, 'cos he was emptying the pockets and laying the bottles on the table, you see. And it was like a chemist's shop! And he says, "Do you mind if I help myself, old boy?"[30]

Things came to a head for Hayes during the summer of 1968, when, in order to try and right himself, he took the drastic step of turning his back on his career: "In the end I just took the phone off the hook, locked the doors and didn't speak to a soul for about ten weeks. After a while I just came round and realized I had got to get myself out of this but it wasn't so easy."[31] Going "cold turkey" was not an unknown route out of addiction among jazz musicians. Miles Davis and John Coltrane had both done so successfully, but in Tubby Hayes's case he clearly needed help. Even deep in the throes of addiction, vanity and ambition continued to dictate his course. Regardless of the lack of work, and in spite of Pete King's blunt dismissals, he still considered there was a slim chance that he could return to the US. Any permanent move would be rendered impossible if he were to become a registered addict. Indeed, despite his body all but breaking down, his biggest fears were not medical but professional. What if the press found out he was using? How could he recover from all the negative publicity? In truth, it wouldn't have taken a serious-minded hack much digging to uncover Hayes's problem – after all, he was a figure legendary for his capacity to indulge. His new seclusion had also provided an even bigger clue: Hayes had rarely if ever been less than 100% reliable in his professional undertakings. Whatever had now taken him off the scene, with nary a word of warning to those who had booked him, must surely be something that even his iron-man constitution couldn't handle.

Life at his Hans Road flat now took on a surreal nature. There were occasional visitors – Tony Ketley, Phil Bates, Thelonious Monk's saxophonist Charlie Rouse, even the Olympic athlete David Hemery, who lived in the apartment above, but Hayes was frequently lost in a miasmic netherworld: sitting around watching an alternating mix of porn and boxing cine films, wolfing down bowls of ice cream one minute, vomiting the next, then craving steak and chips. In between these bizarre episodes he even attempted a little practice but it seemed pointless. Old friends like Tony Ketley tried to tempt him out, but the most he could do was sit and doze in the local cinema or steal into Harrods to buy chocolate ginger.[32]

This little self-indulgent bubble didn't take long to burst. During a raid on his flat on the afternoon of August 19th, Hayes was arrested and charged with possession of diamorphine before being taken to Charing Cross Hospital. The following day he made a brief appearance at Marlborough Street Magistrates Court and was remanded on bail of £50 with a surety of a further £50. The case was due to be heard on September 11th.

Inevitably, news of the arrest flashed across the national press the following morning, with headlines like "Jazzman on Bail" giving indication enough as to how Fleet Street viewed the saxophonist's plight. Despite the sensational copy, the arrest had actually come as a relief. Hayes could at last now tackle his drug dependency with professional assistance, but, even with this weight now finally off his mind, the forthcoming court appearance would doubtless bring with it yet more unwanted press coverage. He also knew he now faced a possible custodial sentence – how long, he wondered, would it be before he was able to resume his career?

Accompanying him to Marlborough Street on the day of the trial, Tony Ketley was surprised to find that, although now under medical supervision, Hayes had wanted to fix before the hearing began. "I remember he went in the gents before he was up before the beak and made a real mess of his shirt, with blood all up the sleeve, so we changed shirts and he wore my clean one."

"It wasn't a good day for Tubby," Ketley maintained. "There were press outside and a TV crew. There was certainly a short clip of the two of us walking into court on that evening's news. Funnily enough, I also remember Jet Harris from The Shadows was on trial that same day, again for drugs."[33]

Giving evidence, the arresting officer Detective Sergeant Norman "Nobby" Pilcher – notorious for his witch-hunts of celebrated drug users, most famously John Lennon – revealed that, along with a quantity of heroin recovered from Hayes's flat, the police had also found a number of syringes. The court was also informed of Hayes's previous arrest for possession of cannabis in 1954.

The saxophonist's defence counsel, Mr Montague Sherbourne, began his address by offering some mitigating circumstances for his client's addiction, citing matrimonial, domestic and health issues as contributory factors. "He desperately tried to cure himself but suffered withdrawal symptoms. He told me that, when he was arrested, he realized the only salvation was to receive treatment."[34]

The defence also stated that Hayes was now a registered addict receiving regular help at the Hackney Hospital addiction unit. When quizzed as to why his client had not sought help for his problems earlier, Sherbourne declared "he asked me to say that he did not go for help because of guilt of it being made known."[35] The knock-on effect on Hayes's career, it was revealed, had been substantial and his earnings had plummeted to around £30 a week. In his summary Sherbourne concluded that after the humiliation of the recent weeks Hayes was now determined to cure his addiction, a situation he strongly urged the judge to consider when passing sentence. Reinforcing this assertion, Pete King was also called as a character witness, with King emphasizing the importance of Hayes's work and reputation, something that must have had a certain hollow ring to it given the Scott club's recent neglect of his talents.

Hayes entered a plea of guilty and in turn received a six-month suspended sentence with a fine of £50 and a further order to pay £5. 5s. costs. The punishment was lighter than might have been expected, and he was visibly relieved. The following morning, several national newspapers carried the story of the reprieve, with the *Daily Express* giving Hayes a fair and welcome chance to state his case. He told the paper's Ian Christie:

> There are all kinds of pressures on you. I never had any illusions that you play any better for taking drugs. You start using them as a stimulant to blot out your problems but they create more problems. I started on the stuff to try and blot out some of the worries on my mind and leave me free to play. I've been around a long time and I'd seen guys hooked on the stuff. I thought at first that I'd never get in that state, it wouldn't happen to me. Then one day you wake up sweating a bit and the next you can't get out of bed. You are using it not as a stimulant but just to be normal.[36]

His relief was equally evident in an interview in *Melody Maker*, published under the somewhat loaded headline of "Agony of Tubby Hayes." "I hope, and believe, this charge was the answer," he confessed to Bob Dawbarn. "It was the jolt I needed. I've had a pretty horrible three weeks but it had given me the opportunity to continue my career and at the same time get treatment and get straight."[37]

With a peculiar sense of timing Fontana had finally chosen to release *Mexican Green* that autumn. To those not aware of the impact of the avant-garde on his work, the recording came as something of a surprise, with the majority of the local critics – Bob Dawbarn in *Melody Maker*, Jimmy Staples of *Crescendo* and *Jazz Journal*'s Steve Voce – finding the album's title track to be as thrilling a performance as anything Hayes had yet released.

Reviewing what he thought was the saxophonist's "best small group LP yet," *Gramophone*'s Alun Morgan perceptively noted, "this is a free as Hayes would want to play, I suspect, for he has his roots deeply entrenched in the music of Charlie Parker and any Parker-inspired soloist seems to recognize the need for familiar footholds."[38]

There were also less cautious critiques: Pete Moon in *Pieces of Jazz* thought Hayes's playing now "too self-consciously new thingish" and criticized his use of over-long solo cadenzas.[39] Ronald Atkins of *Jazz Monthly* was also lukewarm, trotting out the same old contentions about the saxophonist's technical skill: "Where [Hayes] falls down is between the notes," Atkins declared. "Rhythmically inflexible and with a hard sound that alters little he often becomes caught in a spiral where one string of notes can be followed by a similar string of notes. Compared to Johnny Griffin, [he] is an academician who seems to have learned jazz from a book."[40] However, all of the afore-mentioned reviews agreed on the merits of the Pyne–Mathewson–Levin triumvirate, which Alun Morgan called "the most satisfying and productive unit that Hayes has had since his earliest days as a band leader."[41]

There was a timely irony to the remarks, as by the time of *Mexican Green*'s release, the band had already split. The last straw had come early in 1968, when Hayes had left the group high and dry in order to try and kick his habit, but he now gave a somewhat different story to the press. Tony Levin's increasing unavailability was cited as one reason for the break-up: "[He] couldn't get to rehearsals and I was never sure he could make all the bookings," Hayes told *Melody Maker*, "[so] we never had enough fresh material because of lack of rehearsals."[42] Mike Pyne's disgust at the state of jazz club pianos was another, but in all likelihood these were probably expedient excuses. The band had been together for close to two years, just long enough for Hayes to crave a change. But despite his sangfroid, the saxophonist cannot have helped but feel the loss of Pyne, Mathewson and Levin. The quartet had undoubtedly been his best unit yet, and had brought him closer than ever to the kind of group empathy he'd witnessed in bands such as Miles Davis's and John Coltrane's. However, unlike Coltrane after the end of *his* classic quartet, there was to be no leap into the unknown for Hayes. Indeed, although he now faced a situation unimaginable just a few years before – that of a positive *glut* of young, gifted players – his next group began with the altogether more cautious recruitment of two former colleagues, Phil Bates and Bill Eyden. This time round, he had chosen just one new face, "a wonderful guitarist called Louis Stewart from Dublin."[43]

Wonderful was certainly the word. After cutting his teeth on the provincial Irish jazz scene, Stewart had gone on to win the prestigious soloist award at the 1968 Montreux Jazz Festival. Following the victory, he had opted to base his career in London, but the right kind of work was proving frustratingly elusive. At the time of his recruitment by Hayes, he had been reduced to playing in the orchestra at the London Palladium, "gazing at Cliff Richard's boots." Although only twenty-four years of age, the guitarist already had plenty of jazz experience behind him, and clearly had the ability to stand out in a crowd, but being asked to become a member of the Tubby Hayes quartet was tantamount to receiving a musical knighthood. "I haven't played anything like this before," he told Tony Wilson of *Melody Maker* shortly after joining. "I'd been working with organ and tenor playing ordinary kind of things but Tubby has been very helpful and patient. Some of Tubby's compositions are quite unusual with different bar lengths and things like that. If Tubby wants to keep me I'll be happy to stay."[44]

Regardless of Stewart's reservations,[45] his leader seemed happy enough, praising him unstintingly in the press. "He handles the difficult 'comping' role unobtrusively and with taste in the absence of a piano," Hayes wrote soon after the band's formation. "In this role he follows Terry Shannon, Gordon Beck and Mike Pyne and when I say that I do not miss the piano, it is meant as the highest compliment."[46]

Securing work for a new band was proving far trickier than of yore. Hayes had let many people down during his drug-related exile and now, with minds still fixated on his recent arrest and trial, he found there were barriers present that simply hadn't been there before. As a result, getting the new quartet out of the starting blocks had required far more patience than normal. Formed in August 1968, the band's public debut finally came three months later on November 4th, when they commenced a week-long support slot opposite T-Bone Walker at Ronnie Scott's. There had already been problems settling the personnel during the weeks leading up to the gig: Bill Eyden had left in order to play a tour with Georgie Fame and for a time Tony Levin had temporarily filled the drum chair. By opening night, Hayes had managed to secure the services of the maverick Tony Oxley, an appointment that promised much but which, it soon transpired, was ill fated. In an echo of Hayes's run-in with Phil Seamen in the early 1960s, the drummer's audacious style and equally heavyweight character actually did more to misbalance the band than improve it and after the week at Scott's he moved on.

There were other problems too. If Oxley had proved too far out, then Phil Bates was the opposite, lacking the daring and drive that Ron Mathewson had brought into Hayes's orbit. Letting Bates go required all the diplomacy the band leader could muster, but by the late autumn Mathewson had returned, bringing with him a suggestion for the band's drum chair.

A young philosophy postgraduate studying at London University had recently moved into the basement flat at 80 Sinclair Road, the house Mathewson shared with Ray Warleigh and the Pyne brothers. Passionate about jazz, he had played drums with a quartet whilst at Oxford, accompanying performers such as Joe Harriott, Bobby Wellins and Jimmy Witherspoon. The young student and Mathewson regularly whiled away their afternoons by playing together, each man finding the other a constant joy and inspiration. Indeed, the bassist thought so highly of his flat-mate's talent that he decided to engineer a meeting with Hayes.

Michael "Spike" Wells was just twenty-two years old in 1968, but already he was a jazz drummer of considerable skill, creativity and individuality. A former chorister, and a student of both classical piano and cello, not only was Wells among the most rigorously trained of all the musicians who would work regularly with Tubby Hayes, he was among the most intellectual. A true polymath, he was the kind of character who could have chosen virtually any vocational path and made a sterling success of it. Indeed, his subsequent life would embrace several contrasting changes of direction, each taken to with genuine dedication and commitment. But in many ways the career decision that followed Ron Mathewson's recommendation would remain his most pivotal of all. However, in a situation that mirrored his own recruitment by Hayes two years earlier, Mathewson's attempts to promote Wells's talents initially fell on deaf ears. "I told Tubby about Spike," the bassist recalls, "and kept saying he's fantastic and he was like 'Who? Who the fuck is he?' Anyway eventually we fixed up a rehearsal in my flat."[47]

"[The audition took place] about two or three weeks after the recommendation," remembers Wells. "I just had that sort of short time to get my head around the fact that I was having the opportunity to join the leading jazz group in the country."[48] Appropriately enough, the young drummer's methods of preparation included the necessary concentration on playing at speed: "I woodshedded a lot, particularly playing fast tempos, which was the one thing I knew he would be merciless about."[49]

After "bullying my wrists" over a feverish three-day practice workout, the day of Wells's trial-by-fire finally arrived. "The mini-cab drew up outside Sinclair Road with Tubby and Louis Stewart in it and they came in."[50] Mathewson paints a vivid picture of what happened next: "Spike's setting his drums up. He was terrified. So we're talking and Spike's just sitting there behind the drums. Tubby turns round and goes 'Blues in B flat' and off we go, some nice medium tempo thing or other and Spike sounds *great.*"[51]

However, unbeknown to the drummer, Mathewson and Hayes had already cooked up a little tension-building wind-up:

> After we stop, Tubby turns to me and Louis and says "Fellas, can I have a word?" And off we go in a huddle, with these serious-looking faces, and Tubby's whispering "Fucking hell. He's terrific! He's in!"

Anyway he goes over to Spike, still with this grim face, and then starts smiling and says "You've got the job!" Spike nearly fell off his drums![52]

For Wells, "the job" was a dream one, not least of all because of the musical freedom it provided. "[Tubby] hired you because he liked something about your playing. And, as long as you provided it, he would let you do what you wanted. He didn't put you into any sort of narrow groove."[53] Indeed, Wells had brought in an approach that was far looser than that of any of Hayes's previous drum incumbents.

> It was a reflection of what was going on in jazz with Miles's band with Tony Williams, as well as Elvin Jones with Coltrane. There were freedoms opened up in the concept of how to play together rather than just accompany. We were all spinning ideas off each other in a rather more democratic way and that was what Tubby liked to get into at that point. It was a challenge for Tubby, but in a positive sense. It wasn't a struggle. He was very stimulated by it, in the sense that he wanted a looser rhythm section that wasn't just going to stick down time in a very regulated way.[54]

Despite his high ideals, Wells's first gig with the quartet that November made for a decidedly undignified debut. Things started badly and got worse. The quartet had been booked to appear at Norwich University and, as none of the band drove, Hayes had hired a mini-cab, which turned up late. Leaving at 5.30 for a concert starting at 8 pm was a tight squeeze, but all being well they could still make it. A traffic snarl-up in Leytonstone put paid to any spare time and as the clock ticked round to 7 pm they had still to escape the outskirts of north-east London. Eventually, after a heroic effort and much cursing, the band arrived at the university around 10 pm. Wells remembers an eager but disgruntled crowd eyeing him expectantly as he hurriedly set up his drums on stage. Finally, at nearly 10.30 pm, the quartet began to play its reduced forty-five-minute set.

If it seemed things couldn't get any worse, the return journey was even more eventful. The band's taxi ran out of petrol on a deserted East Anglian road, but as the cabbie strode bravely off into the night to get help, petrol was the last thing on Hayes's mind. It had been over six hours since his last fix and he had run out of heroin. After a few more fraught hours, with a restless, sweating saxophonist to placate, the quartet eventually limped back into London in the early hours. The final indignity came when the cheque Hayes had given Wells bounced. "I thought 'Welcome to the big time!'"[55]

The first few gigs with the new Tubby Hayes quartet taught Wells a great deal about his leader, both musically and personally. Although now a registered addict, there were still issues with his drug intake. "At one level it enabled him to function, at another it was damaging. It was nothing for him to open his door to you with a needle in his arm. No one said anything about it. It was just something he did."[56] The drummer also recalls fairly frequent attempts to cure the drug dependency by obliterating it with alcohol. "He used to drink heavily to try and compensate. He tended to do one or the other. When he was using he wouldn't drink but if he tried to come off it was heavy vodka and cokes."[57] And, like Charles Mingus and John Coltrane, Hayes's oscillating weight now necessitated him having two wardrobes, "a fat one and a thin one."[58] Even his nickname came in for a new twist: "We now dubbed him Tubular or Tubey," Wells remembers.[59]

In addition to these self-inflicted pressures, there was the ever-present threat of rearrest, not only as a user but as a potential dealer. "Nobby" Pilcher, the arresting officer from the previous August, continued to hover like a spectre, in Wells's words, "forever on Tubby's back hoping to nick him." Pilcher took his business seriously, but amid the air of intimidation, he'd occasionally provide moments of sheer comedy.

> One night Nobby arrived at Hans Road with another policeman
> and found it very dimly lit – there was a blue light on, as it happens,
> very appropriately. Tubby, my then girlfriend Wivi-Ann and I, and
> a few others, were having a take-away. In the middle of this rather
> stern lecture, Tubby noticed something and turned to Nobby and
> uttered the unforgettable words: 'Excuse me officer, but you're
> standing in my meat pie."[60]

With his drug intake regulated, if not yet wholly under control, Hayes's personal life at last looked as if it might steady. Then, on November 21st, 1968 he received the shattering news of the sudden death of Joy Marshall. The singer had been found alone in her flat, apparently the victim of an accidental overdose of barbiturates. She was thirty-two.

Although they were no longer a couple at the time of her death, Marshall's passing hit her ex-boyfriend like an express train. That same evening, he was uncharacteristically late for the quartet's gig in Walthamstow, arriving drunk and maudlin, finishing the evening by vomiting over the promoter's open diary.[61] Booze might temporarily mask his grief, but those who knew Hayes well saw that he had lost the closest thing he'd ever had to a soul-mate. Tony Ketley thought that, of all the women in Hayes's life, Joy was the only one who had offered something that had genuinely affected him.

> Tubby was a strong character and he liked his own way, but Joy
> was strong too and could fight back. She was incredibly possessive.
> I remember her hauling me out of a meeting at work demanding
> to know where Tubby was, screaming at me. Things were fiery
> between them, but she genuinely loved him and cared for him and

I think, because he couldn't dominate her, the relationship meant much more to him.[62]

As with the passing of his friend Johnny Butts, Hayes chose to commemorate Marshall musically, dedicating a new composition to her memory, appropriately titled 'Song For A Sad Lady'. A little over two years had elapsed since he had written 'A Dedication To Joy'. They were years that were to leave a deep scar.

As 1968 closed the new quartet clocked up its first round of London gigs, playing familiar venues including the Three Tuns in Beckenham, the Copper at Tower Bridge and the Hopbine in North Wembley (a bootleg recording of which exists) and, if not quite as absurdly over-packed with incident as Spike Wells's Norwich University debut, these engagements also had their share of ups and downs. To the drummer's abject disappointment, Ron Mathewson had proved far less "available" than he'd first appeared, and his absence required a list of deps, some less suited to the job than others.

> I remember one bassist being booked on a gig and me getting very excited because he'd always been a favourite of mine. In the end, he was next to useless as he was too pissed to hold it together. I was getting very disillusioned by this and feeling very much like the band wasn't what I'd thought it might become a few weeks before when I'd joined. Tubby was great though and said "Come on and play! Ignore him. I'm just listening to you anyway" which did sort of lift me.[63]

Fortunately, Mathewson was on hand two weeks later on December 18th when the new Tubby Hayes quartet made its BBC *Jazz Club* debut, sharing the bill with the bands of Joe Harriott and Art Ellefson.[64] The repertoire was that which the group were playing nightly on gigs, mixing hard bop, tinges of free improvisation and, in Hayes's new 'Song For A Sad Lady', a fashionable dash of rock rhythms. Spike Wells in particular found his leader at his most unconvincing when making such attempts. "I don't think eight-to-the-bar rhythms were really Tubby's natural thing, but, again it's what people were doing then. All the great players on the Blue Note label had started to put sort of rock and roll sounding tracks on their albums."[65]

11 The Beginning of the End (1969–72)

Tubby was a big deal for me and to see him propped up in bed with long hair and all that really got to me. So I told him and he just said "Come on, we'll have none of that!" He just laughed it off.

Stan Robinson

The final year of the 1960s was one of consolidation for Tubby Hayes. 1968 may well have marked a personal watershed, but after Joy Marshall's death steadying his drug intake was made doubly hard. The addiction unit at Hackney continued to provide the crutch necessary to successfully regulate his habit, but Hayes's compulsive and gargantuan appetite for life – those "addictive tendencies" – inevitably surfaced in other forms. As the New Year dawned, it did so in bouts of binge-drinking, accompanied by outbursts of anger and, rare for Hayes, musical incoherence. Stranded on the South coast after a gig that January, he and Louis Stewart had nearly come to blows.[1] Disarmingly apologetic once he'd calmed down, Hayes knew that there was only so far he could push Stewart: the guitarist's ultimate riposte was to simply threaten to leave and move back to Dublin.

If this were a time to take personal stock, it was also a good juncture at which to look back over the preceding decade of his career. Although the British jazz scene had now changed considerably since his arrival nearly twenty years earlier, the high regard for Hayes from both musicians and the public remained unaltered. Even with his work now thinner on the ground than it had been a few years before, there was no doubting his continued eminence. The publication of the 1969 *Melody Maker* jazz poll results on March 1st confirmed this: he had retained his tenor title – his tenth win in the category – and had again been voted the paper's Musician of the Year.[2]

Just ahead of the publication of the poll results, as part of a new series of articles titled "Second Opinion," *Melody Maker*'s Christopher Bird (a *nom de plume* for the Musicians' Union's Brian Blain) took the opportunity to examine Hayes's career at length. As one of the less obsequious local jazz writers, Bird wasn't afraid to address the old argument that Hayes's outward extroversion actually masked a less assured musical character. Taking the saxophonist's legend apart with remarkable candour, he postulated that his subject

> was never as confident as he seemed. Superficially, yes, he was ready to take on any of the American giants, but musically his Achilles heel was his unwillingness to leave things out; it seemed as if he had to state every change directly rather than concentrate on a melodic line and imply the harmony more often. This, of course, is the characteristic of the really confident jazz musician.[3]

If the main thrust of the critique was ultimately little more than an eloquent update of the "too many notes" diatribes, prudently Bird chose to close his overview by expressing his hope that Hayes's "psychological hurdle," musical verbosity, could finally be surmounted and that "[he] will mature completely and unconditionally into one of the truly great jazz musicians – not just a world class player, as has often been stated, but an artist of the highest class."[4]

Despite the occasional sniffiness of the critics, Hayes continued to be enormously popular with grassroots audiences. Reviewing the quartet's gig at the Torrington in North Finchley the very same week that Hayes had been awarded the *Melody Maker*'s bouquets, the paper's Alan Walsh put his finger on what continued to make Hayes such an enduring draw for local jazz fans: his charisma. "Once more [proving] there is no more exciting tenorist in Europe," Walsh reported, "[he] has what so many good tenor players lack – a sense of showmanship and presentation."[5]

Indeed, even after his very public trial and conviction, Hayes had retained his ability to sell himself, both within and outside of jazz. Even more importantly, he'd at last reconciled his feelings about session work. Just a few years earlier he'd baulked at how much time he was spending in the studios, thinking that it was somehow undermining his talents as a jazz player. But with his work on commercial projects now more diverse than ever, he had at last struck a balance that was sustainable. During 1969 there were regular sessions for BBC Radio One's *Late-Night Extra* with the David Francis Tentette alongside soundtrack work on various film projects, including, most famously, *The Italian Job*, featuring a score tailor-made by Quincy Jones for a group of British jazzmen also containing Tony Coe and Peter King. He had also made an appearance on an album by Family, a band exploring the new sub-genre of progressive rock. And, most bizarrely of all, he featured on the

LP *Hymns-A-Swinging*, a production co-starring the Mike Sammes Singers – a staple part of the UK's radio diet – and the Ted Taylor Organsound, on which traditional hymns were given a surreal 1960s make-over.[6]

Even within his natural jazz orbit, he occasionally found himself in the position of "flown in" guest star. In May he depped for Ronnie Scott in the international Clarke–Boland Big Band at the Vienna Jazz Festival, and a month later he appeared at the Queen Elizabeth Hall with the John Mayer–Joe Harriott Indo-Jazz Fusions, playing the principal part in Mayer's new suite 'Tenor Rhapsody'.

Keen to build upon his continuing popularity, he had also set in motion the relaunch of his big band.[7] Spurred on by the example of Maynard Ferguson's British band – which via regular mainstream TV appearances had successfully launched the Canadian trumpeter's bravura style to a wider public – this time around Hayes envisaged a unit far more flexible than its predecessors. There were cues from across the Atlantic too: Buddy Rich and Woody Herman had effectively reinvented themselves – and the big band genre – by annexing contemporary pop material, whilst the unexpected rise of Blood, Sweat and Tears had shown that the listening public was now happy to embrace music that offered a level of written sophistication drawn directly from jazz. "What I want to do with this band is rather different to any of the big bands I've had before," Hayes told the press. "There's quite a bit of money gone into it – copying, stands, management and that sort of thing – and I see no reason why we can't go into the late night broadcasting field as well as jazz. There is no reason why we can't develop a softer, rather more commercial side."[8]

Those brought in to collaborate with Hayes on the new band's pad, which encompassed music by Lennon and McCartney, Burt Bacharach, Sergio Mendes and the Fifth Dimension, included old hands like Harry South and Les Condon, but there was also new blood in the shape of Dick Walter, a young composer and arranger who was soon to make a substantial mark in television writing. Walter later remembered how "very open to any suggestions" Hayes had been, in particular enthusing about composers such as Burt Bacharach, an attitude that initially surprised him.[9]

In recruiting the remainder of the band Hayes demonstrated a similarly up-to-date attitude. Indeed, his choices revealed that he had been paying close attention to the local jazz scene. Ronnie Scott's recent flop, The Band, featuring John Surman, Tony Oxley and Kenny Wheeler, among others, had shown first the novelty and then the folly of centring a group almost wholly on new stars; consequently, Hayes was far more cautious in his appointments. Familiar faces – Les Condon, Harry Klein, Keith Christie *et al.* – were to be mixed with a judicious smattering of new talent, including trombonist Dave Horler and New Zealand tenorist Brian Smith. The latter remembers Hayes's call as being both unexpected and straight to the point: "He asked if I would like to play in his big band he was getting together – I was really knocked out

The Tubby Hayes Quartet, St Helene Hotel, Guernsey, Monday April 28th, 1969. Spike Wells, Jeff Clyne and Louis Stewart accompany the boss on flute. Courtesy Robin Millard.

to be asked," the saxophonist remembers. "The first sax section rehearsal was at his flat that was behind Harrods. We used his bed as a music stand."[10]

The new band made its public debut in April 1969, with a shake-down gig at the Bull's Head in Barnes on the 21st followed later the same week by an appearance on the BBC's *Jazz Club*. Although the entire cast was under heavy scrutiny, perhaps the biggest weight rested on the shoulders of Spike Wells, who had never before played with a big band. The leader had been somewhat apprehensive as to how Wells's loose post-Elvin Jones style would fit a bigger line-up, but to his delight the drummer acquitted himself marvellously, even eliciting praise from the band's dyed-in-the-wool session-men. "Tommy Watt, the arranger, came down [to the first gig] and he said something quite interesting," Wells remembers: "'Most big band drummers sound like they're driving the band from the bridge whereas Spike sounds like he's down in the engine room'. I was rather pleased with that!"[11]

The new band also broke the hiatus on Hayes's recording career. It had been two years since he had recorded an album under his own name and he was beginning to experience the same kind of air-locked frustration with Fontana that he'd felt during the latter days of his earlier Tempo contract. Nevertheless, when he approached Jack Baverstock in the spring of 1969, he wasted no time in setting out his stall: as well as taping the quartet, he wanted to record a session by the big band, augmented on some titles with strings, aimed at capturing a wider audience. Baverstock liked both ideas, but was especially keen to push the commercial project, hastily scheduling a session for May 27th.[12]

The concept may have served Hayes's and his producer's commercial intentions perfectly, but it held little appeal for some of the musicians involved, as Ian Hamer recalled: "What I regret about that is that we never actually recorded our music. The only thing we ever did [record] was Jack Baverstock's idea, where we're all playing the pop tunes of the time. I think we did '[The Other Man's] Grass is Always Greener' [on our gigs] but very few of the others we ever played on a jazz date."[13]

Indeed, playing a repertoire including such fare as 'These Boots Are Made For Walking', 'This Guy's In Love With You' and 'Hey Jude', the studio regulars among Hayes's crew were operating in familiar middle-of-the-road territory and could be forgiven in thinking that a band they'd originally joined for kicks was starting to resemble their day job.

Spike Wells, however, thought otherwise: "It *was* quite a commercial record as far as arrangements were concerned but I have to say I thought it was one of the best things I'd ever heard Tubby do. In terms of solos, they were beautiful. He played superbly [and] I think he genuinely liked [playing] these slightly Latin American things."[14]

Fontana released the album under the title of *The Orchestra* the following year, and although it certainly makes for a somewhat anticlimactic conclusion to Hayes's time with the label, forty-five years later it's difficult to remain quite so hard-boiled about its contents. There are many beautiful bursts of Hayes's tenor, some all the more effective for their brevity, and the whole is no more offensive to jazz fans' ears than some of Stan Getz's contemporary productions on the Verve label.[15] As can be expected, the music is played with a panache and professionalism that is entirely characteristic of Hayes's approach to all his projects, commercial or otherwise. In some instances, his recastings show familiar material in an all new light: for example, Barbra Streisand's 'Free Again' comes up freshly minted as a soaring tenor ballad, while on 'These Boots Are Made For Walking' Hayes's growling flute fights its way out of a chart that is as funky as anything Roland Kirk ever set to disc.

The record is not a wholesale success, though, and occasionally the pop material simply refuses to budge over into the jazz vernacular, the worst offender being a version of The Beatles' 'Hey Jude', during which the leader can find almost nothing of worth on a distinctly pedestrian chart. At the time of writing, *The Orchestra* remains one of the few Hayes albums not to have reappeared on CD. However, the project has left its mark, one that Hayes himself might have approved of given the album's original commercial intentions: in a bizarre twist, 'Hey Jude' ended up being reissued on vinyl during the jazz-friendly DJ boom of the 1980s, sampled principally for Spike Wells's thundering introduction, and has since gone on to achieve a certain underground cult following.

The BBC had also earmarked the Tubby Hayes big band for two new programmes that summer: *Jazz Workshop*, a radio series giving several key British musicians the opportunity to broadcast thirty minutes of music in whatever instrumental contexts they chose, and *The Jazz Scene*, a television slot showcasing the best of the local talent, to be recorded in the new colour format.

Recorded at BBC Maida Vale on July 25th, and packing no less than eighteen musicians into five performances ranging through big band, nonet, sextet and quartet, the *Jazz Workshop* broadcast (released on CD by the Mastermix label during the early 1990s) was the single most diverse piece of work Hayes had recorded since the sessions for the *Tubbs* album back in 1961. Reviewing the show for *Crescendo* magazine, Brian Gladwell thought the results showed the leader trying just a shade too hard to be all-inclusive. "Perhaps to demonstrate his awareness of current trends, [he] seemed to garnish his playing with the occasional freak-out."[16] The programme had closed with an expanded update of '100% Proof' – appropriately renamed '200% Proof' – utilizing a four-man bass and drums team of Ron Mathewson, Jeff Clyne, Spike Wells and Tony Levin, and allotting the solo space equally between Hayes and Ronnie Scott. The arrangement's free-form climax found both tenorists fully embracing the "current trends," and sounding more like Coltrane and Pharoah Sanders than the super-slick hard boppers of yore. It was another reminder of how radically the two saxophonists' musical landscape had altered since their days together in the Jazz Couriers.

In an interesting "compare and contrast" piece written about the two men for *Jazz Journal* that summer, Steve Voce attempted to identify what now lay at the heart of their playing:

> Scott's tenor playing has always made an interesting comparison with Tubby Hayes, as has been shown when they've worked together. Whereas Hayes is a more pyrotechnic player who makes full use of his fluency, Scott has a more direct and solid approach, his pithy tone and more angular phrasing producing the same results as Tubby's restless agility. In the welter of Griffin, Rollins and Henderson-inspired tenors of today, it probably escapes a lot of listeners that Ronnie and Tubby are thoroughbred romantics in the line of Getz, Hawkins and Webster, as well as supplementing their styles from the music of later men.[17]

Therein lay the rub. Whilst the abandoned climax of '200% Proof' had shown a highly energized use of some of the more obvious traits of the new wave, there remains something of a false ring to it all. All Scott and Hayes had really done in "supplementing" their music was to take a few of the latest devices and graft them into their established methods. Indeed, the fashionable free-for-all blowing that had marked out much of the territory of the post-Coltrane avant-garde was not a natural home for musicians who had already worked so hard to play by purely harmonic rules: they remained intensely curious about the new music, but its influence was unlikely to leave much of a lasting impact on their own playing. "Tubby never quite cracked the Coltrane language," Spike Wells later maintained. However, eight days after taping the *Jazz Workshop* session, Hayes participated in a further BBC broadcast under Harry South's leadership, during which he went head to head with Alan Skidmore, a young tenorist whose bellowing, intense style *had* synthesized the best of all the post-Coltrane saxophonists. The energy, fire and commitment in Skidmore's playing instantly struck a chord in Hayes – here was a player who might just be able to assist in finding his own route towards the cutting edge.

As the son of one of the UK's best-known tenor saxophonists, rising through the ranks of the modern jazz business had been a sometimes trying experience for Skidmore junior. At first, being the offspring of a famous father had helped open doors – he was a player who, simply through osmosis, had an instinctive grasp of jazz saxophone playing – but when his own musical tastes began to reach for the outer limits during the mid-1960s, many of those same doors slammed shut. Whereas Jimmy Skidmore had been all rosy-toned, easy swing, his son had taken the message of John Coltrane's early sixties work as a starting point, but opportunities to develop this style were few and far between, especially in the UK.

For much of the decade Skidmore had divided his time between R&B bands and studio work, forging close musical ties with several of the most adventurous local jazzmen – Kenny Wheeler, John Surman and Tony Oxley amongst them. Together they had realized that new music required a new scene, where innovation was encouraged rather than regarded with suspicion, and for a time they found a spiritual home at "The Old Place," Ronnie Scott's former Gerrard Street premises, which after Scott and Pete King's departure for Frith Street in 1965 had become a hub of musical exploration. They also looked to continental Europe – lured by its promise of greater musical freedom, radio station patronage and better fees. Ironically, success abroad brought belated recognition at home: when Skidmore's quintet featuring Wheeler and Oxley swept the board at the Montreux Jazz Festival in the summer of 1969 – with the leader winning the best soloist award – there was a sudden clamour of interest from some unlikely quarters, as Skidmore remembers.

> I was very influenced by the *very* late Coltrane when he was doing that amazing stuff that nobody could quite figure out, and I had begun to get a pretty big name for myself in Europe doing that kind of thing, so when I came back [to London] it became known in the business that I was doing that free sort of thing. Tubby then started to check it out. He loved it. He was really very enthusiastic about

it and so was Ronnie – the pair of them – and they kind of looked to me. It felt really very strange, very weird; for years I'm looking up to them as my heroes and then *this*.[18]

Given this mutual admiration, the recruitment of Skidmore to the Tubby Hayes big band in the summer of 1969 was almost inevitable. However, the appointment had much more to it than face value. Together with Brian Smith, Hayes now had two of the local frontrunners on his own instrument within his own unit, a situation that both illustrated the breadth of his musical vision and continued the time-honoured tradition of band leaders effectively annexing any potential opposition. Hayes may not have been quite as canny as King Oliver when he had enrolled the young Louis Armstrong, nor as naïve as Coltrane had been when, towards the end of his life, he began to augment his quartet with ranks of would-be avant-gardists of varied ability, but the effect was the same: he now had a direct conduit to what was happening up at the youthful cutting edge. Skidmore and Hayes would pay long visits to the factory of renowned saxophone mouthpiece manufacturer Berg Larsen, spending hours looking for the elusive holy grail of the perfect mouthpiece. However, alongside this enthusiasm for new sounds, the younger man also saw signs of something else in Hayes, far more troubling than mere vanity. "You'd begin to notice that he was short of breath on gigs. He wasn't playing those really long solos any more. It was beginning to change."[19]

One of Skidmore's earliest gigs with Hayes was a recording for the BBC's new TV series, *The Jazz Scene At Ronnie Scott's* in August 1969. Although the BBC themselves appear not to have retained a copy of the programme, a grainy video duplication has passed among collectors and is now available to view on YouTube (Tubby Hayes at Ronnie Scott's 1970 – it has been misdated by whoever posted it). To *see* as well as hear the Hayes band at this point is fascinating. Looking alarmingly un-Tubby, the leader is a captivating study in contrast – cool and professional one minute, wildly animated and sweating the next. His sidemen make for even more interesting viewing, a disparate collective of personal images united by what the BBC costume department must have thought the very latest in sartorial hipness – garish open-necked shirts and cravats. The musical highlights are fortunately less time-bound, with the exception of 'Song For A Sad Lady' which, even by this point, was already beginning to sound like an idea whose novelty had waned. The jewel is undoubtedly Hayes's gorgeous reading of Duke Pearson's ballad 'You Know I Care', played with more than a hint of Getzian flair.

To accompany the launch of the new series, *Radio Times* published a profile of Hayes, complete with a cartoon of the saxophonist by Philip Castle that wouldn't have disgraced the animations of Terry Gilliam. Alongside the usual questions about his background and upbringing, Charles Fox probed a little deeper for an opinion on the latest jazz trends: "What I really like,"

Hayes said revealingly, "is the way the rhythm is more varied, not just the old ching-ching-ching."[20]

The quartet had also begun recording a new album for Fontana that summer, but, whereas the recent big band project had gone off without a hitch, this time things were more problematic. Louis Stewart's relative inexperience hadn't proved much of an issue on the band's live engagements, but, in the rather more calculated environment of the recording studio, the guitarist found his nerves less easy to ignore. Attempting to alleviate his feelings with alcohol only made matters worse. In his own particularly volatile frame of mind – the result of an oscillation between drink and drugs – Stewart's boss didn't take things lightly, with at least one of the days in the studio ending in a blazing row.[21] Several sessions in June and July – some bringing Mick Pyne back in – yielded nothing that Hayes saw as useful and the resulting tapes have remained unreleased. "I'm sure if we heard them now, we'd like them," Spike Wells says, "but Tubby just wasn't happy with it at all."[22]

With Pyne now permanently replacing Stewart, on September 26th the band recorded a radio session for another new BBC series, *Jazz In Britain*, during which the presenter Miles Kington praised Hayes for being one of the few veteran British modernists "to have recruited their sidemen from among the new generation."

"I don't think he's risen to any sort of challenge in doing this," Kington continued. "He's simply responded naturally to the presence of new, exciting blood, which represents a tribute to both sides. Many of his contemporaries have sunk into a comfortable premature old age but Tubby Hayes has refused ever to admit that he sounds less than young. In a lesser player this might be pathetic, but with Tubby Hayes one feels that he derives as much challenge as ever in the act of squeezing the best out of a harmonic framework."

Supporting Kington's last point, the broadcast contained none of the garish freak-outs Hayes had recently indulged in with the big band, and, if anything, the repertoire, balancing standards with original material, looked back to the glory days of the early 1960s.

The time seemed right for a little retrospection. Indeed, as he stood at the dawn of the 1970s, Hayes had a great deal to look back upon. British jazz had moved in almost unbelievably huge strides in the previous ten years: Joe Harriott's free-form, Stan Tracey's *Under Milk Wood*, the Spontaneous Music Ensemble, Mike Westbrook's band and the nascent jazz-rock of Nucleus had, in barely a few years, charted a course which had taken the nation's jazzmen from emulation to innovation. Britain's jazzmen were now not merely international contenders but international *contributors*. By the end of the 1960s, two British musicians – John McLaughlin and Dave Holland – were working and recording with Miles Davis, a dream appointment that would have been all but impossible without Tubby Hayes's pioneering example. Although his own triumphs in America may not have led to a permanent departure for foreign shores, as had been so often predicted earlier in the decade, there was no doubt that Hayes had done British musicians of all stripes a huge service in alerting the world that their country could – and *did* – produce world-class jazz talent. This achievement may well have assured him a place in history, but, as the coming years were soon to reveal, Hayes could no longer rely on reputation alone.

The new decade began promisingly with a rare out-of-town tour for the big band, organized by Hayes's new manager Don Norman. The first date, at the Lafayette Club in Wolverhampton on January 26th, 1970 went as well as could be expected, although the leader had been plagued by breathlessness for most of the evening. One of the band, bassist Dave Green, even suggested Hayes try the inhaler he'd been issued with for his asthma, but it was little help.[23] The following night in Birmingham, Hayes's condition was worse still. "Tubby just suddenly looked terrible. We weren't quite sure what was wrong,"[24] Peter King remembers: "In the break, [he] came off unable to breathe. We were so worried about him."[25] "He couldn't make more than about sixteen bars, a chorus at the very most and he'd slump down into his chair," recalls Alan Skidmore. "But he was still there, he was still doing the gig and it was frightening. He was absolutely done for and I had to stand up and take over from him."[26] During the interval, as the players flocked to find out what was wrong, Hayes asked King to take over the band for the second set: "I felt honoured and very humbled that out of all the great players in the band he turned to me in his time of crisis, but the lasting memory is of our fears about Tubby's sudden physical collapse. It turned out to be the beginning of the end for him."[27]

It appears that Hayes tried to soldier on after his return from Birmingham, although Spike Wells's diary lists a number of gigs in the following weeks that probably never took place.[28] Serious bronchial problems certainly prevented his participation in a BBC *Jazz Club* broadcast by the big band on February 21st and two weeks later on March 7th *Melody Maker* ran the story that he had finally been taken into the Royal Free Hospital in Grays Inn Road, under observation for an "unidentified infection"[29] and would "not be in a condition to blow for some considerable time." Supporting this, Don Norman issued a statement saying that it looked likely that Hayes would be out of action for at least two or three months and that he was unable to commit to any bookings before June.

Although the press had not hinted at the seriousness of Hayes's condition, he was now gravely ill. The infection that had floored him had attacked his heart, lungs and liver, and an explanation as to how it had been contracted was agonizingly slow in coming. However, it eventually transpired that, although his drug intake was now less than it had ever been, the illness may have been the result of his earlier use of a soiled syringe, with the infection simply lying dormant until triggered by Hayes's inconsistent lifestyle. No one could really be sure. Dorothy Hayes was informed by the specialists that even something as mundane as an unclean razor blade may have been the culprit,[30] but whatever the cause it was clear that Hayes's body would take a long time to strengthen again.

For an individual as restless as Tubby Hayes, languishing in hospital was especially difficult. Indeed, fifteen weeks of mind-numbing inactivity even began to affect his appearance. He now sported an impressive beard, which in addition to his flowing locks, made him all but unrecognizable. Visiting times broke the monotony, although, as saxophonist Stan Robinson discovered, Hayes didn't want to be pitied. "Tubby was a big deal for me and to see him propped up in bed with long hair and all that really got to me. So I told him and he just said 'Come on, we'll have none of that!' He just laughed it off."[31]

With so much time on his hands, Hayes at last had opportunity to take stock of the musical world around him. Whilst this sabbatical may well have proved personally therapeutic, for his erstwhile sidemen the saxophonist's sudden indisposition had called for some quick thinking, as Spike Wells remembers:

> I was actually quite lucky up until this point work-wise. As well as Tubby's band, I was working in Ronnie Scott's sextet and we worked often at the club and as a result I was accompanying some of the Americans there. Mick, Ron and I then went off to Sweden for a while with Stan Getz. I was also doing stuff with Humphrey Lyttelton but I strongly got the feeling that Tubby thought I owed him my first loyalty, I suppose because I got my "break" with him, and that he expected me to be there when he was back playing. But then Ronnie's band folded, and the things with Humph ended and so, without those and Tubby's work, I had to think of my options.[32]

Never a man to do things by halves, Wells decided that it was time for an altogether more radical change of direction. "To be honest, I was bored with some bits of the lifestyle of jazz at this time and I wanted to do something to go alongside it, and so I decided to study law with a view to becoming a solicitor."[33] News of the drummer's "defection" made it into *Melody Maker*, which ran an article titled "The Musical Obituary of Spike Wells."[34] "It was all a bit over-dramatic," Wells remembers. "In reality I was just doing something else alongside the playing. I was still gigging and I certainly hadn't lost any enthusiasm for the actual performance."[35]

When he finally emerged from hospital that summer, Hayes was interviewed by *Melody Maker*'s Max Jones.[36] The veteran writer found his subject – freshly shaved and with his oversized clothes hanging off a much thinner frame – "in pretty good shape." Nevertheless, when Jones enquired as to his current state of health, he received an uncharacteristically cautious answer: "I've got to build up my strength again and watch the ticker. I'm making progress and I'm an out-patient at the hospital. I still get pretty breathless if I walk upstairs or up a hill. I do quite a bit of walking where I'm staying with friends in the suburbs." Hayes also confessed that he was still unable to play the tenor: "I hope to be back on it soon. It's right by the bed and I keep looking at it because that horn's my first love." In the meantime he'd begun to build up his musical muscles with the flute and had "noticed no ill-effects so far."

In truth, Hayes's initial reaction to his new-found freedom was much less measured than he had led Jones to believe. As his friend Tony Ketley recalled, the summer of 1970 was "a barmy period for Tubby." "He went a bit potty in some ways, after all these months in hospital."[37] With typical forthrightness, he began a brief relationship with guitarist Dave Goldberg's widow Sylvia, a journalist who had earlier been married to Ketley, "moving in with her for a time in Pinner, but it didn't last all that long."

His drug intake was now marginal, but he had been advised that further heroin use would only lead to more medical complications. In a final effort to permanently clean himself up, he moved in with Harry and Harriet South, going "cold turkey" for the second time in as many years. This time it worked. One part of the "addictive tendencies" at last appeared to have been banished forever but, as usual, Hayes proved to be every bit his own worst enemy. In lieu of heroin, other substances now entered the picture.

One of Hayes's heroes, Stan Getz, had recently decamped to London, seeking respite from years of alcohol abuse. But whenever the two men hung out they did little to aid their shared need to calm down. Hayes would visit Getz's hotel suite, and the pair would allegedly take LSD, an experience that found them staring into an empty bath and seeing incredible hallucinatory images.[38] According to Tony Ketley, Hayes was also drinking far too much, in spite of the recent warnings: "I can remember him walking into this pub and ordering two double vodkas and the barman asking if it was one each. Tubby then drunk them both down. It was like 'I'm out of hospital and I don't give a damn.'"[39]

It wasn't until part-way through the autumn of 1970 that Tubby Hayes felt strong enough to begin performing in public. With typical boldness, he threw himself straight back in at the deep end, scheduling three big band engagements for early November: The Bull's Head at Barnes, Jackie Sharpe's Downbeat Club and a broadcast on BBC Radio One's *Jazz Club*. With a jam-packed audience eager to welcome Hayes back, the return to the band's old stamping ground in Barnes was a guaranteed success. But, despite taking things much easier on the stand, the leader was still not prepared to suffer fools, as fan Bernie Collett witnessed. As he made a last-minute adjustment to one band part, Hayes's directions were clear for all to hear:

> He was reading out loud a score of notes ending with B natural. The room was full but quiet – then some smart arse shouted "Never mind B natural – just be quick." Tubbs then stopped and looked at the bloke and said "If you fuckers can do any better you are

welcome to come up here and try." Needless to say, no more was said.[40]

Although he was now ostensibly well enough to take gigs, Hayes continued to do his best to conceal the strain the work placed upon him. He remained an out-patient at Hammersmith Hospital, principally for the doctors to monitor his liver, which, compounded by his hard drinking and previous jaundice problems, had been the most prominent casualty among the organs attacked by his recent infection. Further tests to ascertain the cause of continued breathlessness had also revealed that, although his lungs had been weakened by the infection and his previous thrombosis, the problem actually stemmed from a faulty heart valve. As the specialists worked out the most effective form of treatment, he was invited to spend Christmas at Don Norman's home at Itchenor, taking the opportunity to visit Bobby Wellins, recently relocated to nearby Bognor Regis.

Since his days as a sideman in Hayes's big band, things had gone from bad to worse for Wellins. Addiction had made him unreliable and, at its worst, difficult to deal with and the phone had simply stopped ringing. His only salvation was the love and support of his wife Isabelle, who at the end of the 1960s had taken him out of London and away from a scene riddled with temptation. Down in Sussex, however, things were far from easy: Wellins had lost most of his teeth, and had been forced to give up playing, finding himself a job in a local fridge manufacturing factory. When news of his plight reached London, a series of benefits held by his former colleagues ensured that Wellins was at least able to receive dental care and retrieve his saxophone. Amid his own personal problems, even Hayes had shown concern, albeit in his own inimitable way. "He used to call and say 'How are you, you toothless tenor player?!'" remembers Wellins.[41]

Christmas dinner with Hayes – the man he described as having the sparkle of champagne – was a bolstering experience for Wellins, although he soon found out that his house guest wasn't paying much heed to doctors' orders. "He was still drinking despite the warnings about his heart. He fell asleep on the sofa after dinner and as his trousers sort of rode up his legs you could see all these sores where he'd spent all that time in hospital. It was awful to see him like that."[42] As he watched Hayes shuffle through the snow back to his B&B that night, Wellins realized that the champagne was now almost flat.

Bobby Wellins's turn back from the brink was undoubtedly a success story, but the New Year brought tragic news of the early deaths of two of Hayes's former colleagues. Altoist Derek Humble – an old friend from the Tempo days – died in February, suffering a massive epileptic fit, the after-effect of an earlier mugging; barely a few weeks later, on March 7th, the Jamaican woodwind virtuoso Harold McNair lost his battle with cancer, aged thirty-nine. The two deaths began an especially bleak period for British jazz, which within a further few years would also claim Joe Harriott, Phil Seamen, Sandy Brown and eventually Hayes himself, all the wrong side of fifty.

By the spring of 1971, with both his career and his health remaining shaky, Hayes was now focusing on his own survival. Existing mainly on meagre record royalties and on payments from the PRS, he was badly in need of a prop. For a short time he taught saxophone and "advanced technique and improvisation"[43] at the Howarth School of Music in Islington, but the income was hardly enough to sustain him. The jazz community rallied round to offer its support on March 21st, with Ronnie Scott's club presenting a benefit evening featuring Stan Getz, Annie Ross and Nucleus which raised a much-needed £650. When he felt strong enough, Hayes continued to make the odd trip to Ronnie's and other London venues, strictly as a listener, but the messages these visits sent out were decidedly mixed. Spike Wells took his old boss to hear Weather Report at Scott's during this period, and recalls how enthusiastic Hayes was at the band's mix of improvisation and electronics, while pianist Brian Dee recalls driving a "cynical" Hayes home after he'd unexpectedly arrived backstage at a concert by Billy Eckstine. "Here, Brian," the saxophonist blurted, "have you got a house? *Yeah?* Well, you would have, wouldn't you!"[44] Another old friend, the journalist Mark Gardner, remembers being shocked by Hayes's appearance at a gig by Dizzy Gillespie and Sonny Stitt: "A crowd of us were just going into a pub as Tubby came out. He looked like death, weighed about seven or eight stone I would guess, and I didn't recognize him. He greeted me warmly and made light of his situation, saying he was getting much better."[45]

The latter remark wasn't at all true. On April 3rd Hayes had visited Hammersmith Hospital for another cardiac assessment, the outcome of which would decide the future course of his treatment. The results did not augur well. He had sustained considerable damage to the mitral valve, which allows an inflow of blood to the left side of the heart, and the condition could not remain untreated. Two courses of action can be considered in such a case: the first is a repair to the valve, a procedure that had first been performed successfully in the 1920s. The valve could also be replaced, an operation which, up until the introduction of the first heart-lung machines in the 1950s, had been impossible. Indeed, the first successful mitral valve replacement had only occurred as recently as 1961.

Patients undergoing the replacement procedure face two potential valve types, one synthetic (or plastic), the other biological, either from a human heart or that of a pig, which has similarities to its human counterpart. Each type of replacement has its pluses and minuses: despite their compatibility, biological valves have a far shorter life span than a prosthetic substitute. The drawback of fitting the latter is an increased risk of cardiac infection. Surgeons often cannot tell exactly which will be the best replacement until they have opened the heart and examined the damage made to the existing valve. In Tubby Hayes's case the damage was thought to be fairly extensive and the news he received in April confirmed that surgery was now not just a possibility but a necessity.

The operation itself would be enormous, necessitating the sawing open of Hayes's ribcage in order to gain full access to the heart. Following a procedure that would last for several hours, he would, quite literally, be stapled back together. There was also no guarantee of its long-term success. The only thing that was certain was that Hayes's life would be forever altered, leaving him facing the proverbial Hobson's choice between a slow painful erosion were he not to undergo surgery, or the equally tedious and agonizing recovery from an operation which, if luck was kind, could at least lead to a more manageable state of health.

The series of events that took place next remains somewhat unclear. Spike Wells's diary lists two visits to see his boss in ward D9 of Hammersmith Hospital early the next month but it appears Hayes may well have been discharged shortly afterwards. Then, in its June 12th issue *Melody Maker* announced that he had been rushed to the hospital on the previous Friday, June 4th, well ahead of the scheduled operation date of July 12th. The operation itself finally took place on Wednesday June 9th. The choice to transplant a biological valve had come as a relief for Hayes, allaying some of his fears about the potential damage of a further infection. Although he now faced months of recovery, surgery had bought him some time, though no one at this point could have known that he would survive for just a further two years.[46]

Following his operation Hayes had moved to a convalescence home in Frimley in Surrey, where under the watchful eye of the nursing staff he began an arduous recovery. His physical movement was initially very limited, and he sported an impressive scar down the length of his thorax, but the doctors were nonetheless happy with his progress. Indeed, the patient's recovery had been so impressive that, after the initial period of medical after-care had passed, he was allowed to return to the family home in Raynes Park at the end of July.

Life back at 34 Kenwyn Road was an odd mixture of the old and the new. The former came from his return to his childhood bedroom, full of memories of his teenage dreams of jazz stardom; the new came in having to cultivate a day-to-day relationship with his mother's second husband Jim Kenyon, a former chemist with whom he had little in common. Escaping into arranging was one way out, but when he wasn't writing, or reading his beloved *Boxing News*, Hayes was listening to music. Miles Davis's *In A Silent Way* was a particular favourite (he found *Bitches Brew* less engrossing), and discs by the Thad Jones–Mel Lewis band, Quincy Jones, Joe Henderson and Stan Getz also received heavy rotation. Once a week, he'd also avidly listen to BBC's *Jazz Club*, finding much of the new music interesting, and name-checking some of the younger players for future use, but experiencing "a good deal of boredom in between."[47]

On a more personal note, he had also been reunited with Liz Grönlund, the young Finnish jazz fan whom he had first met in 1962. Although she had never forgotten him, Grönlund had taken a dismissive view of the saxophonist's drug problems and had not seen him in years. She'd known he'd been very ill, but when he visited her flat in Gloucester Place that Christmas to see Jimmy Deuchar, she was unprepared for the shock of seeing him in his postoperative state. "I remember very clearly him walking in at 89 [Gloucester Place] with Don Norman. [He had] long hair [and was] very stooped."[48]

Off the wagon: a cheerful Tubby Hayes in hospital, 1971. Courtesy Liz Grönlund.

To her surprise, the attraction Grönlund had felt eight years previously was still there. This time around she was even more struck by her former lover's natural good humour, still present amid the worrying health issues: the bluster of the old Tubby Hayes had somehow disappeared. With his short-lived relationship with Sylvia Goldberg now over, and stuck back at home with his mother and stepfather, Grönlund's company was like a breath of fresh air to Hayes. He made it clear that he wanted to see her again. She visited the Hayes house over the festive period, finding the saxophonist stifled by all the maternal attention, recalling that Dorothy's controlled vision of a suburban idyll even extended to the garden: "I remember seeing these bright flowers in the garden and it was winter. Then I realized they were plastic!"[49] Seated in the living room, she and Tubby talked long into the night, with the saxophonist confessing his fears for the future: "He had great difficulty to accept that he couldn't do things he was able to do before."[50]

Although regaining his form was to prove slow-going, by the end of 1971 Hayes was finally well enough to play again. On December 27th he returned to the Bull's Head for a session with the Tony Lee Trio, his first gig in over a year, repeating the journey on New Year's Eve to appear with Dave Horler and Phil Seamen. But, despite a highly partisan turnout for both gigs, Grönlund remembers that even stepping onto the Bull's familiar stage was enough to make Hayes anxious: "I went with him and I was so scared because he looked a fragile person. He had put on weight but he still had difficulty breathing, but all went well. He played one or two numbers only. That was the starting point again, because after that he got his confidence back."[51] Jazz critic and musician Jack Massarik was also in the audience on one of these nights and remembers the shock of hearing "a frail and untubby Tubby [who] played a couple of numbers, sounding like a shadow of his former self."[52]

Hayes's colleagues, however, were merely happy to have him back where he belonged, whatever his form, and although a far cry from the technical whirlwind they'd known previously, he showed he was still capable of the odd surprise. One night he turned up at the Bull's Head to hear Ronnie Ross, who invited him on-stage: "I happened to have my alto with me," remembered Ross, "and he just picked it up and started jamming with us, any tune at all, it didn't matter. Whatever you suggested he would say 'Yes, yes' and played his ass off."[53]

The New Year – and the new start – began appropriately enough with notice in the press. *Melody Maker* flagged up the comeback on January 8th, 1972, publishing the welcome news that Hayes was now fit enough to undertake a short Scandinavian tour the following month. On the 29th the paper printed a more expansive interview conducted by Max Jones, with the veteran journalist happy to report that his subject was "well on the way to recovery." "Tubbs looks and acts as though he'd almost his old boisterous self again. But proceeding with caution. He has turned a lot of corners and can see a long, clear straight ahead of him. He is eating keenly but laying off the drink, except for the odd pint of his favourite draught beer." Hayes went on to explain that he was still having trouble catching his breath and that – as with his pestering cough – even a slight affliction was now much harder to shake off. He also revealed how relieved he was to have been fitted with a human heart valve rather than a synthetic one. "He says you can hear the other kind working," reported Jones, "which could be tricky I should imagine."[54]

Alongside his questions about Hayes's health, Jones was also curious about the saxophonist's future musical plans. Had he heard anything of late that was of practical musical use?

> I think you've got to assimilate a lot of these contemporary ideas, not just the avant-garde jazz but the current rock sounds – all of today's music. Since I was last in the business, for instance, the concept of the rhythm section had changed. A whole lot of rhythmic possibilities are suggested by the best of rock music and the Brazilian things. Yes, I like a good deal of it. I mean I'm interested in the rhythmic trends and the use of electronic instruments and effects. I feel if you incorporate what you want of the present-day sounds

– the rhythms especially – you can still have your orchestrations and your solo playing as you want them.[55]

For the time being, however, his own music would have to wait. As he rebuilt his strength over the coming months, non-jazz composing work for TV and advertising jingles helped tide him over, while the more immediate need of a regular outlet for playing solved itself almost by default. On a Sunday night early in January, he visited the Bull's Head to sit in with pianist Bill Le Sage's Bebop Preservation Society (BPS). The evening went so well that Le Sage asked whether Hayes would like to make it a full-time association, an offer too good to refuse.

Tired of the mix-and-match sloppiness of many local groups,[56] Le Sage had formed the BPS in 1971, a decision that caused a few observers to scratch their heads in wonder. On the face of things, to form an out-and-out bebop band – and one that traded so unashamedly on nostalgia – at a time when virtually everybody else on the jazz scene was hell-bent on progression might have seemed like lunacy, but there were precedents: Dizzy Gillespie, Sonny Stitt, Thelonious Monk and Art Blakey had launched *The Giants Of Jazz* the previous year, finding not only the ready audience that such a starry assemblage of names could guarantee, but also a healthy new appreciation of modern jazz in its original form.

Although working with the BPS was initially satisfying for Hayes ("blowing with Pete King and Hank Shaw keeps me on my toes"[57]), and its gigs were infrequent enough to not prove too demanding, eventually Hayes's vanity got the better of him. Away from the limelight on the BPS's pub gigs, he had been happy enough to take only a modest portion of the musical plaudits, but when the band appeared at Ronnie Scott's opposite Roland Kirk during February, on home ground and opposite an old hero, things began to take a different turn. "[He got] stronger and started to extend his playing time on each tune," the band's bassist Spike Heatley remembers. "That was the problem. Playing with Pete and Hank, there was no way he would [allow himself to] be overshadowed."[58] He hung on for a few more gigs, including a concert at Ealing Technical College and a recording for BBC TV's *Late Night Line-Up*, but by early March Hayes had effectively rowed himself out of the band.[59]

On his showing with the BPS it appeared almost as if it were straight back to business as usual for Hayes, but away from the nostalgic recreations of a bygone era much had changed, certainly in the world around him. Indeed, Great Britain in the early 1970s was a nation gripped by uncertainties, almost as if the sunny can-do optimism that had characterized the previous decade had simply melted away as the clocks chimed in the new decade. Unemployment was at its highest level for twenty years and there were a whole range of other issues, political, fiscal and social, affecting the country: the escalation of sectarian violence in Northern Ireland, the introduction of decimalization, Britain's entry into the EEC, and paranoia about immigration among them. Of all these problems, however, it was to be rabid trade unionism that was to provide the tone for much of the early 1970s – a period often characterized by power cuts, industrial action, three-day weeks and states of emergency. The epic Miners' Strike which lasted for seven weeks from January 1972 had even succeeded in plunging the jazz scene into darkness: drummer Trevor Tomkins remembers that an attempt to record an edition of BBC's *Jazz Club* had to be aborted when the studio lights suddenly went out.[60] Ronnie Scott's club had struggled to present Stan Kenton's band under the same circumstances,[61] whilst at other venues promoters had tried ingenious ways to circumvent the blackouts: gigs at the Torrington in North Finchley, for example, carried on only due to an investment in a number of car batteries and arc lights.

In some oddly correlated way, this sense of claustrophobic gloominess even extended to the artwork on the latest British jazz albums. Norma Winstone's *Edge Of Time* boasted a disturbing and surreal cover painting depicting a cracked egg suspended above a strange landscape, whilst Mike Westbrook's *Metropolis* featured a photograph of an anonymous dual carriageway stretching away into London, street lights barely lifting the early morning murk. The cheerful, multicoloured bursts on the sleeves of records released barely a few years before, like Jeff Clyne and Ian Carr's *Springboard*, Westbrook's *Love Songs*, and even Tubby Hayes's *Mexican Green*, had seemingly disappeared forever.

This new austerity couldn't have contrasted more incongruously with the indulgence and pomp now to be found within the UK's pop charts. Barely a few years earlier it had been easy to make a distinction between the "serious" aspirations of the jazz scene and the more transient nature of public tastes, but now, as pop music splintered off into all manner of images, fashions and styles, the lines had become far more blurred. Indeed, it was sometimes hard to tell where adventurous improvised jazz ended and progressive rock began. At one extreme lay the more earnest rock acts, such as ELO and Emerson, Lake and Palmer, whose ambitious concepts meant that their music either enchanted its listener with its sophistication or bored them with its self-indulgence. Then there were the fantasists like David Bowie, who had effectively created an alternative persona with the release of his landmark *Ziggy Stardust* album in 1972. Running in parallel, the movement of glam-rock had given the world performers with a diverse range of musical identities, ranging from Marc Bolan and T. Rex to Roxy Music, Slade and Mud, Gary Glitter and Alvin Stardust, each boasting outrageously overblown personal images.

Given the pervasiveness of fashion, no one could remain innocent of the crime of the times, not even jazz musicians. Just as they had incorporated some of the more recent musical developments, some among the elder generation of British jazzmen started to visually reflect the new trends: so much so that, where there had once been a clear sartorial distinction between those inside the jazz camp and those outside it, now there was none. Gone were the bum-freezer suits and college-boy haircuts – the uniform of the early sixties modernist – replaced instead by sideburns, shaggy beards and long hair. Alan Skidmore's band, for example, was now visually indistinguishable from one of its rock-playing contemporaries. But, whilst loon pants and paisley shirts may well have suited some of the younger generation, they patently didn't look good on everyone. Indeed, new clothes couldn't really mask the fact that, for some players, nothing much had really changed. The photographs of Tubby Hayes taken during the latter part of his life are sometimes unrecognizable as those of a man who'd once looked sharp as a tack. Everyone had grown used to the weight loss, but with bouffant hair, a swinging medallion and a safari suit, there was now a faintly comic look to his appearance – a kind of Jason King for the jazz set.

For Hayes, the Scandinavian trip that February was the biggest test of his physical endurance he had faced since his comeback. As his interview with Max Jones made clear, the days of non-stop activity were now well and truly over; consequently, the tour comprised just a handful of dates, sensibly paced over the course of a week. On February 12th he played a concert at the Institute of Technology in Gothenburg, accompanied by the Arne Domnerus band, after which he spent a few days in Oslo, broadcasting with the Thorlief Orstereng–Helge Hurum big band and performing with a local trio at the Down Town Key Club. Finally, there was a one-off engagement at the Guldhatten restaurant in Stockholm on February 18th.

Arriving in Oslo, Hayes and Liz Grönlund were greeted by an old friend, the journalist and musical philanthropist Randi Hultin, who had once more kindly agreed to accommodate the saxophonist for a few days. Hultin also took the opportunity to interview her house guest, painting a picture of a man very much changed from the infectious hedonist who had enlivened her parties just a few years before:

> It's still hard on him even to walk and he is not allowed to carry anything, not even his tenor. Tubby has stopped smoking but is allowed to drink a little beer and light wine. He must be careful though. He has trouble if he walks too fast and gets pains in his chest. However, when he plays he feels good [saying] "The sound is no problem. That doesn't disappear because of the operation, but it's the phrases that give me trouble. I cannot phrase the same way I did before [as I] haven't got enough breath."[62]

Off the record, Hultin also noted that the radio big band engagement had taken a particularly heavy toll on Hayes, with the physical energy required to conduct and play on just four numbers (including the inevitable '100% Proof') leading to a serious nasal haemorrhage the following evening.[63] "He never spared himself," Hultin remembered in a letter years later,[64] echoing the sentiment that many felt about Hayes's final years – that he had begun to become some sort of musical martyr.

As was customary with all her guests, before he left Oslo, Hayes signed Hultin's guest book, for what would prove to be the final time:

4.20 A.M. 17 FEB. 72.

It has been much too long since my last visit to your beautiful home. Much has happened in the meantime – but you and yours remain as beautiful and understanding as ever – even more – if that is possible!

Thanks for EVERYTHING!

Relax when you can and FOREMOST Love and Peace to you ALWAYS

Tubby

The following evening's engagement at the Guldhatten in Stockholm was recorded in its entirety by Swedish Radio, with several tracks finally being released in the late 1990s by the Storyville label. A few weeks after his first post-operative gig, they provide a valuable freeze-frame of Hayes's playing in the early stages of his comeback.

Performing with a sympathetic rhythm section of Staffan Abeleen, Niels-Henning Ørsted Pedersen and Alex Riel – a unit that had already accompanied such guests as Ben Webster, Dexter Gordon and Don Byas – the saxophonist sounds in remarkably fine voice and offers a playlist full of ready allusions to his latest enthusiasms. 'Without A Song' – including the Coltrane-esque altered harmonies first used by Joe Henderson – successfully balances hard bop know-how and new-thing revision, whilst the ballad 'I Thought About You' is played with a grace and elegance that recalls one of his earlier heroes, Stan Getz. Including a lightning sprint through 'Rhythm-A-Ning', the faster-paced items taped that night tellingly reveal that, although he could no longer make such tempos a feat of musical endurance, Hayes had lost none of his fundamental technical ability. Nor, despite his protestations to Randi Hultin and others about a lack of breath, is there much to indicate that his phrasing had been impaired by the recent surgery. The only miss-hit he makes – as much a sign of the times as an indictment of his ability – is on 'C Minor Bird', the sort of boogaloo/funk shuffle that Blue Note had done and dusted a few years earlier, which, although played spiritedly enough, shows his desire to keep on trend at its most base.

After reading the accounts of a distinct downturn in Hayes's technical skills in his final years, listening to the Guldhatten recordings is actually somewhat disconcerting. For one, they sound neither like those of a man who had survived a life-threatening condition and undergone major surgery barely a few months before, nor do they sound as if the player in question had suffered a debilitating nose-bleed barely hours earlier. In fact, rather than sounding pale and dimmed, Hayes appears in remarkably rude health. Off the stand, however, he was far more vulnerable. During his stay at Randi Hultin's home, he had opened up to the journalist about his relationship with Liz Grönlund. They were in love, he confessed, adding "I couldn't manage without her."[65] Not only did he love Liz, he needed her. Walking any distance was still a problem and he continued to take a whole host of medications to aid his battle-scarred organs. Above all, he knew that a return to the bachelor-pad existence he'd led after Joy Marshall's death was now impossible. He could no longer afford to go it alone.

When he discussed the possibility of his moving into Grönlund's flat in Gloucester Place, it all made sense. He was desperate to leave the family home in Raynes Park, where his mother's fussing nature was all but suffocating him, to get back to town, to within a cab-ride of Ronnie's and all that he had known for his entire professional life. But he also craved normality and the kind of domestic stability that he had never really known nor previously much cared for.

Once he'd moved in, to her surprise and delight, Grönlund found that the Tubby Hayes she had met and fallen in love with – the hip, streetwise professional – had sides that he'd rarely shown to anyone.[66] He was equally happy drawing her silly cartoons or playing with her pets – mynah bird Nappy and cat Noddy – and he refused to take himself seriously, even when faced with the uphill struggle to regain his health. He'd make her laugh by sitting in bed with a tea cosy on his head, or posing outrageously in front of the mirror. Along with his impressive operation scar, Hayes also now sported a hernia, requiring him to wear a truss. Strapping himself in, he would turn to Liz and say "This is the best saxophonist in the country, you know."[67] But there was also a tinge of bitterness in among the humour, for although Hayes's reputation remained intact, the remuneration that had once gone along with it had all but melted away.

12 It'll Be Me Next (1972–73)

He'd obviously got in a cab, came to see us and made a special trip. There was something about his demeanour, that we kind of had the feeling that was the last time we were going to see him. He had a kind of resignation about him.

Peter King, *BBC Jazz Legends*, 2001

Like others of his ilk, Tubby Hayes faced a tough time coming to terms with the lack of opportunities for straight-ahead jazz in the early 1970s. Put purely and simply, the work – what there was left of it – was no longer especially glamorous or particularly well paid. And there was no longer any room – or even need – for a single dominating figure within the local jazz scene, as Hayes had been in the early 1960s. If he had needed any confirmation of this situation, he need only have looked at the results of the *Melody Maker* jazz poll published in February 1972, in which he had made no showing at all in any of the categories, an omission hitherto unimaginable.[1] In such straitened circumstances, there were two choices: players could look around them, bemoan the fact that their monopoly was gone, and weep disconsolately into the nearest beer glass, or they could use their survival skills to creative effect. Hayes chose the latter. Indeed, if one looks at both the gig listings in the back pages of the *Melody Maker* in the spring of 1972 and the saxophonist's own work diary for that same period, the same venues crop up week in, week out. Not the Festival Hall or Ronnie Scott's but the Hope and Anchor, Islington, the Swan at Stockwell, the Queen's Head, Clerkenwell, the Kensington, the Hopbine, the Jolly Cockney, the Phoenix, the Torrington, backroom pub gigs each helping to create a tiny but culturally valuable circuit. The big names of the Brit-Bop generation – Stan Tracey, Phil Seamen, Hayes – had all now become fixtures on this scene, existing under the radar of a jazz press fascinated with the latest developments in fusion.

Men like Hayes and Tracey had been around far too long to give much regard to critics' arguments about one type of jazz versus another, but nevertheless both found their practical situation extremely worrying. Humour sometimes diffused the tension. "[Tubby] used to want to be a country station master when he thought the business was too difficult," Tracey remembered years later. "Doing everything himself, selling tickets, waving flags, operating the level crossings, lighting the fire in the waiting room."[2] However, despite these imaginary diversions, there were times when good cheer alone was not enough to carry them across the divide.

Tracey had made the last of his contracted albums for producer Denis Preston in 1970 and work was now impossibly hard to come by, to the extent that he had signed on the dole. The last straw came when he was asked to retrain for other work and instead decided to apply for a job as a postman. Tracey's wife Jackie destroyed the application form and with characteristic industriousness set about getting something done, not only about her husband's plight, but about the circumstances of the entire creative jazz community in London. Together with Hazel Miller, she launched the umbrella organization Musicians Action Group, promoting a series of weekly gigs in Stockwell under the highly appropriate banner of Grass Roots. Straight away, any stylistic prejudice was outweighed by the practicalities of survival, and old contemporaries of Tracey's now found themselves sharing a bandstand with players of a quite different mind-set, including the pioneers of the Little Theatre generation, such as Trevor Watts and John Stevens.[3] But if the effect were transformational for some, others remained distinctly suspicious. Brian Blain remembers Phil Seamen eyeing Tracey warily at one South London pub gig around this time, sneering "I hear you've gone over to the other side. Well, let's see if you can still play."[4]

By the middle of 1972, Tubby Hayes had also begun to fraternize with "the other side," building the relationship from a dialogue which ironically enough had begun on a gig shared with Phil Seamen. Opportunities for the two veterans to work together again were becoming more frequent, and when Hayes played a guest spot at the drummer's regular gig at the Hope and Anchor in Islington in February, word of the reunion quickly spread. John Stevens was among the faithful who had come to pay obeisance and listening to his old heroes he struck upon the idea of forming what he termed "a free jam band," uniting the best of the older and newer generations.

On paper, the drummer's choices made for a highly unusual line-up: Kenny Wheeler and Trevor Watts had both been cornerstones of Stevens's Spontaneous Music Ensemble, as had Jeff Clyne, but the real masterstroke was the inclusion of the Holy Trinity of British bop: Tubby Hayes, Stan Tracey and Phil Seamen. There were connections, however. "Lots of the people have played together at one time or another. There's a mutual respect," Stevens told *Melody Maker*'s Richard Williams,[5] but, respect or not, surely such a top-heavy mix of musical personalities would cancel out any potential success? Speculation and cynicism were rife and for some of Hayes's regular colleagues, the meeting with Stevens and co. was nothing but a flirtation, with Spike Wells going on to describe it baldly as the saxophonist's latest attempt to "get in on the act."

Whereas players like Hayes and Tracey found new opportunities and stimulus within the avant-garde, for the BBC the movement's power had become far too pernicious and subversive. When the corporation effectively banned the more extreme forms of improvised music from its *Jazz Club* programme in April 1972, the resulting debacle in the pages of *Melody Maker* resembled nothing so much as the Trad versus Modern wars of the previous decade, with everyone from Humphrey Lyttelton to John Stevens getting drawn in. "It seems to me that a society which values the cultural contributions of a Tony Blackburn above that of an Evan Parker is in grave trouble," wrote pianist Chris McGregor, striking a polemic pose. With so much antipathy in the air, it hardly seemed possible that John Stevens's new collective would get off the ground. For the drummer, however, the timing was just right: the BBC debate proved that jazz was becoming far too polarized – it was time for everyone to come back to the negotiating table, ready to play. He had certainly found a sympathetic ear in Tubby Hayes. Recalls Trevor Watts,

> I remember him being quite enthusiastic about the concept and [he was] also an encouraging musician to those around him, including myself. I think he and Phil Seamen found it a refreshing change. It was great to see that kind of involvement from someone who belonged to a generation of musicians that in general were a little sceptical to the freer things. Tubby seemed very open at that point in his life, and I never felt intimidated by him in any way – he never gave off any bad "vibes" whatsoever.[6]

Reviewing Stevens's band's first performance at the 100 Club on May 22, 1972 (which had been simply advertised as a "jam session" in the pages of *Melody Maker*), *Jazz Journal*'s Martin Davidson began by expressing the fears of many: "Nobody knew what would happen – whether these seven could produce something cohesive or utter shambles. After all, who could predict the results of a fusion of two boppers, two new-thingers and three in-betweeners?"

"The real surprise," Davidson continued, "was Tubby Hayes, who fitted into the free context so perfectly that it was hard to imagine that he had been anywhere else."[7] In 2009 a recording of the gig made by Trevor Watts was finally released on CD under the appropriate title of *Split The Difference*, and at last afforded the chance to flesh out the bare bones of the *Jazz Journal* review.[8] Over two lengthy improvised numbers, the music ebbs and flows in a totally organic way, with no one player stealing the limelight. Besides the novelty of hearing Hayes in this context, perhaps the most surprising aspect of the performance is that so much of it continues to swing. Indeed, there is nothing that resembles the cartoon-like, tempo-less aggression that had elsewhere come to characterize the avant-garde. "I think there's more time-no-changes playing than actual free textural playing," Jeff Clyne commented after hearing the music again. "I suppose looking back at it now, it might seem almost mainstream but at the time it was quite daring."[9]

There is also something quite wonderful in realizing that this burst of collaborative creativity features three-quarters of the band who had recorded *Tubby's Groove* thirteen years before. Times had changed, but Hayes wasn't about to be left behind.

As the Musicians Action Group and Grass Roots initiatives got going, Hayes was busy planning his own comeback. Although he'd been featured on a string of pub gigs with players including Tony Lee, Brian Lemon and Alan Branscombe since the beginning of the year, he'd yet to reform his quartet proper. He'd also been noticeably absent from the airwaves, but as spring broke, he finally emerged from this limbo, recording his first BBC *Jazz Club* appearance since 1970 on April 3rd, as a guest with the Tony Kinsey trio. The reception he received following Humphrey Lyttelton's opening announcement spoke volumes – almost as much in affection for this type of jazz as it is for Hayes himself. With Liz at his side, he also now felt well enough to take a few out-of-town jobs. There were still caveats regarding his health, however – drink was to be taken only in moderation and the stronger brews were strictly off limits. In the wrong kind of company, though, he would still fall spectacularly off the wagon. One night, returning from the Bull's Head, he arrived at Gloucester Place absolutely steaming, pounding on the door and shouting for Liz to let him in, only to find out he was at the wrong flat.[10] Drink could also have other stimulating effects. Following a gig with Tony Lee in Paignton, Hayes wanted to explore the sounds that could be made by closing two of the guesthouse's squeaking doors simultaneously. Desperate to get some sleep, Liz was not impressed.[11]

After what had finally amounted to a two-year hiatus, the Tubby Hayes quartet's first gig together again came on April 20th, with the band returning to a familiar old haunt, the Torrington in North Finchley. Inevitably, the gig drew a packed crowd, eager to witness the next phase in the saxophonist's relaunch. There was even a hint of nostalgia about the proceedings, as *Melody Maker*'s Christopher Bird noted:

> [A]t the risk of sounding mawkish, I can only say that whatever Mike Pyne, Ron Mathewson, Spike Wells and Tubbs had done, just to be in on this reunion would have been almost a magical experience, and there was such an atmosphere of joyful affection, "glad to be here" good spirits and downright musical respect on stage that almost everything that took place was almost beyond criticism.[12]

The evening had undoubtedly been a success but, beneath the sentimental reactions to Hayes's return, those closest to the saxophonist could instantly hear a difference. Spike Wells remembers thinking that his boss had finally begun to "take things a little more steadily." "He'd realized that the style he'd made his own in the middle-sixties was a very punishing one as far as breath control goes. He probably thought that if he eased up on that he might be able to play more imaginatively or reflectively. That was the trend as time went on."[13]

The *Sunday Times*'s Derek Jewell also thought along similar lines when he heard the quartet accompanying American vocalist Joe Williams at Ronnie Scott's the following month: "He's slimmer [than before] and his music likewise is more fine drawn. Once he so loaded his solos with explosions that the effect could be confusingly top-heavy. Now he's all light and shade, firing his bursts more calculatedly and with greater effect."[14]

For one thing, Hayes no longer had to worry about the quality of any of his sidemen, the source of some of his fill-all-gaps hyperactivity in the past. Although Spike Wells was now deeply ensconced in his legal studies and couldn't guarantee his availability, his replacements were all first-class. Alan Jackson, Tony Oxley and Bryan Spring all worked with the quartet that summer and, with Ron Mathewson now frequently working abroad with altoist Phil Woods, various new bass players were also passing through the band's ranks, including Roy Babbington, Daryl Runswick and Chris Laurence.

With Runswick and Tony Levin replacing Mathewson and Wells, the quartet finally made its overdue return to BBC's *Jazz Club* on September 30th. The majority of Hayes's broadcast appearances since his comeback had been much lower-key affairs – he had been part of someone else's band or a guest playing another composer's work – but now, with the recent press reports of his new-found post-operative maturity ringing in his ears, the pressure was on. Choosing to play only his own compositions, superficially all appeared well, with Hayes offering up exactly the sort of bite-sized chunks of virtuosity that writers such as Derek Jewell had latterly picked up on. However, under-pinning everything, there was now a deep sense of melancholy, with one new theme, a ballad titled 'An Unexpected Pleasure' (apparently named in honour of a pre-show joint[15]), offering an affecting blend of lyricism and harmonic complexity reminiscent of Joe Henderson's recent work. As the melody unfurls into a gentle swing, the saxophonist's tone sounds like a voice about to break down in tears, but rather than subtracting from the music's impact, this frailty actually enhances it. Content to leave aside the dazzling set-piece tear-ups he'd delivered in his prime, Hayes was at last wearing his heart unashamedly on his sleeve.

Despite the debilitating after-effects of his surgery, Hayes generally preferred to make light of his concerns to his fellow players. Some of his older colleagues could see all too well how illness had reduced him, physically at least, to a shadow of his former self. Those players who had only begun

Dick Brennan, Tubby, Tony and Olga Lee and Liz Grönlund, Devon, Summer 1972. Courtesy Liz Grönlund.

working with him after his comeback had less to go on. Daryl Runswick was one of the very few of Hayes's new musical accomplices to gain a deeper insight into how much the saxophonist's life had changed since his operation. The bassist was young – barely into his middle twenties – and lived a lifestyle less frenetic and harmful than Hayes had done at the same age, almost an archetype of the new breed of players who hadn't had to go through the piteous rites of passage and insularity experienced by their predecessors. Runswick was well aware of just how ill Hayes had once been, but a gig the two men played in Hull during the autumn of 1972 provided especially grisly proof of how much he continued to suffer beneath a veneer of "courage and cheerfulness."

Runswick had picked up Hayes for the long drive northwards.

> When we arrived in Hull, we found ourselves in a school hall, I think, with a flat floor. Some rostrums needed moving into place for us to set up on, and helping to drag them across the floor I ricked my back. I was in pain throughout the gig and when we set off for home afterwards I had difficulty driving. To make matters worse, a pea-souper fog had come down, so we crawled gropingly along, past midnight, and were still in Yorkshire. Finally, about 1 am, Tubby took pity on me and suggested we stop in Doncaster for the night. He booked us into a hotel where we shared a twin-bedded room.

As he tried to get comfortable, and cursing his twisted back, Runswick then witnessed a sight which put his own pain into withering perspective:

I was horrified to see that Tubby had to sleep sitting up in bed; if he lay down his lungs filled up with liquid. His breathing as he slept was like a boiling kettle. Also he showed me, and let me touch, the heavy metal wiring – it seemed to me as thick as a dry-cleaner's coat hanger – they'd used to fix his rib cage back together after the op, which was still in his chest, lumping up visibly under his skin.[16]

Regardless of his ongoing health issues, Hayes's itinerary that autumn looked decidedly promising. Along with a string of guest appearances, the free improvisation collective assembled by John Stevens earlier in the year also had more work in the book. As the drummer had made clear when interviewed in *Melody Maker*, the group wasn't hustling for gigs – it preferred to operate in a more casual and organic manner, coming together only when all the players could commit. However, they did now have a name: Splinters, an especially suitable moniker for a unit whose members had broken away from a variety of jazz schools.[17] The band were beginning to build a following, bridging a gap between the audiences for bop and free, and providing a new lease of jazz "stardom" for its older hands. Everything appeared to be going better than expected. Then came sudden and tragic news: on October 13th, nine days before their next gig, Phil Seamen was found dead in his Lambeth flat, aged just forty-six.

The drummer's frail body had finally been halted by years of drug abuse, and as word of his passing spread instantly through the usual jungle telegraph there was incredulity as well as grief. Seamen had been the ultimate iron man, somehow always bouncing back from the brink. Was he really gone? Recording a television session with Harry South when he heard the news, Hayes was stunned.[18] Indeed, to all his friends, Phil's death had a sickening ignominy to it – found slumped in a chair, alone – was this the way things were supposed to end for a man who'd given so much? The tragedy also brought out a side of Hayes Liz Grönlund hadn't yet seen much of – his temper. When she prevaricated about whether or not she should attend Seamen's funeral, he exploded.[19] It all then came out – the fears, the memories, the sense of undignified loss. Phil had represented a whole way of life, of handling oneself and taking care of business, that was fast disappearing and which could never be duplicated. It felt as if an era was beginning to end.

Splinters' next gig in Stockwell on October 22nd went ahead as planned, although the musicians knew that, without Seamen, the original guiding rationale was now gone. The following day, attending the drummer's funeral at Golders Green, Hayes suddenly turned to Jeff Clyne and remarked, "It'll be me next." Clyne laughed it off, but for a fleeting moment he saw an intimation of mortality in his once robust old boss that chilled him.[20]

The death of Phil Seamen only added to a sickening roll call of British jazzmen being called before their time. That same year, another old friend, Bobby Breen – the lisping firecracker who'd done so much to enliven Tubby

The Bull's Head, Barnes, autumn 1972. Courtesy Liz Grönlund.

Hayes's first band in the 1950s – fell terminally ill. Joe Harriott had also been hospitalized, fatally stricken with cancer. As the jazz scene recoiled at this bleak news, and perhaps already foreseeing his own demise, Hayes thought it was time to make good his connection with another colleague who had grown distant. Although he had been among the first to offer assistance following his operation, Ronnie Scott had remained an ambiguous presence in Hayes's life. Once inextricably linked, the two tenorists' lives now seemed too disparate, too separate, to dovetail together as they'd done in the days of the Jazz Couriers. Liz Grönlund would later suggest that Scott even harboured feelings of jealousy about Hayes's talents. Nevertheless, when he was asked to assemble a big band to tour with singer Jack Jones that year, Scott had telephoned Hayes, who readily accepted. The old friendship was briefly revived and, travelling between gigs in Scott's car, the elder man sensed a new vulnerability in his once bellicose former partner. Hayes was weaker, and was becoming increasingly worn down by the constant need to make compromises. "Paradoxically, the illness that restricted his breathing dissipated his energy and had, for me, succeeded in making him sound better than ever," Scott observed soon after Hayes's death. "The artist in the man took over from the craftsman."[21]

As 1973 began, Hayes was pacing himself like never before. There were barely a handful of gigs in January, only one of which found him leading his own band. He briefly travelled abroad again in February, this time alone, making an appearance at the Molde Jazz Festival in Norway, but feeling increasingly breathless and weary, virtually any kind of travel was now becoming almost impossible. Even his UK engagements were beginning to shrink within an ever closer radius of London. The Bull's Head remained a frequent port of call, with the quartet making an appearance to celebrate Hayes's thirty-eighth birthday on January 30th. A few days later, on February 4th, he was back at Barnes for a lunchtime slot before he and Tony Lee headed to Southend for an evening gig at the Top Alex, a noisy side-street pub whose jazz nights were presented by ex-Flamingo emcee Bix Curtis. Technically, Curtis had retired from the club game, but together with local promoter Kenny Baxter he had recently decided to help stage local Sunday-night sessions bringing in as many of his old friends as money would allow. In a situation familiar to all working jazzmen, Hayes and Lee had agreed to a compromise to help keep down the costs, appearing with a local bassist and drummer, John Moule and Trevor Taylor. Someone – possibly Curtis himself – also had the foresight to record the evening and, although lo-fi, the resulting tape is a fascinating example of Tubby Hayes's playing in its final phase. The programme mainly comprises standards – often delivered segue à la Sonny Rollins, leading Lee and the rhythm section into a sometimes desperate guessing game – but, despite the safe-ground repertoire and a clearly audible lack of breath, Hayes still delivers. Irrespective of his physical condition, for the local musicians the opportunity to work with the saxophonist was a boon. Trevor Taylor remembers how open he found the guest star and treasures the memory of Hayes telling him that his cymbal work sounded like that of Tony Williams.[22]

Even in the midst of his own failing health, Hayes continued to do his bit to help other musicians in trouble. On February 11th he appeared at Ronnie Scott's with his big band at a benefit for Alan Skidmore, then hospitalized following a serious car accident. On a bill also featuring Howard Riley's trio and Stan Tracey's new band Tentacles, it was the band's first public appearance since 1970, an event that, as Hayes told the press, "signifies the culmination of my complete recovery."[23] It turned out to be a hollow prediction. The night after the gig at Scott's, the quartet, with Tony Levin replacing Spike Wells, appeared at the Banyan Tree in Liverpool. Despite the group giving an excellent account of itself, the long round trip all but knocked Hayes out. He was too exhausted to make the next Splinters gig at Notre Dame Hall the following Friday and did little for the next ten days. On February 26th, he had recovered enough to join the Ian Hamer Sextet on a gig at the Bull's Head, performing a sprawling set captured by Liz Grönlund's tape recorder.[24] The trumpeter's music was now moving into more progressive areas – bringing in the avant-garde as well as jazz-rock – but, as the tape reveals, this shift didn't suit all members: there is far too much of Alan Branscombe's Fender Rhodes and much of the music takes an age to get going, churning away rather remorselessly over one-chord vamps. However, a lengthy version of Freddie Hubbard's 'Straight Life' boasts a Hayes solo that ranks among the best of his later efforts, full of the growling multi-phonics and lines that spiral away from the harmony in a way that presages future developments. How he was able to conjure such brilliance in his reduced physical condition is staggering. "Aspects of his playing were already pointing to the way [Michael] Brecker would be playing in the years ahead," Pete King once remarked of Hayes's later music.[25] Although not strictly accurate, the general sentiment nonetheless still holds: far from being the spent force some jazz history books would have us believe, Tubby Hayes was still pushing ahead, whatever the setting. The only thing that was tempering these enthusiasms was his health and, by the early spring of 1973, it was clear to everyone that Hayes was far from well.

The same week as his gig with Ian Hamer, Hayes made a guest appearance with John Critchinson's trio near Cheltenham (a cheerful letter to Hayes reveals his fee to be £30[26]), shocking all those present with his weight loss and breathlessness. Equally alarming was the saxophonist's request for two bottles of Newcastle Brown Ale for breakfast the following morning, "just to get the motor running."[27] Even more disturbing was his condition during a recording for BBC's *Jazz Club* at Maida Vale on March 5th, during which he debuted a new composition dedicated to Liz, the ballad 'Solweig'. The broadcast marked the big band's return to the airwaves but, despite his superficial delight at the occasion, the rehearsal run-through had very nearly floored the leader: trumpeter Leon Calvert vividly remembers seeing him carried up the stairs from the basement studio for the obligatory pre-show drink.[28]

Nevertheless, he still refused to take things easy. Indeed, the old adage that the show must go on could have been invented for Hayes during this time, although by this point the show had begun to have an almost nightmarish quality to it. Three nights after the BBC recording, on March 8th, the quartet made an appearance at Bix Curtis's Top Alex venue in Southend, playing two sets opposite John Picard and Kathy Stobart. Curtis's letter of engagement for the gig[29] makes interesting reading: Hayes's band were to be paid the princely sum of £70 ("payable in cash on the night, without tax or signature") with the leader invited to jam with Picard and Stobart "should you feel up to it."

Although he made it through the night, a surviving tape of the gig makes for almost depressing listening, especially when one realizes it is the last recorded appearance of the classic Pyne–Mathewson–Wells edition of the Tubby Hayes quartet. For once, the leader sounds uncharacteristically dimmed, taking clipped, grimly determined solos and picking tempos that settle around the middle. His announcements also indicate a less than happy

On-stage at the Top Alex, Southend-on-Sea,
Sunday February 4th, 1973. Courtesy Trevor Taylor.

atmosphere. Introducing 'Trenton Place' he implores a noisy crowd to listen to Mike Pyne (fighting a woefully out-of-tune piano) and he has to contend with Curtis's frequent and irritating interruptions about the venue's catering facilities.

The final jam session, which puts Stobart, Picard and Hayes together with local men Digby Fairweather (yet to emerge as one of the UK's most prominent mainstream jazz figures) and Kenny Baxter is nothing less than surreal. Into this melee, Hayes had also invited the American avant-garde saxophonist Gary Windo, then living in London and carving a formidable reputation for his work with Chris McGregor's Brotherhood of Breath. Windo's shrieking, post-Pharoah Sanders style sounds completely at odds with everything else on-stage. Indeed, hearing it in juxtaposition with Fairweather's Braff-like cornet is truly bizarre, and one might ask why Hayes tolerated such an outré stylist. Beneath all the surface ferocity, however, Windo was by all accounts a sweet and benevolent individual who recognized Hayes's manifest desire to keep abreast of all manner of musical trends. He was also an incredible practical help, happily stepping in to drive Hayes to gigs if his favoured taxi company couldn't oblige.[30]

At the close of the night, Hayes made a bee-line for Kenny Baxter. The two men had known each other since the early 1950s, and Baxter could sense something on his friend's mind.

> It was great to see him and I remember saying to him "good to see you back on the beer" because he'd had a few drinks, but he wasn't his old self. At the end of the gig – I always remember this – I remember him getting in the back of the van and saying to me "I think I may have to go into hospital again, so don't call me." And that was it; that was the last time he played in Southend and the last time I saw him.[31]

It appears that Hayes may well have already realized he didn't have long to live. Although he kept his fears from Liz, he was less secretive with others, and, as spring edged towards summer, he began a round of unannounced visits to old friends, as if to say his farewells. Among the first he called on was the recuperating Alan Skidmore, still undergoing daily physiotherapy following his road accident. Skidmore's wife Kay answered the door of their Borehamwood home one afternoon to find Hayes and Tony Kinsey. To her house-bound husband, the reunion was a delight. Still unable to walk properly he spent most of the evening on the floor of the living room and it appeared that Hayes was intent on joining him: "We had a right old time. Got the whiskey out and we had a few beers and things like that. There was the old 'wahey' and loads of laughter," Skidmore remembers. "Afterwards, it felt almost as if he came over to say goodbye. It was a weird feeling."[32]

Peter King, Stan Tracey and Ronnie Scott were among those who also received similar valedictory visits. Hayes had played Frith Street – opposite the French rock band Troc – at the end of April, but when he called in on Scott unexpectedly a few days later the elder man instinctively sensed this was something much more than a professional courtesy call. The tour with Jack Jones the previous year had brought the two men closer, close enough for Hayes to open up. Scott wrote later that year:

> As he was leaving he said something to me that I will always remember. The exact words are important only to me, but the implication was that he held me in some regard and that my playing had influenced him in his formative years. I know that he wanted me to know this because he felt he may not have had too much time left. I became upset and a little embarrassed and I tried to tell him

that he had paid me the greatest compliment I could ever hope to receive. Because it came from Tubby Hayes.[33]

A few days later, on April 22nd, the Tubby Hayes quartet played what turned out to be its final out-of-town gig at the Top of the World Club in Stafford. Certain aspects of the jazz scene had changed out of all recognition since Hayes's career had begun twenty-three years earlier, but this final engagement had an all-too-familiar ring to it. Local journalist John Watson remembers "a dreadfully out of tune and battered upright piano had been provided for Mike Pyne. Tubby told the promoters that, sadly, he really had no option but to cancel the gig – the piano was unplayable." Thankfully Watson was able to save the day by providing his own electric piano. "Tubby was delighted and very grateful, but to me it was a tremendous honour."[34]

Once on the stand, Hayes had continued to deliver, albeit in a much less expansive manner, and he had now taken to sitting down on gigs. However, the ongoing inconsistency of his health meant that many promoters were now averse to booking him too far in advance. The quartet had a mere handful of gigs in the diary for May and June, including the Corn Exchange, Brighton on May 12th, Fulham on May 30th and Ravenscroft Park on June 7th, but there was little else on the horizon.[35] The Brighton engagement formed part of a mini-festival featuring George Melly and the band Back Door, organized by the Ronnie Scott club, and, in principle at least, everything looked straight-forward. But from the moment Gary Windo's van pulled up outside 89 Gloucester Place that Saturday afternoon it was apparent that things would not go to plan.

Hayes had awoken as usual, climbing out of bed and taking his prescribed medication – a ritual dubbed "pill time" by Liz – as he had done every morning since leaving hospital. But all was not well. The breathlessness he'd felt of late was far worse – his chest felt as if it were in a vice and the breastbone that had been sawn and then stapled back together seemed as if it might burst open at any moment. He'd been coughing up blood during the night and, although he was sweating, he felt cold to the touch. Struggling out of his pyjamas, he made light of things with Liz. It would pass, he said, there was no need to worry. He'd be fine once they got on the road to the gig.

The steps up to the street from the flat had always been a bit of an ordeal, but today they felt like climbing the north face of the Eiger. Liz and Gary Windo helped. Although he accepted it, Hayes hated this. It embarrassed him – he wasn't an invalid, he was still a young man. Indeed, anyone seeing him that day, with his long hair, droopy moustache and trendy clothes might have mistaken him for a pop star rather than a jazz musician. But, even if he looked every inch the man-about-town, he certainly didn't feel it. Settled as best he could in the back seats of the van, he sat quietly as Windo began the customary drive-round to collect the rest of the band. By the time they reached Shepherd's Bush to pick up Spike Wells, Hayes was shivering. As the drummer undid the rear doors he was confronted with the sight of his leader huddled under a blanket, his skin a slight shade of blue. When he expressed his concern, Hayes waved it off. Liz was here, he said, so he'd be OK and, after all, there was a gig to do. Windo and Wells continued loading the drums onto the roof of the van and then they were off, trailing through the London suburbs towards the A23, Brighton, and the music.

Alongside the worries about Hayes's health, the journey contained another drama: one of Wells's drums had worked its way loose, crashing onto the road, an accident necessitating a quick stop, but by the time they finally arrived at the gig the focus was once more on the leader. Everyone in the van agreed that he looked dreadful. Coughing and unable to catch his breath, he nevertheless continued to brush away all the fuss. He'd be fine, he said, undoing his saxophone case. Then, as he had done thousands of times over the last two decades, he slipped the crook of the saxophone into its body, and shimmied on the mouthpiece. Around his neck was one of the ornate psychedelic patterned saxophone slings that Liz had hand-made for him and with hands still shaking he clipped it to the instrument. A quick lick of the reed and the horn was in his mouth. He silently ran his fingers up and down its keys, feeling the pearl buttons and the familiar, peculiarly satisfying, suction as the pads smacked against the open tone holes. He then blew, expecting, as it always had, that gorgeous, deep, cello-rich sound to emerge. But there was nothing, save a sharp pain in his chest. He coughed, feeling liquid massing somewhere in his throat. He tried again. This time there was not much more than a puff of air, spewing out along the sides of the mouthpiece like a deflating balloon. It was no good. He couldn't get a note, any note, let alone the "too many notes" that had once marked him as the ultimate saxophone athlete. With half an hour to go before he was due on-stage, he now stood unable to make a sound, cursing his musical impotence. Rousing himself once more – gripped inside with the determination that had taken him across many obstacles in both his professional and personal life – he closed his eyes and tried again. Nothing. Finally he felt a hand on his shoulder. It was Liz. She looked at him, her eyes betraying both pity and pain. "Come on darling," she said. "Let's go home."

Whilst the trio of Mike Pyne, Ron Mathewson and Spike Wells played on – joined for some of the set by Gary Windo – Liz and Tubby made their way to Brighton railway station to begin an agonizing journey back to London. On the train, they sat holding hands, silent in the knowledge that something was badly wrong. Tubby had experienced trouble blowing before, but never like this. His chest pounded up and down as he fought to catch his breath. He spluttered his answers to Liz, as if literally running out of steam. She thought back to the previous night, to the blood on the pillow.

The ride to Victoria Station seemed to take an eternity and by the time they arrived, Tubby was exhausted. He'd briefly managed to get some sleep but rest of any kind had eluded Liz. She steadied him as he tried to get out of his seat and down onto the platform. The couple stood there for a moment,

Liz taking her boyfriend's weight almost fully with the arm she'd outstretched around him. She surveyed the station concourse. It was Saturday night, the weekend, with the capital alight with those just going out for the evening. Her heart sunk: to her these other people's lives – *anyone* else's life – seemed in that moment almost completely carefree. Who could know the horror she was feeling as she held on tight to the wheezing, pallid man beside her? She knew they had to get home, but Tubby was clearly unable to walk unaided. Summoning her ingenuity, she spotted a parcel trolley and placed his hands on it. Together they headed towards the taxi rank. Were it not so upsetting, it would almost be laughable: a young man, so obviously fashion-conscious, shuffling awkwardly along as if he were in his dotage rather than his prime.

Eventually the taxi arrived outside Gloucester Place and Liz began the reverse journey to that which had begun the day, this time taking all of her man's weight and carrying him down the steps. Somehow, she didn't exactly know how, they managed to get inside the flat. Tubby was coughing still, bringing up clots of blood. As carefully as possible she undressed him, helped put on his pyjamas and put him to bed. She'd better call an ambulance, she said. No, he replied – he didn't need one. He'd be all right. He just needed rest. A good night's sleep would put it all right, she'd see. But Liz had known her boyfriend for long enough to spot any bluster. Tubby was scared. She could see it in his eyes and in the trembling body that felt so cold next to her. She held him – as tightly as she dare given his pain – and the night went on like that. More breathlessness, more choking, more empty reassurances.

Sunday passed by as if in slow motion. For all her concern, by now Liz was becoming almost irritated at Tubby's fake confidence. Sitting up in bed, he countered her at every turn with affirmations that he'd feel fine tomorrow. In reply, she would insist that he needed professional help. And so it went, until Monday. By then, he was almost too weak to object to anything and finally Liz telephoned for help. That same day Edward Brian Hayes entered Hammersmith Hospital for the second time in two years. As news of his collapse and admittance spread to his friends and colleagues, and the cardiologists tried to find out just what was wrong with their patient, Liz was left feeling numb. The man in ward B4 was so much more than case number 372188, so much more than a virtuoso saxophonist and an esteemed musical figure. He was all those things certainly, but above all, he was her world.

* * *

There was almost a familiar ring to it all. Indeed, Tubby Hayes's health had been an issue ever since the autumn of 1965, when he'd first collapsed under the strain of an exhaustive workload. Since then, there had been battles with thrombosis, jaundice and heroin addiction, with each affliction marking the way towards the eventual diagnosis of his faulty heart valve. Throughout all these trials, he had continued to display a self-determination and courageousness that impressed everyone who encountered him. However, this time things were different. Two years before, when the doctors had told him that a heart valve replacement was necessary to save his life, he had taken a characteristically can-do attitude to the procedure, spending months prior to the operation cleaning himself up, cutting down on the vices and taking stock. Thus, the patient that received a new mitral valve in the summer of 1971 was a very different one to that who potentially faced further surgery now. After the first operation, Hayes had been advised in no uncertain terms that his life would never be quite the same again. Walking, sleeping, playing, drinking – everything – had been affected. A tranche of medications may well have ensured a certain level of stability, but, as positive and brave as he undoubtedly was, Hayes was not superhuman. The replacement valve was failing. The initial success of the transplant had given great hope, but there was a risk in using a human valve rather than a synthetic substitute: Hayes's body was now simply rejecting it. It left only one real course of action. Although the hospital had been able to steady his breathing and alleviate certain of the symptoms that had caused him so much discomfort, only further surgery would prolong his life. The odds this time around were far less encouraging than two years previously. After agonizing about whether to undergo the operation or simply let things take their natural course, he finally agreed. Assuaging her worst fears, Liz received a supportive letter from cardiologist Celia Oakley on May 24th: "Tubby is making some forward progress and his morale seems to be excellent. I too hope that we can really get him back to a reasonable state of health."[36] He would never be truly well again – but he might survive.

To the fellow musicians who visited him during the last weeks of May 1973, Hayes presented a mixed picture: although he had made it clear that "he didn't want to know about going through all that again," Ian Hamer remembered the saxophonist being optimistic about the forthcoming operation. "In really good spirits" he had even joked with the trumpeter about the oxygen bottle by the side of his bed, saying he'd found a new way of getting high.[37] Others, however, encountered a less ebullient reaction, with one, clarinettist Vic Ash, recalling the atmosphere at Hayes's bedside as "depressing."[38]

Visiting was strictly limited, with Liz keeping a quiet eye on those who might cause further anxiety in an already delicate situation. Tubby didn't need a queue of well-wishers this time around – he just wanted to get it over with. Even his family were kept somewhat at arm's length. Keen to retain a sense of decency, Hayes had called Rose to let her know about the situation and had asked after his son's welfare.[39] Richard was now in his teens, and Lewis was eight, the age at which Tubby had begun to show a serious interest in music. But the opportunity to repair the relationship with their father was now gone.

Hayes had certainly begun to contemplate his own mortality and – if things should work out – his future. Liz remained at his side as often as visiting hours would allow, talking about their plans. Hayes wanted to spend summers in the Channel Islands, taking less stressful commercial work in between his jazz gigs. "I wanted to be optimistic like he was. I didn't even think in those terms – of dying,"[40] remembers Grönlund. There was also plenty of boredom. Cassette tapes of artists such as Joe Henderson, John Coltrane and Woody Shaw kept Hayes occupied between visitors[41] and, incredibly, amid all the worries, there were times of laughter. One day Liz arrived to find a bevy of young girls peering through the ward doors, giggling and pointing. They'd heard there was a famous musical personality in the hospital, they explained, and had mistaken Tubby for Gary Glitter! Hayes was not amused.

Liz also had her hands full dealing with the phone calls, letters and cards wishing Hayes a speedy recovery. His first wife Maggie was among those to send best wishes ("Take care Tubbs and all the breast!"[42]) and he received supportive letters from both his parents. Typically, Dorothy wrote with the kind of concerns that only a mother can express: "[I] await anxiously every evening to hear the 9 o'clock bulletin – firstly what they have done to you, and how you are feeling. Secondly, what you are having for supper"[43] while Tubby's father – a man who had been a remote figure for most of his adult life, but who had undoubtedly stirred the beginnings of his immense musical talent – penned an unusually affectionate letter on June 6th: "You know that I am very close to you and will do anything that is possible to build you up and get you back again on your feet. My love and thoughts are with you always."[44]

Outside of Ward B4, life carried on. The BBC had broadcast a pre-recorded edition of *Jazz Club* on May 24th featuring Hayes with the Dave Hancock big band. It was to be his last appearance on the programme, an event heavily tinged with irony given how well he sounded.[45] There were also the rallying cries of those musicians wanting to assist Hayes in his hour of need, just as there had been a few years before during his first illness. First to offer their help – and indicative of just how valued Hayes was across the entire spectrum of British jazz – were the Musicians Co-operative, who organized a benefit gig at Ronnie Scott's featuring Evan Parker, Howard Riley and Keith Tippett on June 3rd. News of Hayes's plight had spread to all corners of the business, to figures from both his past and present. Jimmy Skidmore – who more than any other musician had been like a father to Hayes – tape-recorded a message urging his friend to go through with the surgery, no matter what.[46]

Hayes's own sidemen also made frequent visits to see their ailing boss. When Spike Wells called in during the last days of May he thought he saw signs that, for all his surface confidence, Hayes was frightened. "Although he appeared quite cheerful, he was clearly worried about having to go through the operation itself. He looked very weak [and] I think he was worried about whether he was going to make it, reading between the lines. In fact, I can clearly remember him saying 'Don't go, Liz' as we were leaving."[47]

The operation was scheduled for Friday June 8th. There would be no visitors that day and accordingly Liz made the most of her last trip to the hospital the night before. The conversation was hopeful, she thought, although Hayes was feeling very sore from the close shave he'd received at the hands of the nursing staff. Sitting up in bed, he looked down at himself and laughed. "I must get this bloody hernia done." Finally, when there was nothing left to say except goodnight, Liz leaned over, kissed him and got up to leave. "He said to me 'Are you coming back later?' and I said yes. That was it."[48]

But there was one final visitor, whose arrival was a total surprise – Ronnie Scott. As he wrote in the sleeve notes to a posthumously issued Hayes album released in 1980:

> It was – as I recall – after 9.00 pm and visiting hours were long over. However, I gave the ward sister some nonsense about being on tour and not having another opportunity to see him, and with some reluctance, she let me in. Tubby's bed was at the end of the room now and we talked for a while in the dimly-lit silent ward and then it was time for me to leave. As I reached the end of the long room, I turned and waved at him and he smiled and waved back. And then the swing doors closed behind me.[49]

Tubby Hayes died following mitral valve replacement surgery at around 3 pm the following day, Friday June 8th, 1973. He was thirty-eight years of age. The supreme irony was that the valve replacement procedure itself had been successful. The patient, however, could not be revived. His blood pressure was too low and his body simply too worn down to be brought round. The surgeons had tried, but there was nothing that could be done. Tubby Hayes – The Little Giant – was gone.

The news spread almost immediately. Liz had called Dorothy, who took a taxi straight to the hospital. She then called Spike Wells, who remembers being half-prepared: "It was shocking but it wasn't totally unexpected, given how he had been when I'd seen him."[50] However, the news hit others considerably harder. Ian Hamer was at a recording session when he heard. "Greg Bowen, Chris Pyne and a few of us were on it and so I told people [who knew Tubby]. I remember Chris Pyne crying on my shoulder. Everybody was just stunned."[51]

John Critchinson received the news just ahead of his regular Friday night gig in Wiltshire. As co-promoter Jack Pennington announced Hayes's death from the stage, Critchinson's wife suddenly burst into tears. "It was really strange," the pianist remembers. "We'd only seen him a few weeks before and now he was gone. It just seemed to affect people instantly."[52]

Reflecting on the loss, Tubby's long-term friend Tony Ketley remembered that Hayes had once told him that he had

> always feared dying in the middle of something. It could have been a movie or a boxing match – he just had this funny little superstition that he didn't want to go like that, not knowing how something would end. Anyway, the week he went, there was a Test

Match between England and New Zealand, which had started the day before. I thought that was ironic.[53]

Saturday morning brought the first printed confirmation of Tubby Hayes's passing. Unsurprisingly, the news had made the national press, although several of the hastily penned obituaries in the tabloids had insensitively and redundantly dwelt on Hayes's problems with addiction.

Anthony Hopkins of the *Daily Telegraph* led the more intelligent tributes with a measured overview of Hayes's achievements, describing him as

> renowned as a musician of rare composing abilities whose technique as a tenor saxophonist rivalled many more famous American musicians and whose qualities as a soloist were recognized as second to none. His musicianship was vigorous and uncompromising and his categorization as the English John Coltraine [sic] is a valid one.[54]

Peter Clayton had also penned a typically eloquent obituary, published the following day in the *Sunday Times*, which recalled how Hayes had "wisely never hung about waiting from critics and others to catch up with him." Clayton nominated the famous 1964 appearance with Duke Ellington as his subject's most noteworthy moment in jazz history, but, accompanying all the retrospection, he also wondered where he might have gone next: "The last time I talked to him about his own playing he was intensely interested to see if the need to pace himself differently, in the physical sense, was going to produce a new style. It's tragic that he was never given time to find out."[55]

Clayton had spent much of Saturday hurriedly taping interviews for a tribute to be broadcast on the BBC's *Jazz Notes* the next night. As well as conducting a three-way discussion with Mike Pyne, Ron Mathewson and Spike Wells, which recalled far happier days – and during which Wells also gave an unstinting condemnation of the press for dragging up the details of Hayes's drug addiction – Clayton had also managed to buttonhole Ronnie Scott and Ronnie Ross for their reactions. Ross had taken the news very badly and had gotten extremely drunk on the Friday night. Barely coherent, he spoke emotionally about his respect for Hayes's talents. "He was the best, not in the country, but in the world. I don't know anybody else who had that sort of fantastic technique and played cascades of notes. But not just notes – they were all melodies." Close to tears, Ross concluded, "It doesn't make sense."[56]

Things were certainly making no sense for Liz Grönlund. She had returned to the flat that weekend. There were the funeral arrangements to organize and what seemed like a million and one phone calls to make or answer. By Monday morning, cards of condolence had begun to arrive. Harriet South had put pen to paper immediately she heard the news: "I cannot phone you right now, I'm trying not to cry. I feel so numbed I don't even know what to say in a letter. I just came home and Harry told me. I don't think I've ever seen Harry so upset."[57] A letter from the Musicians' Union expressed the sentiment that "the 'profession' will always be indebted to Tubby as one of the 'greats' in the jazz field of entertainment."[58] Along with the official recognitions came condolences from some who Liz hadn't even stopped to think may have noticed. The boss of Key Radio Cars, the taxi firm they'd used almost daily, sent a handwritten letter expressing his sadness and, representative of the thousands of semi-professional and amateur jazz musicians who looked upon Hayes as a hero, Tony Cave of Stafford's Overdrive Jazz Unit conveyed his thoughts in a card: "I hope you will find some strength and comfort from knowing that the man you loved was deeply admired by many, many people. His music has given me some of the most pleasurable moments of my life and Tubbs will live on in his music, as all great artists have done."[59]

Published a week after Hayes's death, *Melody Maker*'s tribute ran under the appropriate title of "Tubby – The Giant of British Jazz" and concluded with the words:

> Edward Brian Hayes will probably go down in the history of British jazz as a great tenor soloist. But he was not simply that, good enough though it might have been for others. In his thirty-ninth year, growing in ability and still anxious to learn more about his craft, he was – as Christopher Bird wrote in MM four years ago –"an artist of the highest class."[60]

At the foot of the page were tributes from several of Hayes's colleagues and friends. John Stevens recalled "a feeling of optimism in his playing and in himself"; Alan Skidmore looked back on "a brilliant musician [and] also a lovely guy"; Tony Levin on "an amazing character whom I shall miss greatly." Stan Tracey and Jackie Sharpe remembered a more personal side – the enthusiasm for boxing and cricket, the humour. "I'll miss Tubby because he was a close friend," wrote Sharpe, "the kind you can't afford to lose."[61]

The day of the funeral arrived: Friday June 15th, a week to the day of Hayes's death. In some ways it was a familiar ritual – the good and the great of London's jazz community turning out to say their last goodbyes to one of their own. Eight months before, for Phil Seamen's funeral, they'd done exactly that, in exactly the same place, Golders Green Crematorium, only this time they were one less in number.

The arrangements for the service had somehow fallen into place, handled by Barnes and Sons of Uxbridge and paid for by Ronnie Scott's,[62] and, like so many struck by grief, Liz had used the organization of the funeral to defer her feelings. She'd done nearly everything – making dozens of phone calls, answering letters – but it had been a truly dreadful week. The messages of support and the press tributes had been wonderful, but none of them could do the one thing that she wanted – take away the pain and bring back the man she loved. In the days following his death, she'd also learned that her boyfriend had died intestate and that it looked likely that there would be legal problems with what constituted his estate. However, none of this mattered today. She'd agreed to ride in the car with Teddy and Dorothy, but hated every moment. For much of the journey the conversation had been about rose bushes – it was a glorious early summer afternoon – and Liz's thoughts soon turned angry. "Typical English," she said to herself. She knew Teddy had been mortified at his son's death, partly through the guilt of never truly getting to know him, but now he wore a stoic mask. Talking about flowers was just a distraction.[63]

The service was due to begin at 2 pm but the muster of musicians was already reaching overflow proportions half an hour or so before: Ronnie Scott, Stan Tracey, John Stevens, Tommy Whittle, Tony Levin, the Skidmores, Evan Parker, Ronnie Ross, Brian Smith, Tony Crombie, Ian Hamer, Annie Ross, Danny Moss and Jeannie Lambe, Jeff Clyne, Eddie Harvey, Dickie Hawdon, Mike Pyne, Spike Wells, Ron Mathewson, Keith Christie, Gordon Beck, Harry Hayes, Colin Purbrook, Stan Roderick, Tony Lee, Pete King, Ken Baldock, Brian Lemon, Stan Sulzmann – the list went on. Then, finally, the conversations stopped, and everyone stood silently, with all eyes on the polished black hearse that slowly drew nearer, the sun glinting on its polished contours.

As Hayes's coffin was lifted out, there was a fleeting moment which some of the mourners saw as symbolic: "I was with Mike Pyne and a lot of the guys," remembers saxophonist Brian Smith, "and a bird came and sat on his coffin. We thought this was really something – being touched by a bird – Charlie Parker – which of course he was."[64] The solemnity was even briefly lifted by Ronnie Scott's notorious wit; Benny Green had slipped a disc the week prior to the funeral and was given special dispensation to be driven to the entrance of the chapel. Lying flat on his back in the rear of the car, Green was helped out feet first, to which Scott observed "Hardly worth going home, is it?"[65]

"The funeral was not spectacular although it was packed out with people," remembers Spike Wells. "I don't remember any music and I certainly don't recall any jazz. It was a fairly simple ceremony."[66] Indeed, there had seemed something oddly incongruous in sending off a man who had been so full of zest in such a pious way. After all the prayers and silent contemplation, it was at last time for the committal, and as the curtains closed, cloaking the coffin from view, all those present – who had been so touched by both the man *and* his music – knew that the odyssey of Edward Brian Hayes was finally over.

Unlike the funeral service, the wake held at Ronnie Scott's club was a far from sober affair. There was plenty of music, even laughter and, as the musicians drank to the memory of their departed friend, more than a few tears. Liz had arranged a buffet and wanted to put a large photograph of Tubby on the bar, surrounded by a floral tribute, a gesture that Ronnie Scott thought too maudlin.[67] Some, including Alan Branscombe, were even talking angrily about how the surgeons had done too little to save Hayes's life, and postulated outrageous conspiracy theories. But amid all the booze and conversation, there was at least one poignant interlude: Annie Ross hushed the room to silence with her version of 'God Bless The Child'.[68] The drinking and banter carried on into the club's regular opening hours, invading that evening's gig by George Melly. Finally, come the small hours it was all over.

It had been the last hurrah for a man that everyone – musicians, jazz critics, fans alike – had admired deeply. What *would* the British jazz scene be like without him?

The weeks and months that followed Tubby Hayes's death had moments of great pride, sorrow, anger and confusion for those who knew and loved him. The obituaries that appeared in jazz magazines across the globe – *Jazz Journal* and *Crescendo* in the UK, *DownBeat* in America, *Coda* in Canada, *Dagbladet* in Norway – had unanimously sung his praises, and there had been affectionate personal tributes in *Melody Maker* from Harry South and Ronnie Scott. But, somehow, something had been lost that couldn't effectively be conveyed in words. It felt like the end of an era. "With the loss of Phil Seamen, Joe Harriott and now Tubby Hayes, jazz in Britain will not be quite the same again," Mark Gardner observed in *Coda* magazine. "Indeed, there are many of us who will never come to terms with Tubby's tragic and premature demise."[69]

For Liz Grönlund the remainder of 1973 seemed like a nightmare. There were those still maintaining that Hayes's death had been caused by the after-effects of his prolonged drug use, but she refused to listen. There had even been talk of an investigative enquiry into the competence of the surgical staff who had carried out the operation, but it all came to nothing. Added to this indignation, Rose Hayes had come to collect her husband's saxophone and music shortly after his death – her legal entitlement as Tubby's next of kin. The visit left Grönlund in pieces.[70] Her doctor prescribed Ritalin and Valium, effectively zombifying her for much of the time. She began to exist in a nether-world of grief and regret, filling her days by assembling scrapbooks of press cuttings about Tubby, drawing love hearts alongside some of the pictures. However, she still couldn't bring herself to listen to him play. The box of tapes and pile of LPs he had left behind sat undisturbed. She knew she wanted to push his music, to ensure that he wasn't forgotten but she had neither the strength nor, having become increasingly reclusive, the contacts. His clothes still hung in the wardrobe, the décor didn't change, the clocks had stopped. Indeed, 89 Gloucester Place was to remain this way for years, a shrine to the memory of Tubby Hayes.[71]

At the end of 1974, eighteen months after his death, Liz tape-recorded some of her memories of Tubby. "I still have a lump in my throat when I talk about him," she confessed. "It is so unbelievable that he is gone, not to come back again. But he's here. I believe so long as you remember a person he must be alive – and he is. I feel his vibrations every day."[72]

Afterword

The Lost Leader: The Legacy of Tubby Hayes

In many ways, he <u>was</u> jazz in this country.

Spike Wells

In November 1973, five months after his death, a plaque commemorating Tubby Hayes was mounted in a quiet corner of Golders Green crematorium, funded by a combination of the proceeds from the various posthumous benefits that had been held in his memory at Ronnie Scott's and elsewhere.[1] It reads:

TUBBY HAYES

JAZZ MUSICIAN AND COMPOSER

DIED 8th JUNE 1973, AGED 38

Long live his memory

and his music

Over the years ahead Hayes's memorial was to be joined by that of his old friend Ronnie Scott, situated barely a few feet away. If you visit the spot today, you'll see commemorative plaques to several other famous names from the world of music and show business, including Val Parnell, the famed impresario and uncle of the bandleader who had been one of Hayes's earliest employers, and Marc Bolan, from the band T. Rex, who died at a tragically young age in a car accident in 1977.[2] Rather conveniently, this unlikely trio – Parnell, Scott and Bolan – effectively map out the changes that had occurred in the professional landscape during Tubby Hayes's twenty-three-year career.[3]

He had begun in the days when a theatre circuit like Parnell's Moss Empire comprised an integral part of a working musician's itinerary. Indeed, some of his earliest gigs with Kenny Baker had been at Moss Theatres. Inspired by men like Scott, Hayes had then been among the first British jazz musicians to take jazz away from the established methods of promotion – the dance band and the variety circuit – and to treat it as an art form as much as an entertainment. Over the next few years, via the example of the Jazz Couriers and his other bands, modern jazz in Great Britain had moved up several notches to the point where, by the early 1960s, it was at last prepared to launch itself unqualified onto the world stage. The timing, however, was anything but propitious: first came the rock and roll explosion, then rhythm and blues, then The Beatles, and quite suddenly, almost overnight, music became polarized, with jazz losing its footing in the wider consciousness. Thankfully, the eclipse was not total; ironically, as the 1970s began, British jazz was more sure of itself and more diverse in its aims than it had ever been, thanks in part to Hayes's example. Nevertheless, it remained unrealistic to expect it to compete with the popular music of the day – the Bolans, the Bowies, the Led Zeppelins. In fact, many of its finest practitioners were barely eking out a living and had never known things so bad. Tragically, some – including Tubby Hayes, Joe Harriott and Phil Seamen – would not live long enough to see any reversal of fortune. Hayes may have possessed musical riches aplenty but he had not died a wealthy man: in 1975 the *Evening Standard* recorded that his estate stood at just £4267.19.[4]

The individual stories of Hayes's closest musical associates during the years immediately after his death make an interesting study in contrasts, mixing equal parts idealism and ignominy. Ronnie Scott continued with his club, as well as forming various bands which – as they had done in the days of the Jazz Couriers – always reflected his latest musical enthusiasms. Central to these, as he had been to Tubby Hayes's musical ambitions, was Ron Mathewson, a player who owed a great deal of his subsequent career success to his old boss.

Spike Wells and Tony Levin both continued to operate inside and outside the profession. Wells had qualified as a solicitor in 1974 and, up until his retirement in the 1990s, he managed to pursue music and law, both at the highest levels. Levin in the meantime played only what he wanted when he wanted and remained faithful to the kind of free-improvised settings that had been all the rage at the time of Hayes's death. Another of Hayes's discoveries, Mike Pyne, on the other hand, had stepped sideways rather than forward, working regularly with Humphrey Lyttelton's band during the 1970s and finding time to revisit his first instrument – the cornet – sometimes in multi-tracked duets. Louis Stewart had also continued to shine, working internationally as a member of bands led by Benny Goodman and George Shearing.

Some of Hayes's other colleagues would not weather so well. Arguably the most original tenor saxophone stylist the UK had ever produced, Bobby Wellins spent most of the early 1970s trying to get his life back together following the heroin addiction that had very nearly killed him. It had taken him out of action and out of London, to the extent that he hadn't even attended Hayes's funeral. Jimmy Deuchar too had gone on to lead a less-than-spectacular career, returning to Scotland before taking commercial gigs in the Far East. Undoubtedly the biggest musical loss was Terry Shannon, the intuitive pianist who had been a key part of virtually all of Tubby Hayes's achievements for close to a decade. After years of abstinence, in the late 1960s he had finally succumbed to serious drug addiction. The episode was short-lived and horrific and afterwards he abandoned London – and eventually playing altogether – for life in rural Lincolnshire.

The bands with which Hayes had been associated at the end of his life also continued to write their own story. Ian Hamer's sextet maintained its sporadic existence, making appearances at the Bull's Head and on the BBC, with Alan Skidmore taking Tubby's place. Splinters, the adventurous free collective dreamed up by John Stevens, simply fell apart, however. The concept had limped on for a while after Hayes's death, with Peter King filling in, but the change of personalities and – according to Trevor Watts – Stan Tracey's quiet dread that he may follow Hayes and Phil Seamen as the band's next casualty, meant things couldn't be the same.[5]

The British jazz scene that Hayes left still had its big hitters – Westbrook, Parker, Tracey, Surman, Tippett to name but a few – but such was its catholicism that no one single figure would have the monopoly in the years ahead, as Hayes had once done. With supreme irony, when the *Melody Maker*'s jazz poll results were announced a few weeks after Hayes's death[6] he was placed fourth in the tenor saxophone category, behind Alan Skidmore, Evan Parker and Brian Smith. Once upon a time, he'd have swept the board, topping several categories, but now, barely a few weeks after his last gigs, he was becoming a footnote, part of the continuum of British jazz rather than its exceptional head. As the 1970s moved onward towards the 1980s, that was how he largely remained: his music was fondly talked of, but perhaps, it could be argued, was no longer relevant.

Virtually all of Hayes's obituaries had stressed the world-class quality of his musical talent, with one calling him "the most eminent European jazz soloist."[7] However, the problem in making any genuine assessment of his gifts was that they have become almost inextricably linked to the romance and folklore of his life story – the chubby teenager who'd blown Ronnie Scott off the stage; the only British soloist authentic enough to export to the USA; the parochial saxophone colossus cut down too early. Even in the twenty-first century, he is still frequently described as "Britain's greatest jazzman," a point that misses the glaringly obvious fact that his career goals were anything but dictated by localism.

So what exactly had he done to elevate himself to this unique position and moreover why had his talents stood out so prominently among those of an entire musical generation that had prided itself on its high standards? The answers lie not in any ability to create a startlingly new jazz voice, but

"Long live his memory and his music." Hayes's commemorative plaque at Golders Green Crematorium. Author's collection.

rather in his gift for doing what others did, but so much better. Indeed, sheer professionalism lies at the heart of virtually everything Hayes ever achieved. Right from the off, he had an uncanny knack for unlocking the cypher of modern jazz. In the early 1950s, he was smack inside the language of men such as Stan Getz, Zoot Sims and the school of "Brothers" who'd emerged from Lester Young's example. Fast-forward to the late 1950s, and the music he made with the Jazz Couriers, both as a writer and a player, revealed an equally keen understanding of the methods of hard bop, one that would only deepen further still during the early 1960s. The purple patch of recording that ensued from this point – a period roughly outlined by the albums *Tubby's Groove* and *Return Visit* – undoubtedly captured Hayes at his career peak. Everything he had worked for was now finally in place: international respect via work in the USA, the immaculate virtuoso technical skill unmatched by any other UK jazzmen, the multi-instrumentalism, the formidable composing and arranging skill. Above all, Hayes had won the respect and admiration of the vast majority of his listeners and fellow musicians, a remarkable achievement in the sometimes fractious world of British jazz.

The most frequently heard compliment about his playing at this juncture was that it sounded "like an American," leaving Hayes in the peculiar position of appearing both a benchmark and an anomaly. Clearly world-class, he nevertheless remained the centrepiece of a very *British* jazz scene, often judged by the same harsh standards that were applied to some of his less able contemporaries. Thus began the oft-heard criticisms of his improvisation containing "too many notes." His garrulous delivery lacked any real substance, some writers maintained. To his credit, Hayes remained largely unmoved by even his sternest detractors. As someone who already possessed a generous helping of self-confidence, he wasn't the kind of person to take it to heart and rarely justified himself in print. After all, if players like Johnny Griffin, Sonny Rollins and Stan Getz considered you an equal, why bother to respond to a petty, non-playing critic sniping from an ivory tower?

The changes that began to transform the British music scene during the mid-1960s, however, were much less easily brushed aside. Hayes was not above vanity and, after a decade of having things pretty much as he wished, the seismic alterations of the post-rock and roll world did not sit easy. When rhythm and blues began to slide into jazz clubs in London, and then took them over, the crowds of adoring fans went elsewhere. Ronnie Scott's was now presenting the "real deal" – genuine American jazzmen – and, despite that fact that without Hayes such a situation certainly wouldn't have existed at all, he began to find himself sidelined. Added to this, the rise of new styles – both inside and outside jazz – presented another threat. Ornette Coleman mystified him. The Beatles irritated him, and even old heroes such as John Coltrane and Sonny Rollins seemed to have lost something in their pursuit of the outer reaches.

Nevertheless, adversity is often a traditional fuel for artistic creativity and with his new band of Mike Pyne, Ron Mathewson and Tony Levin, Hayes now came up with a compromised music that took on board some of the innovations of the day, albeit one that still contained enough of him to be recognizable. The album made by this band, *Mexican Green*, is frequently cited as Hayes's true musical masterpiece – and it is. All the elements that he mastered are present – the burnout tempos, the lyrical balladry, the naturally sophisticated sense of harmony – but there were also enough new things present to prove that change wasn't all bad. The collective improvisation on the title track alone proved hands down that Hayes was refusing to stand still. Indeed, when more than one critic posthumously compared his musical journey to that of his idol John Coltrane, it wasn't just expedient flattery.

The two men had a great deal in common. Their careers had both been alarmingly brief and both had suffered at the hands of critics fond of using their considerable technical skills as sticks with which to beat them. If Hayes ultimately lacked Coltrane's visionary zeal, he nonetheless displayed a similar appetite for self-development. Coltrane had been forced to reconsider his approach in the wake of men such as Ornette Coleman and Albert Ayler, and Hayes did the same, never quite travelling as far as his hero (on record at least) but clearly prepared to abandon some of what he'd taken as rote in order to annex new ground.

There is another point of comparison to be made with Coltrane. Lionized as the American is for his later music, and for the spiritual quest so overtly and inextricably linked with it, he is still perhaps best remembered for the intimidatingly complex super-developments of bebop harmony which he had pioneered in the late 1950s. Indeed, even in the early twenty-first century, nearly fifty years after his death, a college-trained saxophone student is more likely to zone in on this part of his legacy – the *Giant Steps* phase – than try to unlock the mystical cypher of records such as *Om* and *Expression*.

One final parallel exists. Just as *A Love Supreme* has sometimes obscured the fact that Coltrane's earlier albums actually contain more diverse – and at times more engrossing – music, the vaunted reputation of *Mexican Green* may have inadvertently done a disservice to some of Tubby Hayes's earlier work. It remains – without qualification – an exceptional record, and is perhaps the first recorded instance of Hayes working with local players unilaterally suited to his aspirations; but in some ways it stands somewhat outside the rest of his discography. It is his last pure jazz album, a record that points towards a further development that ultimately never came, but that also ironically looks backwards at the same time. In fact, the piece on the album that best exemplifies the folkloric legend of Tubby Hayes – saxophone virtuoso – is not the open-ended title track but 'The Second City Steamer', a performance typical of the hard bop workouts he'd indulged in earlier in the decade.

Now is also a better time to evaluate just how "authentic" Hayes really was. Although it remains possible to argue that via a combination of factors – poor engineering, uninterested record labels and bad timing among them – he never really made an album that consistently captured what he did at its best, there is no doubting the impact Hayes could have at a live gig. The music recently unearthed from gigs at venues such as the Dancing Slipper, the Hopbine and others has confirmed that in general he operated at his best away from the confines of the recording studio. This situation was by no means peculiar to British musicians – one need only look at the discography of Sonny Rollins to see something similar – but even these candid releases reveal the axis on which Hayes's music had always wobbled. Listening to the best of British jazz from the 1950s to the 1970s, be it by Tony Kinsey or Alan Skidmore – to pick two extremes – and there is rarely any doubt about the country of origin. To make so sweeping a statement might seem a little like critical suicide, or at the very least require a lengthy technical caveat to qualify it, but in some almost unfathomable way, it remains a truism.

The work of the Jazz Couriers has long been recognized as having its roots not solely in the hard bop of men such as Art Blakey and Horace Silver but also in the Palais band apprenticeship of its members, and even Hayes's later bands – including those during the early 1970s – continued to have something uniquely British about them. Despite all the critical raves, his big band of the early sixties, for example, didn't *really* sound like anything from across the Atlantic. Nor did his quintet with Jimmy Deuchar quite have the same idiomatic relaxation as a band full of men from Pittsburgh, Detroit and Chicago. Like the music heard on *Mexican Green*, both were highly successful British *reflections* of American trends rather than slavish impersonations.

However, this is not a criticism, more an observation. If jazz is, as is so often said, music able to reflect every aspect of its performer's persona, then why not his or her country of birth? Critics rarely lambasted Django Reinhardt or

Stéphane Grappelli for sounding so unmistakably European, but Hayes was less fortunate, simply because he largely operated on the British jazz scene, a circuit under the scrutiny of an especially duplicitous music press. The narrow-mindedness of many local jazz journalists, particularly during the 1950s, meant that even a musician as outwardly "American" as Hayes could come in for a rough time. On the one hand he was praised – his latest record was as good as anything by Johnny Griffin – but on the other he'd find himself hauled over the coals for being slow in finding his own original methods.

Hayes, of course, should have been congratulated for his technical achievements rather than pilloried for them. Indeed, the very idea of a British jazzman being compared so favourably to a top American soloist had been rare up until his example. In the late 1940s, around the time Hayes began playing, the likelihood of an English soloist getting anything more positive than a polite pat on the back had been distinctly remote. However, there was also an unintentional irony to all the games of critical pigeonholing. Although jazz writers were to remain fond of aligning him with all manner of American saxophonists – from Sonny Rollins to Benny Golson – by the dawn of the 1960s Hayes had begun to do the hitherto impossible by sounding both like and *un*like any of the major contemporary American saxophonists. He continued to borrow from players like Johnny Griffin and John Coltrane, but what he contrived to do with these borrowings was much more than parrot-fashion mimicry. It was at this point that Hayes truly came into his own, and his recordings really began to sound like the products of a major-league jazz talent. Listening to the album *Tubby's Groove*, for example, one hears a player who sounds neither inferior to nor less effective than Griffin, Sonny Stitt or Stan Getz, but just different.

But there was an irony to such an achievement. Hayes was part of a generation of British players who had baulked at the lack of opportunities to get to the music's source – America – and yet in many ways operating at a remove had actually helped. Being away from the melting pot of New York enabled them to make a far more measured assessment of musical trends, albeit one governed by the speed at which they could access the latest records. The albums made by both the Jazz Couriers in the late 1950s and the Tubby Hayes Quintet a few years later reveal the rapidity of this ascent up the learning curve. But, even if an English player could effectively synthesize the newest music from America, as Hayes had definitively proved, the culture from which it came was less readily absorbed.

Some of the first wave of British bebop pioneers, such as Denis Rose and Laurie Morgan, had realized this early on and quickly opted out of what they saw as a hopeless game of phoney mimicry. They weren't Americans and ergo they would never be able to *play* or *behave* exactly like them. Tubby Hayes was never prepared to concede this point. Illustrating this belief at its most base, bassist Jeff Clyne recalled with affectionate amusement how his leader's demeanour on stage would change from week to week depending on which American jazz group was in town. However, these hip pretensions were played out against a background of transport cafes, rain-sodden drives to Manchester and jazz clubs run in pub back rooms. That Hayes was not only able to maintain his self-belief in such surroundings but was actually able to inspire those around him is nothing short of amazing. In considering this point, we are drawn to a renewed appreciation of what was perhaps his greatest contribution to British jazz: that of being a wholly unique catalyst.

Talk to any musician who worked with Tubby Hayes and sooner or later the notion of "leading by example" comes up. Whether it was with the Jazz Couriers or his final quartet, Hayes consistently gave his all and clearly expected the same of those he employed. Indeed, Allan Ganley thought he gave more in Tubby Hayes's band in two years than he did in John Dankworth's over fifty. As Spike Wells confirms, if you proved you had the necessary talent to make a real contribution on the bandstand, there were no limits.

But Hayes was not just a leader of bands – he was a leader of an entire movement. It's impossible to leaf through the pages of magazines such as *Jazz News* or the *Melody Maker* from the early 1960s and avoid either his photograph, a review of one of his recordings or an article detailing his latest musical movements. He had certainly become the most ubiquitous face in British modernism, and to some had come to define a whole genre. "In many ways, he *was* jazz in this country," maintains Spike Wells.[8] It is easy to see why. He had a good image, an easy way with the public and had inspired a certain familiar affection, even in non-specialist listeners. As writer Peter Clayton had observed in the *Sunday Telegraph* in 1964, they may not have understood fully what he was doing but his conviction and charisma were enough to win them over. Of all his many characteristics, it was the latter that had come in most handy in building a following. He had been among the first British modernists to abandon the veneer of po-faced aloofness the music cultivated during the bop boom, and to let the audience in. "The thing has to be sold," he once remarked. "I don't think you can get modern jazz across by exhibitionism, but a lot of guys don't communicate *at all*."[9] Not only had he realized that modern jazz required salesmanship, he had recognized that it was localism that was sabotaging much of its potential success.

> The trouble with most British musicians is that they lack confidence in themselves. They persistently underrate their own abilities and also the ability of an audience to respond to their music. Once I've created a little receptive atmosphere by introducing the tune, it's up to the people to make some effort to meet the musicians as well.[10]

Hayes had also led the way to a greater realization of what being professional truly meant. It was no good looking on your doorstep for the work, recognition and plaudits that you *thought* you deserved – you had to think in far broader, international terms. The impact of this positive attitude on his own career is well known, but it also fuelled the beginnings of British jazzmen *en masse* getting a far better deal at home and abroad. Indeed, without his example much of what subsequently became possible for later generations of British musicians would have been inconceivable. In fact, it would not be at all far-fetched to suggest that Tubby Hayes changed not only the international face of British jazz, but also the entire *profession* of music in the UK.

So what of Tubby Hayes the person rather than the professional musician? As this study has proven in several instances, he was certainly not a saint. Nor was he a particularly consistent sinner. Like most high achievers he alternated peaks of stunning success with troughs of stupid mistakes – some personal, a few professional – and he had the good grace to remain approachably human throughout both. His character flaws included narcissism and an unwillingness to yield to others, both traits ingrained in childhood. Ironically, they also numbered among his greatest strengths. Musically, he had always wanted to sound good. Natural talent helped, but he was a hard worker as well as an idealist, dedicated to pursuing something until he could fully grasp it, the very reason why the physical after-effects of his illness so dented his confidence. Peter King once recalled Hayes's desire to remain at the cutting edge as a "macho thing." Self-centredness had also made him a strong leader, one who knew his direction almost instinctively, and yet this deep-rooted reluctance to let others have their way could sometimes unbalance his playing. The interplay of free jazz, in particular in Splinters, could only have come at a time when *he* was ready for it. A few years earlier, such a collective effort would have taken the spotlight from him and that simply would not do.

His biggest personal drawback was his impulsiveness, which overruled virtually everything in the first fifteen years or so of his professional life. Whatever he wanted – or thought he *needed* – be it one more pint, a shot of this or that, or an available woman – he indulged in with unrelenting passion. Spike Wells recalls this appetite for life as "similar to what they say about Charlie Parker."[11] Ronnie Scott had called it "burning any and every available candle at both ends"[12] while another critic spoke of Hayes's attitude to living as "a contagious knees-up."[13] Although there was much tolerance and even admiration of Hayes's prodigious cravings, there were times when it all became too much, even for those who loved him ("he could sometimes be a bit of a nuisance," the Ronnie Scott club's solicitor Wally Houser once wrote euphemistically[14]), and the shouts of "wahey" and encouragement to "go on, have another double"[15] became more of a test of endurance than endearment. Nevertheless, he was quick to publicly condemn his own actions after his infamous drugs trial in 1968, and expressed deep embarrassment that he had let so many people down. When he chose to, Hayes could also display a far more sensitive side, that of "a very tender man" as Mike Pyne once described him.[16] Others who remembered a more considerate side included the late Jeff Clyne; one of the first things the bassist was keen to tell the author during his interview was that Hayes had once made a special trip across London just to give his new-born son a teddy bear, called, inevitably, Tubby Teddy.[17]

He was also not without regrets or guilt. The only time he ever let rip at Les Tomkins it left the journalist – one of his oldest friends – in shock, but Hayes was straight on the phone the next day, explaining that it wasn't Tomkins's fault and that he'd caught him at a bad time.[18]

Without doubt, the most painful emotions for Hayes came during his relationships with the opposite sex. He knew that he and his first wife Maggie had married too young and was genuinely pleased that towards the end of his life they had again become friends. He also spoke with genuine disappointment that his marriage to Rose had also failed, truthfully acknowledging that his obsessive workload had been the root cause. The ensuing relationship with Joy Marshall gave him some of the best and worst times of his life and, even though they had separated by the time of her death in 1968, the impact of her sudden passing left him heartbroken. Finally, in Liz Grönlund, he'd found something that had eluded him for most of his life – the love of a woman that didn't somehow deplete him, but instead provided something resembling a conventional home life for the very first time. Hayes had begun life firmly under his mother's wing, and maintained a lifelong closeness to Dorothy that he had never enjoyed with his father; in some ways, Grönlund, older and yet less hard-bitten, offered a return to the securities of childhood.

Tubby had also failed to achieve a satisfying father–son bond with his own children, Richard and Lewis. By all accounts he rarely mentioned them after leaving Rose, and had severed all direct contact by the late 1960s. After his death, Rose gradually revealed more about their marital difficulties to her sons, citing both Hayes's desire to live in the US and his drug habit as the deciding factors in their break-up. But whilst Richard was just old enough to grasp the impact of these human dramas, Hayes's youngest son Lewis was left to piece together a picture of the man who was his father by collecting his records. Although no one saw any particularly dark demons lurking within him, Lewis was clearly a troubled soul, suffering bouts of depression before dying of a sleeping tablet overdose in December 1989, just a few weeks shy of his twenty-fourth birthday.[19]

Tubby had bequeathed one thing to his sons, though: artistic precocity. After becoming obsessed with comic books, Richard Hayes published his first novel, *The Secret Army*, in 1977, aged just sixteen, subsequently becoming a successful author.[20] Lewis's success was equally impressive: during the mid-1980s he and his stepfather Jim Campbell formed Master Mix Records, scoring a massive commercial hit with a remix of the dance track 'I Found Lovin'' by the Fatback Band. Echoing his father's trait for winning awards, when sales reached 200,000 copies Lewis was presented with a BPI Silver disc.

This study has also revealed that Tubby Hayes was a man of many parts, not all of them visible to the public. He had a photographic memory, particularly about sporting fixtures. He was also a skilled artist; teenage sketches and immaculately hand-drawn comic books survive, as do rather more ad-hoc drawings made during his final few months with Liz Grönlund at Gloucester Place. He loved boxing and enjoyed collecting cine films of old fights. He was a Chelsea FC supporter and also adored cricket, following Surrey throughout his life. In fact, the impression one gets when hearing about Hayes in his rarer and more sedate moods is that he was an ordinary man, who just happened to have been blessed with an extraordinary musical gift. He was also extraordinarily courageous, never more so than in battling the heart condition that eventually killed him. Indeed, the very same determination that had so helped him overcome the prejudices and insecurities of his early career undoubtedly helped him live longer than he perhaps might. But bravery alone was ultimately not enough to stave off the inevitable end.

Tubby Hayes the man ceased to be in 1973, but in the years after his passing, Tubby Hayes the musical legend continued to grow. However, for a while the legend was more apocryphal than tangible, and anyone wishing to examine than music of a man who had left such impressive tales of artistic achievement in his wake would have found themselves frustrated at the lack of evidence. Only two of his albums remained in print during the mid-1970s – the Philips re-release of *100% Proof*, issued shortly before his death, with its ghastly cover portrait of the latter-day moustachioed Hayes looking for all the world like a saxophone-playing porn star, and the ubiquitous Music for Pleasure reissue of *The Jazz Couriers In Concert*. Scouring the second-hand racks could bring up his albums on Tempo and Fontana, but Hayes's music was now in danger of falling into the worst kind of posthumous limbo that can befall a creative musician – that of being talked about but rarely heard.

Perhaps even more worrying was the lack of interest among fellow musicians. Despite the fact that he had acquired an almost cult-like following in the saxophone section of the National Youth Jazz Orchestra (NYJO) during the early 1970s, no one even knew where Hayes's pad containing arrangements for his big band had got to since his death.[21] Some of it was rumoured to be with his widow. Others had heard that it had been destroyed. Surely something as culturally important as this couldn't just be left languishing in someone's loft?

Fortunately, the time for a revival of interest in Hayes's music was just around the corner. As the seventies gave way to the eighties, jazz fashions like fusion had grown tired and predictable and young jazz musicians were again looking to their forebears for inspiration. Fuelling this new wave of revivalism was a reissue boom – record labels were making the most of their back catalogues by repackaging the work of all manner of jazz names, resulting in a new generation encountering the sounds of hard bop for the first time, marvelling at the energy of a music that had so entranced the Jazz Couriers thirty years before. Some of the genre's originators were still out there on the road, including Art Blakey whose dynastic Jazz Messengers now featured two young brothers from New Orleans, Wynton and Branford

Marsalis, who had almost overnight restored the image of the music. Not only were the Marsalises precociously steeped in the jazz of the 1950s and '60s, they also looked the part. The sharp-suited, classic look that Tubby Hayes and his generation had fought so hard to emulate was back. More importantly, so was the music.

Just as it had done three decades earlier, this influence permeated to young British jazzmen, amongst them Clark Tracey and Alec Dankworth, the sons of two of Tubby Hayes's erstwhile colleagues. Indeed, Tracey's mid-eighties quintet was exactly the sort of band Hayes himself would have thrived in – musically sharp, taking the greatest delight in playing the most challenging music as if it were no more taxing than a mere warm-up. The group even played 'Suddenly Last Tuesday', a composition from the repertoire of the old Hayes quintet, taken at a suitably kamikaze tempo.

Ironically, though, it wasn't one of these young lions who took the first step in relaunching the music of Tubby Hayes, but an old playing partner – Bobby Wellins. Although he has made a return to full-time playing in 1976, the saxophonist occasionally needed to teach in order to get by. When one of his students played him Hayes's recording of 'Cherokee', it all came back. "I suddenly felt ashamed that I had never made any attempt to pay tribute to such a superlative improviser and a dear friend," Wellins wrote shortly afterwards.[22] He began to mull over the idea of attempting to resuscitate the Hayes big band. At first, it looked almost impossible – nobody knew where the charts had ended up, but after a few helpful phone calls to Jackie Sharpe and Harry South, Wellins discovered the majority of the library was still with Rose Hayes, simply gathering dust. As the pieces of the jigsaw fell together, Wellins was able to secure the financial assistance of the Arts Council of Great Britain, and finally, on Tuesday May 6th, 1980, the Hammersmith and Fulham Jazz Festival presented a concert billed as a "Tribute to Tubby Hayes." Although lack of rehearsal and unsuitable acoustics did their best to sabotage the set, the reception given the band – which included old hands like Spike Wells, Ron Mathewson and Peter King – was justification enough. Tubby Hayes's music was out of limbo, at last.

As if the Hammersmith gig had somehow magically uncorked the bottle, Hayes's legacy underwent a remarkable renaissance during the early 1980s. The year after the concert, Spotlite Records released an album of previously unissued concert recordings to great critical acclaim,[23] an event followed soon after by the Mole Jazz label's reissue of two of the saxophonist's best albums from the old Fontana catalogue, *Mexican Green* and *Tubbs' Tours*.[24] The BBC even dusted down the Tubby Hayes big band episode of *Jazz 625* for a brave weekend of jazz television in 1984,[25] a decision resulting in fans and musicians too young to have ever heard Hayes play in person encountering his music for the first time. The opportunity to play it also arose again when Jack Sharpe gained permission to use Hayes's arrangements full-time, leading to the formation of a new band featuring a clutch of rising jazz stars, including Guy Barker, Dave Bishop and Jamie Talbot. The Sharpe band's week-long engagement at Ronnie Scott's club in 1989 – with added starter Jimmy Deuchar – was just like old times. The music had clearly stood the test of time and for older fans there was something especially heart-warming about watching a youthful tyro like Dave Bishop tearing into Hayes's test-piece '100% Proof'.[26]

Hayes's music in its recorded form had also become enormously collectable. Original pressings of his Tempo albums now changed hands for three-figure sums, an ironic situation that especially tickled the man who'd produced them back in the 1950s, Tony Hall. For those unprepared to sell the family silver, an enterprising label from East London, Jasmine Records, began to license the Tempo sessions and release them on facsimile vinyl. This renewed interest increased as the LP format made way for the new technology of the compact disc. Newly discovered sessions began to appear, rescued from dusty old tapes retrieved from long-defunct venues like the Hopbine[27] and, in 1990, an album by Hayes's quartet, taken from BBC *Jazz Club* tapes and appropriately titled *For Members Only*, became a best-seller on the back of airplay from the new radio station Jazz FM.[28]

That same year there was the first attempt at a book detailing Hayes's work, *Tubby Hayes: A Discography*, by Barbara Schwarz, a modest but key study outlining a professional life lived very much in the recording studio.

The twenty-fifth anniversary of Hayes's passing in 1998 was marked by the long-overdue springing of the locks on the Fontana archives. Greeted by the critics as if they were long-lost friends, *Late Spot At Scott's* and *Down In The Village* were finally re-released on CD,[29] and there was the welcome news that further unheard studio tapes – allegedly including out-takes from the *Mexican Green* sessions – had now been located.[30]

As the twenty-first century began, interest in Hayes's work only deepened. In 2001 he was the subject of a *Jazz Legends* documentary on BBC Radio 3,[31] with Peter King adding his wry personal reminiscence, and, over the next few years, there were extensive retrospective appreciations published in magazines including *Record Collector*[32] and *Jazz Review*.[33] The culmination of these events was undoubtedly on the day in 2005 that would have been Hayes's seventieth birthday: his story was central to a new BBC TV documentary series, *Jazz Britannia*, and there were yet more reissues of his long-sought-after Fontana albums, together with newly uncovered live sets capturing Hayes at his mid-sixties prime.[34] DJ Gilles Peterson had even relaunched Hayes as an unlikely dance-floor hero, turning a new generation of listeners on to the insistent groove of 'Down In The Village'.[35] Perhaps even more heartening was a burgeoning interest from younger players. Prominent saxophonists Theo Travis and Gilad Atzmon both name-checked Hayes as a formative influence, whilst pianist Gareth Williams declared that seeing the rerun of the Tubby Hayes big band's *Jazz 625* show in the early 1980s had been the catalyst that inspired him to become a jazz musician. For nostalgic fans, the biggest kick, however, was the formation in 2000 of the band Celebrating the Jazz Couriers, for which tenorist Mornington Lockett transcribed the original Hayes–Scott arrangements to be played by a new line-up including ex-Oscar Peterson drummer Martin Drew and – some said the reincarnation of Hayes himself – the precocious saxophonist Nigel Hitchcock. The band proved a tremendous success on the UK club and festival circuit, recording two albums that not only proved the durability of the music, but how it could stimulate a quite different generation of players. And, in a victory that mirrored the triumphs of its inspiration, the group won the Best Small Band category of the Hamlet Jazz Awards in 2002.[36]

However, some critical prejudices die hard and Hayes was still open to a lambasting by those who misunderstood his genius. The Penguin Guide to Jazz, first published in 1992, gave the saxophonist the sort of qualified entry that would have done Edgar Jackson or Danny Halperin proud, describing him as "a fascinating but problematical player [who] often left a solo full of brilliant loose ends and ingenious runs that led nowhere in particular."[37] It was the old "too many notes" contention all over again. When Jazz Review printed an article in 2000 titled "The Ten Most Important British Jazz Musicians of All Time"[38] and Hayes was omitted, there was something akin to a minor riot in the magazine's letters page. "Musicians, critics and fans alike recognized Hayes as perhaps our most creative jazz artist so how could he be left out?" wrote one outraged reader. Tubby Hayes clearly continued to inspire enormous affection and these objections prompted the magazine to publish an extensive article on Hayes – accurately titled "The Lost Leader."[39] Going some way to redressing the balance, Barry Witherden asked Pete King and Tony Hall if they saw any players on the current UK scene who had something of Hayes in them. The nominees were Peter King and Mornington Lockett, but Witherden was forced to conclude, correctly and without romantic sycophancy, that "Hayes has been inspirational rather than influential." The distinction was a subtle one.

The Jazz Review article also raised the intriguing proposition of where Hayes would have gone next had he lived; his former manager, Pete King, opined that "he'd now be the equal of Rollins and Brecker in celebrity and stature." One can appreciate King's sentiments, but his proposition is not an entirely convincing one, as we shall see.

The "what if?" parlour game, beloved of jazz writers and fans, is easily played when considering, say – to pick two obvious examples – Clifford Brown or Eric Dolphy. Both men died alarmingly young, after all too brief a time in the spotlight, and both were obviously broadening and honing their art when their lives were cut short. Could the same truly be said of Tubby Hayes? In the years immediately prior to his death, illness had forced him to make many compromises in his playing and he made no secret of the stultifying frustration he felt at no longer being quite his old self. Reaction to this varied: from the critics there was almost a sense of satisfaction to be derived in the tempering of his formidable technical skill; for the fans, regardless of whatever form he was now in, Hayes was simply back where he belonged – on the bandstand. For the saxophonist, however, it all added up to his now being merely a faint echo of what he had once been. This is a valid point. Mention the name Tubby Hayes and the music most listeners will instinctively think of will be that of him in his pomp, tackling hard bop at helter-skelter speeds and proving his international mettle. It's unlikely to be the music he made late in his career with John Stevens and Splinters.

Ultimately, there is no answer to what Hayes would have done next musically – there can't be, although some possible clues can be found in the work of those of his contemporaries who outlived him. If one looks at the work of Stan Tracey and Peter King, two prominent examples from Hayes's immediate circle, one sees that after the experiments of the early 1970s, which saw the grafting of some of the language of the avant-garde onto their already classic styles, both men returned to a more natural mode of expression. Whether they had been enriched by the experiences playing in free settings or not is debatable, but they were certainly more mature performers, more at ease with what *was* present in their music than ever before. Perhaps Hayes would have done the same, making a gradual retreat back inside and playing to his strengths. It's impossible to imagine him – or indeed *anyone* – continuing to play the sort of funk-derived fusion found in his early '70s compositions such as 'She Insulted Me In Marrakech'. However, when listening to Peter King's recordings from the early 1980s, in particular the albums *East 34th Street* and *New Beginning*, one hears a suggestion of the sort of music he might have made – sophisticated, deeply rooted in harmony and with enough structural variation to provide a new challenge.

If such a fantasy is cheering, then the question of exactly *where* Tubby Hayes would have played had he lived is less warming. Again, recourse to the working itineraries of his surviving colleagues – and those who emerged in their wake – provides the best indication.

For much of the first two-thirds of Tubby Hayes's career, his focus had been on America, specifically on playing in New York and getting the opportunity to play the cognoscenti at their own game. However, almost as soon as he had proved this was possible, the rules of the game changed. By the close of his career in the early 1970s there was no longer a desperate need for British players to seek out the music at its source, simply because times had changed. The jazz-soloist-as-commuter idyll that Hayes had envisaged in the mid-1960s had never truly caught on and, for all their undoubted authenticity, the surviving players from his generation, Peter King and Bobby Wellins for example, have never really cracked America. Instead, into the early twenty-first century, they continue to operate mainly across the UK club and festival circuit, with the occasional dash to Europe or the Far East.

At home, another erstwhile colleague, Stan Tracey, enjoyed towards the end of his life a respect and stature that could have so equally have been afforded Hayes. Nevertheless, the work opportunities that accompanied the plaudits remained frustratingly limited. Indeed, if one looks at Tracey's elevated status as one of the most creative jazzmen to have come from the United Kingdom, and at his hugely important body of compositional work, it seems inconceivable that right up to within months of his death he should have still been honouring a monthly gig at that most grassroots of all London jazz venues, the Bull's Head at Barnes. However, one can easily imagine Tubby Hayes doing the same, not simply because he's somehow indelibly linked to the Bull's Head and its rich tradition of solid British modern/mainstream, but because, like as not, the pub-jazz circuit that he, Tracey and Phil Seamen were working in during the early 1970s continues to have a central part to play in British jazz.

It's odd to think of this giant-slaying talent, who'd once followed John Coltrane into the Half Note and who'd been head-hunted by Art Blakey, having prospects no more starry than this. One wonders how Hayes's ego would have coped. But, then again, it's perhaps best that we'll never know.

So what remains of Tubby Hayes's legacy? Is it to be found in his insistence that the nationality of your birth need not be an excuse for developing a convincingly authentic jazz voice? Is it in his equally passionate dedication to technical excellence, which irreversibly raised the standards expected of jazz musicians from these islands? Or is it in his belief that a musician could do it all – master several instruments, compose, arrange – and not dissipate his or her energies or become faceless? Or is it simply to be found in the sure and certain fact that – four decades after his death – we're still talking about him? In truth, it's probably a combination of all of these. The great majority of British jazzmen now have a technical and idiomatic command that is imperceptible from that of musicians born in the USA, and since Hayes's death there have been several musicians from the UK who've successfully demonstrated a skilful ability to juggle multi-instrumentalism and writing – Alan Barnes springs immediately to mind. But there has never been an individual who has engendered quite the same affection as Tubby Hayes did.

His music is more readily available than at any time – including, rather perversely, during his own lifetime – and he's no longer simply a near-mythical figure. Indeed, with a better understanding of both his strengths and weaknesses, in some ways he now appears more tangible than ever, standing as a genuine example of the oft-heard phrase "larger than life." Perhaps, then, it's Hayes's general spirit that is his true legacy – a "can do" attitude from which we can still learn much of value. "It's no good waiting for somebody to put something in your lap," he once observed. "You've got to go out and do it for yourself."[40] Amen.

Over sixty years have passed since Tubby Hayes played his first professional note and we live not only in a different world to that of the early 1950s, shrunk by social media, the internet and all the other technological advances that invade our daily lives, but in one where so many more things are possible. You can go and learn to be a jazz musician at college: you no longer have to glean whatever you can from a few prized records or in back-of-the-bus conversations. You can wish for an international career in jazz music without it seeming an impossible goal. You can go through the horrors of drug addiction and not be seen as a pariah, and you now stand a far better chance of surviving heart surgery than ever before. Maybe it is because Tubby Hayes fought to overcome all these things, and did so when none of them had any given certainty of success, that we continue to take inspiration from his story. Ultimately he wasn't "the English John Coltrane," nor was he by any stretch of the imagination a man who altered the course of his chosen art. He didn't give rise to a school of imitators (indeed, the jury is still out on whether he left any real musical heir[41]), nor did he leave a body of recorded work that truly matches in volume his reputation and legend. What he was – and will remain – was a man who emerged from an ordinary background to do truly extraordinary things.

Notes

Introduction

1. Julian Joseph, *BBC Jazz Legends*, July 13, 2001.
2. Bob Dawbarn, *Melody Maker*, February 20, 1965.

1. A Face Not Built for Gloom

1. Publicity brochure of Hayes Orchestra circa 1935, now in the possession of Liz Grönlund.
2. *Jazz Notes*, BBC Radio 2, June 10, 1973.
3. Tape recorded conversation between Dorothy Hayes and Liz Grönlund, circa 1976.
4. John Fordham, *Jazz Man: The Amazing Story of Ronnie Scott and his Club*, London: Kyle Cathie, 1994.
5. Vic Ash, *I Blew It My Way: Bebop, Big Bands and Sinatra*, London: Northway Publications, 2006.
6. John Martin, "The Little Giant of the Tenor Sax," *Jazz News*, September 10, 1960.
7. Other famous ex-Rutlish pupils over the years would include Prime Minister John Major, animator Raymond Briggs and murderer Neville Heath.
8. www.en.wikipedia.org/wiki/rutlish_school
9. Email to author, July 31, 2007.
10. Telephone conversation with author, September 12, 2007.
11. Ibid.
12. Letter to author, July 30, 2007.
13. Ibid.
14. This is now in the possession of Liz Grönlund, as are other childhood sketches by Hayes.
15. Letter to author, July 30, 2007.
16. Telephone conversation with author, September 12, 2007.
17. Martin, "The Little Giant of the Tenor Sax."
18. Edwina Coven, "Larger-than-Life Profile; Tubby Hayes," untraced magazine clipping circa 1969 in Liz Grönlund's scrapbook.
19. Martin, "The Little Giant of the Tenor Sax."
20. "How Some of Today's Top Men Started," *Melody Maker*, October 29, 1966.
21. "Hear Me Talkin'," *The Jazz Scene*, BBC, August 21, 1966.

22. Coven, "Larger-than-Life Profile."

23. Martin, "The Little Giant of The Tenor Sax."

24. Ibid.

25. Dudley Herbert, telephone conversation with author, September 12, 2007.

26. Conversation with author, December 16, 2006.

27. Telephone conversation with author, September 12, 2007.

28. Letter to author, July 30, 2007.

29. Martin, "The Little Giant of the Tenor Sax."

30. Coven, "Larger-Than-Life Profile."

31. Charles Fox, "Tubby Hayes, the End of the Old Ching-Ching-Ching," *Radio Times*, September 25, 1969.

32. Tape recorded conversation between Dorothy Hayes and Liz Grönlund circa 1976.

33. Coven, "Larger-Than-Life Profile."

34. "Hear Me Talkin'," *The Jazz Scene*, BBC, August 21, 1966.

35. Les Tomkins, "The Tubby Hayes Story," *Crescendo*, June 1963.

36. Tomkins, email to author, August 15, 2007.

37. "It was Music in the Anton Manner," *Melody Maker*, July 15, 1950.

38. Tomkins, email to author, August 15, 2007.

39. Sleeve notes to CD reissue of *Tubbs*, Universal Impressed Re-pressed 983 1887 (2005).

40. Harvey, telephone conversation with author, August 30, 2007.

41. Sleeve notes to *Tubby Hayes and The Jazz Couriers featuring Ronnie Scott*, Tempo TAP 15, 1957.

42. Sleeve notes to Tubby Hayes Quintet, *Down In The Village*, Fontana 680 998 TL, 1963.

43. Email to author, August 8, 2006.

44. Letter to author, July 30, 2007.

45. Interviewed by author, April 21, 2004.

46. "Blind Date," *Melody Maker*, June 15, 1968.

47. Maurice Burman, "I'm an Aquarius and that Helps," *Melody Maker*, February 7, 1959.

48. *Melody Maker*, April 28, 1951.

2. Boy Wonder Tenorist

1. Vic Ash, *I Blew It My Way: Bebop, Big Bands and Sinatra*, London: Northway Publications, 2006.

2. John Robert Brown, "No Motorways at All," *Jazz Review*, July 2002.

3. Interviewed by author, September 3, 2007.

4. Ash, *I Blew It My Way*.

5. George Melly recalled the fun of this in the BBC documentary *Smokey Dives*, BBC2, transmitted April 2001.

6. Quoted in Dominic Green, *Benny Green: Words and Music*, London: London House, 2000.

7. Interviewed by author, May 30, 1999.

8. Quoted in Green, *Benny Green*.

9. *Melody Maker*, July 28, 1951.

10. Interviewed by author, May 30, 1999.

11. Phil Seamen interviewed by Harry Frost, London, August 28, 1969 (unpublished).

12. Interviewed by author, May 30, 1999.

13. *Melody Maker*, July 14, 1951.

14. "Terry Brown," *Jazz at Ronnie Scott's* (JARS), September 1988.

15. Ibid.

16. Ibid.

17. John Martin, "The Little Giant of the Tenor Sax," *Jazz News*, September 10, 1960.

18. Interviewed by author, April 19, 2009.
19. Ibid.
20. "There's been a Revolution says Ambrose," *Melody Maker*, April 4, 1953.
21. *New Musical Express*, spring 1953 (undated clipping in Hayes's scrapbook).
22. Martin, "The Little Giant of the Tenor Sax."
23. Interviewed by author, April 19, 2009.
24. Interviewed by author, September 3, 2007.
25. Interviewed by author, September 3, 2007.
26. Interviewed by author, April 19, 2009.
27. Email to author, January 9, 2012.
28. Interviewed by author, April 19, 2009.
29. Ibid.
30. Ibid.
31. Telephone conversation with author, August 30, 2007.
32. Maggie Hayes, interviewed by author, April 19, 2009.
33. Telephone conversation with author, August 30, 2007.
34. "Well Played Vic!" *Melody Maker*, April 24, 1954
35. Interviewed by author, September 3, 2007.
36. In an interview for *The Wire* in 1983, Tracey was quoted as saying "It was in [the Kenny Baker band] that I had my first smoke through Tubby. He turned me on in a place called Goole." Stephen Gove-Humphries and Philip Hanson, "Stan Tracey," *The Wire*, autumn 1983.
37. "Tubby Hayes Facing Drugs Charge," *Melody Maker*, October 30, 1954.
38. Louis Barfe, "Jazz Parnell: Master of Many Trades," 2005, www.transdiffusion.org
39. "Tubby Hayes and Wife Fined in Drugs Case," *Melody Maker*, November 20, 1954.
40. Undated clipping in Hayes's scrapbook.
41. "Jazz Honours List," *Record Mirror*, January 8, 1955.
42. Sleeve notes to *Tubby Hayes and The Jazz Couriers featuring Ronnie Scott*, Tempo TAP 17, 1957.
43. Barry Witherden, "The Lost Leader," *Jazz Review*, January 2001.
44. "Hayes to Tour and Record with 9-piece," *Melody Maker*, February 12, 1955.
45. *Record Mirror*, undated clipping in Hayes's scrapbook.
46. "Benny Green . . . Introduces you to the 'Little Giant'," *New Musical Express*, March 25, 1955.
47. Ibid.
48. *Melody Maker*, May 14, 1955.
49. *New Musical Express*, undated clipping in Hayes's scrapbook.
50. "Enter The Tubby Hayes Band," *New Musical Express*, undated clipping in Hayes's scrapbook.
51. Ibid.
52. "Tubby Hayes Orch. A Success," *Music Mirror*, undated clipping in Hayes's scrapbook.
53. "Battle of the Bands at – Southsea," *Melody Maker*, April 9, 1955.
54. Interviewed by author, September 3, 2007.
55. "The Musicians Pay Tribute . . ." *Melody Maker*, June 16, 1973.
56. Interviewed by author, September 3, 2007.
57. John Robert Brown, "No Motorways at All," *Jazz Review*, July 2002.
58. Ibid.
59. Sleeve notes to *Jack Sharpe Big Band – Catalyst*, Frog CDFRG 716, 1987.

3. '56 not '45

1. Mark Gardner, "The Jazz Record Producers – No. 1: Tony's Tempo," *Jazz Journal International*, August 2008.
2. *New Musical Express*, undated clipping in Hayes's scrapbook.
3. *Jazz Monthly*, September 1955.
4. *Melody Maker*, October 15, 1955.
5. *Jazz UK*, February/March 2009; Peter Vacher, "Global Bop,"
6. Interviewed by author, September 3, 2007.
7. Ibid.
8. At the close of the session, Tony Hall had also taken the opportunity to have Hayes and the rhythm section record two titles with trumpeter Dizzy Reece, 'Please Call' and 'Now's The Time', in order to complete the Jamaican's debut album, *A New Star* (Tempo LAP 3). Neither performance is particularly outstanding, but as an early showing of the front-line of Hayes and Reece they have some discographical merit; both men were to feature on arguably Hall's greatest production coup, the LP *Blues In Trinity*, recorded for the Blue Note label three years later.
9. Hamer, interviewed by author, April 3, 2004.
10. *Music Mirror*, February 1956.
11. Conversation with author, July 23, 2005.
12. Benny Green, "Edward, My Son!" *New Musical Express*, February 10, 1956.
13. *Melody Maker*, June 25, 1955.
14. *New Musical Express*, April 18, 1956.
15. "Russo," *Melody Maker*, February 4, 1956.
16. Roy Carr, "Tough Times at Tempo," in *A Century of Jazz*, London: Hamlyn, 1997.
17. *Jazz Monthly*, February 1957.
18. "Benny Green . . . Introduces you to the 'Little Giant'," *New Musical Express*, March 25, 1955.
19. Jack Massarik, "Mr. 100 Percent," *Jazzwise*, September 2005.
20. *Melody Maker*, February 9, 1957.
21. *Jazz Monthly*, July 1957.
22. "Tubbs Recalled by Jack Sharpe," *Jazz at Ronnie Scott's* (JARS), July/August 1987.
23. Carl Carter, "Archer Street: The Boulevard of Broken Dreams!," *Beat*, late 1956.
24. Interview for *BBC Jazz Session*, November 11, 1960.
25. *Jazz From London*, Acrobat AMCD 4368, 2012.
26. Telephone conversation with author, August 30, 2007.
27. Richard Cook, "Reminiscing with Tony," *Jazz Review*, June 2001.
28. Kitty Grime and Val Wilmer, *Jazz at Ronnie Scott's*, London: Hale, 1979.
29. John Martin, "The Little Giant of the Tenor Sax," *Jazz News*, September 10, 1960.
30. *Melody Maker*, January 19, 1957.
31. Quoted in innumerable articles and sleeve notes to the saxophonist's albums including the 1987 CD reissue of *No Room For Squares*, Blue Note CDP 7 84149 2.
32. Telephone conversation with author, August 16, 2008.
33. Brian Nicholls, "Jazzman's Diary," *Jazz Journal*, July 1957.
34. Benny Green, "The Jazz Couriers: The End of the Old Order and the Beginning of the New," *Jazz News*, February 1958.
35. Interviewed by author, March 3, 2011.
36. Interviewed by author, September 3, 2007.
37. Barry Witherden, "The Lost Leader," *Jazz Review*, January 2001.
38. Jack Massarik, "Remembering Ronnie," *Jazzwise*, December 2006/January 2007.
39. Sleeve notes to Tubby Hayes, *Tubbs; A Tribute*, Spotlite SPJ 902, 1980.
40. Telephone conversation with author, August 16, 2008.
41. *Jazz Journal*, January 1958.

42. *Twenty-Five Years of Ronnie Scott's*, BBC2, 1984.
43. Hayes recalled that he was sacked from Six-Five Special for not adapting himself to the music. He and Scott were also participating in various rock and roll recordings with Tony Crombie at this point.

4. The End of the Old Order

1. Maurice Burman, "I'm an Aquarius and that Helps," *Melody Maker*, February 7, 1959.
2. Brian Nicholls, "Jazzman's Diary," *Jazz Journal*, April 1958.
3. Sleeve notes, *The Jazz Couriers In Concert*, Tempo TAP 22, 1958.
4. Brian Nicholls, "Jazzman's Diary," *Jazz Journal*, April 1958.
5. "Anglo-American Exchange," *Crescendo*, August 1966.
6. *The Eighth Wonder*, Tempo EXA 82, 1958.
7. Ibid.
8. *Jazz Monthly*, February 1959.
9. Bob Dawbarn, "End this Sneer Campaign," *Melody Maker*, July 26, 1958.
10. Maurice Burman, "Ronnie Scott's says: Our Critics are at Fault," *Melody Maker*, August 23, 1958.
11. Interviewed by author, September 10, 2007.
12. Burman, "I'm an Aquarius and that Helps."
13. Interviewed by author, September 10, 2007.
14. Roy Carr, "Tough Times at Tempo," in *A Century of Jazz*, London: Hamlyn, 1997.
15. Richard Cook, "Reminiscing with Tony," *Jazz Review*, June 2001.
16. Sleeve notes to Dizzy Reece, *Blues In Trinity*, Blue Note BLP 4006.
17. Mark Gardner, "The Jazz Record Producers – No. 1: Tony's Tempo," *Jazz Journal International*, August 2008.
18. Sleeve notes to Dizzy Reece, *Blues In Trinity*, Blue Note BLP 4006.
19. Conversation with author, December 16, 2006.
20. Cook, "Reminiscing with Tony."
21. Telephone conversation with author, August 16, 2008.
22. Sleeve notes to *The Couriers Of Jazz*, London LTZ-L 15188, 1960.
23. Sleeve notes to *The Couriers Of Jazz*, Carlton LP 12 116, 1959.
24. "The Test: Stan Tracey," *Jazz Review*, October 2000. Tracey remarked "That's Ronnie and Tubby? It didn't sound like either of them. They're usually more robust players than what I heard there. Tubby usually played a lot more notes than that, as did Ronnie."
25. Kitty Grime and Val Wilmer, *Jazz at Ronnie Scott's*, London: Hale, 1979.
26. Maurice Burman, "I'm an Aquarius and that Helps," *Melody Maker*, February 7, 1959.
27. "Flamingo Flare-up," *Melody Maker*, March 7, 1959.
28. Ibid.
29. Interviewed by author, September 10, 2007. Despite Clyne's claims that these visits were "pre-Beatles," John Lennon, Paul McCartney and Ringo Starr had all performed at the Cavern by this time, although not yet collectively.
30. Derek Ansell, unpublished sleeve note to *The Jazz Couriers Live In Morecambe*.
31. Tippin' – *The Jazz Couriers Live In Morecambe 1959*, Gearbox GB 1514.
32. *Jazz Journal*, August 1960. The timing of the issue didn't exactly help: the album appeared under the immense shadow of *Tubby's Groove*, recorded some months later, but which, with the unfathomable wisdom typical of record companies, was issued first.
33. In his biography *Joe Harriott: Fire in His Soul*, London: Northway Publications, 2011, Alan Robertson actually uses this quote as a chapter title.
34. Reported in Robertson, *Joe Harriott: Fire in His Soul*.
35. *Jazz Britannia*, Episode 1 'Stranger on the Shore', BBC4, transmitted January 28, 2005.

36. Michael Pearson, "Head and Heart," *Jazz FM The Magazine*, issue 21, 1993.
37. Conversation with author, February 3, 2007.
38. Brian Blain, "I remember Phil . . ." *Jazz FM The Magazine*, issue 15, 1992.
39. *Jazz Journal*, March 1960.
40. *Jazz Monthly*, March 1960. Tony Hall nonetheless still held his faith in the end product: in what would be the last of his transatlantic album deals, he licensed *The Last Word* to the American Riverside label who issued it under the title *The Message from Britain* on their Jazzland subsidiary in 1961. With a certain amount of irony, the American press reviews were more favourable than those at home; Metronome's Richard Moses called the album "an outstanding record of its kind" and added that he considered both Hayes and Scott "major league players."
41. Bruce Turner, *Hot Air, Cool Music*, London: Quartet, 1984.
42. Sleeve notes to The Jazz Couriers, *The Last Word*, Tempo TAP 26, 1960.
43. John Martin, "The Little Giant of the Tenor Sax," *Jazz News*, September 10, 1960.

5. Now It's Who Have *They* Got?

1. *The Club That Ronnie Built*, BBC Radio 3, 1999.
2. Benny Green, *Jazz Decade: London*, London: Kings Road Publishing, 1969.
3. *Desert Island Discs*, BBC Radio 4, January 31, 1976.
4. Sleeve notes to *Tubby Hayes Quartet – For Members Only*, Miles Music MMCD 086, 2002.
5. Email to author, January 26, 2008.
6. Sleeve notes to *Tubby Hayes Quartet – For Members Only*, Miles Music MMCD 086, 2002.
7. Telephone conversation with author, July 29, 2007.
8. Sleeve notes to Tubby Hayes, *Tubby's Groove*, Tempo TAP 29, 1960.
9. Interviewed by author, September 10, 2007.
10. Telephone conversation with author, August 16, 2008.
11. Mark Gardner, "The Jazz Record Producers – No.1: Tony's Tempo," *Jazz Journal International*, August 2008.
12. Sleeve notes to Tubby Hayes, *Tubby's Groove*, Tempo TAP 29, 1960.
13. Ibid.
14. Ibid.
15. Ibid.
16. Bob Dawbarn, "Here's Tubby at his Best," *Melody Maker*, May 7, 1960.
17. John Martin, "Tubby is Groovy," *Jazz News*, August 5, 1960.
18. Tony Hall, telephone conversation with author, January 24, 2009.
19. In an article titled "Britain has Taken to Blue Note Jazz" (*Melody Maker*, July 10, 1961), Bob Dawbarn asked Lion if he had further plans to record British artists. "I am afraid it is too difficult to promote non-Americans," the producer replied. "It is a great shame, but the public did not really take to our recordings of Dizzy Reece."
20. Gardner, "The Jazz Record Producers."
21. Interviewed by author, September 10, 2007.
22. "In My Opinion," *Jazz Journal*, August 1961.
23. Interviewed by author, September 10, 2007.
24. Even Coltrane's previous contract, signed with Prestige Records in the spring of 1957, seems ostentatious when set beside Tempo's budget; he received a $300 advance on each album.
25. Unpublished interview, late 1990s.
26. "Peak Hour T.V. for Tubby Hayes," *Jazz News*, March 11, 1960.
27. Richard Hayes, letter to author, September 2013.

28. Interviewed by author, September 10, 2007.

Seamen sometime tired of all the tenor sax pyrotechnics. In *Fire in His Soul*, John Robertson's excellent biography of Joe Harriott, the drummer's dislike of musicians who "played a lot of quavers" – as did Hayes – is recalled by trumpeter Les Condon: "He called them iddle-diddle players and he said I was one of them. He gave me a hard time for it. He took me to hear African bands to hear how they played. That's what he was into."

29. Ibid.

30. John Martin, "The Little Giant of the Tenor Sax," *Jazz News*, September 10, 1960.

31. Telephone conversation with author, April 15, 2008.

32. Telephone conversation with author, January 24, 2009.

33. "News in Brief," *Melody Maker*, December 3, 1960.

34. David Nathan, "No Tuba For Tubby," *TV Times*, March 1962.

35. "Trad is Sad – says Jimmy Deuchar," *Melody Maker*, September 9, 1961.

36. Sleeve notes to Tubby Hayes, *Tubbs*, Fontana TFL 5142, 1961.

37. Ibid.

38. Ibid.

39. *Melody Maker* broke the story of Hayes's new two-year Fontana contract in its March 25th issue, accompanied by a picture of the tenorist and Jack Baverstock at one of the recent sessions. The label was keen to capitalize on the popularity of it new signing and recorded Hayes again on March 31st, when the quartet took part in a *Jazz News* Poll-Winners concert at the London Palladium. The three Hayes performances released on an LP shared with Cleo Laine and John Dankworth shortly afterwards – 'Ah-Leu-Cha', 'Young and Foolish' and 'All Members' – make a solid and occasionally spectacular footnote to the studio recordings on *Tubbs*.

40. Available on Tubby Hayes, *New Edition – Rare Radio Recordings 1958–62*, Acrobat ADDCD 3097.

41. "Now – It's Who Have *They* Got?" *Melody Maker*, June 17, 1961.

42. Bob Dawbarn, "Tubby Achieves World Status," *Melody Maker*, June 17, 1961.

43. Kitty Grime, "The Talents of Tubby," *Jazz News*, June 28, 1961.

6. Down in the Village

1. Allan Ganley, Interview with author, April 1, 2004.

2. The composition, titled "Combined Operation," was premiered at *An Evening with John Dankworth* at the Royal Festival Hall on July 8, 1961.

3. "You Can't Live on Three Jobs a Week says Tubby Hayes," *Melody Maker*, August 12, 1961.

4. "A Great Day for British Jazz," *Disc*, September 2, 1961.

5. As a footnote to his recent UK reviews, the year after Tubby's initial US triumph, Epic Records released his first Fontana album in the USA, under the title *Introducing Tubbs*, garnering a three-and-a-half-star rating in *DownBeat*'s March 15, 1962 issue. The critical tenor was surprisingly agreeable, especially from a writer who, unlike his UK counterparts, lacked any sort of sycophantic parochial pride in a home-grown hero. Ira Gitler wrote that Hayes was "closer to [Hank] Mobley . . . but his is a harder-punching, more relentless attack" and he also concurred with his English counterparts about Hayes's vibes skills ("he does not approach his saxophone prowess, although he is more than adequate"). Gitler thought that the album's quartet numbers were the most convincing. "This is not the best Hayes can do, but it's still better than good."

6. Business was booming both at home and abroad; on August 6, 1961 the quartet plus guest vocalist Frank Holder played the Belgium Summer Jazz Festival in Ostend and

on the 17th Hayes made a guest appearance on Dudley Moore's new TV series *Strictly for the Birds*.

7. This letter is now in the possession of Tubby and Rose's son Richard.
8. "New York Is the Only Place for Jazz," *Melody Maker*, October 7, 1961.
9. "Tubby a Triumph in USA," *Melody Maker*, September 30, 1961.
10. Dan Morgenstern, *Metronome*, December 1961.
11. "New York is the Only Place for Jazz," *Melody Maker*, October 7, 1961.
12. *Jazz Legends*, BBC Radio 3, July 13, 2001.
13. Tenor saxophonist Bobby Wellins has alluded to this in several conversations with the author, although he is unsure of the American's identity.
14. *Jazz Legends*, BBC Radio 3, July 13, 2001.
15. "New York is the Only Place for Jazz," *Melody Maker*, October 7, 1961.
16. Stanley Dance, "Lightly and Politely," *Jazz Journal*, November 1961.
17. *Jazz News*, October 18, 1961.
18. Sleeve notes to Tubby Hayes, *Tubby The Tenor*, Epic LA 16023, 1962.
19. Ibid.
20. Gordon Jack, "Dave Bailey," *Jazz Journal*, September 2002.
21. These offcuts were finally released together with the original album's contents on the CD *Tubby Hayes and Clark Terry – The New York Sessions* (CBS 466363 2) in 1990. The album was withdrawn from sale soon after, owing to copyright issues.
22. The reactions of writers such as Green and *Melody Maker*'s Bob Dawbarn were fuelled as much by Hayes's back-story as by the music to hand, but American critics had no need for such sycophancy. John S. Wilson's review of Tubby the Tenor in *DownBeat* on July 5, 1962 awarded the album a paltry two stars and declared "if nothing else, this disc proves that Britain is producing soloists who can be just as long-winded as any of our home-grown products. Minutes of aimless diddle-daddle pile up, ingratiation wears thin and fluency proves more of a bore than a boon."
23. Benny Green, "Jazz Record Reviews," *The Observer*, May 1962.
24. Sleeve notes to Tubby Hayes, *Tubbs In NY*, Fontana TFL 5183, 1962.
25. Before returning home, Hayes honoured another New York jazz tradition by visiting the apartment of Baroness Pannonica de Koenigswarter, the legendary patron to the city's jazz community. As was the house rule he appended his three wishes in her guest book:
    1. To be out there playing with the best musicians
    2. For my wife and kid to have everything they want
    3. For everybody to be happy
    These wishes, together with those of other visitors to the Baroness's home, were finally published in book form as *Three Wishes: An Intimate Look at Jazz Greats*, Baroness Pannonica de Koenigswarter, New York: Abrams Image, 2008.
26. BBC Scotland's *The One O'Clock Gang* on October 20, 1961, ATV's *All Kinds of Music* on the 24th (alongside the never-to-be-assembled-again line-up of Edmund Hockridge, Carol Carr and The Mudlarks) and the poppy *Go, Man, Go!* on the 27th.
27. Tony Brown, "Tubby on Telly," *Melody Maker*, November 25, 1961.
28. Bob Dawbarn, "What Happened?" *Melody Maker*, November 18, 1961
29. Danny Halperin, "The Recent Musical Shock," *Jazz News*, November 22, 1961.
30. Interviewed by author, March 3, 2011.
31. Sociologically minded musicologists would probably reason that the confusion left in the wake of the avant-garde was symptomatic of the state of America at the time. The Kennedy administration was big on image, and with promises about the space race clearly had its eye on the future, but it was at the helm of a sick country, battered by civil rights issues, scared out of its wits by the threat of nuclear annihilation and, for all its brash confidence, deeply uneasy with its own course. Kennedy himself had been the figurehead everyone had looked to start a new age: young, handsome and gifted with

charismatic rhetorical skills, his potential was enormous, but his time in office was smeared with personal controversy, and in leaving America with the grisly burden of military intervention in Vietnam, his political legacy was to be forever blood-stained.

32. Danny Halperin, "Looking Back," *Jazz News*, December 6, 1961.
33. Tony Hall, "Hayes Quartet Break up Next Month," *Disc*, January 30, 1962.
34. Hayes, Dudley Moore and Don Rendell played opposite Jaspar at the Marquee on January 28, 1962 and the Belgian also appeared on the final episode of *Tubby Plays Hayes*, screened on February 5th.
35. Ketley, telephone conversation with author, August 28, 2008.
36. Clyne, interviewed by author, September 10, 2007.
37. Tony Hall, "The Spirit is Really Something, says Tubbs," *Disc*, March 10, 1962.
38. Humphrey Lyttelton best summed up this confusion when introducing the bassist on a BBC broadcast: "Freddy Logan has a Dutch birth certificate, an Australian passport, a British driving licence, a Scottish name and a German car!"
39. Interviewed by author, April 1, 2004.
40. David Ash, "Little Giant on a High Note . . ." *Daily Express*, February 23, 1962.
41. In a review of a Hayes CD in *Jazz at Ronnie Scott's* (JARS) November 1998/January 1999, Davis recalled meeting Hayes in the summer of 1962 and complimenting him on his soprano playing, to which the saxophonist replied that he'd now abandoned the instrument, adding "it's in a cupboard somewhere."

During the course of research for this book a further unissued studio recording of 'In The Night' – apparently intended for release as a single – came to light, containing a Hayes solo even more impressive than that on the March 7th broadcast.

42. Bob Dawbarn, "Tubby's Quintet May be Britain's Greatest Ever," *Melody Maker*, March 17, 1962.
43. John Howes, "The New Tubby Hayes Quintet," *Jazz Journal*, May 1962.
44. Interviewed by author, April 1, 2004.
45. Mike Hennessey, "Sending a Message," *Jazzwise*, May 1998.
46. *Jazz at Ronnie Scott's* (JARS), November 1998/January 1999.
47. It was later taken up by the Acid Jazz circle centred upon DJ Gilles Peterson, and appeared on Peterson's Impressed CD compilation, which in 2002 introduced a new audience to several slices of hitherto rare British modern jazz.
48. Bob Dawbarn, "Tubby Hayes – Our Best!" *Melody Maker*, December 8, 1962.
49. *Jazz Journal*, October 1963.
50. "You Have to Work Harder in the States," *Melody Maker*, July 7, 1962.
51. Available on Tubby Hayes, *New Edition – Rare Radio Recordings 1958–62*, Acrobat ADDCD 3097.
52. Val Wilmer, "Talkin' with Tubby," *Jazz News and Review*, August 1963.
53. Email to author, August 27, 2011.
54. Sleeve notes, Tubby Hayes and the All-Stars, *Return Visit*, Fontana TFL 5195, 1963.
55. Ibid.
56. Ibid.
57. *Jazz Monthly*, September 1963.
58. *Jazz Journal*, August 1963.
59. *DownBeat*, May 9, 1963. Hayes himself thought this review at odds with the content of the record. "The album I made one year before with Clark Terry and Eddie Costa was a much better record but *DownBeat* gave it a lousy review."
60. *Jazz*, November–December 1963.
61. "Tubby Answers the Jackpot Question," *Melody Maker*, June 30, 1962.
62. On August 2nd he was voted eighth in the tenor saxophone section of the International Critics Poll in *DownBeat*, just behind Hank Mobley and just ahead of Stanley Turrentine. However, news of Tubby's tenor saxophone talent hadn't reached everywhere yet; the

Northamptonshire Advertiser that summer noted that promoters at a local gig "hope to bring the maestro of the trombone – Tubby Hayes and his full group to Wollaston."

63. As summer slipped into autumn the workload barely slackened. In collaboration with Chet Baker and Stan Tracey, during late August 1962 Tubby was busy providing the soundtrack music for the Susan Hayward film *Stolen Hours*, then being filmed at Shepperton studios. There was also an evening at Ronnie Scott's endorsing Trixon vibraphones on August 29th before the quintet began a new six-day tour covering the Midlands and the North, taking in an appearance on ABC-TV's pioneering religion and jazz programme *Sunday Break in Manchester* on September 2nd.

64. Ganley, interviewed by author, April 1, 2004.

65. Ibid.

66. Interviewed by author, September 6, 2008.

67. David Nathan, "No Tuba For Tubby," *TV Times*, March 1962.

68. In an interview with the author, Maggie Hayes actually used the word "matronly" to describe her successor. April 19, 2009.

69. Edwina Coven, "Larger-Than-Life Profile," clipping from untraced magazine circa 1969 in Liz Grönlund's scrapbook.

70. "We are Not Unfair to Jazz says B.B.C." *Jazz News*, May 9, 1962.

71. Indeed, the pages of the music press in the dying days of the year effectively repeat the patterns of the preceding twelve months, variously containing news of his late triumphs (the Anglo-American Four Brothers with Ronnie Scott and guests Al Cohn and Zoot Sims at the Dankworth club on December 23, 1962): favourable reaction to his recordings (the review of *Down In The Village* in *Melody Maker* on December 8th); adverts for typical out-of-town gigs (the Athenian Restaurant in Scarborough on December 9th); vociferous critique ("Could someone please explain what has happened to Tubby Hayes? [His] playing up here was ragged and uncouth" wrote one *Melody Maker* reader of a recent gig in Staffordshire) and fans' pipe dreams ("I suggest to Miles Davis that he employs Britain's Tubby Hayes," D. Smith wrote to *Melody Maker* on December 29th).

7. Tubby Hayes Loves You Madly

1. Les Tomkins," The Tubby Hayes Story," *Crescendo*, June 1963.

2. "Disc Discussion," *Crescendo*, March 1963.

3. In another interview that year, Hayes expressed mystification over the new *Coltrane* album, telling Val Wilmer of *Jazz News* "I have been a bit disappointed because at one time I thought John Coltrane could really do it. He'd zoom through the changes and all that, but now I hear him sticking to two chords and so on, and with his ability it seems like he's wasting his time. I've bought most of his albums but I never seem to play them now. For example I heard him do 'Out Of This World', a nice tune with good chord sequences and he only uses two chords all the way through."

4. This apocryphal story has been quoted among musicians.

5. This earthier approach was also echoed locally in the short-lived co-operative band headed by Ronnie Scott and Johnny Dankworth, The Seven Souls, a group that aimed unashamedly to "please dancers" with "uncomplicated arrangements with a strong beat."

6. Interviewed by author, April 21, 2004.

7. Korner's own guitar playing and singing were as gravelly and authentic as one could have imagined and early on he made the sensible decision to surround himself with musicians who could best frame his raw gifts. The list of young jazzmen who passed through his Blues Incorporated line-up in the sixties formed an impressive litany of future stars: saxophonists Ray Warleigh, Art Themen, John Surman, Brian Smith,

Lol Coxhill and Alan Skidmore, trombonist Chris Pyne, drummers Phil Seamen and Ginger Baker, guitarist John McLaughlin, bassist Danny Thompson, organist Graham Bond and pianists Johnny Parker and Mike Pyne among them.

8. In a nod to the boom, that winter Ronnie Scott's club began to organize its own R&B nights. The venture was short-lived, and struck some of the players involved as ironic; playing jazz they previously hadn't been allowed to within a country mile of Gerrard Street.

9. "Jazz Singles," *Melody Maker*, March 16, 1963.

10. Interviewed by author, April 1, 2004.

11. Ketley, telephone conversation with author, August 28, 2008.

12. Bob Dawbarn, "Tubby's Students Find a Groove," *Melody Maker*, April 27, 1963.

In bassist Danny Thompson, the band already had one member clearly capable of great things. "I remember we used to play Jimmy Deuchar's [fast] arrangement of 'Suddenly Last Tuesday' and he was making it. He was about the only one who was actually!" Hayes later confessed. Thompson had also mightily impressed Freddy Logan, who offered a glowing endorsement in *Melody Maker*: "I hope to teach him as much as possible about chords. He is so promising that I don't think it will take long."

13. Sleeve notes to *Tubby Hayes Quartet – For Members Only*, Miles Music MMCD 086, 2002.

14. Unpublished interview, circa late 1990s.

15. *Melody Maker* wondered openly about the possible dividends of a potential hit: "What happens if it makes the pop charts? Will Tubby become a sort of modern Acker Bilk?"

16. "Blind Date," *Melody Maker*, June 8, 1963.

17. *Melody Maker*, June 1, 1963.

18. *Evening News*, May 30, 1963.

19. Bob Dawbarn, "Non Stop Tubby," *Melody Maker*, June 1, 1963.

20. John Wickes, *Innovations in British Jazz*, Chelmsford: Soundworld, 1999.

21. Interviewed by author, April 1, 2004.

22. Sleeve notes to *Tubby Hayes Quartet – For Members Only*, Miles Music MMCD 086, 2002.

23. Val Wilmer, "Talkin' with Tubby," *Jazz News and Review*, August 1963.

24. Bob Dawbarn, "Dying? Only in the West End," *Melody Maker*, December 14, 1963.

25. Les Tomkins, "The Tubby Hayes Story," *Crescendo*, June 1963.

26. Ibid.

27. "Beat Crazy – that's Britain!" *Melody Maker*, July 27, 1963.

28. *Melody Maker*, August 10, 1963.

29. Sleeve notes, Ronnie Scott, *When I Want Your Opinion, I'll Give It To You*, Jazz House, JHAS 610, 1997.

30. Email to author, March 20, 2005.

31. Ibid.

32. Tomkins brokered a deal with Ronnie Scott's Jazz House in the mid-1990s and the label's first release in its Archive Series in 1995 comprised five tracks by Tubby recorded between 1963 and 1966, including two from the recordings he made of the Hayes quintet in late 1963. A further agreement with Harkit Records led to three more Hayes recordings from December 1963 appearing on CD in 2005. At the time of writing Tomkins's tapes have also been issued by Candid Records.

33. "One of the reasons why the provincial scene is so bad is because they still try to run the clubs in dingy back room of pubs," Harry South opined in *Melody Maker* that December. Bob Dawbarn, "Dying? Only in the West End," *Melody Maker*, December 14, 1963.

34. Brian Blain, "Controlled Excitement, Lyrical Improvisation," untraced magazine article in Liz Grönlund's scrapbook, circa late 1962.

35. "The Right Honorable Member for Jazz," www.harkitrecords.com.

36. After Gilmour's death in the early 2000s, Paul Adams of Fellside Recordings took on the daunting task of cataloguing the surviving tapes stored in the recordist's garage, work which, over ten years on, is still in progress. Gilmour was far from a model of discographical order, but fortunately he had the good sense to store his tapes safely.

37. *New Musical Express*, February 14, 1981. Further discussion about Hayes's posthumous recorded legacy will feature in later chapters, but, as an opener in the campaign to unearth the many hours of private tape by Tubby that exist, the Dancing Slipper session established high expectations.

38. The introduction was lifted verbatim from Hayes's string arrangement of 'The Party's Over', recorded for the BBC's *Light Programme* trial in May 1963.

39. Other items were recorded but no new music was added to the subsequent CD reissue in 1999.

40. Only a poor-quality audio snippet of *Juke Box Jury* exists but Hayes's BBC debut with his big band has survived in its entirety.
    Answering Humphrey Lyttelton's question as to whether he would like to take the band on the road permanently, Hayes replies "There's too many mothers in this band," a witty in-joke reducing the band to fits of laughter but which whizzes over the heads of many listeners.

41. He had begun by scoring *The Criminal* in 1960, followed by *Saturday Night, Sunday Morning* in 1961. In 1963 he had completed the music for the classic Dirk Bogarde feature *The Servant*, a film typical of the new wave in British cinema.

42. Bob Dawbarn, "Ten Years of the Johnny Dankworth Orchestra," *Melody Maker*, December 7, 1963.

43. The two would reunite – appropriately enough in legal chambers – to recreate the duet on ITV's *Monitor* special on the Dickens suite shown on December 22, 1963.

44. 'The Simple Waltz' was released by the Jazz House label in 1995 (*Tubby Hayes: Night and Day*) whilst 'Opus Ocean' and 'The Sweetest Sounds' were issued by Harkit Records in 2005 (*Tubby Hayes: Live In London, Volume 1*).

45. Notably the albums *My Funny Valentine, Four and More, Miles in Berlin* and *Miles in Tokyo*.

46. Sleeve notes, Tubby Hayes Quartet, *Mexican Green*, Fontana SFJL 911, 1968.

47. Interviewed by author, April 1, 2004.

48. Tubby Hayes Quintet, *Dancing in the Dark*, Savage-Solweig SS-002, 2011.

49. Issued commercially on CD by the Candid label as *Inventivity*, CCS 790101, 2010.

50. Watching Gonsalves in action was fascinating; half stooped before the microphone, with a tortured expression contorting his face as he played, the saxophonist appeared to be on some deeply personal mission. Ellington even once remarked, "For the avant-garde, I have Paul Gonsalves." But whereas the playing of some of his admirers like Archie Shepp and David Murray was to become spikily political, Gonsalves didn't have a belligerent bone in his body and was a soft man who struggled throughout his life to shake off his addictions. Drugs and alcohol would often demolish him, and the relationship he enjoyed with his employer during their lengthy association was more akin to a father's resigned toleration of a wayward son's excesses than an exercise in sharp band-leading discipline. Sometimes Gonsalves would prop himself up on his tenor and go to sleep, miming his way through as much of the evening as he could get away with. Ellington periodically tired of this and would rouse the saxophonist to play an extended feature in an effort to gain his sobriety. Periodically he would fire Gonsalves but he was usually back on the bandstand the next night, a central part of the disparate magical family of Ellingtonians.

51. In *Jazz Journal* in August 1961, Hayes was quoted as saying "I like his playing so much, such a terrific amount of feeling. Gonsalves could never be mistaken for anyone else."

52. "Don't Worry Looking, There's No Part," *Melody Maker*, April 26, 1969.

53. "Hear Me Talkin'," *The Jazz Scene*, BBC, August 21, 1966.

54. "The Night Tubby Blew with Duke," *Melody Maker*, February 22, 1964.
55. "Don't Worry Looking, There's No Part," *Melody Maker*, December 13, 1969.
56. Ibid.
57. "Tubs Trumps!" *Crescendo*, March 1964.
58. "Brits with the Duke," *Jazz at Ronnie Scott's* (JARS), September/October 1998.
59. *Melody Maker*, February 23, 1964.
60. Ibid.
61. "Disc Discussion," *Crescendo*, April 1964.
62. Ibid.
63. "Tubby Hayes Rides High on the Duke's Bandwagon," *Sunday Times*, February 16, 1964.
64. Sinclair Traill, "Editorial," *Jazz Journal*, March 1964.
65. "The Night Tubby Blew with Duke," *Melody Maker*, February 22, 1964.
66. Paul Gonsalves and Tubby Hayes, *Just Friends*, Columbia, SCX 6003, 1966.
67. "Brits with the Duke," *Jazz at Ronnie Scott's*, September/October 1998.

8. The Best of Both Worlds

1. Despite the purists' tongue-clucking, Ellington's blessing deeply affected Hayes. The story has two interesting postscripts: first, that shortly after the concert Hayes received a bootleg recording of the show from an anonymous fan and, secondly, that Gonsalves returned the favour ten days later by appearing together with Hayes on an album hastily organized by Jack Sharpe, *Just Friends*, a record that sadly has something of the air of a missed opportunity to it. The concert tape is extremely lo-fi and distorted with Hayes only really audible when accompanied by Ellington and the rhythm section, although one can clearly hear the leader remark to the audience that "Tubby Hayes wants you to know that he too loves you madly."
2. The admiration was mutual and there was a welcome televisual endorsement for Hayes that same week when Getz appeared on the popular show *On the Braden Beat*. Taking part in a blindfold test, the American was convinced that Tubby was Sonny Rollins.

   However, the American's visit had left those who got to know him with mixed feelings, full of admiration for his music but perplexed by his truculent character. Towards the end of the run there had been an almighty three-way row between the tenorist and his hosts, who had at last tired of their guest's big-time attitude. The air was cleared, but only just and, for the remaining days, Getz was in continual pain due to a dislocated neck bone, a situation that Scott and King probably thought he deserved. But there was still one twist of karma to come. The day after their guest left, Scott slipped a disc whilst getting into his sports car, an injury he famously attributed to "bending over backwards to please Stan Getz."
3. Stan Robinson, conversation with author, July 26, 2009.
4. The morning after Getz's last London gig, Hayes flew to Germany for three days of concert and radio work with the Kurt Edelhagen big band, and the surviving radio transcriptions reflect the recent brush with his hero. A glorious 'Easy Living' is Hayes at his ballad best while a large-scale adaptation of 'You For Me' (from *Tubbs In NY*) is an unqualified success. The two remaining items, however, illustrate the chasm between the guest's conception and that of Edelhagen's musicians. The quartet version of 'Secret Love', with its four-square piano improvisation, falls down almost immediately after Hayes's solo, and 'In The Night', re-scored as a flute feature, is given a rather twee and stiff reading.
5. These guest singers included Joy Marshall, Madeline Bell and Barbara Moore. *Crescendo's* review from June 1964 notes, "Well-chosen material [and] Tubby's friendly compering contributed greatly to the pleasingly informal atmosphere of the show" but aside from press coverage nothing survives from the series.

6. *Melody Maker* announced the launch on February 29, 1964. The new series was then unnamed but was eventually titled *Jazz 625*.

7. Neither programme has been screened since that initial airing, but, according to Henebery, they may well still exist: "The early ones survive because they were recorded on telerecordings, on film. With a lot of VT the philistines at the Beeb just wiped the tapes."

8. *Mark Time!* Fontana TL 5217. Described in *Melody Maker* as "an ultra-cool male version of Annie Ross," Murphy wasn't a crooner in the Sinatra/Bennett mould but rather a witty, satirical and hip humorist who'd twist songs alarmingly to suit his own ends, something that had led Rodgers and Hammerstein to launch a successful legal challenge to have his version of 'My Favourite Things' withdrawn from sale.

9. Recalling the collaborative ethos of the band, Ian Hamer noted: "It wasn't like being in a regular big band, which we'd all done and which you could get to hate sometimes if the music was crap. A lot of the brass players were busy doing sessions. We were all busy but if a gig came in with Tubby, I wouldn't take a session. We were earning enough money anyway doing sessions, so doing the big band was like a night-off playing our own music."

10. Sleeve notes to Tubby Hayes Orchestra, *Tubbs' Tours*, Fontana TL 5221, 1964.

11. King late recalled something of the background to the piece: "It was around the time when the great, sort of, Freedom Now! was being expounded everywhere. And I wanted to say the word now in African and I called my brother up [Eddie, a speaker of over forty different languages] and he said, 'What do you mean in African? There's like 380 different African languages!' And I said what's the most commonly used one and he said Swahili, everybody understands Swahili. He said 'What do you mean now? Do you mean now or do you mean Now! Right this minute!?' I said, that's what I mean. He said the word for that is Sasa-Hivi and it sounded just such a great title."

12. He made his recording debut on the instrument in 1959 on London Jazz Quartet, Tempo TAP 28.

13. Sleeve notes to *Tubby Hayes Quartet – For Members Only*, Miles Music MMCD 086, 2002.

14. Matt Monro, *Love Is Everywhere*, Parlophone PMC 1151, 1961.

15. John Martin, "The Little Giant of the Tenor Sax," *Jazz News*, September 10, 1960.

16. Allegedly it was McNair who taught Hayes the famous humming and playing trick that Roland Kirk had popularized during the early 1960s.

17. Bob Dawbarn, "Big Band Knockout!" *Melody Maker*, December 19, 1964.

18. *Jazz Beat*, January 1965.

19. *Jazz Monthly*, February 1965.

20. Interviewed by author, April 1, 2004.

21. Ibid.

22. Ibid.

23. When one considers the sheer risible nature of the film it is small wonder that Amicus eventually sunk into the kind of sub-species of rubber dinosaur-filled fantasy which kept Doug McClure working after *The Virginian*. The box office takings were unimpressive, it was banned in Finland and a tie-in single with Roy Castle barely reached the chart. However, largely due to Hayes's participation the film has gained a cult following, the passionate nature of which was never better gauged than in summer 2009 when a limited edition 7" single of the three Hayes soundtrack items, 'Bailey's Blues', 'Give Me Love' and 'Voodoo', was pressed by Trunk Records, selling out within weeks.

24. Eventually released on the album *Inventivity* in 2010.

25. "Benny Golson at the B.B.C." *Jazz Monthly*, September 1964.

26. Bob Dawbarn, *Melody Maker*, August 22, 1964.

27. Max Jones, "Tubbs Tomorrow," *Melody Maker*, September 19, 1964.

28. Chris Roberts, "Shout for Joy at The Flamingo," *Melody Maker*, June 9, 1962.

29. In his autobiography *Flying High*, King details their marriage with sometimes disquieting candour. Even those outside London jazz circles remember Marshall's reputation; drummer Spike Wells, then a student at Oxford University and playing in a local trio accompanying guest artists from London, remembers a visit by King which ended with the saxophonist desperately searching for an all-night party to attend rather than go home and face his wife's temper.

30. Whilst in Boston, Hayes visited the Berklee School of Music, bastion of jazz education in the US, another forceful reminder of how far advanced America's example could be. "We couldn't half do with one here," he wrote on his return to the UK. "I know I'd like to have learned it all in the first place instead of battling through the dark as I did." *Melody Maker*, December 26, 1964.

31. *Melody Maker*, December 26, 1964.

32. In the final weeks of 1964, there was still work aplenty. On December 21st and 22nd the big band made two London appearances, one at the Flamingo, on a benefit gig for Club XI founder Harry Morris. New Year's Eve was spent on an all-nighter at Scott's in the company of Ben Webster.

33. Peter King, *Flying High: A Jazz Life and Beyond*, London: Northway Publications, 2011.

34. Email to author, August 13, 2007.

35. Sleeve notes to *Tubby Hayes Quartet – For Members Only*, Miles Music, MMCD 086, 2002.

36. Another who was impressed was the Welsh pianist Gareth Williams – eventually to become one of the best jazz keyboard players in the UK. Stuck at home during the school holidays, Williams saw Hayes and his band of smart, hip, suited young men and decided that jazz was for him. Williams later dedicated one of his albums to Tubby.

37. Bob Dawbarn, "Tubby Does it Again," *Melody Maker*, February 20, 1965.

38. Interviewed in *Melody Maker* in the summer of 1965, Pete King of Ronnie Scott's was also concerned about the noticeable absence of new talent: "The worrying thing is the lack of young players. Peter King, Alan Branscombe, Brian Dee and Gordon Beck were the last batch of good young jazzmen and they've been professional a few years."

39. Les Tomkins, "My After-thoughts: Tubby Hayes Reflects on the Experience of Playing in America for the Fourth Time," *Crescendo*, August 1965. The unabridged interview recording was finally released in 2005 on *Tubby Hayes – Live In London Volume 2*, Harkit Records HRKCD 8109.

40. Les Tomkins, "The Tubby Hayes Story," *Crescendo*, June 1963.

41. "The Musicians Pay Tribute . . ." *Melody Maker*, June 16, 1973.

42. *Smokey Dives*, BBC2, transmitted April 2001.

43. *Jazz Britannia*, Episode 2 'Strange Brew', BBC4, transmitted February 4, 2005.

44. "REACTION with Tubby Hayes," *Melody Maker*, April 10, 1971.

45. "Tubby Hayes Vamps till U.S. Gov't Okays Engagement in Manne-Hole," *Variety*, June 8, 1965.

46. Leonard Feather, "Tubby Hayes – Victor Feldman," *DownBeat*, August 26, 1965.

47. Leonard Feather, "Shearing Flips as Tubby Hayes Plays," *Jazz Beat*, June 1965.

48. Tomkins, "My After-thoughts."

49. *DownBeat*, August 12, 1965. Feather also asked Hayes to take part in *DownBeat's* famed Blindfold Test, and his comments make interesting reading. As usual, the journalist had chosen a provocative set of records with which to test the listener, including tracks by Lionel Hampton, Yusef Lateef, James Moody, Coleman Hawkins, Herbie Mann and Joe Harriott. Hayes's responses were far from predictable; he liked the Hampton track and gave Hawkins a five-star thumbs up, but was disappointed by the floppy commercial efforts of Herbie Mann. As Feather had hoped, it was the avant-garde selections that prompted the Englishman's most pointed reactions. Harriott was given a lukewarm reception and a disc from the new-wave altoist Byron Allen was dismissed almost instantly: "I don't know, maybe I'm a bit old fashioned or something, but I

do like to hear a little bit of form and a little bit of beauty in anybody's playing. He sounded as though he could play the saxophone, but because he was trying to find something new, he was going deliberately out of his way to get these extraneous noises going." Hayes was clearly unafraid to criticize the latest trends whilst still in the music's homeland: The drumming on Byron's record, by one Ted Robinson, put him in mind of an earlier put-on of the new wave of percussionists by Albert Heath, delivered for the amusement of his dubious colleagues: "[Heath] was joking but this sounded just the same, only I think this guy was serious. One star."

50. Feather, "Shearing Flips as Tubby Hayes Plays."
51. Ibid.
52. *Jazz Legends*, BBC Radio 3, July 13, 2001.
53. Tomkins, "My After-thoughts."
54. Michael Shera, "Jazz in Britain," *Jazz Journal*, July 1965: Opening a concert for organist Jimmy Smith at the Royal Festival Hall, the band received a grouchy review in *Jazz Journal*: "Hayes's tenor playing reached a peak some years ago, and technically is hard to fault. Unfortunately, he continues to cram as many notes as possible into every bar at up tempo and takes such long solos that one loses interest before the end. The audience applauded politely at the end, but it was Jimmy Smith they came to hear."
55. Mike Hennessey, "Sending a Message," *Jazzwise*, May 1998.
56. Steve Voce, "It Don't Mean a Thing," *Jazz Journal*, October 1965.
57. Bob Dawbarn, "Tubby: Just How Much Work Can a Man Do?" *Melody Maker*, October 2, 1965.
58. Jack Carter and Dave Doubble, "Commonwealth Jazz '65," *Crescendo*, November 1965.
59. "Anglo-American Exchange," *Crescendo*, August 1966.
60. "Danger! . . . If the Animals Get Too Far Out?" *Melody Maker*, August 14, 1965.
61. The day after the Hammersmith Jazz Jamboree concert, Harry South's band and Georgie Fame reassembled at the Paris Studios for a live BBC *Jazz Club* broadcast, during which Humphrey Lyttelton introduced the vocalist as "a young man who's equally popular among jazz fans and pop-pickers." On his three numbers, 'Down For The Count', 'Lil Darlin'' and 'Little Pony', Fame sounds audibly nervous, but as Lyttelton notes, the young singer was performing in front of his idol, Jon Hendricks, present in the studio in between his own sets at Annie's Room.
62. J. G. Jones, a fan who wrote to *Crescendo*, had even more reason to be peeved than most – he and a party of local musicians got up at 5 am to drive from Cwmbran in Wales!
63. "This *Was* a Big Band Jamboree," *Crescendo*, December 1965.
64. "Tubby Tales the Honours at Jamboree," *Melody Maker*, November 13, 1965.
65. Conversation with author, June 5, 2008. There was humour too: Hayes announced '100% Proof' with a knowing smile: "We don't have too much time, so we're gonna play one more tune, which only lasts a couple of minutes."
66. Peter King, email to author, May 25, 2007.
67. The opening bill at Frith Street that winter wasn't exactly a commercial sure-fire bet, and presented the exotic multi-instrumentalist Yusef Lateef, a musician who had little following outside the US. It was another act of faith on Scott and King's part, and the opening night itself, like that in Gerrard Street in 1959, was a further close-run thing. The club's electrical network was still incomplete and stray wires hung dangerously loose. Then there was a plumbing problem resulting in a single working toilet comprising the club's unisex facility. "It was very bohemian, really very French," Scott recalled with amusement some years later. The proprietor and his partner had even tried to accelerate the pace of the transformation of their premises from bomb-site to presentable venue by plying the Irish workforce with "uppers." The club, *Melody Maker* noted, finally opened for business two hours later than planned, but with no front door.

68. Tubby Hayes, *Live in London Volume 1*, Harkit Records HRKCD 8072, 2004. Reviewing the album in *Jazzwise* magazine the saxophonist's former producer Tony Hall found "this is a very different Tubby Hayes from the one I worked with on Tempo" and noted a "20-minute, exhaustive exploration of the changes of By Myself, where he's mostly in another world."

9. Addictive Tendencies

1. As Pete King recalled, Tubby's attitude to laying off was typically casual: "The rest of us would take our saxes on holiday and practise every day for fear of losing our touch. Tubby would just shove his in the case and kick it under the bed until he got back."
2. Mark Gardner, "Drummer Tony Levin," *Jazz Journal*, November 2007.
3. Sleeve notes, Tubby Hayes Quartet, *Addictive Tendencies*, Rare Music Recordings RM 028, 2006.
4. Sleeve notes, Tubby Hayes Quartet, *Mexican Green*, Fontana SFJL 911, 1968.
   For Hayes, the experience had come as a very welcome surprise. The only thing he couldn't quite believe were his own ears, as he remarked on a live recording a few weeks later: "I'd had a few drinks, I wasn't too sure if I was imagining things, but the people I was with said 'Yeah, he sounds good'."
5. Interview with Danny Thompson by Peter Vacher, July 8, 1994, now stored in the British Library Archival Sound Recordings.
6. Ibid.
7. Mark Gardner, "Bang the Drum for Tony: He's Soaring to Stardom," *Birmingham Sunday Mercury*, April 17, 1966.
8. It's probably slightly unfair to further pillory Shannon over this point. He was a fine modern jazz pianist, fully conversant in the language of hard bop, but by the mid-1960s, with the advent of Bill Evans and even younger pretenders like Herbie Hancock, things were fast changing. Shannon was cut from the same cloth as men like Sonny Clark and Tommy Flanagan and like them he could handle the modal approach well enough but ultimately lacked a commitment to something new. If all this makes the pianist sound like something of an anachronism by 1965 it should be pointed out that he still continued to play highly creatively within his own remit.
9. Archival Sound Recordings interview with Danny Thompson by Peter Vacher, July 8, 1994, now stored in the British Library.
10. Brian Priestley, "Pyne Branches Out," *Melody Maker*, January 30, 1971.
11. Phone conversation with author, July 18, 2008.
12. Gardner, "Bang the Drum for Tony."
13. Gardner, "Drummer Tony Levin."
14. Priestley, "Pyne Branches Out."
15. BBC *Jazz Notes*, June 10, 1973.
16. Tubby's long announcement prior to 'Alone Together' – edited out of the CD issue – reveals both his sense of pride in his new sidemen and his sense of humour. He jokes about Thompson's work with Alexis "Cornflakes," about Pyne's recruitment after his former pianist was "taken suddenly drunk" (a favourite Ronnie Scott quip) and notes Levin's day job commitment to "rush back and sell beds and carpets and all that kind of thing." The drummer remembered that Tubby's outrageous behaviour was in evidence from the very start of their working relationship. "He was a heavy character in many ways, he really was. He could be funny. One night in Manchester he was very drunk and he told me he wanted to drive my car. Now he couldn't drive, but he was so drunk he wanted to try. I just didn't let him have the keys. It was funny because the next morning I said to him 'You tried to drive my car last night, remember?' He

looked blank and said 'I don't remember any of those things I do when I'm pissed'."
Conversation with author, December 2, 2007.

17. Rather, what Hayes had actually done was to use Coltrane and his group as some sort of inspirational benchmark, or as an invitation to be daring by his own standards. Any resemblance is largely superficial: his use of multi-phonics (multiple notes produced simultaneously on an instrument designed to play only single tones) and occasional recourse to a series of major scale fragments, sometimes moving in a sequence of ascending intervals of minor thirds and sometimes in more random patterns, may sound initially Coltrane-like, but players such as Sonny Rollins were also using these devices.

18. *Independent on Sunday*, December 18, 2005.

19. "Anglo-American Exchange," *Crescendo*, August 1966.

20. "Ornette: Noise or Music – the Controversy Continues," *Melody Maker*, May 7, 1966.

21. Email to author, August 13, 2007.

22. Email to author, June 29, 2004.

23. Sleeve notes, Tubby Hayes Quartet, *Addictive Tendencies*, Rare Music Recordings RM 028, 2006.

24. Email to author, January 21, 2005.

25. *Jazz Britannia*, Episode 2 'Strange Brew', BBC4, transmitted February 4, 2005.

26. 'Hear Me Talking', *The Jazz Scene*, BBC, August 21, 1966.

27. *Melody Maker*, October 9, 1965.

28. Clipping from untraced newspaper in Liz Grönlund's scrapbook.

29. Derek Jewell, "What Makes Tubby Run?" *Sunday Times*, November 1966. One can sympathize entirely with Hayes: by the mid-1960s his CV as a session musician was becoming ever more diverse. In the past five years he had appeared on albums by, among others, Shirley Bassey, Matt Monro, Peter and Gordon, The Polkadots, Susan Maughan, Caterina Valente and even comedian Charlie Drake. Later on in the decade he would record with Ringo Starr.

30. With the exception of a few provincial jaunts, including Manchester's Club 43 on March 19, 1966, his own outfit had largely been on hold, but there had been occasional gigs with Harry South. A sold-out rematch with Georgie Fame at the Marquee at the end of April led to the collapse of several fans due to intense heat and overcrowding, although, on a more positive note, it confirmed Tubby's faith in the commercial potential of a bigger unit.

31. "No Room at the Bull?" *Crescendo*, June 1966.

32. "Anglo-American Exchange," *Crescendo*, August 1966.

33. Gardner, "Drummer Tony Levin."
   The vibes cull didn't instantly enter the jazz public's consciousness; Hayes was still figuring in their respective section in the *Melody Maker* poll into the early 1970s. Several writers have also incorrectly suggested that he concentrated upon the instrument when his heart valve problems occurred later in life, but after 1966, they were a thing of the past.

34. Voce mentions this in his obituary for Hayes in *Jazz Journal* in July 1973.

35. Tubby Hayes Orchestra, *100% Proof*, Fontana, TL 5410, 1967.

36. Clyne, interviewed by author, September 3, 2007.

37. Ibid.

38. Looking at *100% Proof* it remains difficult not to think in somewhat jingoistic terms. Brash, confident and assertive, the music leaps off the disc with larger-than-life character that matches the renewed confidence in Great Britain at the time. Indeed, by the summer of 1966, a very British cultural revolution had already taken place; London had suddenly found itself at the centre of all things new and artistic, from Carnaby Street to the Little Theatre Club. Bright new fashions and Technicolor pop music were everywhere. The Beatles had grown from a novel group of talented young men

to increasingly innovative voices in their own right, and their new album, *Revolver* – brimming with ground-breaking ideas and studio trickery new to pop – was their best to date, garnering *Melody Maker*'s LP of the Year award. Other bands like the Kinks and the Small Faces celebrated everyday English culture rather than ignoring it, and, for the first time since World War II, the country's musical community galvanized itself with truly home-grown resources. It wasn't only happening in music. Harold Wilson's popular Labour government, who had promised the White Heat of British modernity, were re-elected with an increased majority that summer and when the England football squad defeated Germany in a historic 4–2 win at Wembley on July 30th a wave of nationalistic pride engulfed the nation. *100% Proof* is a vibrant souvenir of this heady time and although Fontana would not issue the album until the middle of the following year – during the vaunted "Summer of Love" – it remains as much a symbol of cultural identity in Britain in 1966 as those iconic photographs of Bobby Moore lifting the World Cup.

39. Barry McRae, "August at Scott's," *Jazz Beat*, September 1966.

40. Tomkins regards this performance as such a success that in 1995 he named the first of the many CDs issued from his archive in its honour.

41. The album may have been popular with Hayes due to it touching wider emotional reaches than Coltrane was then doing – the stark Spanish/Greek evocation of 'El Barrio' occupied one end of the spectrum, the gentle romanticism of the ballad 'You Know I Care' was at the opposite. There was a Monk-like blues, 'Isotope', and the convoluted title track that succeeded in conveying the composer's early experiences of "anger and frustration" in "the maze of New York." The album ended with a glittering run-through of 'Night And Day', with Henderson positively dancing to Elvin Jones's all-encompassing accompaniment. *Inner Urge* is simply a masterpiece, one of the dozen or so truly indispensable tenor-led quartet albums, and a recording that deserves a place in any collection purporting to represent the finest in jazz.

42. Interview with Danny Thompson by Peter Vacher, July 8, 1994, now stored in the British Library Archival Sound Recordings.

43. Richard Hayes, letter to author, September 2013.

44. Ibid.

45. Ibid.

46. Ibid.

47. *People in Places: Everything's Cool*, BBC1, televised April 9, 1970.

48. Sleeve notes to Tubby Hayes, *Live at The Hopbine*, Harkit Records HRKCD 8195, 2005.

49. Apparently Lyons taped every session at the Hopbine but his archive seems to have disappeared, with only a handful of the tapes left in the possession of the surviving musicians. Lyons was even rumoured to have later burnt his entire collection.

50. Mathewson, telephone conversation with author, July 19, 2005.

51. Sleeve notes to Tubby Hayes, *Live at The Hopbine*, Harkit Records HRKCD 8195, 2005.

52. Mathewson, telephone conversation with author, July 19, 2005.

53. Gardner, "Drummer Tony Levin."

54. Brian Priestley, "The Musical Obituary of Spike Wells," *Melody Maker*, October 24, 1970.

55. Bob Dawbarn, "Caught in the Act," *Melody Maker*, November 5, 1966.

56. Oddly enough, following a critical review of a performance with Phil Seamen that autumn Hayes wrote to *Melody Maker* stating, "I believe certainly believe that, with a few exceptions, the standard of bass playing and drumming in this country is inferior, not only to most Americans, but also some Continental musicians. Tell me where we have a Niels-Henning Ørsted Pedersen, a Peter Trunk or Roman Dylag. Or, on drums, an Alex Riel or John Christiansen [sic]." It is somewhat surprising that he did not mention his own trio of Pyne, Mathewson and Levin.

57. Fittingly the LP taped at this concert was released in the spring of 1967, just as Hayes was about to embark on a more expansive tour under Burman's auspices. The somewhat mixed response it received in the press gave the first real indication as to how Hayes's following might take his loosened approach. "[He] produces a controlled orating scream with its roots in the Trane style of a few years back," wrote Graham Boatfield in *Jazz Journal*, an opinion supported by *Melody Maker*'s Bob Dawbarn, who wrote of "a touch of 1960 Coltrane" to Hayes's soloing.

58. A desire to convey the excellence of this music is enough to prompt the author to quote his own words from the press release accompanying the issue of the double CD: "[it] surely ranks with Coltrane's *Chasin' The Trane* and Rollins' *Live At The Village Vanguard*. It is simply a masterpiece. Everyone who thinks they know Tubby's music should own it."

59. Conversation with author, December 2, 2007.

60. One of the bandleader's announcement – edited for the CD issue – centred around introducing Ron Mathewson and might be termed a typical example of what he had described a month earlier in *Melody Maker* as his "verbal diarrhoea." He even jokes about this on the mic ("it sort of passes the time and I get my hands warm") but goes on to call his new sidemen "three fine young jazz musicians of whom I'm very proud of and pleased to have working with me"; when his description of his young bassist's apprenticeship in a Dixieland band raises a laugh from one member of the audience he cautions them that "It takes all types, man."

61. Interview track included on Dexter Gordon, *American Classic*, Elektra E1 60126, 1982.

62. For Coltrane the form anchored some of his best early work (*Blue Train*), and an album from his middle period (*Coltrane Plays The Blues*) appropriated the form with the saxophonist's personalized sense of harmony. His epic 1961 solo *Chasin' The Trane* (with its raw imperfect execution, initially dismissed by Tubby as "fluffing") was one of the first indications of a definite shift towards the avant-garde and as Coltrane's music became more and more intense, and less and less connected to sequential harmony, he still retained the blues form, albeit hitting quite different emotional bases to anyone else, as can be witnessed on 'Pursuance' from his 1965 album *A Love Supreme*.

Rollins too had etched up his share of blues triumphs, most notably the style-defining thematic improvisation of 'Blue Seven' from *Saxophone Colossus*; other examples include the manic 'Ee-Ah' from *Sonny Boy*, 'Sonnymoon for Two' from his *Village Vanguard* album, 'Blues For Philly Joe' on *Newk's Time*, the delicious 'Sumphin'' recorded with Dizzy Gillespie, and, the same year Hayes played at Rochester, the avant-garde-tinged *East Broadway Rundown*.

Stan Getz, not on the face of things a likely candidate for such earthy expression, had also clocked up the bebop wizardry of 'Crazy Chords', taking the blues through all twelve keys, and the stomping 'Blues For Mary Jane', the high spot of his marvellous 1956 Verve album *The Steamer*.

63. With no little irony, when Levin released the Rochester recordings he titled the album *Addictive Tendencies*. "Hear it once and you'll be hooked!!!" read the advertising.

64. The final few days ahead of his US trip included a diverse range of jazz activity. Depping for Bobby Wellins, he recorded a BBC *Jazz Club* session with Stan Tracey's quartet on Monday December 12, 1966, playing music from the pianist's forthcoming album *With Love From Jazz* (the prospect of hearing Hayes in this setting is mouth-watering, and although a tape is known to survive, even Tracey's discographer has failed to prise it from the hands of one especially obfuscating collector), and there was a further *Jazz Goes to College* television recording at Bristol University with the Ronnie Ross big band. Tubby's own quartet played its final gig of 1966 on Wednesday December 14th, returning to the Phoenix in Cavendish Square.

65. Sleeve notes, Tubby Hayes Quartet, *Mexican Green*, Fontana SFJL 911, 1968.

66. With cruel irony, Butts was never to hear the final album release of *100% Proof*, a record on which his playing is outstanding. It was issued six months after his death.
67. Sleeve notes, Tubby Hayes Quartet, *Mexican Green*, Fontana SFJL 911, 1968.
68. Mark Gardner, "Caught in the Act," *DownBeat*, March 23, 1967.
69. Gardner, "Drummer Tony Levin."
70. Conversation with author, December 2, 2007.
71. Gardner, letter to author, March 2, 2007.

10. The Other Scene

1. Clyne, interviewed by author, September 3, 2007.
2. According to an article in *Jazz UK* magazine in May 1998, Re-Dial's mastermind Richard Cook had "enough unissued Hayes material to make up an album, plus unreleased complete takes from studio sessions such as the one that produced the celebrated *Mexican Green*."
3. Sleeve notes, Tubby Hayes Quartet, *Mexican Green*, Fontana SFJL 911, 1968.
4. Ibid.
5. Brian Blain, "Tubby – the British Bossman," clipping from untraced magazine in Liz Grönlund's scrapbook.
6. Telephone conversation with author, August 31, 2007.
7. Sleeve notes, Tubby Hayes Quartet, *Mexican Green*, Fontana SFJL 911, 1968.
8. Wells, interview with author, April 27, 2004.
9. Ibid.
10. Email to author, August 13, 2007.
11. Whereas John Coltrane could – and *would* – abandon much of what he'd already learned in order to pursue music built almost purely on intuition, Hayes was never wholly convinced by free playing, something that aligns him more closely to Sonny Rollins than to Coltrane. Like Hayes, Rollins's relationship with the avant-garde was never entirely satisfying. Already among the most free-wheeling of jazz improvisers, he gained nothing by associating with players whose harmonic skills were considerably inferior. Even the looseness of post-Coleman and Coltrane rhythm sections didn't entirely suit him: *East Broadway Rundown*, the album Rollins made in 1966 with Jimmy Garrison and Elvin Jones, spends much of its extended time without any sense of real coherence; as if bereft of anything to contrast with, Rollins suddenly finds himself with a shade too much freedom. The best Rollins of the period, namely the album *On Impulse*, ironically finds him with a more conventional rhythm section, which acts as a backdrop against which he is able to perform with far greater daring than with Garrison and Jones.
12. Savage-Solweig SS-002 – *Tubby Hayes Quartet* – Lament, 2010.
13. The band's late album, *Miles Smiles*, was released in the UK that summer and met with unconditional acclaim. "As usual Miles Davis is in the van of jazz progress; positive achievement I mean, not the shrill shriek of protest," wrote Mark Gardner in *Jazz Journal*. "This music is refined, intricate, sophisticated but within the grasp of anyone with ears to hear and emotions to be stirred." Some of Davis's long-standing colleagues had a rather harder time coming to terms with such freedom; Sonny Rollins's visit to the Ronnie Scott club that March proved that, for all his daring, the great tenorist had been more unseated by the avant-garde than inspired by it. As on previous visits Rollins's performance across the engagement – and the few out-of-town dates that followed – contained moments of brilliance as well as those of startling incoherence. Ronnie Scott recalled a gig in Liverpool where the saxophonist reached a musical standstill almost as soon as he began and never recovered, going off to a slow handclap. The following night in Manchester, however, found Rollins in devastating form, piling

wave upon wave of intimidating improvisational genius onto an audience who couldn't get enough.

14. Mark Gardner, "Drummer Tony Levin," *Jazz Journal*, November 2007.
15. Max Jones, "How to Lose £1,200 in 5 Months," *Melody Maker*, November 25, 1967.
16. Baxter, telephone conversation with author, August 16, 2007.
17. Pauline Clark, "Why Tubby Is Knarked," clipping from untraced newspaper in Liz Grönlund's scrapbook, circa 1967. In this interview with Clark, Hayes also delivered definitive harangues about both the avant-garde and current pop music. "To my mind, so much of it is a fake. Good jazz comes from a disciplined knowledge of harmony, chords and good time-keeping. A jazzman must know all this before he goes in for the avant garde."

"But Tubby is not against experiment," Clark went on, "and local jazz fans at the Tropicana tomorrow will no doubt hear his own brand of avant garde as it is his policy to introduce a touch of it to his more conventional compositions. Neither is he unsympathetic towards the new interest in jazz shown by some of the modern pop singers. He greatly respects Georgie Fame, for instance, and believes he has an important contribution to make in jazz.

"The Beatles? Well, I don't know about them. They'll never really make the grade as jazz musicians, but some of their experimental ideas in their latest records when developed could produce some interesting new ideas." Closer to home, Joy Marshall's latest Decca LP *How About These?* featured a familiar mix of Lennon and McCartney, Motown and Bacharach, whilst pianist Gordon Beck's *Experiments With Pops* album also faced the challenge head-on, albeit in a far more subversive way.
18. *Jazz Journal*, July 1967.
19. *Jazz Monthly*, July 1967.
20. The mainstream media was also doing as much as it could to fuel the largely artificial notion that the world was experiencing a Summer of Love, full of free-blown creativity. The boom was largely manufactured, with all and sundry leaping on the hippy bandwagon with a willing abandon. Indeed, for all those who bought Scott McKenzie's anthemic single 'San Francisco', and thought it an innocent soundtrack to the peace and love revolution, there were others who realized that drug-fuelled visions of a utopian existence were as divisively destructive as they were liberating. "If you're really hip, you don't get involved with LSD and things like that," George Harrison told *Melody Maker*, but when Paul McCartney publicly admitted using the hallucinogen that summer, followed shortly by the arrest of Rolling Stone Mick Jagger on drugs charges, the now all-too-common public denouement of pop stars' sins began in earnest. Jagger in particular was turned into something of a martyr, a theme his band quickly seized upon in the promotional film for their new single 'We Love You'. The Stones made very unconvincing hippies and for the first time in their short careers appeared visibly out of step with the times.

Jazz had its own hippy guru in Charles Lloyd, the poetic saxophonist and flautist who had emerged from Cannonball Adderley's band to take Coltrane's post-modal message to a college audience, and in whom Hayes took some interest. Unlike his Ivy League contemporaries, Lloyd sported an Afro and wore a kaftan and his mix of free improvisation, vague exoticism and rock borrowings soon brought him to the same position that Dave Brubeck had occupied a decade earlier, that of a fashionable jazz name to be dropped casually into conversation if one wanted to appear to be connected with the times. When Lloyd visited London in June, Bob Dawbarn concluded: "The psychedelic wrapping will do a lot of good bringing people into the fold, but there's a very tangy jazz package underneath it all."
21. Richard Hayes, letter to author, September 2013.
22. Ibid.

23. If John Coltrane's passing left jazz unsure of which direction it was headed, the death by overdose of Brian Epstein on August 27, 1967 left The Beatles equally exposed. After the group had retreated to the studio in 1966, Epstein's role as the band's manager had seemed increasingly pointless. Addiction to barbiturates didn't help an already troubled soul, and disenfranchised, he retreated into a world of self-loathing. Although Epstein may have seen himself as irrelevant to the future of his charges, his death hit The Beatles hard. "I knew we were in trouble then," John Lennon later confessed. "I thought 'We've fuckin' had it now'." The band had been visiting the transcendental meditation guru Maharishi Mahesh Yogi in Wales at the time of Epstein's death, and in the months that followed it was apparent to those in The Beatles' inner circle that post-*Sergeant Pepper*, their direction was increasingly erratic and self-indulgent. When they began filming the TV special *Magical Mystery Tour* that autumn, the organization was chaotic, and, with Paul McCartney frequently taking the reins, the once-balanced dynamic between the group began to alter radically.

24. Younger English players such as Alan Skidmore and Evan Parker – yet to really make their mark – were already taking Coltrane's cipher apart, but for Tubby Hayes the process had proved far harder. The impassioned roar of the Coltrane quartet at its height wasn't the kind of thing you could readily examine and carefully unpick. Even Alan Skidmore, one of the saxophonist's close musical followers, later admitted that his faithfully accurate style came principally from a total immersion in Coltrane's recorded output rather than from painstaking analysis. It also came from a genuine love of something new. Tubby Hayes and Ronnie Scott were both fascinated with Coltrane (Scott claimed that an experience listening to the saxophonist in New York during 1965 was among the most profound of his entire musical life) but learning this new language in its pure form meant the unlearning of musical rules they considered sacrosanct. Both may have been energized by Coltrane's inspiration but after a decade of pacing players like Stan Getz, Zoot Sims and Hank Mobley it was inconceivable that there would be an overnight sea change.

25. "Tubby Hayes Taken Ill – Misses Tour," *Melody Maker*, October 28, 1967.

26. Bob Dawbarn, "Agony of Tubby Hayes," *Melody Maker*, September 21, 1968.

27. *Phil Lives*, BBC Radio Derby, 1983.

28. *The Chant of the Weed*, BBC Radio 3, March 18, 2000.

29. Conversation with author, February 15, 2011.

30. *Jazz Britannia*, Episode 1 'Stranger on the Shore', BBC4, transmitted January 28, 2005.

31. Dawbarn, "Agony of Tubby Hayes."

32. Telephone conversation with author, August 31, 2007.

33. Ibid.

34. "Tubby Hayes Fined on Drug Charge," *The Guardian*, September 12, 1968.

35. Ibid.

36. Ian Christie, "How I Got Hooked – by Tubby Hayes," *Daily Express*, September 12, 1968.

37. Dawbarn, "Agony of Tubby Hayes."

38. *Gramophone*, November 1968.

39. *Pieces of Jazz*, autumn 1968.

40. *Jazz Monthly*, November 1968.

41. *Gramophone*, November 1968.

42. Dawbarn, "Agony of Tubby Hayes."

43. Ibid.

44. Tony Wilson, "Louis – New Face with the Tubby Band," *Melody Maker*, November 16, 1968.

45. Conversation with author, May 14, 2011. Although Stewart possessed all the necessary talent, he was characteristically unsure of whether he was yet ready for the job – only

after a last-minute prompting by his wife did he nervously telephone to offer his services.

46. "Why No Mention of Louis?" *Melody Maker*, March 15, 1969.
47. Telephone conversation with author, July 18, 2008.
48. Interviewed by author, April 27, 2004.
49. Ibid.
50. Peter Vacher, "Priest who Plays, Drummer who Prays," *Jazz UK*, October/November 2007.
51. Telephone conversation with author, July 18, 2008.
52. Ibid.
53. Interviewed by author, April 27, 2004.
54. Ibid.
55. Ibid.
56. Ibid.
57. Ibid.
58. Ibid.
59. Telephone conversation with author, August 16, 2007.
60. Interviewed by author, April 27, 2004.
61. Telephone conversation with author, August 10, 2007.
62. Ibid.
63. Wells, interviewed by author, April 27, 2004.
64. Compere Humphrey Lyttelton clearly made a mental note of Hayes's new discoveries: within six months Wells had begun a short-lived tenure with the trumpeter's band.
65. Interviewed by author, April 27, 2004.

11. The Beginning of the End

1. Louis Stewart revealed this story to the author on a gig they performed together in Edinburgh in May 2011.
2. "Young Stars Pushing Through," *Melody Maker*, March 1, 1969. Despite the headline, the paper concluded "there is still no-one to seriously challenge Tubby Hayes as Musician Of The Year."
3. Christopher Bird, "Tubby Hayes: Second Opinion," *Melody Maker*, January 18, 1969.
4. Ibid.
5. Alan Walsh, "Caught in the Act," *Melody Maker*, March 8, 1969.
6. Unsurprisingly, the original LP on the Davjon label has acquired collectable cult status, and has even been reissued, as an odd, even surreal, sidebar to Hayes's main discography.
7. Hayes also dropped in on a big band of a different stripe on February 27, 1969 as part of the Musicians' Union Campaign for Live Music master classes, launched on the thoroughly unsuspecting Medway Dance Orchestra in Chatham, Kent.
8. Christopher Bird, "Tubby's Back, and This Time He Means Business," *Melody Maker*, May 3, 1969.
9. From an article on Cameron on the former Vinyl Vulture website (www.vinylvulture.co.uk). Quoted by kind permission of Oliver Lomax.
10. Email to author, April 16, 2004.
11. Interviewed by author, April 27, 2004.
12. If the Summer of Love two years earlier hadn't really impinged on the odyssey of the average British jazzman, by the summer of 1969 there had begun a far more conciliatory phase. Hayes wasn't the only one prepared to renegotiate his boundaries. Old ideologies were crumbling and there were reminders everywhere that change was necessary for survival: Miles Davis's late album, *Filles De Kilimanjaro*, borrowed

heavily from rock and effectively ended the run of classic acoustic jazz by his famed "second great quintet." In its place would emerge something altogether darker and more streetwise. There were also signs that things couldn't go on as they were closer to home. When African percussionist Guy Warren guested with the Don Rendell–Ian Carr quintet on a series of university concerts, his radical, Dadaist approach totally sabotaged the equilibrium of a band weighted a little too heavily on the academic side. For Carr, it was the beginning of the end of his faith in straight-ahead jazz, leading to the formation of the jazz-rock group Nucleus shortly after.

Tenorist Dick Morrissey and guitarist Terry Smith – two of the finest mainstream/modern players on the London jazz circuit – had also jumped ship to play with soul singer J. J. Jackson, ahead of forming their own jazz-rock outfit If, and even older figures were bending to popular taste: Hayes's former boss, the impresario Vic Lewis, recorded the album *Beatles My Way* that summer.

13. Interviewed by author, April 4, 2004.
14. Interviewed by author, April 27, 2004.
15. The albums *What The World Needs Now* and *Didn't We* most notably.
16. Brian Gladwell, "Radio and TV Notebook," *Crescendo*, October 1969.

There were other observers who took an equally cynical viewpoint. Humphrey Lyttelton – regular compere of the weekly BBC *Jazz Club* programme – found himself increasingly presenting music that reeked of contrivance, as he revealed to Richard Cook in *Jazz Review* magazine in 2001: "If there was a band like, dare I say Tony Oxley's or John Stevens's, I'd sneak round and look at the music, and it was all things like electrical circuits and drawn symbols, but quite often you'd see a little section in the circuit which said 'freak out'."

17. Steve Voce, "It Don't Mean a Thing," *Jazz Journal*, July 1969.
18. Interviewed by author, April 21, 2004.
19. Ibid.
20. Charles Fox, "Tubby Hayes, the End of the Old Ching-Ching-Ching," *Radio Times*, September 25, 1969.
21. Stewart recalled this with obvious regret during a conversation with the author on a gig in 2011.
22. Interviewed by author, April 27, 2004.
23. Telephone conversation with author, November 7, 2013.
24. *Jazz Legends*, BBC Radio 3, July 13, 2001.
25. Sleeve notes to *Tubby Hayes Quartet – For Members Only*, Miles Music MMCD 086, 2002.
26. Interviewed by author, April 21, 2004.
27. Sleeve notes to *Tubby Hayes Quartet – For Members Only*, Miles Music MMCD 086, 2002.
28. Stoke on Trent on January 30th, the Torrington in North Finchley on February 9th and a recording at the Bull's Head on February 9th.
29. "Tubby Hayes in Hospital," *Melody Maker*, March 7, 1970.
30. "Memories of Tubby" (letter from Harry South), *Melody Maker*, June 30, 1973.
31. Conversation with author, July 17, 2009.
32. Interviewed by author, April 27, 2004.
33. Ibid.
34. Brian Priestley, "The Musical Obituary of Spike Wells," *Melody Maker*, October 24, 1970.
35. Interview with author, April 27, 2004.
36. Max Jones, "Return of Tubby Hayes," *Melody Maker*, August 15, 1970.
37. Telephone conversation with author, July 19, 2006.
38. Liz Grönlund recalled this incident when interviewed by the author, September 6, 2008.

39. Telephone conversation with author, July 19, 2006.
40. Email to author, September 8, 2006.
41. Conversation with author, February 14, 2011.
42. Ibid.
43. A half-page advertisement for this appeared in *Crescendo* in January 1971.
44. Conversation with author, October 12, 2013.
45. Letter to author, March 2, 2007.
46. By eerie coincidence, a vital part of the operating procedure included the use of a mitral valve dilator – commonly known as a Tubbs dilator.
47. Max Jones, "Proceeding with Caution," *Melody Maker*, January 29, 1972.
48. Liz Grönlund, tape recording circa 1975
49. Interviewed by author, September 6, 2008.
50. Ibid.
51. Liz Grönlund, tape recording circa 1975.
52. Jack Massarik, "Mr. 100 Percent," *Jazzwise*, September 2005.
53. "The Musicians Pay Tribute . . ." *Melody Maker*, June 16, 1973.
54. Jones, "Proceeding with Caution."
55. Ibid.
56. Chris Welch, "Le Sage – Preserving Bebop," *Melody Maker*, January 29, 1972.
57. Jones, "Proceeding with Caution."
58. Email to author, October 22, 2010.
59. Richard Williams, "Caught in the Act," *Melody Maker*, March 25, 1972.
60. Telephone conversation with author, April 3, 2012.
61. John Fordham, *Jazz Man: The Amazing Story of Ronnie Scott and his Club*, London: Kyle Cathie, 1994.
62. Randi Hultin, "Tubby's Back Again," clipping from untraced magazine in Liz Grönlund's scrapbook.
63. Randi Hultin, *Born Under the Sign of Jazz*, London: Sanctuary Press, 2000.
64. Letter from Hultin to Hayes's discographer Barbara Schwarz, August 25, 1983.
65. Hultin, *Born Under the Sign of Jazz*.
66. Interviewed by author, September 6, 2008.
67. Ibid.

12. It'll Be Me Next

1. *Melody Maker*, February 26, 1972. Hayes's tenor crown had been won by Alan Skidmore.
2. *Jazz UK*, March–April 2002.
3. The Grass Roots policy was effectively outlined by the bookings that first month: the Brotherhood of Breath, Mike Osborne, the Tony Oxley/Paul Lytton duo, Tracey's own trio with Dave Green and Bryan Spring and a new band under the pianist's leadership, Tentacles, mixing the best of the newer faces including Alan Skidmore, Harry Beckett, Art Themen and Paul Rutherford.
4. Brian Blain, "I Remember Phil . . ." *Jazz FM The Magazine*, issue 15, 1992.
5. Richard Williams, "Stevens: Getting in a Jam," *Melody Maker*, July 22, 1972.
6. Email to author, June 29, 2004.
7. Martin Davidson, "Jam Session at The 100 Club," *Jazz Journal*, July 1972.
8. Reel Recordings RR013.
9. *Jazzwise*, June 2009.
10. Interviewed by author, September 6, 2008.
11. Ibid.
12. "Caught in the Act," *Melody Maker*, April 29, 1972.

13. Interviewed by author, April 27, 2004.
14. *Sunday Times*, May 14, 1972.
15. Liz Grönlund, interviewed by author, September 6, 2008.
16. Letter to author, February 7, 2011.
17. Exactly who came up with the band name remains moot; Clark Tracey recalls it being bandied about at this point during meetings between John Stevens, Hayes and his father at the family home in Streatham and thinks it may well have been Stan's idea.
18. Insert to *The Phil Seamen Story*, Decibel Records BSN 103, 1973.
19. Interviewed by author, September 6, 2008.
20. Interviewed by author, September 10, 2007.
21. Ronnie Scott, "Tubby's Contribution to Jazz in this Country was Second to None," *Melody Maker*, June 23, 1973.
22. Conversation with author, February 20, 2013.
23. *Melody Maker*, February 10, 1973.
24. Other leaders with whom Hayes had made sideman appearances since the beginning of 1972 included Harry South, Duncan Lamont, Ray Premru–Bobby Lamb, Dave Hancock, Kenny Wheeler and David Francis.
25. Barry Witherden, "The Lost Leader," *Jazz Review*, January 2001.
26. Now in the possession of Liz Grönlund.
27. John Critchinson, conversation with author, March 14, 2013.
28. Conversation with author, May 24, 2004.
29. Now in the possession of Liz Grönlund.
30. In another incident revealing Windo's kindness, following Alan Skidmore's accident in 1972, Skidmore's wife Kay remembered that among the many well-wishers calling up, Windo was the only one who had asked how *she* was doing.
31. Telephone conversation with author, August 31, 2007.
32. Interviewed by author, April 21, 2004.
33. Scott, "Tubby's Contribution to Jazz."
34. John Watson, email to author, August 22, 2011.
35. Details from Spike Wells's work diary.
36. Dr Celia Oakley, MD, FRCP. This letter is now in Liz Grönlund's scrapbook.
37. Interview with author, April 4, 2004.
38. Interviewed by author, July 15, 1999.
39. Grönlund, interviewed by author, September 6, 2008.
40. Ibid.
41. Grönlund still has these cassettes.
42. From a card now in Liz Grönlund's scrapbook.
43. Ibid.
44. Ibid.
45. Especially as he tore into the opening number, his own composition 'Grits, Beans and Greens'. The theme boasted some awkward harmonic twists, prompting pianist John Horler to apologize to Hayes afterwards, thinking he hadn't played it well enough. "Don't worry," the composer told Horler. "I have trouble getting round it too."
46. Peter Clayton, "The Man who was Tubby," *Sunday Times*, June 10, 1973.
47. Interviewed by author, April 27, 2004.
48. Interviewed by author, September 6, 2008.
49. Sleeve notes to Tubby Hayes, *Tubbs; A Tribute*, Spotlite SPJ 902, 1980.
50. Interviewed by author, April 27, 2004.
51. Interviewed by author, April 4, 2004.
52. Conversation with author, March 14, 2013.
53. Telephone conversation with author, July 16, 2008.
54. Anthony Hopkins, "Tubby Hayes Dies at 38," *Daily Telegraph*, June 9, 1973.
55. Peter Clayton, "The Man who was Tubby," *Sunday Times*, June 10, 1973.

56. BBC *Jazz Notes*, June 10, 1973.
57. Letter now in Liz Grönlund's scrapbook.
58. Ibid.
59. Ibid.
60. *Melody Maker*, June 16, 1973.
61. "The Musicians Pay Tribute . . ." *Melody Maker*, June 16, 1973.
62. The funeral costs of £192.50 were settled by Ronnie Scott's Jazz Ventures.
63. Grönlund, interviewed by author, September 6, 2008.
64. Email to author, May 16, 2004.
65. Dominic Green, *Benny Green: Words and Music*, London: London House, 2000.
66. Interviewed by author, April 27, 2004.
67. Grönlund, interviewed by author, September 6, 2008.
68. Ibid.
69. *Coda*, October 1973.
70. Interviewed by author, September 6, 2008.
71. Grönlund's neighbours Robert Savage and Vivien Van Namen both remember that 89 Gloucester Place was left exactly as it had been when Hayes had lived there well into the 1980s.
72. Liz Grönlund, tape recording circa 1975.

Afterword

1. "In Brief," *Melody Maker*, December 1, 1973.
2. According to Richard Hayes there is a nice but possibly exaggerated story of the young Bolan apparently hanging around one night outside the 100 Club in Oxford Street, allegedly with no money to get in and hear Hayes. Tubby supposedly spotted Bolan and invited him in as his guest, adding he should "sit on the side of the stage and pretend to be part of the band."
3. Edward Brian Hayes had been born a child of the mid-1930s and grown up in a Britain at war, and which still had an Empire. The Britain he died in in 1973 was quite different, a land of power cuts, glam-rock and *Love Thy Neighbour*. Although it had survived rather than thrived, British jazz was among the post-war success stories: it was never out of the woods for long, and the financial privations its musicians faced would never really go away, nor would there ever again be the kind of work-on-tap, both in jazz and heavily jazz-related, that had proliferated in the 1950s and '60s, but in terms of its confidence and diversity of aims things had never been healthier.
4. "Jazzman's £4000," *Evening Standard*, February 10, 1975.
5. Watts, email to author, June 29, 2004.
6. *Melody Maker*, June 30, 1973.
7. *Jazz Journal*, July 1973.
8. Interviewed by author, April 27, 2004.
9. "You Must Please the Audience," *Melody Maker*, January 28, 1961.
10. Brian Blain, "Controlled Excitement, Lyrical Improvisation," clipping from untraced magazine, 1962.
11. Interviewed by author, April 27, 2004.
12. Sleeve notes to Tubby Hayes, *Tubbs; A Tribute*, Spotlite SPJ 902, 1980.
13. Brian Case, *New Musical Express*, February 14, 1981.
14. "An appreciation of the late, great, Tubby Hayes by Wally Houser." Jim Godbolt, *Ronnie Scott's Jazz Farrago*, London: Hampstead Press, 2008.
15. Sleeve notes to *Tubby Hayes Quartet – For Members Only*, Miles Music MMCD 086, 2002.
16. BBC *Jazz Notes*, June 10, 1973.

17. Interviewed by author, September 3, 2007.
18. Les Tomkins, "Tubby Hayes," *Crescendo*, July 1973.
19. Richard Hayes, email to author, April 4, 2014.
20. Richard Hayes published a further three books between 1978 and 1980. His Amazon Author Central page offers this succinct précis of his writing career: "Described by *The Guardian* newspaper as "a compulsive raconteur [who] can handle his characters and plot like plasticine," Richard's first novel, *The Secret Army* (UK 1977 [Macmillan Children's Books] and USA 1979 [The Viking Press]) was published when he was sixteen. Three further novels and a TV series format for London Weekend Television followed. Since then, Richard has worked extensively in book and magazine publishing while also developing further projects. Recent credits in the comic book industry have included short pieces for anthologies such as *Meanwhile* and *The Comics Creators Guild Annual* (both published by Soaring Penguin) and "*Manhunt*" for *Commando* (D.C. Thomson)."
21. Saxophonist Dave Bishop joined NYJO barely a few weeks after Hayes's death and remembers the affection with which its members recalled Hayes, who had occasionally been brought in to coach the band.
22. Press release for the 2nd Hammersmith and Fulham Jazz Festival 1980.
23. Tubby Hayes, *Tubbs: A Tribute*, Spotlite SPJ 902, 1980.
24. *Tubbs' Tours*, Mole 4 and *Mexican Green*, Mole 2. Both were produced for re-release by Hayes's friend, Peter Bould. After Hayes's death *Mexican Green* had achieved near-iconic status, and its initial reissue in 1981 alerted a new generation – one free of any preconceived ideas as to how Hayes's music had developed – to its myriad delights. It also allowed for a far more considered appraisal of its contents. Surprisingly, the critical tenor hadn't altered much over the intervening fourteen years, as Brian Case of *NME* noted: "Giant Steps had taken [Hayes] about as far as he wanted to go, but he continued to take an informed interest in the avant-garde, despite a suspicion that much of it was intrinsically boring. [*Mexican Green*] represents the pinnacle of late, small-combo Tubby Hayes. Despite the more free-ranging rhythm section, only the title track takes much advantage of the absence of deadlines and wider tonal spectrum. The opening pairs the leader's warped-iron legato with Mathewson's shuddering arco to dramatic effect, and there are powerful moments of piano thunder and Rollins-like tenor drainpipe tonalities, but it is the sections of swing, swagger and yell that remain in the mind."

    It also helped inspire some younger musicians including the saxophonist Theo Travis. In an article in *Jazzwise* magazine (October 2003, "Turning Point: Viva Tubby") Travis names *Mexican Green* as his favourite album, describing how "[the music is played] by a band that is very schooled in hard bop. It's got changes and swings – they manage to do that, even though there are whole sections where they are improvising – playing chords and changes, but unscripted. In fact, you might not know except it says it on the record sleeve. It's a tell-tale sign of how unified the band was, they were so coherent and together, and you find out so much about who they are as musicians and how the group works." Travis also noted how the mix of the album had inspired one of his own recordings – a nice example of parochial influence from a player of the post-Brecker generation.
25. Televised on BBC2, Saturday July 28, 1984.
26. Jack Sharpe Big Band, *Roarin'*, Ronnie Scott's Jazz House JHCD 016, 1991.
27. *Tubby Hayes, Live 1969*, Harlequin Records HQ 3006, 1986.
28. In *Jazz at Ronnie Scott's* (JARS) magazine in November 1990, Graham Griffiths of New Note Distribution reported that "exceptional sales" of the album *For Members Only* on Miles Music were directly attributable to recent airplay on Jazz FM.

29. In a review reflecting the general response to these reissues, *Jazzwise* magazine (issue 13, June 1998) opined "both CDs constitute an unanswerable rebuttal to those who consider world-class UK jazz a recent phenomenon."

30. Ronald Atkins, "Blast from the Past," *Jazz UK*, May 1998.

31. *Jazz Legends*, BBC Radio 3, July 13, 2001.

32. Steve Ingless, "The Swinging Giant," *Record Collector*, August 2004.

33. Barry Witherden, "The Lost Leader," *Jazz Review*, January 2001.

34. Between 2000 and 2011 no fewer than fifteen releases of newly discovered material were issued by a variety of labels.

35. *Impressed* with Gilles Peterson, Universal 064 749 2, 2002.

36. There have been similar projects in the succeeding years, including recreations of the Tubby Hayes Big Band at the Brecon and Southport Jazz Festivals, featuring former members Alan Skidmore and Peter King. The reissues and new issues have also continued apace with some startling discoveries being made, most notably the session tapes sent to Blue Note by Tony Hall in 1960, which, remastered and released by Candid Records as *Tubby's New Groove*, took the distinction of winning Reissue of 2011 in *Jazzwise* magazine. Liz Grönlund too finally agreed to grant access to the archive recordings Tubby left with her, with a new label – Savage-Solweig – launched specifically aimed at releasing the treasures it contains. Thus far, it has issued three albums – *Tubby Hayes Quartet: Lament*, Savage-Solweig SS-001 (2010), *Tubby Hayes Quintet: Dancing In the Dark*, Savage-Solweig SS-002 (2011) and *Tubby Hayes Big Band: Rumpus*, Savage-Solweig SS-003 (2015) each containing thrilling examples of the leader doing what he did best, in front of cheering fans. With issues like these, in many ways, things have never looked brighter for the music of Tubby Hayes.

37. Richard Cook and Brian Morton, *The Penguin Guide to Jazz on CD, LP and Cassette*, London: Penguin, 1992.

38. *Jazz Review*, August 2000.

39. Witherden, "The Lost Leader."

40. Les Tomkins, "The Tubby Hayes Story," *Crescendo*, June 1963.

41. Interviewed by the author in 2004, Spike Wells thought that Barnes had something of Hayes's irrepressible energy. The author would also nominate Peter King and Alan Skidmore.

Selected Discography

The discography that follows is by no means a complete one, but rather it offers a general guide to the most important sessions of Tubby Hayes's career, including his entire studio recorded output as a leader for the Tempo and Fontana labels. Whilst the focus is mainly upon Hayes's work with his own bands, there is a small selection of sessions where he appears as a sideman with leaders including Vic Lewis, Dizzy Reece and Ian Hamer.

Those readers wishing to explore Hayes's recorded work further are directed to *100% Proof – The Complete Tubby Hayes Discography*, a forthcoming collaboration between the author and Canadian discographer C. Tom Davis, to be published by Names and Numbers. This study not only includes details of his appearances on a wide variety of commercial albums but also looks at his film soundtrack recordings, BBC radio broadcasts and advertising jingles.

At the time of writing, only two of Hayes's 1960s albums remain unissued on CD – his second session with Paul Gonsalves, *Change of Setting* and his easy-listening big band effort from 1969, *The Orchestra* – but given Hayes's ongoing appeal it is likely that an enterprising label may yet see this gap in the market.

I've also attempted to include all of the CD releases of newly discovered music issued in the last ten or so years, made at Ronnie Scott's, The Hopbine, The Dancing Slipper and other venues by keen amateur recordists such as Les Tomkins and Allan Gilmour. These make a fascinating and frequently engrossing sidebar to the central action of Tubby's studio discography.

As is the nature of what comprises – or, indeed, what's left of – the record industry, album products sometimes come and go with alarming rapidity and it's impossible to guarantee that what's listed here will remain in catalogue forever. I've attempted therefore to capture exactly what is available at the time of writing. When one considers how few of Hayes's records were available barely a decade ago, things have improved considerably. Happily, yet more releases, including further previously unheard music from his own tape archive, are in the pipeline.

Simon Spillett
January 2015

Abbreviations

(afl) alto flute
(alt) alternate take
(ann) announcer
(arr) arranger
(as) alto saxophone
(b) double bass
(bcl) bass clarinet
(bg) bass guitar
(bs) baritone saxophone
(btp) bass trumpet
(cel) celeste
(cl) clarinet

(d) drums
(dir) director
(elp) electric piano
(fl) flute
(flg) flugelhorn
(frh) french horn
(gt) guitar
(hp) harp
(mel) mellophonium
(o) oboe
(p) piano
(perc) percussion

(picc) piccolo
(ss) soprano saxophone
(tb) trombone
(timp) timpani drums
(tp) trumpet
(ts) tenor saxophone
(tu) tuba
(vb) vibraphone
(vcl) vocal
(vl) violin
(vtb) valve trombone

KENNY BAKER SEXTET
Kenny Baker (tp); Vic Ash (cl, as); Jimmy Skidmore (ts); Tubby Hayes (ts); David Milne (p); Allan McDonald (b); Pete Bray (d)

EMI Studios, London, July 24, 1951

> CE 13516 I Can't Get Started
> CE 13515 I Only Have Eyes For You

Parlophone E R3452 (78rpm)

VIC LEWIS AND HIS ORCHESTRA
Dave Loban, Ronnie Baker, Les Condon, Colin Wright (tp); Lad Busby, Johnny Watson, Jack Botterill, Laurie Franklin (tb); Ronnie Chamberlain, Bernard Allen (as); Les Wigfield (ts); Tubby Hayes (ts, bs); Brian Rogerson (bs); Don Riddell (p); Dave Willis (b); Kenny Hollick (d); Gerry Mulligan, Johnny Keating (arr); Vic Lewis (dir)

Decca Studios, London, January 13, 1954

> DR18500 Sextet
> DR18501 Walkin' Shoes

Decca LF 1157 Vic Lewis – Mulligan's Music
PROPERBOX 117 – Tubby Hayes – The Little Giant (CD)

VIC LEWIS AND HIS ORCHESTRA
Personnel and location as above

January 14, 1954

> DR18502 Line For Lyons
> DR18503 Nights At The Turntable
> DR18504 Bweebida Bobbida
> DR18505 Limelight

Decca LF 1157 Vic Lewis – Mulligan's Music
PROPERBOX 117 – Tubby Hayes – The Little Giant (CD)

VIC LEWIS AND HIS ORCHESTRA
Personnel and location as above

January 20, 1954

> DR18505-1 Westwood Walk
> DR18506 Bark For Barksdale

Decca LF 1157 Vic Lewis – Mulligan's Music
PROPERBOX 117 – Tubby Hayes – The Little Giant (CD)

VIC LEWIS AND HIS ORCHESTRA
As above but Dave Power (tp) replaces Condon. Add Roy Garnett (perc)

Sheffield Town Hall, January 23, 1954

> Bill's Blues[a][b]
> Jolly Rogers[a]
> Moonlight In Vermont[a]
> Too Marvellous For Words (Tubby Hayes and rhythm section only)[a][b]
> You'd Be So Nice To Come Home To[a]
> Bweebida Bobbida[a][b]
> Peanut Vendor[a][b]
> Sextet[a][b]
> Jump For Joe[a]
> The Creep[a][b]
> Walkin' Shoes[a][b]
> Limelight[a][b]
> Bark For Barksdale[a][b]
> Intermission Riff[a][b]

a Hep 20 – Vic Lewis In Concert
b PROPERBOX 117 – Tubby Hayes – The Little Giant (CD)

TUBBY HAYES AND HIS ORCHESTRA
Jimmy Deuchar, Dickie Hawdon (tp); Mike Senn (as); Tubby Hayes (ts); Jackie Sharpe (ts, bs); Harry South (p); Pete Blannin (b); Lennie Breslaw (d)

Decca Studios, London, March 10, 1955

> VOG 48 Jordu
> VOG 49 Orient Line
> VOG 50 May Ray
> VOG 51 Monsoon

Tempo EXA 14 – Tubby Hayes and his Orchestra – The Little Giant
PROPERBOX 117 – Tubby Hayes – The Little Giant (CD)

JIMMY DEUCHAR ENSEMBLE
Jimmy Deuchar (tp); Ken Wray (tb); Derek Humble (as, bs); Tubby Hayes (ts); Victor Feldman (p); Lennie Bush (b); Phil Seamen (d)

Decca Studios, London, April 26, 1955

> VOG 2497 Treble Gold
> VOG 2498 Basshouse

IPA Special
Final Selection

Tempo LAP 2 – Jimmy Deuchar Ensemble
PROPERBOX 117 – Tubby Hayes – The Little Giant (CD)

TUBBY HAYES AND HIS MEN
Personnel and location as March 10th but Dave Usden replaces Deuchar

April 29, 1955

VOG 62 I Let A Song Go Out Of My Heart[a][c]
VOG 63 Sophisticated Lady[a][b][c]
VOG 64 Deuces Wild[b][c]

a Tempo EXA 17 – Tubby Hayes and his Orchestra
b Tempo A113 (78rpm)
c PROPERBOX 117 – Tubby Hayes – The Little Giant (CD)

TUBBY HAYES AND HIS ORCHESTRA
Personnel and location as above but Bill Eyden replaces Breslaw

July 14, 1955

VOG 196 Fidelius
VOG 197 Tootsie Roll

Tempo EXA 17 – Tubby Hayes and his Orchestra
PROPERBOX 117 – Tubby Hayes – The Little Giant (CD)

DIZZY REECE QUINTET
Dizzy Reece (tp); Tubby Hayes (ts); Harry South (p); Pete Blannin (b); Bill Eyden (d)

Decca Studios, London, July 14, 1955

VOG 198 Now's The Time
VOG 199 Please Call

Tempo LAP 3 – Dizzy Reece – A New Star
PROPERBOX 117 – Tubby Hayes – The Little Giant (CD)

TUBBY HAYES QUARTET
Tubby Hayes (ts); Harry South (p); Pete Blannin (b); Bill Eyden (d)

Decca Studios, London, July 29, 1955

VOG 82 Dance Of The Aerophragytes
VOG 83 There's No You
VOG 84 Imagination
VOG 85 Peace Pipe
VOG 86 Evil Eyes
VOG 87 There'll Never Be Another You
VOG 88 Opus De Funk
VOG 89 Straight Life

Tempo EXA 27 & EXA 28 Tubby Hayes – The Swinging Giant Vol. 1/2
PROPERBOX 117 – Tubby Hayes – The Little Giant (CD)

TUBBY HAYES AND HIS ORCHESTRA
Personnel as July 14, 1955 but Ian Hamer replaces Usden. Add Bobby Breen (vcl, perc)

The Royal Festival Hall, London, February 18, 1956

> VOG 599 The Little Giant/Orient Line[a c]
> VOG 600 Plymouth Rock[a c]
> VOG 601 Room 608 (Tubby Hayes, Dickie Hawdon and rhythm section only)[a c]
> VOG 602 Doggin' Around[b c]
> VOG 603 Sophisticated Lady[a c]
> VOG 604 Mambo Tittoro[a c]
> VOG 605 I'll Remember April (Breen vcl)[b c]

a Tempo TAP 2 – British Modern Jazz Scene 1956
b Tempo (E) EXA 36 – Modern Jazz Scene 1956
c PROPERBOX 117 – Tubby Hayes – The Little Giant (CD)

TUBBY HAYES QUINTET
Dickie Hawdon (tp); Tubby Hayes (ts); Harry South (p); Pete Elderfield (b); Bill Eyden (d)

Decca Studios, London, July 17, 1956

> VOG 919 Ode To Ernie
> VOG 920 Foolin' Myself
> VOG 921 No, I Woodyn't
> VOG 922 Message To The Messengers
> VOG 923 Hall Hears The Blues
> VOG 924 Nicole

Tempo TAP 6 – Tubby Hayes Quintet – After Lights Out
PROPERBOX 117 – Tubby Hayes – The Little Giant (CD)

JAZZ AT THE FLAMINGO
Ronnie Scott, Tubby Hayes (ts); Harry Klein (bs); Terry Shannon (p); Lennie Bush (b); Tony Crombie (d)

The Railway Arms, West Hampstead, London, July 31, 1956

> VOG 943 Night In Tunisia
> VOG 945 Laker's Day

Tempo TAP 5 – Jazz At The Flamingo
PROPERBOX 117 – Tubby Hayes – The Little Giant (CD)

BIX CURTIS' JAZZ FROM LONDON
Bert Courtley, Hank Shaw (tp); Ken Wray (btp); Vic Ash (cl); Tubby Hayes (ts, vb); Jimmy Skidmore (ts); Dill Jones (p); Lennie Bush (b); Bill Eyden (d); Bix Curtis (ann)

Unknown venue, circa early 1957

> Blue 'n' Boogie
> Salute To The Bandbox
> Birk's Works
> Caravan

Acrobat ACMCD 4368 – Jazz From London 1957 (CD)

TUBBY HAYES AND THE JAZZ COURIERS

Jimmy Deuchar (tp[1]); Tubby Hayes (ts, vb); Ronnie Scott (ts); Terry Shannon (p); Phil Bates (b); Bill Eyden (d)

Decca Studios, London, August 8, 1957

> VOG 2111 The Theme/Through The Night Roared The Overland Express[1][a][c]
> VOG 2112 Royal Ascot[1][a][c]
> VOG 2113 On A Misty Night[a][c]
> VOG 2495 On A Misty Night (alt)[b][c]
> VOG 2114 Cheek To Cheek[a][c]

a Tempo TAP 15 – The Jazz Couriers featuring Ronnie Scott/Tubby Hayes
b Tempo TAP 17 – Speak Low (anthology)
c Acrobat ACSCD 6002 – Tubby Hayes – The Complete Tempo Recordings 1955–1959 (CD)

TUBBY HAYES AND THE JAZZ COURIERS

Personnel and location as above but omit Deuchar

August 15, 1957

> VOG 2290 Oh, My!
> VOG 2291 Plebus
> VOG 2292 Reunion
> VOG 2293 A Foggy Day
> VOG 2294 The Theme

Tempo TAP 15 – The Jazz Couriers featuring Ronnie Scott/Tubby Hayes
Acrobat ACSCD 6002 – Tubby Hayes – The Complete Tempo Recordings 1955–1959 (CD)

THE JAZZ COURIERS

Personnel as above

The Dominion Theatre, London, February 16, 1958

> VOG 3071 What Is This Thing Called Love?
> VOG 3072 Some Of My Best Friends Are Blues
> VOG 3073 The Serpent
> VOG 3074 Guys And Dolls
> VOG 3075 Time Was
> VOG 3076 Speak Low
> VOG 3077 Cheek To Cheek

Tempo TAP 22 – The Jazz Couriers in Concert
Acrobat ACSCD 6002 – Tubby Hayes – The Complete Tempo Recordings 1955–1959 (CD)

TUBBY HAYES

Tubby Hayes (as, ts, bs, vb, p); Phil Bates (b); Bill Eyden (d)

Decca Studios, London, March 1958

> VOG 3089 Time Was
> VOG 3090 Blues For Those Who Thus Desire
> VOG 3091 The Eighth Wonder

Tempo EXA 82 – Tubby Hayes – The Eighth Wonder
Acrobat ACSCD 6002 – Tubby Hayes – The Complete Tempo Recordings 1955–1959 (CD)

DIZZY REECE QUARTET/QUINTET/SEXTET

Dizzy Reece (tp); Donald Byrd (tp[1]); Tubby Hayes (ts); Terry Shannon (p); Lloyd Thompson (b); Art Taylor (d)

Decca Studios, London, August 24, 1958

> 1001 Blues In Trinity[1 a b c]
> 1002 Color Blind[b c]
> 1003 Just A Penny[1 b]
> 1004 Round About Midnight (omit Reece)[a b c]
> 1005 Eboo[1 b]
> 1006 Close Up[a b c]
> 1007 Shepherd's Serenade[1 a b c]

a Blue Note BLP 4006 – Dizzy Reece – Blues In Trinity
b Blue Note (Japan) TOCJ 4006 – Dizzy Reece – Blues In Trinity (CD)
c Acrobat ACFCD 7502 – Dizzy Reece – The Complete Recordings 1954–1962 (CD)

DIZZY REECE QUARTET

Dizzy Reece (tp, perc); Tubby Hayes (ts, bs); Lloyd Thompson (b); Phil Seamen (d)

Decca Studios, London, October 2, 1958

> VOG 3469 Main Title (Nowhere To Go)
> VOG 3470 The Escape and Chase
> VOG 3471 The Search (On The Scene)
> VOG 3472 The Sunset Search (Nowhere To Go)

Tempo EXA 86 – Dizzy Reece – Original Jazz Themes for the Ealing Film "Nowhere To Go"
Acrobat ACFCD 7502 – Dizzy Reece – The Complete Recordings 1954–1962 (CD)

THE JAZZ COURIERS

Tubby Hayes (ts, vb); Ronnie Scott (ts); Terry Shannon (p, cel); Jeff Clyne (b); Bill Eyden (d, timp)

Decca Studios, London, November 1958

> Mirage
> After Tea
> Stop The World, I Want To Get Off!
> In Salah
> Star Eyes
> The Monk
> My Funny Valentine
> Day In, Day Out

Carlton 116 – The Couriers Of Jazz
Acrobat ACSCD 6002 – Tubby Hayes – The Complete Tempo Recordings 1955–1959 (CD)

THE JAZZ COURIERS
Personnel as above

The Tivoli Restaurant, Morecambe, Lancashire, March 15, 1959

> Tippin'
> For All We Know
> Embers
> Cherokee

Gearbox Records GB 1510 – The Jazz Couriers – Live In Morecambe 1959

LONDON JAZZ QUARTET
Alan Branscombe (as, ts, vb, p); Tubby Hayes (as, ts, fl, vb); Jack Fallon (b); Tony Crombie (p, d)

Sonatape Studios, London, May 14, 1959

>   Wait And See
>   The Toff
>   Lakeland
>   Sadie's Song
>   Copper On The Beat
>   Let Nature Take Its Course
>   Slick Riff
>   Big Ben Bounce
>   Mirage
>   Autumn In Cuba
>   Fishin' The Blues
>   Cheekie Chappie
>   London Lament
>   The Baron's Blues

Tempo TAP 28 – London Jazz Quartet
Acrobat ACSCD 6002 – Tubby Hayes – The Complete Tempo Recordings 1955–1959 (CD)

THE JAZZ COURIERS
Tubby Hayes (ts, fl, vb); Ronnie Scott (ts); Terry Shannon (p); Kenny Napper (b); Phil Seamen (d)

Decca Studios, London, June 26 and July 3, 1959

>   If This Isn't Love
>   Easy To Love
>   Whisper Not
>   Autumn Leaves
>   Too Close For Comfort
>   Yesterdays
>   Love Walked In

Tempo TAP 26 – The Jazz Couriers – The Last Word
Acrobat ACSCD 6002 – Tubby Hayes – The Complete Tempo Recordings 1955–1959 (CD)

TUBBY HAYES QUARTET
Tubby Hayes (ts, vb); Terry Shannon (p); Jeff Clyne (b); Phil Seamen (d)

Decca Studios, London, December 1959

>   Tin Tin Deo
>   Embers
>   Like Someone In Love
>   The Surrey With The Fringe On Top
>   Sunny Monday
>   Blue Hayes

Tempo TAP 29 – Tubby Hayes – Tubby's Groove
Acrobat ACSCD 6002 – Tubby Hayes – The Complete Tempo Recordings 1955–1959 (CD)

TUBBY HAYES QUARTET
Personnel and location as above

Tin Tin Deo (alt)
Visa
Supper At Phil's
Symphony
Hooks' Way
The Trolley Song

Candid CCD 79554 – Tubby Hayes – Tubby's New Groove (CD)

TUBBY HAYES AND HIS ORCHESTRA
Tubby Hayes (ts); Stan Roderick, Eddie Blair, Jimmy Deuchar, Bobby Pratt (tp); Don Lusher, Jimmy Wilson, Keith Christie, Ray Premru (tb); Alfie Reece (tu); Johnny Scott (picc); Terry Shannon (p); Jeff Clyne (b); Bill Eyden (d)

Philips Studios, London, March 21, 1961

Love Walked In
Tubbsville
Cherokee

Fontana TFL 5142 – Tubby Hayes – Tubbs
PROPERBOX 176 – Tubby Hayes – Little Giant Steps (CD)

TUBBY HAYES AND HIS ORCHESTRA
Tubby Hayes (vb); Johnny Scott (fl, afl); Bill Skeat (fl, cl); Bob Burns (cl, bcl); Al Newman (cl, bcl); Harry Myers (o); Terry Shannon (p); Dave Goldberg (gt); Jeff Clyne (b); Bill Eyden (d)

Philips Studios, London, March 22, 1961

S'posin'
The Folks Who Live On The Hill

Fontana TFL 5142 – Tubby Hayes – Tubbs
PROPERBOX 176 – Tubby Hayes – Little Giant Steps (CD)

TUBBY HAYES QUARTET
Tubby Hayes (ts); Terry Shannon (p); Jeff Clyne (b); Bill Eyden (d)

Philips Studios, London, March 23, 1961

The Late One
R.T.H.
Falling In Love With Love
Wonderful! Wonderful!

Fontana TFL 5142 – Tubby Hayes – Tubbs
PROPERBOX 176 – Tubby Hayes – Little Giant Steps (CD)

TUBBY HAYES QUARTET
Personnel as above

The London Palladium, March 31, 1961

Ah-Leu-Cha
Young And Foolish

All Members

Fontana TFL 5151 Tubby Hayes/Cleo Laine – Palladium Jazz Date
PROPERBOX 176 – Tubby Hayes – Little Giant Steps (CD)

TUBBY HAYES ORCHESTRA WITH JACK COSTANZO
Tubby Hayes (ts) with orchestra including Jimmy Deuchar (tp); Tommy Whittle, Ronnie Scott (ts); Phil Seamen (d); Jack Costanzo (perc)

Philips Studios, London, August 22, 24 and 25, 1961

> Southern Suite Part I: Penitentiary Breakout
> Southern Suite Part 2: Chase and Capture

Fontana TFL 5190 – Costanzo plus Tubbs – Equation in Rhythm
PROPERBOX 176 – Tubby Hayes – Little Giant Steps (CD)

TUBBY HAYES QUARTET/QUINTET
Tubby Hayes (ts); Eddie Costa (vb); Horace Parlan (p); George Duvivier (b); Dave Bailey (d)

799 7th Avenue Studios, New York City, October 3, 1961

> You For Me[abcd]
> Airegin[abcd]
> Soon[abcd]
> Doxie[abcd]
> Soho Soul[c]

a Fontana TFL 5183 – Tubby Hayes – Tubbs In N.Y.
b Epic LA 16032 – Tubby Hayes – Tubby the Tenor
c Columbia CK 45446 – Tubby Hayes with Clark Terry – The New York Sessions (CD)
d PROPERBOX 176 – Tubby Hayes – Little Giant Steps (CD)

TUBBY HAYES QUARTET/QUINTET/SEXTET
Personnel and location as above but add Clark Terry (tp, flg)

October 4, 1961

> A Pint Of Bitter[abcd]
> Opus Ocean[abcd]
> A Simple Waltz[c]
> Half A Sawbuck[c]
> You're My Everything[c]

a Fontana TFL 5183 – Tubby Hayes – Tubbs In N.Y.
b Epic LA 16032 – Tubby Hayes – Tubby the Tenor
c Columbia CK 45446 – Tubby Hayes with Clark Terry – The New York Sessions (CD)
d PROPERBOX 176 – Tubby Hayes – Little Giant Steps (CD)

THE TUBBY HAYES BAND
Tubby Hayes (ts, vb); Bobby Pratt, Eddie Blair, Jimmy Deuchar (tp); Keith Christie (tb); Ken Wray (vtb); Alan Civil (frh); Johnny Scott (as, fl); Vic Ash (ts, cl); Bob Efford (ts, o); Harry Klein (bs, bcl); Gordon Beck (p); David Snell (hp); Freddy Logan (b); Allan Ganley (d)

BBC Studios, Maida Vale, London, February 21, 1962

> Take Your Partners For The Blues
> Peace

Down In The Village
Souriya
Early Morning Afterthoughts

Gearbox Records GB 1502 – Tubby Hayes Band – BBC Jazz For Moderns

TUBBY HAYES QUINTET
Tubby Hayes (ts, vb); Jimmy Deuchar (tp); Gordon Beck (p); Freddy Logan (b); Allan Ganley (d)

Ronnie Scott's Club, London, May 17, 1962

Half A Sawbuck
Angel Eyes
The Sausage Scraper/Quintet Theme
My Man's Gone Now
Yeah!/Quintet Theme

Fontana TF 5200 – Tubby Hayes Quintet – Late Spot At Scott's
PROPERBOX 176 – Tubby Hayes – Little Giant Steps (CD)

TUBBY HAYES QUINTET
Tubby Hayes (ss, ts, vb); Jimmy Deuchar (tp); Gordon Beck (p); Freddy Logan (b); Allan Ganley (d)

Ronnie Scott's Club, London, May 18, 1962

Johnny One Note
But Beautiful
The Most Beautiful Girl In The World/Quintet Theme
Down In The Village
In The Night
First Eleven/Quintet Theme

Fontana 680 998 TL – Tubby Hayes Quintet – Down In The Village
PROPERBOX 176 – Tubby Hayes – Little Giant Steps (CD)

TUBBY HAYES AND THE ALL STARS
Tubby Hayes (ts, vb); James Moody (ts, fl); Roland Kirk (ts, fl, nose fl, manzello, stritch); Walter Bishop Jr (p); Sam Jones (b); Louis Hayes (d)

A&R Studios, New York City, June 23, 1962

25190 Stitt's Tune
25191 I See With My Third "Eye"
25192 Medley (If I Had You/Alone Together/For Heaven's Sake)
25193 Afternoon In Paris
25194 Lady "E"

Fontana TL 5195 – Tubby Hayes and the All Stars – Return Visit!
Smash 27026 – Tubby Hayes – Tubby's Back In Town
PROPERBOX 176 – Tubby Hayes – Little Giant Steps (CD)

TUBBY HAYES QUINTET
Tubby Hayes (ts, vb); Jimmy Deuchar (tp); Terry Shannon (p); Freddy Logan (b); Allan Ganley (d)

Philips Studios, London, circa February 1963

 267284-1F Sally
 267284-2F I Believe In You

Fontana TF 397 (45rpm)

TUBBY HAYES TRIO
Tubby Hayes (vb); Freddy Logan (b); Allan Ganley (d)

Ronnie Scott's Club, London, November 7, 1963

 Spring Can Really Hang You Up The Most

Ronnie Scott's Jazz House Archive Series JHAS 602 – Tubby Hayes – Night And Day (CD)
Candid CCD 79108 – Tubby Hayes – Night And Day (CD)

TUBBY HAYES QUINTET
Tubby Hayes (ts); Jimmy Deuchar (tp); Terry Shannon (p); Freddy Logan (b); Allan Ganley (d)

Ronnie Scott's Club, December 3, 1963

 If You Knew
 As Close As You Are
 Two Bass Hit/Quintet Theme

Harkit HRKCD 8109 – Tubby Hayes – Live In London Volume 2 (CD)

TUBBY HAYES QUINTET
Tubby Hayes (ts); Jimmy Deuchar (tp, mel); Terry Shannon (p); Freddy Logan (b); Allan Ganley (d)

The Dancing Slipper, West Bridgford, Nottingham, December 4, 1963

 All Of You
 Don't Fall Off The Bridge
 Modes and Blues
 Blue Flues

Spotlite SPJ 902– Tubby Hayes – A Tribute: Tubbs
SPJ-CD-902 – Tubby Hayes – A Tribute: Tubbs (CD)

TUBBY HAYES QUINTET
Tubby Hayes (ts); Jimmy Deuchar (tp); Terry Shannon (p); Freddy Logan (b); Allan Ganley (d)

Ronnie Scott's Club, London, December 16, 1963

 Half A Sawbuck

Ronnie Scott's Jazz House Archive Series JHAS 602 – Tubby Hayes – Night And Day (CD)
Candid CCD 79108 – Tubby Hayes – Night And Day (CD)

TUBBY HAYES QUINTET
Tubby Hayes (ts, fl); Jimmy Deuchar (tp); Terry Shannon (p); Freddy Logan (b); Allan Ganley (d)

Ronnie Scott's Club, London, January 31, 1964

> The Simple Waltz[a][b]
> The Sweetest Sounds[c]
> Opus Ocean/Quintet Theme[d]

a Ronnie Scott's Jazz House Archive Series JHAS 602 – Tubby Hayes – Night And Day (CD)
b Candid CCD 79108 – Tubby Hayes – Night And Day (CD)
c Harkit HRKCD 8109 – Tubby Hayes – Live In London Volume 2 (CD)
d Harkit HRKCD 8072 – Tubby Hayes – Live In London

TUBBY HAYES QUINTET
Tubby Hayes (ts); Jimmy Deuchar (tp, mel); Terry Shannon (p); Freddy Logan (b); Allan Ganley (d)

The Dancing Slipper, West Bridgford, Nottingham, February 12, 1964

> As Close As You Are
> Dancing In The Dark
> Younger Than Springtime
> Suddenly Last Tuesday/Quintet Theme

Savage-Solweig SS-002 – Tubby Hayes Quintet – Dancing In The Dark (CD)

TUBBY HAYES QUINTET WITH CAT ANDERSON AND ROLF ERICSON
Cat Anderson (tp); Rolf Ericson (flg[1]); Tubby Hayes (ts); Jimmy Deuchar (tp, mel); Terry Shannon (p); Freddy Logan (b); Allan Ganley (d)

Ronnie Scott's Club, London, February 14, 1964

> (Inventivity)/Billie's Bounce
> Oleo/Quintet Theme
> Mean To Me[1]
> Split Kick[1]

Candid CCS 79101/2 – Tubby Hayes – Inventivity (CD)

PAUL GONSALVES/TUBBY HAYES
Paul Gonsalves (ts); Tubby Hayes (as, ts, vb); Jimmy Deuchar (tp, mel); Les Condon (tp); Keith Christie (tb); Jackie Sharpe (bs); Stan Tracey (p); Lennie Bush (b); Ronnie Stephenson (d)

Lansdowne Studios, London, February 25, 1964

> Tupa
> Amber Mood
> Just Friends
> Pedro's Walk
> Baby Blue
> Souriya
> Mini Minor

Columbia SC 6003 – Paul Gonsalves/Tubby Hayes – Just Friends
Vocalion CDSML 8482 – Paul Gonsalves/Tubby Hayes – Just Friends/The Johnny Scott Orchestra – London Swings (CD)

THE TUBBY HAYES ORCHESTRA
Tubby Hayes (ts, fl, timp); Ian Hamer, Bert Courtley (tp); Jimmy Deuchar (tp, mel); Keith Christie (tb); Ken Wray (vtb); Alan Branscombe (as); Peter King (ts, cl); Bobby Wellins (ts, cl); Jackie Sharpe (bs, cl); Terry Shannon (p); Freddy Logan (b); Allan Ganley (d)

Philips Studios, April 20, 1964

> The Scandinavian
> Pedro's Walk
> Raga
> In The Night

Fontana TL 5221 – The Tubby Hayes Orchestra – Tubbs' Tours
Universal 983 1886 – The Tubby Hayes Orchestra – Tubbs' Tours (CD)

THE TUBBY HAYES ORCHESTRA
Personnel and location as above but Les Condon replaces Courtley, Ronnie Ross (as, bs, bcl) replaces Branscombe. Add Benny Goodman (perc)

April 26, 1964

> Parisian Thorofare
> Sasa-Hivi
> Israel Night
> Russian Roulette
> The Killers Of W.1

Fontana TL 5221 – The Tubby Hayes Orchestra – Tubbs' Tours
Universal 983 1886 – The Tubby Hayes Orchestra – Tubbs' Tours (CD)

TUBBY HAYES QUINTET/SEXTET WITH KENNY LYNCH
Tubby Hayes (ts); Jimmy Deuchar (tp, mel); Terry Shannon (p); Freddy Logan (b); Allan Ganley (d); Kenny Lynch (vcl[1])

Shepperton Studios, June 20, 1964

> Bailey's Blues
> Give Me Love[1]
> Voodoo

Trunk Records TTT 005

THE TUBBY HAYES QUINTET WITH SAL NISTICO
Sal Nistico (ts); Tubby Hayes (ts); Jimmy Deuchar (tp, mel); Terry Shannon (p); Freddy Logan (b); Allan Ganley (d)

Ronnie Scott's Club, London, July 12, 1964

> Friend's Blues
> Just Friends

Candid CCS 79101/2 – Tubby Hayes – Inventivity (CD)

TUBBY HAYES QUARTET
Tubby Hayes (ts); Johnny Fourie (gt); Kenny Napper (b); Johnny Butts (d)

Ronnie Scott's Club, London, September 13, 1964

On Green Dolphin Street

Harkit HRKCD 8072 – Tubby Hayes – Live In London (CD)

JIMMY DEUCHAR QUARTET WITH TUBBY HAYES
Jimmy Deuchar (tp); Tubby Hayes (ts); Terry Shannon (p); Albert Stinson (b); Benny Goodman (d)

Ronnie Scott's Club, October 3, 1964

Stella By Starlight/Theme

Candid CCS 79101/2 – Tubby Hayes – Inventivity (CD)

TUBBY HAYES AND THE RAY SANTISI TRIO
Tubby Hayes (ts, fl); Ray Santisi (p); John Neves (b); Joe Cocuzzo (d)

WGBH-TV, Boston, USA, November 27, 1964

Nobody Else But Me
Sometime Ago
Opus Ocean
Sonnymoon For Two

Fresh Sound FSR-CD 839 – Tubby Hayes – England's Foremost Tenor Sax Meets U.S. Jazz Greats (CD)

TUBBY HAYES AND THE PAUL GONSALVES ALL-STARS
Tubby Hayes (ts, fl, vb); Paul Gonsalves (ts); Ray Nance (tp, vl); Tony Coe (as, ts, fl, cl); Ronnie Scott (ts); Jackie Sharpe (bs); Terry Shannon (p); John Lambe (b); Ronnie Stephenson (d)

Lansdowne Studios, London, February 15, 1965

Change Of Setting
Royal Flush
Child's Fancy
Min And Madge Blues
Deb's Delight
Tubby's Theme (Soft And Supple)
Speedy Gonsalves
Don't Fall Off The Bridge

World Record Club WRC T 631 – Tubby Hayes and the Paul Gonsalves All-Stars – Change Of Setting

TUBBY HAYES QUARTET
Tubby Hayes (ts, fl); Terry Shannon (p); Jeff Clyne (b); Benny Goodman (d)

Ronnie Scott's Club, London, February 18, 1965

Mini Minor
Alone Together
Sometime Ago

Tentoten TTT CDS 759 – Tubby Hayes – Intensity (the 1965 tapes) (CD)

TUBBY HAYES WITH THE TOMMY WHITTLE QUARTET
Tubby Hayes (ts); Tommy Whittle (ts[1]); Kenny Powell (p); Ron Mathewson (b); Dick Brennan (d)

The Hopbine, North Wembley, London, March 13, 1965

> Night And Day
> It Never Entered My Mind
> No Blues
> On Green Dolphin Street[1]

Harkit HRKCD 8195 – Tubby Hayes – Live At The Hopbine (CD)

TUBBY HAYES QUARTET
Tubby Hayes (ts, fl); Terry Shannon (p); Jeff Clyne (b); Benny Goodman (d)

Ronnie Scott's Club, London, March 23, 1965

> I'm Old Fashioned[a b]
> A Weaver Of Dreams[c]
> Nobody Else But Me[c]

a Ronnie Scott's Jazz House Archive Series JHAS 602 – Tubby Hayes – Night And Day (CD)
b Candid CCD 79108 – Tubby Hayes – Night And Day (CD)
c Harkit HRKCD 8072 – Tubby Hayes – Live In London (CD)

TUBBY HAYES QUARTET
Tubby Hayes (ts, fl, vb); Gordon Beck (p); Jeff Clyne (b); Johnny Butts (d)

BBC Studios, London, Summer 1965

> Tubby's Blues#1
> The Song Is You
> The More I See You
> Speak Low
> Tubby's Blues#2
> Tubby's Blues#3
> Bluesology
> Detour Ahead
> Who Can I Turn To?
> Tubby's Blues#4
> Tubby's Blues#5
> A Taste Of Honey
> Alone Together
> I Never Know When To Say When
> Tubby's Blues#6
> Tubby's Blues#7
> Bye Bye Blackbird
> Time After Time
> In The Night
> Tubby's Blues#8

Art of Life Records AL 1016-2 – Tubby Hayes Quartet – Commonwealth Blues (CD)

TUBBY HAYES QUARTET
Tubby Hayes (ts); Gordon Beck (p); Jeff Clyne (b); Johnny Butts (d)

Ronnie Scott's Club, London, December 11, 1965

By Myself

Harkit HRKCD 8072 – Tubby Hayes – Live In London (CD)

TUBBY HAYES QUARTET
Tubby Hayes (ts, fl); Mike Pyne (p); Danny Thompson (b); Tony Levin (d)

The Dancing Slipper, West Bridgford, Nottingham, March 28, 1966

Alone Together
Here's That Rainy Day
What Is This Thing Called Love?
By Myself
Spring Can Really Hang You Up The Most
A Taste Of Honey

Harkit HRKCD – Tubby Hayes Quartet – Live At The Dancing Slipper (CD)

TUBBY HAYES ORCHESTRA
Tubby Hayes (ts, fl, vb); Kenny Baker, Ian Hamer, Greg Bowen, Les Condon, Kenny Wheeler (tp); Keith Christie, Nat Peck, Johnny Marshall, Chris Smith (tb); Roy Willox (as, fl); Ray Warleigh (as, fl); Ronnie Scott (ts, cl); Bob Efford (ts, cl, bcl, o); Ronnie Ross (bs, bcl); Gordon Beck (p); Jeff Clyne (b); Ronnie Stephenson (d)

Philips Studios, London, May 10, 1966

Bluesology
Sonnymoon For Two
Night In Tunisia

Fontana TL 5410 – Tubby Hayes Orchestra – 100% Proof
Universal 938 1885 – Tubby Hayes Orchestra – 100% Proof (CD)

TUBBY HAYES ORCHESTRA
Personnel and location as above

May 12, 1966

Milestones

Fontana TL 5410 – Tubby Hayes Orchestra – 100% Proof
Universal 938 1885 – Tubby Hayes Orchestra – 100% Proof (CD)

TUBBY HAYES ORCHESTRA
Personnel and location as above except Harry Klein and Johnny Butts replace Ross and Stephenson

May 13, 1966

Nutty
100% Proof

Fontana TL 5410 – Tubby Hayes Orchestra – 100% Proof
Universal 938 1885 – Tubby Hayes Orchestra – 100% Proof (CD)

TUBBY HAYES QUARTET
Tubby Hayes (ts, fl); Mike Pyne (p); Bruce Cale (b); Tony Levin (d)

BBC Paris Studios, London, June 23, 1966

Change Of Setting
Lament
A Taste Of Honey
Make Someone Happy

Marshmallow MMEX-149-CD – Tubby Hayes – The Shadow Of Your Smile (CD)

TUBBY HAYES QUARTET
Tubby Hayes (ts); Mike Pyne (p); Bruce Cale (b); Phil Seamen (d)

Ronnie Scott's Club, London, August 9, 1966

Night And Day

Ronnie Scott's Jazz House Archive Series JHAS 602 – Tubby Hayes – Night And Day (CD)
Candid CCD 79108 – Tubby Hayes – Night And Day (CD)

TUBBY HAYES WITH THE LES CONDON QUARTET
Tubby Hayes (ts); Les Condon (tp); Mike Pyne (p); Ron Mathewson (b); Tony Levin (d)

Bristol University, November 18, 1966

Freedom Monday
When My Baby Gets Mad – Everybody Split

77 LEU 12/21 – Peter Burman Presents Tubby Hayes – Tony Coe: Jazz Tete A Tete
Progressive PCD-7079 – Peter Burman Presents Tubby Hayes – Tony Coe: Jazz Tete A Tete (CD)

THE TUBBY HAYES QUARTET
Tubby Hayes (ts); Mike Pyne (p); Ron Mathewson (b); Tony Levin (d)

The Little Theatre, Rochester, Kent, December 4, 1966

Walkin'
Alone Together
Off The Wagon
When My Baby Gets Angry, Watch Out!
What Is This Thing Called Love?

Rare Music Recordings RM 028 – Tubby Hayes – Addictive Tendencies (CD)

THE TUBBY HAYES QUARTET
Tubby Hayes (ts); Mike Pyne (p); Ron Mathewson (b); Tony Levin (d)

BBC Paris Studios, January 23, 1967

Dear Johnny B.
Dolphin Dance
A Dedication To Joy
Mexican Green

Miles Music MMCD 086 – Tubby Hayes Quartet – For Members Only (CD)

THE TUBBY HAYES QUARTET
Tubby Hayes (ts, fl); Mike Pyne (p); Ron Mathewson (b); Tony Levin (d)

Philips Studios, London, February 2 and March 3, 1967

  Dear Johnny B.
  Off The Wagon
  Trenton Place
  The Second City Steamer
  Blues In Orbit
  A Dedication To Joy
  Mexican Green

Fontana SFJL 911 – Tubby Hayes Quartet – Mexican Green
Universal 983 1983 – Tubby Hayes Quartet – Mexican Green (CD)

THE TUBBY HAYES QUARTET
Tubby Hayes (ts); Mike Pyne (p); Ron Mathewson (b); Tony Levin (d)

The Little Theatre, Rochester, Kent, April 2, 1967

  Lament
  What Is This Thing Called Love?
  Nancy With The Laughing Face
  Mexican Green

Savage-Solweig SS-001 – Tubby Hayes Quartet – Lament (CD)

THE TUBBY HAYES QUARTET
Tubby Hayes (ts, fl); Alan Branscombe (vb, p); Jeff Clyne (b); Tony Levin (d)

BBC Studios, April 20, 1967

  Thinking Of You
  The Shadow Of Your Smile
  Pavanne
  Nobody Else But Me
  I'm All Smiles
  Ricardo
  What's New?
  Autumn Leaves

Marshmallow MMEX-149-CD – Tubby Hayes – The Shadow Of Your Smile (CD)

THE TUBBY HAYES QUARTET
Tubby Hayes (ts); Mike Pyne (p); Ron Mathewson (b); Tony Levin (d)

Playhouse Theatre, London, August 7, 1967

  For Members Only
  You Know I Care
  Second City Steamer

Miles Music MMCD 086 – Tubby Hayes Quartet – For Members Only (CD)

THE TUBBY HAYES QUARTET

Tubby Hayes (ts, fl); Mike Pyne (p); Ron Mathewson (b); Tony Levin (d)

Playhouse Theatre, London, October 11, 1967

Off The Wagon[a]
Finky Minky[a b]
This Is All I Ask[a b]
Second City Steamer[a b]
Change Of Setting[b]
Conversations At Dawn[a b]
Nobody Else But Me[a b]

a Mastermix CDCHE10 – Tubby Hayes Quartet – For Members Only (CD)
b Miles Music MMCD 086 – Tubby Hayes Quartet – For Members Only (CD)

THE IAN HAMER SEXTET

Ian Hamer (tp, flg); Keith Christie (tb); Tubby Hayes (ts, fl); Harry South (p); Kenny Napper (b); Bill Eyden (d)

BBC Studios, London, December 3, 1967

Freakin' Out
Conversations At Dawn
Corpus
Cambridge Crescent
Tobago

Jasmine JASCD 641 – The Ian Hamer Sextet – Acropolis (CD)

THE TUBBY HAYES BIG BAND

Tubby Hayes (ts); Greg Bowen, Ian Hamer, Les Condon, Kenny Wheeler (tp); Keith Christie David Horler, Bill Geldard (tb); Peter King (as); Brian Smith (ts); Harry Klein (bs); Louis Stewart (gt); Ron Mathewson (b); Spike Wells (d)

The Torrington Arms, North Finchley, May 8, 1969

Song For A Sad Lady
Dear Johnny B.
March Brown
Rumpus
You Know I Care
Seven Steps To Heaven
The Inner Splurge

Savage-Solweig SS-003 – The Tubby Hayes Big Band – Rumpus (CD)

THE TUBBY HAYES ORCHESTRA

Tubby Hayes (ts, fl, afl); Derek Watkins, Greg Bowen, Tony Fisher, Ian Hamer (tp); Les Condon (tp, flg); Keith Christie, David Horler, Bill Geldard (tb); Roy Willox (as, fl, cl); Bob Efford (ts, fl, cl, o); Louis Stewart (gt); Alan Branscombe (p, vb, perc); Ron Mathewson (b, bg); Spike Wells (d) plus unidentified string section and soprano voice on some titles

Philips Studios, London, May 27, 1969

Up, Up And Away
The Other Man's Grass Is Always Greener

Emily
These Boots Are Made For Walking
Free Again
Here, There And Everywhere
Song For A Sad Lady
Mas Que Nada
The Gentle Rain
Hey Jude
The Windows Of The World
This Guy's In Love With You

Fontana 63909002 – Tubby Hayes – The Orchestra

TUBBY HAYES BIG BAND, NONET, SEXTET AND QUARTET
Tubby Hayes (ts); Ian Hamer (tp, flg); Greg Bowen, Les Condon (tp); Kenny Wheeler (tp, flg); Chris Pyne, David Horler, Bill Geldard (tb); Peter King (as); Alan Branscombe (as); Ronnie Scott (ts); Harry Klein (bs); Louis Stewart (gt); Mike Pyne (p); Ron Mathewson, Jeff Clyne (b); Tony Levin, Spike Wells (d)

BBC Studios, Maida Vale, London, July 25, 1969

The Inner Splurge (big band)
Octuple Blast (nonet)
200% Proof
Conversations At Dawn (sextet)
For Members Only (quartet)

Mastermix CHECD 00105 – Tubby Hayes – 200% Proof (CD)

TUBBY HAYES QUARTET
Tubby Hayes (ts); Mike Pyne (p); Ron Mathewson (b); Spike Wells (d)

BBC Playhouse Theatre, London, August 6, 1969

Where Am I Going?
Mainly For The Don
Grits, Beans And Greens

Harlequin HQ CD 05 – Tubby Hayes – Live 1969 (CD)

THE TUBBY HAYES BIG BAND
Tubby Hayes (ts); Greg Bowen, Ian Hamer, Stuart Hamer, Les Condon (tp); Kenny Wheeler (tp, flg); either Keith Christie or Chris Pyne, David Horler, Bill Geldard (tb); Peter King (as); possibly Alan Branscombe (as); Alan Skidmore (ts); Brian Smith (ts, fl); Harry Klein (bs); Louis Stewart (gt); Mike Pyne (p); Ron Mathewson (b); Spike Wells (d)

The Torrington Arms, North Finchley, October 26, 1969

Mainly For The Don
The Other Man's Grass Is Always Greener
A Song For A Sad Lady
100% Proof

Jasmine JASCD 602 – Tubby Hayes – Blue Hayes (CD)

THE TUBBY HAYES QUARTET
Tubby Hayes (ts); Mike Pyne (p); Ron Mathewson (b); Spike Wells (d)

The Hopbine, North Wembley, December 23, 1969

 Introduction[a][b]
 Off The Wagon[a][b]
 For Heaven's Sake[a][b]
 Where Am I Going[a]
 Vierd Blues[a][b]
 Walkin'[a][b]

a Harlequin HQ 3006 – Tubby Hayes – Live 1969
b Harlequin HQ CD 05 – Tubby Hayes – Live 1969 (CD)

TUBBY HAYES WITH THE TONY LEE TRIO
Tubby Hayes (ts, fl); Tony Lee (p); Tony Archer (b); Dick Brennan (d)

The Hopbine, North Wembley, February 8, 1972

 Symphony
 Autumn Leaves
 A Certain Smile (omit Hayes)
 I Thought About You
 Sonnymoon For Two

Acrobat ACMCD 4383 – Tubby Hayes – Symphony: The Lost Session (CD)

TUBBY HAYES WITH THE STAFFAN ABELEEN TRIO
Tubby Hayes (ts); Staffan Abeleen (p); Niels-Henning Ørsted Pedersen (b); Alex Riel (d)

Guldhatten, Stockholm, Sweden, February 18, 1972

 Off The Wagon
 Without A Song
 Vierd Blues
 I Thought About You
 C Minor Bird
 Rhythm-A-Ning

Storyville STCD 8251 – Tubby Hayes Quartet – In Scandinavia (CD)

TUBBY HAYES QUARTET
Tubby Hayes (ts, fl); Mike Pyne (p); Daryl Runswick (b); Tony Oxley (d)

The Hopbine, North Wembley, London, May 2, 1972

 Someday My Prince Will Come
 Seven Steps To Heaven
 Alone Together

Gearbox Records GB 1523 – Tubby Hayes Quartet – Seven Steps To Heaven

SPLINTERS
Kenny Wheeler (tp, flg); Trevor Watts (as); Tubby Hayes (ts, fl); Stan Tracey (p); Jeff Clyne (b); John Stevens, Phil Seamen (d)

100 Club, London, May 22, 1972

One In One Hundred
Two In One Hundred

Reel Recordings RR 013 – Splinters – Split The Difference (CD)

THE IAN HAMER SEXTET
Ian Hamer (tp, flg); Keith Christie (tb); Tubby Hayes (ts, fl); Alan Branscombe (p, elp); Daryl Runswick (b, bg); Spike Wells (d)

BBC Studios, London, July 2, 1972

Greenwell's Glory
Challoners Wood
Sienna Red

Jasmine JASCD 641 – The Ian Hamer Sextet – Acropolis (CD)

THE IAN HAMER SEXTET
Ian Hamer (tp, flg); Keith Christie (tb); Tubby Hayes (ts, fl); Alan Branscombe (p, elp); Ron Mathewson (b, bg); Spike Wells (d)

BBC Maida Vale Studios, London, March 26, 1973

Mayday!
Challoners Wood
Acropolis
Hamer-philia

Jasmine JASCD 641 – The Ian Hamer Sextet – Acropolis (CD)

Index

9 781781 791738